Managing Millennials

A Wiley Brand

Managing Millennials

by Hannah L. Ubl, Lisa X. Walden, and Debra Arbit

BridgeWorks, generational experts, thought leaders, and consultants

A Wiley Brand

Managing Millennials For Dummies®

Published by: **John Wiley & Sons, Inc.,** 111 River Street, Hoboken, NJ 07030-5774, www.wiley.com

Copyright © 2017 by John Wiley & Sons, Inc., Hoboken, New Jersey

Media and software compilation copyright © 2017 by John Wiley & Sons, Inc. All rights reserved.

Published simultaneously in Canada

No part of this publication may be reproduced, stored in a retrieval system or transmitted in any form or by any means, electronic, mechanical, photocopying, recording, scanning or otherwise, except as permitted under Sections 107 or 108 of the 1976 United States Copyright Act, without the prior written permission of the Publisher. Requests to the Publisher for permission should be addressed to the Permissions Department, John Wiley & Sons, Inc., 111 River Street, Hoboken, NJ 07030, (201) 748-6011, fax (201) 748-6008, or online at http://www.wiley.com/go/permissions.

Trademarks: Wiley, For Dummies, the Dummies Man logo, Dummies.com, Making Everything Easier, and related trade dress are trademarks or registered trademarks of John Wiley & Sons, Inc., and may not be used without written permission. All other trademarks are the property of their respective owners. John Wiley & Sons, Inc., is not associated with any product or vendor mentioned in this book.

LIMIT OF LIABILITY/DISCLAIMER OF WARRANTY: WHILE THE PUBLISHER AND AUTHOR HAVE USED THEIR BEST EFFORTS IN PREPARING THIS BOOK, THEY MAKE NO REPRESENTATIONS OR WARRANTIES WITH RESPECT TO THE ACCURACY OR COMPLETENESS OF THE CONTENTS OF THIS BOOK AND SPECIFICALLY DISCLAIM ANY IMPLIED WARRANTIES OF MERCHANTABILITY OR FITNESS FOR A PARTICULAR PURPOSE. NO WARRANTY MAY BE CREATED OR EXTENDED BY SALES REPRESENTATIVES OR WRITTEN SALES MATERIALS. THE ADVISE AND STRATEGIES CONTAINED HEREIN MAY NOT BE SUITABLE FOR YOUR SITUATION. YOU SHOULD CONSULT WITH A PROFESSIONAL WHERE APPROPRIATE. NEITHER THE PUBLISHER NOR THE AUTHOR SHALL BE LIABLE FOR DAMAGES ARISING HEREFROM.

For general information on our other products and services, please contact our Customer Care Department within the U.S. at 877-762-2974, outside the U.S. at 317-572-3993, or fax 317-572-4002. For technical support, please visit https://hub.wiley.com/community/support/dummies.

Wiley publishes in a variety of print and electronic formats and by print-on-demand. Some material included with standard print versions of this book may not be included in e-books or in print-on-demand. If this book refers to media such as a CD or DVD that is not included in the version you purchased, you may download this material at http://booksupport.wiley.com. For more information about Wiley products, visit www.wiley.com.

Library of Congress Control Number: 2017936221

ISBN 978-1-119-31022-8 (pbk); ISBN 978-1-119-31024-2 (ebk); ISBN 978-1-119-31023-5 (ebk);

Manufactured in the United States of America

10 9 8 7 6 5 4 3 2 1

Contents at a Glance

Table of Contents

Introduction

If we were in the business of doling out participation awards, we'd give you a shiny red ribbon just for picking up this book. Sadly (or fortunately?) for you, we're actually in the business of information — generational information to be specific. In this book, our focus — as you may have guessed by the not-so-subtle title — is Millennials. Prepare yourself for a meticulously crafted story about the generation everyone loves to hate, replete with tools, techniques, and strategies to help you better lead and manage this infamously unmanageable generation.

At its core, *Managing Millennials For Dummies* is intended to be a truth-teller and problem-solver for anyone who manages, leads, or works with Millennials. We won't kid you (or ourselves) by claiming this book is the #1 solution or the be-all and end-all cure for your Millennial woes. Humans are complicated, and contrary to popular belief, Millennials are in fact human. As Millennials ourselves, trust us when we say we get the challenge. We feel your pain. We sympathize, we empathize, and we also know when to tell it like it is. As generational researchers and management consultants, we hear the good, bad, and ugly about Millennials, and we work tirelessly to dispel myths and shed light on truths. This book is a collection of all our best work around recruiting and retaining the Millennial generation. We hope that you'll use this tool as suits you best to find out more about this slippery generation, cull actionable strategies to improve your Millennial management style, and maybe, just maybe, leave with a changed perception about this complicated generation (and by that we mean you'll stop hating them).

Managing Millennials For Dummies is not intended to be read as a step-by-step manual. We get that as managers trying to lead four (and sometimes five) generations in the workforce, you've got more than enough on your plate. So instead, treat this book as a choose-your-own-adventure, but with more intellect and less redirection.

Side note: Though this book is all about unwrapping the layers behind the Millennials, we also strongly believe that they need to learn about you, their manager, and the other generations as well. That said, we can only cover so much in the span of one book. We've incorporated a few chapters on Baby Boomers, Gen Xers, and post-Millennials, but the majority of the content and strategy is focused around understanding and managing the Millennial generation.

About This Book

Although this book is called *Managing Millennials For Dummies,* you don't need to be a manager to glean something valuable from these pages. Whether you're a CEO; a retiree who's curious about the "why" behind your Millennial children; a manager seeking to improve recruiting and retention efforts; or an entry-level, inquisitive Millennial who just wants to learn more about your own generation; this book is for you. All we ask is that when you turn to any given section, you come ready to take off your own generational lens and commit to seeing the world through Millennials' eyes.

Another thing we ask of you? If you can, set your preconceived doubts and skepticism aside. Trust us when we say that we know managing Millennials is no easy feat. We know this not only because we *are* Millennials, but also because we *manage* Millennials. Most importantly, we know because we've talked to thousands of managers on the front lines who are dealing with this newest addition to the workforce. Some are struggling and some are thriving, but all are just trying to do their very best. While we've seen Millennials get the short end of the stick (they certainly aren't winning any popularity contests) and also praised as the best thing that's ever happened to the modern world, the truth, as usual, lies somewhere in the middle. Within these pages, we've found ways to shed light on this truth. We celebrate the greatness of Millennials, show you how to manage the not-so-greatness away, and give you a road map for building a cohesive, collaborative, and connected cross-generational team.

Perhaps the most unique aspect about this piece of writing is that it's a bit of a generational Russian nesting doll (stay with us here): It's a book about Millennials written by a group of Millennials who work in a company that researches everything and anything Millennial, as well as all things generational. As a heads-up for the odd Millennial hater who may have picked up this book, we actually think Millennials are great. If you were hoping for some more Millennial bashing, you most definitely have not come to the right place. We believe that while Millennials may not have deserved all those participation trophies, they're most certainly worthy of some understanding (plus, we didn't give those trophies to ourselves, people!).

In true Millennial fashion, we ran with not "two heads are better than one," but with three. Tapping into our collaborative spirit, your Millennial authors represent a three-pronged perspective on this generation: Hannah Ubl, a Young Millennial; Lisa X. Walden, an Old Millennial; and Debra Arbit, a Millennial/Gen X cusper.

Foolish Assumptions

We took the liberty of making a few assumptions about you, fair reader. Yes, we know what people say about assuming, but please forgive us! We assume that you

>> Are a leader, manager, or have a managerial mindset

>> Manage Millennials and find yourself struggling

>> Want to improve your multi-generational management skills

>> Think Millennials are gems, or at least cloudy gems, that need some buffing (if you are here to read about how terrible Millennials are, you'll need to find another book)

>> Have a general curiosity about generations broadly, and Millennials in particular

If any of the above are a fit, then you've come to the right place. Please fill free to jump around and choose the sections that best fit your unique need.

Conventions Used in This Book

When writing, we skewed toward keeping it simple. In so doing, we adopted a few conventions to make reading an enjoyable and confusion-free experience:

>> When we refer to Millennials, we're talking about the cohort born between 1980 and 1995.

>> Nearly all elements of the book are grounded in U.S. generational theory, so the Millennials we refer to work in the United States.

>> In our eyes, managing and leading are of equal importance, so we use both verbs throughout the book.

Icons Used in This Book

Throughout your exploration of this content, you'll find a few markers along the way. Our approach calls out certain elements throughout the book. The images in the left-hand margin of the book are signs to pay attention. Here are what those icons look like and mean.

TIP

This icon alerts you to a tip or action that will make managing Millennials easier.

WARNING

This icon serves as a flashing light to alert you to potential missteps and mishaps. Heeding the warning is a good idea.

REMEMBER

If we want to remind you of previously stated knowledge, or just how capable of a manager you are, you'll know it when you see this icon.

Beyond the Book

If you're more of a bullet-point, "give me the a skimmed virtual version so I can read it on my phone while in line at the grocery store" kind of person, we've got you covered. To view this book's Cheat Sheet, simply go to www.dummies.com and search for "Managing Millennials For Dummies Cheat Sheet" to find a handy electronic reference guide that answers the most common generational questions.

Where to Go from Here

Your adventure has only begun, and we look forward to where it takes you! Before exploring the wealth of knowledge these pages have to offer, remember to walk (or read) without judgment and be willing to change your perspective by donning different generational hats. This book is designed for you to choose the adventure, plot your course, and curate the information that is most useful to you and your endeavors.

If we could wave our magic wands and cast a spell, we'd have you read this entire book cover to cover. Alas, we are mere muggles, and aren't imbued with such powers, so we'll tell you this: Read what matters most to you. We know that time is of the essence, and we've written this content for busy people on the go. This book is "skippable," crafted so you can jump around to any section of the book and pull bite-sized pieces of information that give you the most bang for your buck. Gray sidebars are intended to give you a dose of the interesting but slightly tangential (not the essential need-to-know) info that should be seen as extra spice, but certainly not your nourishing generational veggies. They'll (hopefully) be fun to read, but not pivotal enough to change the course of your management approach.

The content within each chapter varies, and the title should very clearly point the way. Some chapters are focused on providing actionable strategies, while others raise awareness and start a dialogue. You may be inclined to skip the awareness chapters (Chapter 2, 3, 4) as unnecessary fluff, but we encourage you to take a look if/when time allows. Awareness is a huge piece of solving the generational management puzzle. If you're well-versed in who Millennials are, skip ahead to the generational clash points in Part 2. If you want to know about a deeper, more nuanced dive into the Millennials you don't usually hear about, skip to Part 3.

Our ultimate goal is for what you read in these pages to trigger an aha moment and inspire you to take a different approach. So, venture on, dear reader. Millennials aren't half as bad or challenging as they may seem, and the information held herein will help you come to that realization, if you haven't already. Turn the page. Your sojourn into the mind of the Millennial awaits you.

1
Getting Started with Managing Millennials

Uncover why managing Millennials can be so tough.

Orient yourself with generational birth years and key events and conditions that shape the people you live and work with.

Gain an understanding of where generational theory comes from and how to use it (and how not to!).

Take a deep dive into the Millennial psyche.

Decode who Millennials really are, how they got that way, and how they show up at work.

Distinguish fact from fiction when it comes to Millennial stereotypes.

Compare and contrast Millennials to Baby Boomers and Generation Xers.

Understand and eliminate your own generational biases when managing Millennials.

IN THIS CHAPTER

» **Introducing the generational timeline**

» **Examining shifts in today's multigenerational workplace**

» **Meeting the Millennials: traits, insights, and subtleties among them**

» **Recognizing clash points**

» **Finding a lot to love about Millennials**

Chapter **1**

Confronting the Millennial Management Challenge

I f you felt the need to pick up this book, page through chapters, or scan a series of helpful lists, you must have a reason. You may love every Millennial you work with and want to learn more about them. You may scratch your head anytime a Millennial asks when he can move up the ladder. You may struggle to motivate a generation that wears headphones at work and longs to bond with you at happy hour over a local IPA. You may be a Millennial yourself who doesn't understand your own generation. Whomever you are, we're glad you're here, because this whole "Millennial thing" isn't made up, and we understand your interest to learn more.

It's no secret that Millennials are winning the generational media popularity contest. In 2015 alone, approximately 44,000 articles featuring Millennials graced the digital newsstands, partly because they're a massive generation, set to comprise 75 percent of the global workforce by 2025. This coverage, bordering on excessive, has given Millennials a pretty notorious PR problem, often slandered as lazy, narcissistic, entitled brats.

Once upon a recent decade marked by neon fashion and big hair, another young generation entered the work arena. They appeared apathetic, wore flannel, rocked out to Nirvana and Run DMC, and entered work determined to succeed and enforce balance. Bosses and colleagues welcomed them with (somewhat) open arms and chuckled with a profound sense of knowing: "Someday we'll figure out these kids, but until then they'll have to figure it out themselves." Now these flannel-wearing kids are Gen X managers and leaders running organizations. The companies who welcomed them reaped the rewards. Others who hoped their few hires would magically turn into Baby Boomers are reeling. They missed out. Companies may face a similar fate if they look to the Millennial generation and wonder, "Do I have to pay attention to you? Do I have to change things just to meet your needs? Maybe we'll wait for the next generation and skip these needy Millennials." While we understand your thought process, fair reader, we know your plight if you gloss over the youngest generation making waves in the workplace.

This chapter will prove that the Millennial struggle is real — first, we'll forecast the current and future generational demographic shifts and then introduce who the Millennial generation is and is not. You'll discover the importance of not just knowing *who* Millennials are but *why* they are the way that they are. Next, we'll pepper your palette with what happens when the next generation clashes with other generations at work before finishing the chapter with giving you a solid glimpse into the future.

Pinpointing Millennials on the Generational Timeline

Understanding the generations begins with acknowledging that the time you're born into influences who you become. Table 1-1 gives a breakdown by generation.

TABLE 1-1   **Generational Breakdown**

Generation	Birth Years	Benchmark Fact
Traditionalists	Pre-1946	Got their news on the radio
Baby Boomers	1946–1964	Television started entering the home
Generation Xers	1965–1979	Grew up during the birth of cable TV
Millennials	1980–1995	Saw the Internet become social for the first time
Generation Edgers (aka: Gen Z)	1996–2010	Grew up on Wi-Fi and smartphones

While it's easy to look at this breakdown and think, "You're just putting people into boxes!" the truth is more complex. For decades, generational theorists have found that the end of one generation and the beginning of another stems from the experiences they have in their formative years. To get a glimpse into some of those major moments, take a nostalgic walk through the timeline of generations past in Figure 1-1.

These years are not static; they're fluid. Here's a brief FAQ:

TIP

>> **These numbers are different than others I've seen — why is that?**

Generational-year breakdowns are not fixed. They're fluid because generational theory is a sociological science and therefore doesn't follow hard rules. These years are determined by the researched truth that the events and conditions that you experience growing up shape who you are. For more about the distinction between sociology and psychology, see Chapter 2.

Before jumping to any conclusions about who generations are, an education in generational theory can set you straight. If you feel like becoming a generational expert who knows all things generational, take a dive into Chapter 3.

>> **What happened to Gen Y?**

If you are excited to read the passage on Gen Y and how different they are from Millennials, or if you're a Millennial who is proud to be Gen Y and not a Millennial, we are sorry to disappoint you. "Gen Y" and "Millennial" are synonymous. When researchers were first puzzling out the youngest generation at work, they named them simply as the successor to Gen X and made fun with the play on words "generation why." Super clever. However, as more research was done, "Millennial" stuck. You can use either moniker you want. Just know that they're the same, and in this book, we mostly use the term "Millennial." (Gen Y is more popular outside of the United States.)

>> **What are their population sizes?**

At their peaks:

- Traditionalists — 75 million

- Baby Boomers — 80 million

- Generation Xers — 60 million

- Millennials — 82 million

Note: Peak population indicates the highest population point of a generation. Information is taken from U.S. Census Data.

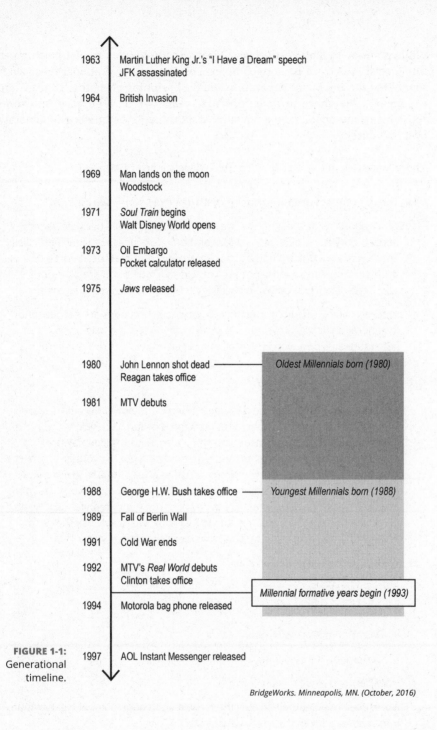

1963	Martin Luther King Jr.'s "I Have a Dream" speech
	JFK assassinated
1964	British Invasion
1969	Man lands on the moon
	Woodstock
1971	*Soul Train* begins
	Walt Disney World opens
1973	Oil Embargo
	Pocket calculator released
1975	*Jaws* released
1980	John Lennon shot dead — *Oldest Millennials born (1980)*
	Reagan takes office
1981	MTV debuts
1988	George H.W. Bush takes office — *Youngest Millennials born (1988)*
1989	Fall of Berlin Wall
1991	Cold War ends
1992	MTV's *Real World* debuts
	Clinton takes office
	Millennial formative years begin (1993)
1994	Motorola bag phone released
1997	AOL Instant Messenger released

FIGURE 1-1: Generational timeline.

BridgeWorks. Minneapolis, MN. (October, 2016)

>> So how technologically savvy are Millennials really?

Here's the truth — all Millennials are not technological geniuses. The oldest Millennials didn't use cellphones until they got out of college, and the youngest of the generation used a cellphone for the first time in middle school. That being said, they've always known a world where they're expected to have a technological know-how beyond the generations that came before them. With each young generation comes another wave of the most technologically adept.

>> How much of the workforce do they comprise?

It's too hard to really pin this statistic down because it's ever-changing, but just as generations before, the younger generation will continue to comprise more of the workforce than older generations. Many have estimated that Millennials will comprise 50 percent of the American workforce by 2020. In 2015, Pew Research Center updated the numbers as shown in Figure 1-2.

Note: Pew Research Center's birth years are ever-so-slightly different from ours, but not so significantly that it impacts the data trends.

Labor Force Composition by Generation
% of the labor force

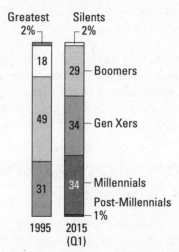

FIGURE 1-2: Labor force generational composition.

"Millennials Surpass Gen Xers as the Largest Generation in U.S. Labor Force" Pew Research Center, Washington, DC (May, 2015) http://www.pewresearch.org/fact;tank/2015/05/11/millennials-surpass-gen-xers-as-the-largest-generation-in-u-s-labor-force/ft_15-05-04_genlaborforcecompositionstacked-2/

Spotting the Coming Sea of Change in the Workforce

The workplace is in the midst of a large transformation: Gregory is undergoing metamorphosis; Dr. Jekyll is becoming Mr. Hyde; the bud is blooming into a flower; the rain shower is becoming the thunderstorm. Needless to say, the generations are shifting quickly and making ripples at work as you read this sentence. It's not enough to look at Millennials in a vacuum, because while you are working to figure out how to best manage them, the other generations are moving around at the same time. Maybe you've felt the shifting sea tides of the oncoming silver tsunami as Boomers leave the workplace en masse, the swells foretelling a perfect storm of Gen Xers surging into leadership, or the tidal wave of Millennials building to overtake the workplace.

REMEMBER

We know you are here to read a book about managing Millennials. The next section focuses more on the other generations and where they currently stand in the workplace as it relates to retirement and leadership. While this may seem irrelevant, it is imperative to not look at Millennials in a vacuum. Understanding what's going on with Boomers and Xers right now is a key component to understanding how to manage Millennials. However, if you are one of the very few people who do not work with any generation other than Millennials, feel free to skip this part and pick up at "Getting Grounded in Millennials 101."

TIP

Why does the generational study of the masses even matter if what actually matters most is the individual? Understanding the individual person will always be an integral factor in becoming a good manager, but an education in impactful generational trends will make you a *great* manager. Instead of thinking of the focus on trends as a generalization or stereotyping, think of it as a necessary foundation to build upon.

Anticipating the silver tsunami: Baby Boomer retirement

Baby Boomers have been lauded for their leadership prowess over the past few decades. A large generation hailed for their level of work ethic is now reaching a pivotal moment in their career paths. Anticipating this massive change — Boomer retirement — in the workforce is critical.

TIP

As a manager, avoid viewing this generation as a group who plans to slow down, settle down, and move on quietly. At work, they are the generation who is looking to develop and change, despite what their age may say about them. To Boomers, age is just a state of mind, and they're looking to managers to understand that. Don't underestimate them and don't dismiss them.

A smattering of startling statistics

As Boomers have redefined every life stage they have entered, retirement will be no exception. Here are the facts:

>> Ten thousand Boomers reach American retirement age every day (Pew Research, 2010).

>> One in four boomers plans to have an encore career (MetLife, 2011).

>> Sixty-six percent of all companies in the United States are owned by Baby Boomers (NextAvenue.org, 2015).

>> Thirty-three percent of Boomers are delaying the age at which they retire (AARP 2015).

>> Boomers report that age 62 is "middle-aged" (Forbes, 2014).

>> The industries that hurt the most when Boomers leave are aerospace and defense, government, and healthcare (multiple sources).

Though some Boomers will be retiring in the next decade, all of them won't be. Remember to align yourself in the right time period — consider that Gen Xers are already in their 50s but so are the youngest Boomers. They have many years ahead of them and aren't looking to retire anytime soon.

WARNING

Some may anxiously anticipate the looming exodus of Boomers over the next decade, because it has the potential to leave a path marked by devastation. As Boomers leave, companies struggle to ensure that they've taken the proper steps to prepare: Is succession planning in place? Do employees fear the departure of Boomers and the consequential brain drain? Are Boomers still engaged as they approach retirement?

The Millennial management challenge

The time is upon you. As Boomers leave, open positions are waiting for the next generation of leaders. While some Gen Xers will seize the available opportunities to succeed, there won't be enough of them to fill the Boomer vacancies. Millennials need to be targeted now as another generation of leaders.

Forecasting the perfect storm of Gen X

When Gen Xers entered the workplace, they had no reason to confidently plan their future careers. After all, as eager adolescents, they were told, "You'll be the first generation who is not going to do as well as your parents." Talk about a way to inspire and uplift a 20-something ambitious worker! If that weren't enough, as they grew up and excelled in their careers, they saw not one, not two, but *three* recessions. Naturally, they seek a stable career, a secure path to success, and a work environment that fosters growth of middle-management. However, many Gen Xers are finding themselves trapped underneath the "gray ceiling." Boomers are working longer than planned, and Xers are stuck with nowhere to go but side to side when all they want to do is move up.

TIP

Very few research houses, organizations, and members of leadership focus on how to retain the best Gen X talent. Gen Xers have been given a list of nicknames, including "the forgotten generation," "the neglected middle-child generation," and "the lost generation." As a manager, view them as anything but those monikers! They are the current and future leadership of organizations and must be understood to create a dynamic multigenerational workforce.

A smattering of startling statistics

Want to impress your friends and co-workers with some facts about everyone's favorite forgotten generation? See the following for some hard-to-believe facts about Gen X:

>> Fifty percent feel stalled in their careers (BBC, 2011).

>> Sixty-eight percent of all INC 500 CEOs are Gen Xers (*Time*, 2014).

>> Forty-four percent of Xers believe it is "useless to plan for retirement when everything is so uncertain" — versus 31 percent of Boomers (Allianz, 2015).

>> Sixty-eight percent of Gen Xers feel that they will "never have enough money to stop working" — versus 43 percent of Boomers (Allianz, 2015).

As you plot how to control the uncontrollable perfect storm of Gen Xers' demographic shift, keep track of the two paths that Gen Xers can chart:

1. **The path to senior level jobs.**

    Many Xers have been waiting patiently in the wings to fill the roles that Boomers will leave vacant. These Xers may likely view the large wave of Millennials eager for leadership as entitled and impatient. A Gen Xer may wonder, "Why should they — who have been working for less time — get a job similar to the level of the one that I've been working toward for 15 years?!"

2. **The path more traveled.**

    Many Xers are perfectly happy in their careers and don't feel the urge to move up the ladder. These Xers will likely be managed by a Millennial someday, if not already. It's important to understand how to groom Millennials to manage a generation other than their own.

The Millennial management challenge

Generation Xers are eager for their next move, so when you look to the next generation of leaders, consider that Millennials aren't the only population to take the reins. Gen Xers are ready. As Xers and Millennials simultaneously move up the ladder, they'll have to master working together. In your current role, strategize how you can seamlessly manage and lead this transition. Additionally, note that most of the people managing Millennials are and will be Gen Xers, not Boomers. The tides are shifting.

Tracking the tidal wave of Millennials in the workforce

We hope that you're ahead of the Millennial wave, or at least riding it, because Millennials already make up the highest percentage of the American workforce. There is a reason that so many articles have been written about this giant generation in the past decade, and one of the biggest reasons is its sheer size.

A smattering of startling statistics

If you've somehow been able to avoid Millennials to date, you won't be able to for long. Millennials are making major waves in today's workforce:

>> Millennials will comprise 50 percent of the American workforce by 2020 (*Forbes,* 2012).

>> Millennials will comprise 75 percent of the global workforce by 2025 (U.S. Census Bureau).

>> Millennials outpace other generations working, comprising 35 percent of the workforce in 2015, according to Pew Research Center, with Gen Xers 1 percent behind (Pew Research, 2015).

>> The majority of Millennials plan to stay in their next job for more than four years (BridgeWorks, 2017).

The Millennial management challenge

The aforementioned statistics don't need a lot of explanation, because the management challenges they cause are likely the reason that you picked up this book. The youngest generation's attitudes and behaviors at work often baffle and confuse leaders and managers into stereotyping them. In numerous chapters, we pick apart where those stereotypes come from and, in turn, why they are far from the truth.

Anticipating Gen Edgers on the horizon

As a sense of calm comes over you because you're feeling a genuine connection managing Millennials, prepare yourself for another generation arriving on the workplace landscape. The oldest Generation Edger is almost done with college, so you're likely working with them already if not preparing to recruit the best of their brightest. You can read much more about Generation Edge in Chapter 16.

A smattering of startling statistics

If you think Gen Edge will act and look just like mini-Millennials, these stats will tell you otherwise:

>> Ninety percent of Gen Edgers want to see more female leaders in the workplace (BridgeWorks, 2017).

>> Top concerns for Generation Edgers going into their careers are 1) financial instability, and 2) not enjoying their job (BridgeWorks, 2017).

>> Gen Z (another name for Gen Edge) is the most ethnically diverse generation in U.S. history, composed of 47 percent ethnic minorities (*Forbes,* 2016).

>> Their attention span is estimated at just 8 seconds, compared to 12 seconds for Millennials (*Forbes,* 2016).

The Millennial management challenge

If you are an Xer struggling to manage the Millennial generation, have hope. You'll likely have an easier time managing Generation Edge because they're going to be similar to your kids. Also keep in mind that Millennials will be managing a lot of this generation, and they're going to be in for a bit of a rude awakening when they realize that they're so unlike the younger generation. Managing across generations will continue to be a challenge for Millennials. So, you, as their manager, are going to be tasked with getting everyone properly trained to manage across the generations, even if the manager is a newbie.

Getting Grounded in Millennials 101

Welcome to your first lesson on Millennials, the generation that likely resulted in you picking up this book to help you navigate any pent-up generational frustrations. We know that Millennials can be a challenging, complex, even sensitive subject, and we aim to be the professors who drive you to think differently. This is Millennials 101, after all, and our mission is to give you "Understanding

Millennials" CliffsNotes so you can better understand the later courses (or sections of the book). For this course, we start with the basics.

Our objectives are as follows:

>> To give you a cursory understanding of Millennials

>> To aid in your ability to bust stereotypes about the youngest generation at work

>> To highlight the need-to-know information about Millennials

To prepare for this course, start viewing the world through the eyes of Millennials. When you do, imagine the following:

>> **You have never known a world without the Internet.** Whether at school computers or work computers, you learned how to master the search line and chat box from a young age. Since then, tech upgrades have been the norm. Your world is in a constant upgrade cycle.

>> **You received participation awards and trophies from a young age** and now everyone makes fun of you about that. But you didn't give them to yourself. And why should you feel ashamed for the celebratory fifth-place ribbon you got in pre-ballet at age 4?

>> **Your teen years were marked with homeland violence,** whether watching 9/11 in eighth-grade homeroom or empathizing with every national and international shooting, riot, or terrorist attack since then.

>> **You want to work hard, but everyone claims you're lazy.** No matter what you do or say, most leaders and older adults have a Millennial lens on when they speak and work with you that is less rose-colored and more of a brown hue.

Can you see it? Are you truly imagining growing up in a world like the one we just described, while at the same time facing the harsh stereotypes of the other generations? If you have your Millennial lens firmly fastened, read on.

Identifying common traits

The Millennial generation, just like Boomers and Xers, has a long list of traits associated with them. In the nature of KISS (keep it simple, stupid), these are the traits most commonly associated with the generation born between 1980 and 1995. *Note:* We don't think you're stupid.

Collaborative

Millennials grew up with "There is no 'I' in 'team'" posters in every classroom and teachers encouraging a group mentality to do great work. Social networking fostered informal group gatherings.

> **How it manifests:** Open workspaces, whiteboard walls, brainstorming sessions, working together in one room even if they're working on different things, regular check-ins, and valuing team goals and team decisions over those of individuals.

> **How others view it negatively:** Other generations can view Millennials as needy, uncomfortable working independently (or unable to do so), constantly distracted, or unfocused.

Tech savvy

Millennials can't remember a time without technological influence. Even if their computer or video game hours were limited, they still had time dictated by how many hours they could spend with a screen. They were the first generation to use the Internet when it went social and the first to get cellphones, and later smart-phones, in their youth.

> **How it manifests:** Striving to use the latest digital devices; seeking tech solutions to streamline work; finding more comfort in text or instant message communication than the phone; and demanding upgrades in their work lives and personal lives, whether in the form of promotion, workspace, or process and procedure.

> **How others view it negatively:** Other generations can view Millennials as distracted, Facebook-obsessed, or unable to have a face-to-face conversation. They can also be intimidated by Millennials' forceful request to use tech platforms that make other generations feel isolated, archaic, or uncomfortable.

Adaptable

Technology upgrades serve(d) as a catalyst for change. Since Millennials' whole world growing up was constantly changing, they learned to be malleable with any future shift. To Millennials, change and disruption — in a broad sense — are critical to success.

> **How it manifests:** When change occurs at work, they are the most comfortable. In fact, most times, they embrace it or seek to make it happen themselves. In the social world, they are progressive like any young generation before them and fight for progressive societal changes.

Identifying common values

Exploring what Millennials value (outside of family, friends, and fortune) can give you extra credit in your Millennial education. For any generation, values drive decision-making. For Millennials, the following three values drive it the most.

Purpose

Most Millennials believe that if you aren't working to make the world a better place, then you aren't an exceptional global citizen. Their parents told them to follow their passions, and the media highlighted what happens when your decisions aren't motivated by those passions (corruption, lies, the disasters of Wall Street and big business, and so on). In purchases they make and places they work, they want to know that their decisions serve a higher purpose — not in a religious sense, but in a "make the world better for those who live in it" sense.

Authenticity

To gain respect with a Millennial, the worst thing to do is construct a façade of non-truths. What were pillars of business etiquette to one generation (three-piece suits, politically correct language, and hiding in an ivory tower) now alienate another generation. Given the media's outreach and social media's exposure of issues and psyches, the world is too transparent to hide behind a suit and tie.

Choice

The rise of customizable everything, from phone cases to sneakers to design-your-major undergrad programs, has instilled in Millennials the justified desire to choose their career paths, office environments, and work environment.

Gaining insight into what Millennials think of themselves

We're going to let you in on a not-so-secret secret: Millennials hate being called Millennials. In 2015, Pew Research Center asked each generation how they felt about themselves. The result: Millennials were the least proud of belonging to their generation, with 60 percent not considering themselves part of the generation. You may wonder why, but ask yourself who would want to see themselves as a generation that is self-absorbed, wasteful, and greedy? (FYI, those were the top traits they used to describe themselves in the survey.)

This is just *one* survey, so if you're wanting to challenge the report's findings, we're with you. It's much more complex than one study. Over the years, we have always relied on qualitative research to support statistics, and writing this book is no exception. Throughout the rest of the pages, you'll see quotes from managers of Millennials and Millennials themselves. To support this notion that Millennials are tired of their stereotypes, here's a sample of what we heard:

> "Everyone says we are lazy, entitled, we get bored and just switch jobs for the sake of switching jobs, and that we are impatient." —*Michael S., Millennial*

> "We want to be CEO day one is the most obvious thing I hear about Millennials. We have a sense of entitlement and need to be in charge." —*Kara F., Millennial and Manager*

The good news? Millennials also view themselves as idealistic, tech savvy, and socially accepting. These are great traits they'll bring with them as leaders who will have their own work to do accepting a younger generation of workers.

TIP

Ask the Millennials you manage whether they like being associated with their generation. Then keep asking questions to uncover the reasoning behind their answer. It's also helpful to tell them what you have loved or admired about the Millennial generation. That may make them more likely to feel proud of the moniker rather than cower away from it. Remember that just because a generation sees themselves one way doesn't mean that others view them with a similar lens.

Steering clear of stereotypes

The Kryptonite of understanding generational differences is stereotyping. As best you can, avoid thinking about or focusing on any common stereotypes that Millennials are

>> Narcissistic

>> Lazy

>> Entitled

>> Trophy-obsessed

>> Needy

>> Impatient

>> Overly sensitive

>> Distracted

GEN X AND BOOMERS HAVE OPINIONS ABOUT THEMSELVES, TOO

In Pew Research Center's 2015 survey, the older the group, the more positively they saw themselves. Maybe you become more generationally proud with age. Maybe the younger generations are more self-critical (we hope this isn't the only case). For your purposes, here are two things to know:

1. Fifty-eight percent of Gen Xers embrace their generational label. We find that if Gen Xers learn more about their generation, they are more willing and prouder to align themselves with their own cohort (Pew Research Center, 2015).

2. Boomers *love* being Boomers. They did in their youth, and they continue to love it today. To them, Baby Boomer does not equal old or out of touch. Unfortunately, other generations can view them that way.

Millennials Less Likely Than Boomers, Gen X to Embrace Generational Label

% of those in each generation who consider themselves to be part of that generation...

Millennial (ages 18-34)	40
Gen X (35-50)	58
Boomer (51-69)	79
Silent (70-87)	18

American Trends Panel (wave 10). Survey conducted Mar 10-Apr 6, 2015. Respondents could select more than one generation label.

PEW RESEARCH CENTER

"Most Millennials Resist the 'Millennial' Label" Pew Research Center, Washington, DC (September, 2015) http://www.peoplepress.org/2015/09/03/most-millennials-resist-the-millennial-labe1/9-2-2015_01/

Don't let us be the only voice; hear from some Millennials themselves about what they really think is true about their generation:

> "I think our generation is so global. We study abroad, we travel, we grew up in a very global society with the Internet, so many things are at our fingertips. I think our perspective is open-minded." —*Alexa S., Millennial*

> "[I think we're] tech savvy [and] eager to do well. I think it's naïve to say we want to be a manager without doing anything. We know what we want and . . . are more realistic than other generations." —*Kara F., Millennial and manager*

Combating Millennial fatigue

Millennials are a hot topic. Google the word "Millennial" and 12 articles will pop up from the past hour — or at least it'll feel like it. The challenge is that the media hasn't really decided how it feels about Millennials. Does it hate them? Love them? Think they're the corporate plague? Or the corporate miracle? Regardless, the word "Millennial" has oversaturated media's conversation.

Have you fallen victim to the Millennial fatigue epidemic? Take this quiz:

>> Do you cringe every time someone says the word "Millennial"?

>> Do you groan when you see your organization has decided to conduct a generational training?

>> Are you tired of reading information about Millennials that doesn't align with the people you work with?

>> Would you rather hear nails on a chalkboard for 5 minutes than sit through a 90-minute presentation on Millennials?

>> Are you wondering when you're going to hear any information about Generation Xers or Baby Boomers?

If you answered yes to any of the preceding questions, we feel your plight. Consider how you can cure your fatigue:

>> Seek out information and articles that avoid negativity, lack bias, and tell the story behind the statistics.

>> Ask the Millennials you manage to lead the Millennial conversation.

>> Spread your generational reading to Gen Xers and Boomers.

>> Hire BridgeWorks to do a generational training that's actually entertaining and helpful (a little self-promotion never hurt anyone, right?).

>> Read this book in chunks, as it's intended to be read.

Recognizing that not all Millennials are the same

Sociology is a powerful way of viewing the world, if you can find the right moments to separate sociology from psychology. There are usually two reactions to studying Millennials:

1. **"People all must be looked at as individuals, not as the masses."**

   Rebuttal: That is true! That's why there are millions of people dedicated to the study of the individual. However, studying the masses in turn can influence the masses. Arguably, you will have a broader reach and more sustainable lens with which to view the world if you have a scope of how a mass demographic acts and reacts at work or in times of change. It's not the be-all and end-all, but it is the foundation with which to view those around you.

2. **"This doesn't describe *me* or the Millennials I work with."**

   Right. As the previous point mentions, generational theory is a study of the masses. Furthermore, we don't believe that all Millennials are the same. Segmentation is at times critical to understand the generation for certain purposes — see Chapter 13 where we split the Millennial cohort into two: Old Millennials and Young Millennials. Further segmentation can be done for whatever market information you're attempting to uncover, but this is a good start. Mass trends are still a helpful tool to serve as your control in the science experiment of "What kind of Millennial are you?"

Differentiating a bad employee from a Millennial

Are you sitting down? We have some big news . . . sometimes, Millennials aren't good employees. Just like every other generation, there are good eggs and rotten ones, but the challenge at times can be separating your own bias and stereotyping from the truth about the Millennial employee whom you work alongside. If you answer yes to two or more of the following questions, there's a good chance that you are dealing with a bad employee, not just a Millennial:

Yes/No Do you keep making excuses to keep him there?

Yes/No Do you find your greatest challenges to be with just one Millennial versus many of them?

Yes/No Do his Millennial colleagues struggle to work with him?

Yes/No Does he fulfill one too many stereotypes of the Millennial generation?

Yes/No Is he oblivious to the way that he fulfills those stereotypes? Even after you've spoken to him about it?

Yes/No Has he been given the honest conversations and tools to change, but you still don't see a difference?

If you circled yes to two or more of the questions in the list, it may be time to put a plan in place and have a tough conversation.

WARNING

The key here is that just because you have one bad Millennial, it may not say anything about the generation as a whole. Resist the urge to take one bad egg's bad behavior out on all of your young employees.

Identifying and Navigating Generational Clash Points

If you've ever had a disagreement, frustration, or challenge moment with a Millennial, there's a chance that you were in the midst of a clash point, or an area in which the generations are likely to collide but each has a valid point of view. The last part of this clash point definition is usually the most important but most often neglected point of generational differences — neither generation, when experiencing a clash, is wrong. In fact, most of the time, both are right. Part 2 of this book takes a deep dive into the following clash points:

>> **Adapting to changes in organizational structure (see Chapter 6).**

   A preview: In the past, a traditional organization flowed in one direction. If you wanted to move up the ladder or communicate up the ladder, there was only one way to go. Boomers mastered the art of navigating this structure, and Gen Xers learned how to adapt to it. Millennials ushered in the expectation that the organization flows in multiple directions, with no limit to the number of ways communication can flow. The misinterpretation of where each generation is coming from can lead to misunderstandings when it comes to a Millennial's loyalty to an organization, expectations of speedy career progression, and respect for the chain of command.

>> **Encouraging and facilitating collaboration (see Chapter 7).**

   A preview: Millennials are known for being hyper-collaborative in school and at work — in their minds, work is best when it is done in teams. This can cause collisions with Boomers who, though they value collaboration, prefer it in a structured environment. Hyper-independent Xers who grew up with the motto, "If you want something done right, do it yourself" may find Millennials' desire to collaborate annoying, inefficient, and laborious.

>> **Supercharging your feedback loop (see Chapter 8).**

   A preview: Giving feedback in such a way that another generation can hear it is no small task. Boomers, eager to receive feedback in their young professional days, ultimately designed the annual review session to illicit feedback, good or bad. Gen Xers loathe the timestamp of a review of feedback that should have happened in the moment, and Millennials opt for a less-formal, less-structured feedback process. Millennials, raised in the self-esteem movement, prefer regular feedback and are concerned not when they don't receive good feedback, but when they don't receive any feedback at all. These different mindsets can cause collisions, especially if you're a manager who just wants the best for the person whom you manage.

» **Motivating Millennials (see Chapter 9).**

A preview: Compensation is a start to motivating Millennials, just like other generations, but it isn't the golden ticket. They have varied motivation factors that can be boiled down to connecting work to a larger purpose, customizing their compensation structure, and giving them opportunities to give back at work. (Yes, some may even be motivated if they can bring their dogs to work.)

» **Dropping workplace formalities (see Chapter 10).**

A preview: Take a look at the change in workplace dress code since the 1960s and you'll have a clear picture of how the formal work world has become informal. Millennials tend to embody multiple facets of the informal — whether dress, communication, body language, or the blend of work and personal life. This flair for the casual at work can turn off other generations, who take pride in the way formalities translate to education, a job, and respect for colleagues.

Discovering What Managers Love About Their Millennials

Millennials may get a bad rap, but what managers are finding out is that they are actually a huge benefit and even a boon to the workplace in many ways. It's true! Hey, maybe you're one of those people who's thinking, "Gosh, you know what, I have so much respect for the Millennials I manage." If you are one of those people, you may be in the minority, but we urge you to speak up. The more people who talk about their positive experiences with Millennials, the more likely Millennials are to continue to step up to the plate rather than feel defeated by the mountains of negative stereotypes about them. In truth, there are many qualities that managers love about Millennials they manage:

"I think they will raise their hands for anything; they get excited about any project as long as they see the impact they can make. My own experience [with Millennials] has been collaborative and understanding of team dynamics; [they are] extremely hard working. I have the privilege to office next to three Millennials, and I see them buck the stereotypes every day. They are co-workers and friends." —*Ann F., manager*

Millennials are heralded for their innovative minds — they're driven to look at how something is done and think, "There is a more efficient and inventive way that we can do this." All generations are innovative in their own right; don't misunderstand us. The difference is the way that Millennials have seen technology as the tool to innovative solutions from a young age. The only way that they could succeed growing up was if they had innovative approaches to work, so now they are quite a creative bunch!

> "I see Millennials bringing fresh perspectives, new ideas, but yet at the same time I see them honoring the legacy in our business." —*Ann M., Manager*

Though one of Millennials' biggest stereotypes is how lazy they are, the majority have a work ethic similar to their Boomer parents' (this is especially true of Early Millennials). Most Millennials really do want to show up, work hard, and get the job done.

> "I believe our organization focuses on the value that our employees get from being who they are and what they bring to the relationship they have with [clients]. It's about a relationship, not doing a task." —*Deb N., Manager*

A side effect of Millennials' desire to push corporate formalities out the window is their welcoming of all things authentic at work. Less intrigued by small talk and more inclined toward close relationships with colleagues, they may alienate some who prefer to keep their personal lives personal, and professional lives professional. Still others, as quoted in this section, may find this a breath of fresh air.

Paving the Path to the Workforce of the Future

Managers and leaders have a responsibility on their shoulders right now: to create a workforce that embraces both the current generations at work and the future cohort of workers. While generational differences can at times be frustrating, the best thing you can do is create as healthy a work environment as possible that includes diversity of thought.

If you're thinking to yourself, "Why do I have to change everything for the young generation?!," we hear your exasperated question. You don't have to change everything because, truthfully, they need to change for you as well. However, consider the moments when you can change to pave a path for the future. It's not very often that someone will look back and think: "Wow, I'm really glad I resisted change at every opportunity." C'mon. Don't be *that* guy (or gal).

To ensure that you are creating the right space for the future workforce, just stick to these basic rules:

>> Have an open mind.

>> The moment you think you've looked into the future enough is the exact moment you need to keep looking.

>> When someone says, "We can't," say, "We can."

REMEMBER

By preparing for the future now, you're learning how to focus on the present, and that means understanding how to motivate and engage every Millennial you manage. In so doing, you'll groom the next generation of leaders on a foundation of their strengths instead of their stereotypes. In turn, they'll take a similar approach when they manage. . . and for many, that management time is now! Millennials are managing and leading Baby Boomers, Gen Xers, Millennials, or even Generation Edge, the generation after Millennials. You know that generations don't stop at Millennials, and it's becoming more important for all managers to learn how generations are shifting. To get a sneak peak at the generation after Millennials, see Part 4.

Chapter **2**

Harnessing Generational Theory to Guide Your Management Practice

I f you're reading this book, there's obviously some reason you gravitated toward the topic of generations. Maybe you're a manager or recruiter looking to better understand the next generation, maybe you're a natural Gen Junkie (someone who's innately interested in the generations topic), or maybe your leader pressed this book into your hands and asked you to take a gander. Whatever the impetus was, we're happy you're here and even happier that you're taking a peek at this chapter. You can think of it as a crash course in the basics of generational theory. It's Generations and Management 101. Whether you've had previous exposure to the generations topic or not, this chapter gives you a guide to improve your management strategy. You'll ground yourself in some of the fundamental concepts of the theory and find out what exactly defines a generation and why.

There's a chance that some readers may skim or avoid this section entirely, and if that's you, that's fair. But in our work, we've found that perceptions around the parameters of the generations can vary widely, and that can impact how well someone can bridge a generational divide. Do you know what defines a Millennial? Is it the year she was born? Or is it a more nuanced definition? You're probably catching this . . . it's the latter. Before diving into the strategies of working with a different generation (we get to that in Part 2), it's useful to have a solid grasp of the central building blocks of this topic first. So if you want to solidify your understanding of generational theory, read on. If you want to have ready responses for the skeptics (or quiet your inner naysayer), read on. If you want to see how generational theory can help not only improve your relationships with Millennial employees, but also positively impact the bottom line, read on. If you want to find out how to spin awareness into strategy, then read on, dear reader, read on.

Wrapping Your Brain around the Generations Topic

Generational theory is an effective way to better understand people from all areas of your life. This book focuses on applying that theory to the workplace and improving Millennial management techniques, but it's a topic that's applicable to all generations, and it's relevant whether you're at the dinner table or the conference table. It isn't, however, the be-all and end-all solution to all things at work, so we want to be clear about what this topic encompasses.

Divvying up what the gen topic is and isn't

What the generations topic is:

>> **A promotion of diversity:** Generations are one form of diversity, and it's a form that leaders and managers gravitate toward for two very special reasons: It's a unique lens of diversity in that it steers clear of any "politically incorrect" blunders, *and* it's also a topic that everyone can relate to. Every person in your office belongs to a generation, so it can feel like an easy, inclusive conversation. By now, we all understand the importance of building a diverse workplace. Promoting generational diversity is just as important as any other form, and you can only expect to build a (functional) multi-generational workforce if you understand the generations within your walls.

>> **An embrace of change:** In many ways, the generations topic is a sneaky way to talk about change. The concept of change alone, in and of itself, is a difficult enough thing to grasp. It's intangible. What does change mean? What's that

change going to be applied to? When you're talking about people, though, it's a little bit easier to have this conversation. It's like telling your toddler that his broccoli is actually like eating tiny trees in an attempt to get him to eat his vegetables (or better yet, tiny trees that are covered in yummy cheese)! The generations topic can make change an easier pill to swallow and, sometimes, even a treat. When else do you get to talk about your favorite childhood toy at a diversity event? By using a generational framework, particularly when it's focused on the next generation, you can introduce the concept of change in a tangible, approachable way.

>> **A shift in perspectives:** As you consider how you may apply generational theory to your own management techniques, think about it as a useful lens — a Gen Lens, if you will — that can help you see your employees more clearly. It's not a complete tool for finite categorization of human beings, but a way to overcome generational blind spots and understand the people you're working with. Putting on your Gen Lens(es) gives you the 20/20 vision you need to gain insight into what makes the people around you tick.

What the generations topic isn't:

>> **A definitive, be-all and end-all, comprehensive solution to manage any and all Millennials:** Humans are complex and multilayered, and the last thing you want to do is put people into boxes. Instead of boxes, you can think of generational categories as unfixed containers that can bend and shift depending on the person. Every person is singular, and if you put people into a neat generational box, it can strip away the complexities that differ from Millennial to Millennial.

>> **A source of managerial prowess:** Understanding your employees through a generational lens is not the sole indicator of an effective manager. Generational insights have to be used wisely and paired with other sets of knowledge and instincts.

Grasping the essential tenants

If you really want to nerd out on the generations, you should pick up any of the classic works written by William Strauss and Neil Howe, who have written foundational academic texts on the ins and outs of generational theory. To give you the CliffsNotes version, we dilute one of the key concepts of their academic tomes here — namely, the essential tenants of how a generation is defined.

ARE YOU A GEN JUNKIE?

Some people who discover the generations topic instantly become fascinated. Just by way of reading this book, you are more likely to be one of these people. To test whether you truly are a Gen Junkie, take this quick quiz. If you answer "yes" (Y) to three or more of these questions, chances are you can include yourself in the pack.

- **Y/N** Have you told anyone else about something you have read in this book yet (or marked something to share later)?

- **Y/N** Are you familiar with these terms: cusper, the Greatest Generation, and Homelanders?

- **Y/N** Have you ever disagreed with someone of a different age and said, "It must be a generational thing"?

- **Y/N** Do you ever fall into an Internet wormhole, clicking article after article about generational differences?

- **Y/N** Read the following: "Eighty percent of Millennials sleep with their . . ." Are you tempted to Google how that statistic ends?*

We'll save you the trouble: Eighty percent of Millennials sleep with their phones.

A *generation* is a group of people born within the span of about 15 to 20 years. This span encompasses the length of roughly one life stage. According to Strauss and Howe, three central pieces define a generation:

» Age location in history

It sounds fancy, but all it means is that a group of people have experienced big historical events, conditions, and trends during the same life stage.

Okay. That was nice and academic, but what does it look like in real life? While coming of age, Baby Boomers can remember how it felt when Neil Armstrong landed on the moon or where they were when JFK was shot. Xers can wistfully list off the first handful of music videos that MTV cycled through and vividly recall the white Bronco car chase. For Millennials, the time the second plane hit the Twin Towers is forever burned into their memories. For each of these events, each generation faced its respective event in the same phase of life, solidifying their age location in history.

» Common beliefs and behaviors

In large part because of these collective experiences, each cohort shares many similar beliefs, behaviors, traits, values, and motivations.

To breathe life into this academic description, here's an example: Baby Boomers, especially older Boomers, grew up in a time of massive growth and amazing social change. They tend to be an optimistic and positive bunch. Xers, on the other hand, saw institutions around them crumble and tend to be a skeptical lot. Millennials were encouraged to share their voices at home and work on group projects in school, making them a highly collaborative bunch.

» Perceived membership

In simplest terms, this is the feeling that you belong to a specific group. Because you belong to a group of your generational peers, you have a common bond. You're in the members-only club.

Whether in a church congregation, a sorority, or a chess club, everyone has belonged to a group and bonded over their similarities (or their differences from those outside of their group). Generationally, Boomers may feel a sense of belonging when they recognize that their preference for professionalism in the workplace extends to others in their generation. Xers can reminisce about being latchkey kids growing up. Millennials remember AOL chat rooms and laugh about some of their embarrassing screen-name choices. The nostalgia factor in the generational game further strengthens this tenet of belonging.

Classifying the different generations

Now that you know that generational bands span about 15 to 20 years, here is the official breakdown of generations by birth years.

Generation	Birth Years
Traditionalists	Born prior to 1946
Baby Boomers	1946–1964
Generation X	1965–1979
Millennials (also known as Gen Y)	1980–1995
Generation Edge (also known as Gen Z)	1996–2010

When you're looking at these birth years, you may be wondering to yourself, "Wait a second. Does this mean that if someone is born on December 31, 1979, and someone else is born on January 1, 1980, that they have two completely different generational perspectives?" Naturally, that would be ludicrous. These birth years are simply a way to frame the generations and serve as a point of reference. It's the events and conditions that occur during a generation's formative years that are most important in defining how that cohort behaves. Because of this, you may see other books or articles that cite slightly different birth years. They aren't set in stone, nor is any aspect of generational theory. It's what you do with these facts and figures that makes the rubber meet the road.

Linking generations to events and conditions

Events and conditions are the heart and soul of generational theory. It is here that we can identify the key influencers that go into forming generational identities. Before diving deeper into this concept, consider using the exercise in Table 2-1 to get your mind in the right place.

TABLE 2-1   **Nostalgia Exercise**

Traditionalists	Baby Boomers	Generation Xers	Millennials	Generation Edgers
World War II	The Beatles	MTV	Chat rooms	Newtown shooting
Radio	Civil Rights Movement	Challenger shuttle disaster	Events of 9/11	Barack Obama
The atomic bomb	Moon landing	The Cold War	Reality TV	YouTube
Alfred Hitchcock	Rosa Parks	Atari	Matthew Shepard killing	#Feminism
LIFE magazine	Sex, drugs, and rock 'n' roll	AIDS	Napster	ISIS
Babe Ruth	Birth control pills	Star Wars	Iraq and Afghanistan wars	Netflix
Citizen Kane	Gloria Steinem	Rise in divorce	Columbine	WiFi
The Great Depression	OPEC oil embargo	Simpson/ Goldman murders	Tattoos, piercings, and body art	Supreme Court decision on same-sex marriage
Henry Ford	John F. Kennedy	Title IX	Facebook	Snapchat
Sputnik	Booming birth rate	Reagan assassination attempt	Twitter	Recession
Pearl Harbor	Vietnam War	Personal computer	Smartphones	Global competition
Other:	Other:	Other:	Oprah Winfrey	Beyoncé
_____	_____	_____	World Wide Web	Affordable Healthcare Act
_____	_____	_____	Other:	Other:
_____	_____	_____	_____	_____
	_____		_____	_____
			_____	_____

TIP

After you've done this activity yourself, consider using it as a team-building tool with your employees.

Exercise instructions: Find your generation and circle two or three events, conditions, or icons from the corresponding list that you feel had an impact on you. The next part is the hard part: Think about how those things influence who you are *today*. It's not just about how it made you feel at the time, which is entertaining and fun, but how it *still* impacts you. If you are up for an extra challenge, ask yourself: How does this event/condition/icon impact who I am at work?

Below this chart you'll find examples of what we've heard members from each generation say in response to this exercise, but don't read those until you've done the exercise yourself. No cheating. You'll be disqualified.

To help move the conversation along, or if you're just curious to know what people typically say, read on:

> ### Traditionalist condition: Radio
>
> *"Unlike kids today who get all their news and entertainment from their phones, we all gathered around the radio growing up. Everything from listening to shows like Superman to a presidential address was all audio, so you had to imagine what you couldn't see. I think that it still makes me better at visualizing things when no picture exists. We may not have had as much information as we do today, but we were still able to make decisions with what we had. At work, I am able to imagine the unseen and make decisions with the information in front of me."*
>
> ### Baby Boomer event: OPEC oil embargo
>
> *"I'll never forget the gas shortage. I was 14, and my dad made me wake up two hours before the gas station even opened — on our assigned day, no less — to get in line just to fill up our tank. Growing up as a Baby Boomer, it felt like there was never enough for us. We were just such a huge generation that it felt like we were too big for the world that was built for us — we had to fight to get not just what we wanted, but what we needed, whether that was gas, a good grade in school, or a job. Today, it has definitely made me a more competitive person. Just like I got to that gas station two hours before it opened, I'm always the first one in the office. I know that if I don't do the job right, there are plenty of others who will."*
>
> ### Generation Xer event: Challenger explosion
>
> *"I'll never forget. I was in eighth grade. The teacher rolled in a TV cart so the whole class could watch the shuttle launch with a teacher on board. Within minutes, the entire classroom was filled with stunned silence as we watched the Challenger explode. I remember being so scared and sad. And then, it didn't end on the day of the explosion.*

Cable news replayed the footage over and over and over, and as the months went on, it was discovered that the cause of the explosion could have been prevented, but someone was trying to save a buck. I think that event still impacts who I am today because I just don't feel like I can trust anyone or any organization. I mean, if NASA is willing to cut corners and put people at risk, who am I to think that my organization wouldn't do the same?"

Millennial condition: Napster/streaming music

"When I started high school, Napster was all the rage. Until that point, if you wanted to hear a song you had to wait until it came on the radio or buy the entire album. Thanks to Napster, you could listen to any song you wanted with the click of a button, whenever you wanted to. And not only that . . . it was totally free! I think this has affected me at work in a few ways: My generation expects immediacy, we want to be able to customize our experience at work and not just do things the way as generations past, and at times it's like we expect to get something for nothing."

Generation Edge condition: YouTube

"I use YouTube so much in my life right now, it's hard to think of a time without it. It's just the greatest tool because I use it to learn how to do anything. I guess my entire generation is self-taught in a way, because if we want to know how to do something, we can YouTube it. And then if we're especially good at it, we can create our own tutorials!"

Understanding the global influence

Of course the events, conditions, and icons a person experiences are inextricably linked to the country he lives in. Some events have implications worldwide, like world wars, but others, like the tripling of the divorce rate and extreme hikes in college tuition, are specific to the United States. Taking this into account, it should be no surprise that the generations topic plays out differently across the globe. A Boomer in the States is going to have different traits than a Boomer in India. Primarily in the West, certain countries show generational similarities across borders in large part due to similar access to technological innovation and shared experiences of international events. However, in more emerging economies like China and India, there can be stark differences from country to country. Research has shown that when it comes specifically to Millennials and Generation Edge, because of globalization and the Internet, there are more similarities than differences across the globe.

Immigration and ethnicity

How does a Millennial whose grandparents and even great-grandparents grew up in the United States differ from a Millennial who is a first-generation immigrant? The answer is slightly complicated. Most simply, generational theory has a cyclical component to it. Research has found that first-generation immigrants tend to behave much like the Traditionalist generation (loyal, hard-working, patriotic, grateful for the job). The second generation tends to behave more like Boomers (pushing for more education, finding ways to get ahead, working within established systems), with the third generation acting more like Generation Xers (questioning the status quo, not totally trusting institutions, finding individual paths). These are only general trends, but they should help give a framework for examining people you work with from an immigration perspective.

REMEMBER

As we mention earlier, people are multilayered and complicated. It is not enough to just throw a generational label on them and move on. The key is to understand that several factors are at play, and immigration and ethnicity are important lenses.

Overcoming the "Yea, Buts. . ."

Generational differences is the one area of diversity where it's considered okay to cast shade, throw people under the bus, and just plain make fun of *perceived* failings. For example: "Millennials are entitled babies, Gen Xers are *so* cynical and apathetic, and don't even get me started on Boomers. What a workaholic bunch, not to mention they can barely figure out how to send an email from their phones!" Can you even imagine saying these types of things about another area of diversity like religion or gender? No way! It's amazing to us too, but it does get that vicious, and sometimes even worse.

The biggest hurdle when attempting to make generational theory part of your management strategy is pushback. One may even call it negativity. When fellow managers see you carrying around this book, they may wonder aloud, or to themselves, "Yea, but . . . aren't all Millennials just entitled kids who got trophies for trying? Why bother?" The next generation of employees is getting hit full force with these stereotypes. New employees are painted with the broad brush not of the Millennial, but the *worst* Millennial. These stereotypes make it so that on day one, your new hire is already fighting an uphill battle.

There will be many a detractor/naysayer to the generational conversation. These lingering questions and pushback may be coming straight from you! Here are some of the "yea, buts" that bubble up most often:

>> **The psychology "yea, but . . .":** This topic doesn't even consider things like whether someone's an introvert or an extrovert.

>> **The life stage "yea, but . . .":** These kids are going to grow up and end up acting just like us.

>> **The outlier "yea, but . . .":** I'm a Gen Xer, and I'm nothing like that.

>> **The stereotyping "yea, but . . .":** Aren't you just putting people into a box?

>> **The tired-of-conflict "yea, but . . .":** Aren't we all just more similar than we are different? We don't need something that's going to drive us farther apart from each other.

In the following sections, we take these piece by piece, objection by objection. Once you can clear your mind of them and overcome any lingering "yea, buts . . .", you'll effectively wipe off the smudge on your Gen Lens and see your direct reports more clearly.

Comparing two key perspectives: Sociology versus psychology

Recap: The psychology "yea, but . . .": This topic doesn't even consider things like whether someone's an introvert or an extrovert.

The first step to addressing this "yea, but . . ." is understanding that generational theory is a sociological science and not a psychological one. It's goal, by definition, is to examine how people act and behave in large groups. The "group" in this scenario refers to a generational cohort. It's the sociological study of how historical events and conditions can impact your generational identity/persona.

Psychology, on the other hand, is focused on the individual. It strives to understand the singular person's mind, his emotional and social reactions, and the unique things that make him tick. What are that person's triggers? What makes him happy? What makes him sad? What motivates his behavior? What singular influences played a role in forming his mind and personality?

So, really, the difference between sociology and psychology is as simple as the difference between the micro and the macro. It's like the difference between what a blue M&M looks and tastes like versus the genre of candy that M&Ms fall into.

REMEMBER

Generational theory is a fluid science; it's completely normal to relate perfectly to a trait or behavioral pattern of your generation and maybe not so much to another. As with any sociological study, there are exceptions and outliers. Generational theory is simply one lens to help people understand one another and the world around us.

WHEN PSYCHOLOGY AND SOCIOLOGY ARE A PERFECT MATCH

Psychology looks at the individual. Sociology focuses on patterns and trends. Both sciences are valid. Both offer useful information, and, in fact, they often work best when paired with one another. In many ways they're complementary, and we frequently recommend that clients pair the two when trying to understand the people they work with. Be it Kolbe, MBTI, DiSC, or any other psychological assessment you favor — far from contradicting the generations topic, it serves as a useful pairing, like a fine red wine with a nice juicy steak. They are meant to go together, and the one makes the other that much better.

Contrasting the concepts of life stage and generations

Recap: The life stage "yea, but . . .": They're going to grow up and be just like us. Isn't this just youth culture?

This particular "yea, but . . ." is a biggie. We aren't going to try and tell you that there isn't even a sliver of truth to this assertion. Of course there are certain attitudes and behaviors that are more about life stage and not necessarily specific to generational personalities. Young people will be young. Teenagers will always have messy rooms. Whether that manifests as bright-eyed and bushy-tailed or impulsive and (sometimes) reckless, there is some element of that youth mentality in any set of young people.

TIP

Before going any further, find out how to differentiate generation versus life stage versus age. For example, compare a 22-year-old Millennial named Lucy to a 32-year-old Millennial named Mina. They work differently and have varied expectations. Mina is sharp, articulate, and respects unwritten rules — that's experience. Lucy speaks about college days and what she hopes she can accomplish quickly in her first year. That's life stage. As true as that may be, these different stages affect their work. If Mina has a mortgage and a child on the way, she may be more inclined to stick with the job longer because security has become more of a priority now that there's more than one mouth to feed. Both of them are collaborative, energetic, and want to make a difference. That's generational.

Whenever you feel tempted to chalk a generational behavior up to life stage, try to silence the following micro "yea, but . . ." life-stage thoughts.

"We all experience these big moments together — we're more similar than we are different!"

The age location that each generation occupied when they were teenagers is essential to their personalities. It is during this period in time that you're making up your mind about how you feel about the world around you. You are impressionable and making sense of everything. An example we like to use is the events of September 11. It goes without saying that 9/11 was an event that changed the game for everyone, regardless of one's generation. But for Millennials, it happened right as they were in their formative (or roughly teenage) years. If you experienced that day as a 60-year-old, it would impact you differently than a middle schooler. For Millennials, the world that had seemed at least relatively safe from the atrocities of global terror was all of a sudden under attack. Their bubble of safety was burst violently, and, for them, the United States was no longer safe from the monstrosities of global terrorism. In the blink of an eye, they too became targets for terrorism, and tomorrow was far from guaranteed.

This "live for today" mentality is one they've carried with them, and it won't change regardless of what life stage they're occupying, because it's a trait that was formulated and hardened during their most impressionable years. As Millennials age into parenthood, retirement, and grandparenthood, this trait is likely to hold steady. They'll always want to make the most of their time in the here and now. Research gurus like Yankelovich and Gallup, among others, have tracked generational characteristics over decades and have found that values for the cohorts have remained consistent regardless of life stage.

"They'll grow up and be just like generations before"

Xers were always told they were going to grow up and behave just like the Baby Boomers. But we've seen something different — even though Xers have aged into another life stage, now with families, homes, and sometimes elderly parents to care for, they've still retained their Xer-like qualities and are even passing them on to their Gen Edge kids.

Millennials have long been cast as a generation averse to growing up and averse to settling down, but once they reach "a certain age," they will. There's this thought that the traditional cycle of life — education, career, marriage, kids, retirement — is the only way to become an adult. Millennials are not embracing this supposed truth like generations past. Generation Xers also caused a ruckus when they started working and insisted on balance. They shook up the traditional path, and Millennials will, too. They already are by deciding to buy a home as a replacement engagement ring because that commitment is more definite — and definitely more practical. What we're working to say is, "No, you can't expect that another generation will act like you once they 'grow up.'"

"Each life stage is basically the same; parenting will always be parenting"

Being a parent now is quite different from being a parent in the 1940s. As Millennials move into the parenting life stage, they're dealing with all kinds of challenges that didn't exist when Boomers were raising Millennials. From online bullying, to battling tech addiction, to the almost weekly school shootings, today's parents have struggles that just didn't exist before. So not only are Millennials being influenced by their distinct generational traits as they enter a new life stage; they're experiencing a life stage that is unique in and of itself because of its location in history.

"We all go through similar life stages in our youth and as adults; it's a part of getting older"

The age at which a life stage is experienced has changed over time. Millennials are just now starting to settle down, buy homes, and become parents. This is happening much later than it did for both Xers and Baby Boomers. They're older parents, and is there any question that this will impact how they raise their kids?

Understanding that the exception proves the rule

Recap: The outlier "yea, but . . .": I'm a Gen Xer, and I'm nothing like that.

You may have heard statements like these:

> "I know a Millennial who hates technology."

> "I'm a Boomer, but I embody all these Millennial traits."

> "I'm an older Xer and identify more with Boomers."

The preceding exceptions by no means disprove generational theory. Over our years in this field, we've seen some recurring objections that fall under the category of the outlier "yea, but . . . ," which you're likely to encounter yourself, either because you're the one thinking it or because it becomes a challenge you encounter as you try to use generational theory in your management strategy. In many cases these examples stick out because they are the outliers, but by and large, the overarching structure of each generation holds true.

The missing trait outlier

The naysayers wear this missing trait outlier like a badge of honor. They know a Millennial who hates technology, a Boomer who's a tech whiz, and a Gen Xer who hates email. Remember that generational theory is not looking to define every single Millennial by exploring a comprehensive list of their traits, beliefs, behaviors, and motivations. You can think of gen theory more like a compass than a map. We're trying to give you a general gauge for a demographic of people, rather than give you the definitive sketch of the Millennial persona. To meet a Millennial who "defies" this or that trait is not only normal but completely expected. It's simply the nature of the study.

The different generation outlier

Occasionally, you may come across someone who's genuinely confused — "I'm a Gen Xer, but I identify with Millennials almost entirely, Boomers a little bit, and Xers not at all." Don't panic. This doesn't mean you should throw the generations topic out the window. When this happens, it can most often be attributed to one or both of these reasons:

>> **Family dynamics:** Who raised this Gen Xer? Was it younger Boomers? Did they grow up with Millennial siblings? If so, this Gen Xer was likely exposed to the events and conditions more typically associated with Millennials and thus, logically, identifies with that generation more than her own.

>> **The "inner generation":** This concept is interesting, and it has more to do with chosen mindset than anything else. For example, there are some Boomers who are so future-focused and age defiant that they truly act and feel like Millennials. On the other hand, a teenager could be so conservative or traditional that she may find more similarities with people in their 70s than her own classmates. We call this a person's "inner generation."

The cusper outlier

Another oft-repeated outlier case is that of the *cusper.* It comes up with those who are born near the edge of two generations and straddle the line, be it Boomer/Xers, Xers/Millennials or Millennial/Edgers. These people often exhibit traits from both generations. Though these people can sometimes feel like the generational conversation doesn't apply to them, they couldn't be more wrong. They have the advantage of two perspectives, being able to see from two generations' vantage points. They are a boon to organizations and often help streamline communication across generational divides. For more on cuspers, see Chapter 13.

Differentiating between stereotyping and recognizing patterns

Recap: The stereotyping "yea, but . . .": With all of these sweeping generalizations, aren't you just stereotyping?

First, we define stereotyping. Forgive us while we do the classic grade school, "Let's look up what this word means in the dictionary" exercise.

> **Stereotype:** *A widely held but fixed and oversimplified image of a particular type of person or thing.*

With this definition, it's easy to see how someone might dismiss generational theory as a way to stereotype swaths of people by age. The big differences between stereotyping and what the generations topic aims to do boil down to the following:

>> **Leading with the negative:** When you're using generations to pigeonhole people in a derogatory way, then you're stereotyping. Millennials are needy. Gen Xers are apathetic. Baby Boomers are selfish. These are some examples of stereotypes. Not only are they negative, but they're painting these generations in a broad stroke, without (and this is important) taking the time to unearth the *why* behind this perceived trait.

>> **Putting people in boxes:** Our goal is not to put people in a box; it's to take the lid off the box and see what's inside. It's just one more tool to help you evaluate and understand what makes a person tick. You never want to use these tools to pin down someone's identity, but rather to open up the way you see others and connect with them.

Taking the negative to a positive

Recap: The tired-of-conflict "yea, but. . .": Aren't we all just more similar than we area different? We don't need something that's going to drive us farther apart from each other.

This is what we like to call the "I'm so exhausted with all of these trainings that talk about how we're different!" outlier. It's a natural place of frustration or burnout. It's tiring studying human behavior *all* the time – with every psychological and sociological assessment out there, a moment may come when you (yes, you) throw up your hands and say one of the following:

>> **"At the end of the day, we're human. We all want the same thing!"** True. We agree that we are all humans driven by basic human instincts like joy, fulfillment, and having enough resources to provide for yourself and your family. We caution taking the all-encompassing approach, however, because we know that managers and leaders have tough jobs, and treating everyone the same can only work for so long. Generational theory is not the one and only solution to develop a thorough understanding of the people you manage, but it can serve as the foundation.

OR

> » **"It's just so negative to talk about how we're different all the time. Can't we talk about how we're similar?"** We encourage re-phrasing this remark as, "We're more alike than we are dissimilar, but those differences matter." We know that using the words "clash" and "difference" can feel divisive at times, but a true understanding of diversity is what leads to inclusion. Understanding how your generation is different from another gives you the opportunity to find even more areas where you are alike.

Using Generational Theory to Build a Better Workplace

As you discover more about generations, you'll apply more to your life. And you'll also realize that you're becoming an even better leader and manager.

REMEMBER

Part of being a great leader is acknowledging that one generation is not better than another. This book focuses on the youngest generation because they're causing the most head-scratching right now. But as is the case with many lenses of diversity, the more diverse the better. Each generation brings their own talents to the table for a more holistic approach to any endeavor.

It's up to you to create a better workplace for your employees, and understanding generational nuances and behaviors gives you that edge to then impact the bottom line and take action.

Impacting the bottom line

People often dismiss generational theory as a soft science, one that is all fluff and no substance. They couldn't be more wrong. Tapping into generational dynamics has far-reaching implications — and yes, financial ones as well. Though it can be easy to slough it off as a touchy-feely topic to help us all just get along, in reality it's a dollars-and-cents, bottom-line issue.

REMEMBER

Still not convinced? Consider this: The generations topic touches every realm of the working world. From recruiting and retention to marketing and selling, generational collisions can cost your organization big bucks. Think about that promising new recruit that you just spent the last year investing in only to see him walk out the door. There is no industry, company, or organizational strategy that wouldn't benefit from generational insight. If you have any doubts, ask yourself whether you're prepared to deal with these generational challenges that are either already here, or just around the corner:

>> **Recruiting:**

- The next generation pipeline of talent is more diverse than ever. Do your recruiting strategies reflect this fact?

- Are your recruiting materials still a verbose booklet and a dense block of text, or are you tapping into social media and next-generation networks to recruit in a creative and dynamic way?

>> **Training:**

- Gen Edge is a visual and resourceful generation. How do you create training that appeals to their unique learning style?

- Millennials seek to collaborate and connect with their colleagues. Do your training programs build in opportunities to make connections, maybe even friendships, for new hires?

>> **Retention:**

- What are you doing to ensure that Xers don't feel stalled in their careers and feel like the only way up is out of your organization?

- The average Millennial tenure at an organization is between three and five years. How are you proactively stemming the tide of Millennial attrition?

>> **Turnover:**

- You just switched to an open-office layout. Why are your Xers and Boomers leaving in droves?

- Are you implementing creative open-door policies that make it easy for ex-employees to return? (Side note: These tend to become some of the most loyal employees. They say, "If you love something, let it go, if it comes back . . ." — you know the rest.)

>> **Succession planning:**

- As Baby Boomers start to retire en masse, do you have a plan for retaining the institutional knowledge that will be walking out the door with them?

- Have you built successful mentorship programs that connect the next generation of leaders with seasoned veterans?

>> **Selling:**

- Xers and Millennials want utmost transparency from their salespeople. Are you adapting to this new style of selling?

- Traditionalists are still looking for time and a personal touch from sales-people. Is your staff prepared to customize their sales approach?

>> **Marketing:**

- Millennials are increasingly responding to companies that wear social responsibility on their sleeve. How are you weaving this into your marketing?

- Baby Boomers are *not* on board with the "you're retiring, take it easy, slow down, and relax" messaging as they move into the next phase of their lives.

Turning the "what" into "so what"

Too often, those interested in the generations topic treat it like an academic study or a fun/interesting hobby and nothing more. They'll soak in this new study or that latest survey, or maybe even read an entire book (cough, cough) and leave it at that. The information they've learned gets stowed away in a one-person tomb. We totally understand — it's a fascinating topic and it can be easy to get lost in the study of people, because people are fascinating. But while we certainly hope this topic is engaging as well as instructive, we want to take things a step further. We want *you* to take things a step further.

We want readers to feel confident to make the leap from awareness to action. Awareness is only half the battle. Action is the other half. We've tried to strike a balanced mix of understanding the why behind the what with strategies to turn the what into action. Because it's not enough to say "Oh, now I get why Millennials love technology," but to instead ask, "How can I tap into their love of technology and use it as an asset for the company?" It's not enough to know that Millennials are integrating work and life without also using that information to reassess realistic (and implementable) changes to your flexibility and formality policies — if not for the organization at large, then at least within your one-to-one relationship with your direct report.

While every chapter in this book will absolutely include strategies to help you turn the "what" into "so what," if you are looking to dive right into the most actionable things you can do right now, we suggest focusing on Part 2 where we break down generational clash points and how to manage through them.

You can think of this book not just as a manual for how to build a stronger workforce, but a manual that comes with a tool set.

Chapter **3**

Breaking into the Millennial Mind

"Millennials win the generational popularity contest!" said no one, ever. Let's face it . . . Millennials have a bad PR problem. They're portrayed, not on a spectrum, but as one of two poles — either the best thing that's ever happened to the working world, or the absolute worst.

At their worst, Millennials are stereotyped as entitled, narcissistic, coddled, lazy, sensitive, tech addicts. These less-than-flattering descriptors form a thick fog of negativity that can be hard to see through. The fog is so dense that even on day 1 of a new job, they're already fighting an uphill battle. It's hard for Millennials to make a good first impression because their colleagues' and managers' opinions are so clouded by the negative associations of what it means to be a Millennial.

On the other end of the spectrum, Millennials are lauded as the greatest thing to happen since sliced bread. They're ascribed almost superhero-like qualities, painted out to be a group of disruptive creatives who will teach all the old stodgy workers how to embrace a new age of working (that includes craft beer happy hours and ping-pong tournaments in the lunchroom). This supposedly positive portrayal actually isn't helping at all. Instead, it breeds resentment in other generations, and let's face it, no generation can live up to such an impossible standard (not to mention that, arguably, some of these attributes aren't all that great).

The truth, as is usually the case, lies somewhere in the middle. In this chapter, we aim for a more centered, balanced, and hopefully fair approach. Over the next few pages, we dive into the pivotal events and conditions that were instrumental in shaping the Millennial identity.

Consider this chapter as you would a booklet on how to learn salsa. It can build the foundation, show you the steps, and make you aware of everything you need to know. But until you actually learn how to partner with someone and put that learning into practice, you're never going to succeed. This chapter focuses on awareness about the formative influences of the Millennial generation. For actionable management strategy, go to Part 2 of this book, where you find out how to address generational clash points.

WARNING

When we say we're "breaking into the Millennial mind," we're talking about Millennials as a *group* and not *individual* Millennials. Generational theory is rooted in the sociological study of large-scale patterns and trends. Keep that in mind as you read this upcoming chapter. We research and analyze the Millennial persona, not individual Millennial personalities (with all the psychological complexities).

Viewing Millennials as Whole Beings

It's unfortunate that Millennials have been restricted to two-dimensional portrayals. While managers, and the general population, would benefit from a full, robust sketch of who Millennials are as a generation, the people doing the sketching are amateur artists making assumptions, and therefore drafting line drawings instead of the full, 3D renderings that Millennials (and every generation) deserves.

Differing depictions of Millennials

Everyone seems to want to throw in their two cents about the Millennial generation. In this section, we outline some of the more common Millennial depictions. Spoiler alert: Though some of these are more favorable than others, they all fail to give an accurate, fair, and thorough accounting of this complex generation.

>> **The media's version:** The media doesn't benefit from reporting on the middle ground (that's not how you sell magazines or get a high click-rate), so the

media's versions of Millennials are either: "These kids are the best thing since sliced bread and are coming to save the world!" or "This new generation will be the destruction of everything good that we've fought so hard to build. They must be subdued!" These extreme versions of Millennials, either on the positive end or the negative end, are what we so often see plastered all over magazines. And you know why? Because the title "Lock down the hatches: Millennials will destroy the working world as we know it" on a cover is a surefire way to make magazines fly off the shelves.

» **The focus-group-of-one version:** This depiction of a Millennial crystalizes when people base their opinions of *all* Millennials on *one* memorable person. They may have encountered a Millennial like Randall: He embodies all the Millennial stereotypes and amps them up to a level that paints his entire generation in a horrible light — he's always on his phone, is never on time, has no work ethic to speak of, boasts about his weekend getting drinks with a band that no one has heard of, frequently shares horrible ideas with upper level management, and so on. Or, they may have encountered a Millennial like Claire, who is seemingly perfect, cutting-edge, full of great ideas, ambitious, and considerate, and therefore makes her generation just so much better than the others. Either way, these scenarios, yet again, echo the two polar opposites of the spectrum. They're based on a focus group of just one.

» **The water cooler version:** It's a sad consequence of human nature that a shared love of talking about bad stuff trumps a shared love of talking about the good stuff. At work, colleagues become comrades when they vent around the water cooler (or Keurig machine): "Can you *believe* he went up to the CEO today?!" or "I'm so frustrated; I need to coach her through *every* step of every project!" or "Why do we keep hiring all these young people if they're just going to leave in two years — it's a waste of time and money!" These conversations tend to be reactionary, tainted by frustration, and only reinforce Millennial stereotyping.

» **The just-like-my-kid version:** This Millennial depiction blossoms from a person (usually a Boomer parent) saying something like: "I have a kid. She's a Millennial. She can do no wrong. She's taught me so much about the world. She knows so much about technology. She's basically brill (that's a cool word I learned from her that is short for 'brilliant'). We should put all our faith in Millennials because they're coming to save us from our wicked (or hopelessly antiquated) ways." Some parental bias is obviously at play here, and so we have another portrayal of Millennials that just doesn't capture the generation as a whole.

Finding the why behind the what

In every one of the examples in the previous section, the data is contaminated. Either the sample size is far too small, the data gatherer is biased in some way (as in the parent-to-kid association), or there's some ulterior motive (the media is looking for click-bait). But perhaps the biggest reason the preceding information borders on inaccurate is that each version depicts *what* a Millennial is and ignores *why* he is that way. "The Why Behind the What" could have been the title of this entire chapter.

Now, as you may imagine, there's no straightforward answer behind the big "why" for the entirety of the Millennial generation. For every individual member, the why behind their actions, preferences, traits, and motivations is a complex and complicated tangle of many different factors. It's an intersection of where they were born, who their parents are, whether they're introverts or extroverts, the kind of education they received, whether they grew up in a small town or a big city, their race and gender, and the list goes on and on. But when we look at Millennials collectively, the root of understanding them as a cohort, or truly "breaking into the Millennial mind" comes from studying the collective experiences they had as they were in the midst of their formative years. (For more on the theory of formative years, see Chapter 2.)

Why You Are Who You Are: Taking a Look at the Formative Years

Experiences that happen during your formative years define who you will become as an adult. So how do we define Millennials' formative years? First you have to look at their birth years. We define Millennials as anyone born between 1980 and 1995 (see Figure 3-1). *Formative years* means different things to different theorists and psychologists, but for the purpose of generational understanding, the term is synonymous with adolescence, or roughly the teenage years, as shown in Figure 3-2. So, the formative years for the entire Millennial generation span anywhere between 1993 and 2014; to pinpoint a Millennial on that timeline, see Table 3-1. (Again, *this is not finite,* but rather a way to start the conversation. Some theorists have posited that formative years stretch out into the early twenties and start as early as seven or eight years old.)

If you question just how important those formative years are, consider a couple examples of how influential these years are to the masses:

>> **Rites of passage:** For centuries, cultures have celebrated the moment when a man or woman reaches a new stage in his or her life. Typically this happens at a tipping point when the person is in the transition stage between childhood and adulthood.

>> **Pop culture teen obsession:** Some of the greatest TV shows and movies, the truly iconic ones across generations, focus on teenagers: *The Breakfast Club, Happy Days, Saved By the Bell* (sidenote: there's a reason *Saved by the Bell: The*

College Years failed in comparison — they were, in a sense, leaving their formative years), *The OC, Fresh Prince of Bel Air.* Your teen years leave a large mark on your life forever, even though they cover such a small amount of time. Cue the "oh my gosh, I have my 15-year high-school reunion coming up and need to look my best" conversations.

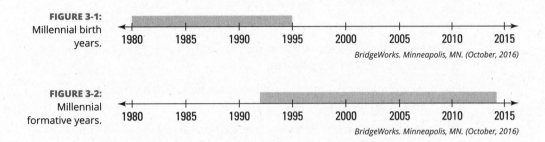

FIGURE 3-1:
Millennial birth years.

BridgeWorks. Minneapolis, MN. (October, 2016)

FIGURE 3-2:
Millennial formative years.

BridgeWorks. Minneapolis, MN. (October, 2016)

TABLE 3-1

Correlating Birth Years to Formative Years

Birth Year	Formative Years
1980	1993–1999
1981	1994–2000
1982	1995–2001
1983	1996–2002
1984	1997–2003
1985	1998–2004
1986	1999–2005
1987	2000–2006
1988	2001–2007
1989	2002–2008
1990	2003–2009
1991	2004–2010
1992	2005–2011
1993	2006–2012
1994	2007–2013
1995	2008–2014

Obviously a lot has happened within that 21-year time span of Millennial formative years. We can't cover everything, but in the upcoming sections, we hit upon the most influential happenings within that timeframe. To whet your appetite, consider the following:

>> Millennials are the first generation to have had access to the Internet throughout the entirety of their formative years.

>> Millennials have never known a time without the PG-13 rating.

>> Millennials were Facebook guinea pigs, first using it in its more experimental phase with .edu email addresses.

>> A black president was in the presidential seat for almost a third of their formative years.

>> Most Millennials can't remember a divided Germany — the oldest Millennials hadn't reached their formative years when the Berlin Wall came down.

>> Millennials are the most educated and the most diverse generation thus far (not considering the post-Millennials).

>> Millennials never lived in a time when personal home computers weren't the norm.

We understand that there's a difference between the lower end of the Millennial scale (kids who have a couple years of work experience at best) and the upper end (settled adults who may have spent well over a decade in the workplace). While we assess the whole 15-year generational band in this chapter, we break down the early versus late Millennial mentalities for you in Chapter 13. There we'll touch on those moments when the differences between early and late Millennials are both stark and pertinent to how you might manage them differently.

Uncovering the impact of technology

Technology is a huge factor in understanding the Millennial persona. Check out this technology timeline of major accomplishments, releases, and launched innovations from 1993 to 2014:

>> **1993:** Pentium Processor; Internet available to anyone with dial-up.

>> **1994:** Sony Playstation; Yahoo; Amazon.

>> **1995:** Java; eBay launched.

>> **1996:** DVD player invented; Nintendo 64; Palm Pilot; Hotmail.

>> **1997:** AOL Instant Messenger; Broadband introduced; Netflix founded; DVD players become available in the United States.

>> **1998:** Google is born; Bluetooth technology launched.

>> **1999:** Napster founded; first modern optical computer mouse introduced; WiFi becomes available to the public; Honda Insight launched, the first mass-produced hybrid vehicle in the United States.

>> **2000:** AT&T introduces text messaging; GPS goes mainstream; USB drives hit the market.

>> **2001:** Wikipedia is launched; first iPod; iTunes.

>> **2002:** First US camera phone released; Friendster goes live and reaches 3 million users.

>> **2003:** Skype; Myspace.

>> **2004:** Facebook launched as "Thefacebook."

>> **2005:** YouTube launched.

>> **2006:** Nintendo Wii; Twitter; Facebook opens to everyone.

>> **2007:** Apple's first iPhone released; Kindle; Netflix starts streaming.

>> **2008:** Google Android; Spotify.

>> **2009:** Uber; Fitbit launched first tracker.

>> **2010:** Apple introduces iPad; Instagram.

>> **2011:** Siri; Snapchat; IBM Watson.

>> **2012:** Google gets Nevada license for driverless car.

>> **2013:** Google Glass; Apple adopts Touch ID technology; Drones go mainstream.

>> **2014:** 3D printing industry boom; first Apple Watch announced.

Ask a person to name one defining trait of the Millennial generation, and you'll usually get some version of tech-savvy (though sometimes the more unkind respondent will say tech-obsessed). Though Baby Boomers and Gen Xers also experienced their fair share of technological innovations, Millennials grew up during a time when the tech world was blowing up and fundamentally changing everything from the way we work to the way we consume media. The technology timeline should give some insight into the major bombshell developments of the era, but ranking among the most influential you can include Internet access becoming widespread, the Internet going social, Napster, smartphones, and at the tail end . . . Uber.

These developments, among so many others in the past 20 years, have left lasting impacts on corporate and social culture. For Millennials especially, certain truths arose because of their development alongside developing technology:

>> **As a collective, they became uniquely adaptable to change.** Millennials have been there for the ride and have grown to adapt with the changing tides. Their youth set them up to become adaptive to a world that was rapidly changing and upgrading around them. They learned to pick up new systems and adjust to the new goings on.

>> **To them, technology is more than just the hardware; it's a way of life.** They have always been connected to the world in a way that generations before them weren't. Further on in this chapter, we discuss social media and how it cemented that concept, but for now we hone in on the way that technological advancements themselves helped to shape the Millennial persona.

>> **Those who hold the information, hold the power.** The Internet fundamentally changed the adage, "Knowledge is power." In the past, experience, networks, and hierarchy contributed to your level of knowledge. Millennials didn't have to buy the full suite of the *Encyclopedia Britannica* to hold the world's knowledge in their hands . . . a quick (but sometimes not-so-quick) dial-up gave them the inside scoop on the topic of their choosing.

>> **The consumer market demanded a new salesperson.** We don't need to tell you that online shopping changed the buying and selling economy. In addition to on-demand shopping experiences, Millennials were also shown how to filter trustworthy brands. No product and no service goes unsurveyed — or in some cases — un-crowdsourced.

We know, technology has influenced everyone. We all use smartphones and are all overdependent on the Internet. A key difference to remember is that for some of the older generations, massive breaks in tech — like the Internet — arrived when they were outside of their formative years. They'd already made some sense of the world around them, and things like iPhones weren't impacting their views of the world. For Millennials, who were experiencing these changes as young teens, the concept of technological innovation became embedded into their brains. For them, the Internet is a basic necessity of life and always has been.

Understanding Millennial reliance on technology

If the power were to go off in your workplace for more than a few hours, continuing the workday would seem ridiculous. No lights, no phones . . . what's the point of being at work? Electricity is not an amenity to the workplace. It's a necessity. You probably agree with this, yes? But wait . . . Traditionalists may not have necessarily felt the same way. "You spoiled kids!" they may have thought. "Pick up a pen and paper. Open up some windows. Life goes on, and you don't *need* those nice amenities to be a productive employee and get your work done."

Apply this example to Millennials and their infamous obsession with technology and always being connected. You may have encountered this before. Say the Internet goes down at work. After you subdue a minor panic, you start thinking of what you can still get done. What's a Millennial's response? "Oh, time to go home or to Starbucks. Right?" Without the Internet, the whole infrastructure that they're used to working in (and living in) is down.

For Millennials, the Internet is nearly always a necessity because they rely on it for

>> **Any and all information:** They grew up using technology to make sense of the world around them. With Google, then Wikipedia, and eventually smartphones, they had constant access to all the information about any subject, topic, or area of expertise they could want. Learning the proper techniques for curling, how to make a Manhattan, or how to ace a Civil War history test never seemed so simple or accessible.

>> **Getting around:** You may have learned the lay of the land in your neighborhood or became a pro at navigation using what some refer to now as "old-timey, printed maps," but Millennials never had to. With GPS technology and smartphones, flexing that muscle in their brains was never necessary. Hence the reason you may know some Millennials who use smartphones to navigate to and from work every day.

>> **Staying connected:** As a generation more globally diverse than ever before, Millennials have friends and family spread out all over the world. What started as messaging your friends on AIM has morphed into Skype, WhatsApp, and FaceTime. For Millennials, these are authentic ways to connect with their peers, near or far.

>> **Collaboration tools:** Crowdsourcing, Yelping reviews, following an event hashtag — the Internet has opened up a world of collaboration where you can

rely on your peers to give you the info you need, rather than being force-fed by those who hold the information or power. In a sense, information has gone democratic.

Millennials will likely always rely on technology to get their work done, whether it's to connect during and after hours or to streamline processes. As a manager, the best thing that you can do is to give them the flexibility to use technology in a way that suits them.

Delving into the need for customization

For Millennials, perhaps the most momentous shift technology has helped bring about is the introduction of the supremely customized world. As an example, take Napster (the first service of its kind, paving the way for current staples like iTunes, Spotify, and Apple Music). For those of you not in the know, Napster was a peer-to-peer file-sharing service for MP3s — usually music. The point here is not the "Wow, we can get so many songs for free without recording them on the radio" thing (though we could certainly go down a rabbit hole about that), but more about the "Wow, I can choose to download any song I want at any time" thing. Instead of needing to buy entire albums, where, for better or for worse, buyers would be exposed to not just the hits but the rest of the songs on the album, Millennials could hand-pick exactly what they wanted to download. Technology and modern advancements blew the door wide open for customization. The ringtones on their phones were hand-selected, and it wasn't just a ringtone . . . it meant something (are you more of a Mario Brothers theme ringtone lady or a Spice Girls' wannabe kind of gal?)

(PHONE) SEPARATION ANXIETY

There are times when reliance on technology can border on dependence. It has led to a generation of people who can't fathom leaving the house without their phones, and who — whether they're late to work or not — will circle back to pick up this ever-important tool. That sound of a text message or ping of alert is such a constant in their lives that the absence creates, in a mild sense, a feeling that something "just doesn't feel right." Over-connectedness certainly carries some unfavorable consequences, and in many cases Millennials are aware of the problem. There has been a recent push for mindfulness and a #unplug movement that encourages letting technology go, if only for a little while, to connect, instead, with the world and the people around you free of digital distraction.

THE END OF WONDER

We have heard the argument that the tech boom has marked the end of wonder. Imagine (see what we did there?) that you are a Traditionalist:

- You don't see the news; you read about it the morning paper.
- You don't watch Superman save the planet; you imagine his cape swirling around Earth as it's described on *The Adventures of Superman* radio show.
- Your access and exposure to all things worldly is limited, so you spend a good deal of time mentally creating what could be.

While Traditionalists were required to wonder in order to paint a picture, younger generations already have a foundation to build upon. Some people deem this new "access-to-any-and-all-information" as a condition that keeps young people away from creative hypotheticals, but might it simply give them a new way to wonder, with more creativity-sparking tools at hand? Now, think of yourself as a young Millennial:

- You've consumed news in snippets via social media or live-streaming events with no filters.
- Every show and movie is at your disposal with on-demand entertainment.
- Gaming platforms allow you to create your own worlds.
- When you have a creative idea, you have a virtual room of input to help you imagine an even better way of doing things.

So goes the argument that with more at your disposal, the more you are pushed to think outside the box and therefore wonder what could be. Someone could debate that you have no original thought if everything is in reaction to something else, but to that we challenge you: When was there a legitimate original thought uninfluenced by any other past experience or person? It's a almost poetic that all our thoughts build upon each other's imaginations. Willy Wonka would be proud.

This need for customization has spilled over beyond the tech world. Fast-casual restaurant chains like Chipotle let you choose exactly how you want your food because you don't need to stick to the stock items on a menu. From a very young age, Millennials have been able to customize their style. Major clothing brands like Nike feature specially customized apparel, designed by you for you so that no one in the world would have anything like it. If you want to take this trend to it's extreme level, Millennials have even latched onto tattoos as a way to customize their skin. They're taking the messaging that they're unique and that there's no one else like them to the nth degree.

BUILDING YOUR PERSONAL BRAND

Technology has opened the door for customization, which has opened the door for personal branding, or customization of all aspects of your appearance. Your ringtone says something about you, your hair says something about you, and even that tattoo of the Deathly Hallows on your forearm is proclaiming something about who you are. In a sense, technology gives Millennials the opportunity to craft a brand, and many have been doing it from a young age. A side effect of growing up with the sharing tools the Internet has made widely available means that you're always self-aware of what you're putting out into the world. Millennials take pride in crafting their personal brand. A well-crafted identity can serve many purposes, whether it's helping them land their dream job, or even as a tool to attract like-minded individuals to a cause.

Technology has led to customization not just of how you buy products, but also how you consume information. On Facebook, you can very blatantly choose who you're friends with and who you're not. Social media feeds can be set up to show only the kind of information you want to see. RSS feeds can be filled with your favorite news sources. This has, of course, led to some negative backlash. The world has become ever-more-polarized because you can just choose to blot out the things you don't agree with. Diversity of opinion is harder and harder to come by, as is patience with views that are divergent from your own.

At work, Millennials seek opportunities to customize their workspace, schedule, and story. In their minds, choice is a crucial factor to staying involved and motivated because it allows them to stay on personal brand in everything that they do.

Revealing their collaborative nature through video games

Another way technology shaped Millennials is the way it encouraged a collaborative mindset, and you can see that through the evolution of gaming. To really understand what gaming means to Millennials, you have to rewind time and look back at Xer formative years and their experience within the gaming world.

Xer video games focused on the individual and, not coincidentally, Gen Xers are a highly independent generation. Xers were the first generation to truly be exposed to video games, and what were they playing? Pong, Tetris, Space Invaders, Donkey Kong, Frogger, Duck Hunt. For the most part, these were solo games. You might hang out while your friend played on his or her Atari, or you might partake in some of the very basic multi-player functions, but that mode was far from fine-tuned, and your access was limited to whoever was in the room and the number of remotes available.

GAMING INCEPTION

The latest evolution of gaming, which perhaps applies more to Generation Edge (the generation after Millennials), is the arrival of Twitch, a collaborative gaming site that is one of the highest-viewed sites on the Internet. On Twitch, gamers can just sit around and watch their friends play games . . . while on the screen they can see another person in a different room playing a game, who is also surrounded by friends watching him or her play the game. It's a way to "hang out" while watching video games. Don't worry . . . we don't get it either.

Millennials, on the other hand, played far more collaborative games than Gen Xers before them. As time progressed, they started to play multiplayer games with up to four players per game, and then ever-improving Internet access enabled Millennials to connect with players across the world. Massively multiplayer games like EverQuest and World of Warcraft allowed them to game with millions of people from all walks of life and every part of the globe. Gaming went mobile with the Game Boy, which evolved into the Nintendo DS, and now smartphone apps allow Millennials to game with anyone from anywhere.

The gaming world is a critical piece of the puzzle to understanding the Millennial collaborative spirit. Collaboration is something that has been a part of their daily existence. So you'd better believe that when they show up at work, they'll approach their job as a team sport. Whether that means collaborating on creative work like writing or even more seemingly mundane tasks like budgeting, Millennials will jump at the opportunity to work together to get the job done.

Dissecting the "upgrade cycle" generation

As Millennials were growing up, one of the constants in an ever-changing world was the rate of change itself. While previous generations have experienced impressive technological innovations (for example, radio and television), Millennials were teens during some of the fastest evolutions in technology the world has seen to date. We've dubbed this phenomenon of the increasing rate of change as the "upgrade cycle," and it applies to everything from the phones in Millennials' pockets to how quickly they can access the Internet, to how quickly they want to move up in organizations, and even to the advancement of human rights.

Here is a snapshot of the key influencers of the upgrade cycle during the formative years (1993 to 2014):

>> **Cellphones:**

- At the outset (1993): Unsightly candy-bar cellphones (size and shape of a candy bar)

- By the end (2014): Slim and sleek iPhone 6 Plus

>> **Home movies:**

- At the outset (1993): VCRs ("Be Kind, Please Rewind")

- By the end (2014): Streaming Netflix on mobile devices

>> **Internet access:**

- At the outset (1993): Toasting a Pop-Tart at home while waiting to connect to less-than-reliable dial-up

- By the end (2014): Ubiquitous WiFi — coffee shop, airport, even on the bus

>> **Music:**

- At the outset (1993): Sitting by the radio to record your favorite song on a mixtape

- By the end (2014): Paying a monthly subscription to stream music at any time, from any device, wherever you are

>> **Video games:**

- At the outset (1993): Taking turns playing Super Mario AllStars on your dope Super Nintendo Entertainment System

- By the end (2014): Watching others play Halo on Twitch

Understanding the rate of change itself

Have you heard the term *planned obsolescence?* It's something that's become part of the Millennial expectation. When this generation gets a new phone, they know it's not a forever phone, because there's always going to be a new have-to-have innovation on the horizon. The rate of change has sped up so quickly that it's actually created segmentations within the Millennial generation itself — the early Millennials may have used a Nokia phone in high school and upgraded to a smart-phone later on. Later Millennials used a smartphone in high school, and an upgraded version of that same touchscreen smart technology in college. This seemingly minor difference in experience shifts educational style preferences, communication amongst friends, and awareness of what's happening in the world.

The cellphones in their pockets weren't the only things subject to the upgrade cycle. Internet access has become better and better. Video games have improved to the point of virtual reality gaming. Even social media networks have upgraded and evolved, offering changing functionalities and uses. Is it any surprise that when Millennials enter the workforce, they may be looking to upgrade their jobs? It's built in as a part of their understanding of the world around them and their place within it.

One of the most pervasive complaints about the Millennial generation is that they're entitled. Employers complain that new hires enter organizations and expect to be promoted within a year or two, even if they've never had experience in that particular industry. The root of this expectation is likely quite obvious to you now: The upgrade cycle shifted not just Millennial expectations about technology, but their expectations about the work world as well. In addition to that, their parents raised them with the message, "You can be anything you want to be," so that desire to move quickly through the ranks makes sense. If they're not reaching their goals within your company, or they feel stagnant after five years, their eyes will wander. It's only natural, because for Millennials, the status quo was always evolving, changing, and being disrupted.

Connecting on speed

In the beginning, there was dial-up. Older Millennials can remember the slow, tedious process of waiting for the all-too-familiar dial-up jingle to go through its ditty, with no guarantee of any connection at the end of its tune. If you did manage to connect, there followed the long periods of waiting for pictures to load, programs to download, basically anything at all to happen. Oh, and if your mom or dad needed to make a call, forget it. Time to switch over to TV for a bit, because the line had to be freed for the phone to work.

Fast forward to now, and it's a completely different ballgame. Access to the Internet isn't constrained to one location. Smartphones in your pocket guarantee that the amazing Internet is almost always accessible. Whether it's through WiFi hotspots or 4G, access to all information, resources, and tools is always at your fingertips, quite literally. It has changed the speed at which we can get things done, and it's broken down physical barriers — work can now be accomplished anywhere, not just at your desktop that's tethered to the Interweb via Ethernet cables.

THE PARADOX OF CHOICE

Evolving technology has vastly expanded choice. When Boomers and Xers purchased their first phone — a landline phone — they could choose between a handful of different types and colors. When Millennials purchased their first phone — a cellphone — there were hundreds to choose from based on brand, style, and color. This upgrade in choice, while appearing like a treasure chest of choices, has had some pretty negative side effects. *The Paradox of Choice,* a book by Barry Schwartz published in 2004, honed in on the anxiety that has resulted from having too many options. Millennials are the first generation to be subjected to the massive amount of choice during their formative years:

- With so many news sources on the Internet, how can you screen for the best, most-trustworthy provider?

- Millennial parents and teachers said you could be anything you wanted to be . . . but how do you choose what you want to pursue and do?

- The world is actually your oyster: How do you decide where you want to go?

- There are 15 flavors of fro-yo but you only get 3 to a cup: an impossible choice! (Okay, that one's not as stressful, but you get our point.)

The following formula has cemented itself in people's minds, and sadly has become inextricably associated with Millennials:

Instant access = instant gratification = spoiled + entitled humans

If any generation had grown up with instant access to all things like Millennials did, they'd probably have developed similar perceptions of the world around them. So before you (or someone you know) gets frustrated and/or annoyed by Millennials, remember that instantaneous access hasn't created an entitled generation, but it *has* resulted in a desire for the following:

>> A flattening of power structures

>> Access to people in positions of power

>> Cutting-edge (or at least modern) tech in the workplace

>> Fast, efficient working style with efficient tools available to speed up the process

Tracking the influence of social media: from Friendster to Snapchat

When examining Millennial events and conditions and how they would shape who this generation became, there was a time when many generational researchers believed that the defining Millennial event would be 9/11. It was a turning point in both American and global history, a moment that shook the world. Millennials were young and impressionable when it happened, so it still stands out as one of the most influential events of the generation. As momentous and impactful as that event was, it turns out that there would be another condition that would be even more influential in defining the Millennial generation as a whole — when the Internet went social.

Check out the following major accomplishments from 1993 to 2014 on this social media timeline:

- » **1993:** Not applicable
- » **1994:** Justin's Links (first blog)
- » **1995:** Angie's List
- » **1996:** Hotmail
- » **1997:** AOL Instant Messenger; SixDegrees
- » **1998:** Google
- » **1999:** Live Journal; Blogger; MSN Messenger
- » **2000:** Craigslist; eHarmony
- » **2001:** Wikipedia
- » **2002:** Friendster
- » **2003:** Myspace; LinkedIn; Wordpress; Skype
- » **2004:** Facebook; Flickr; Yelp
- » **2005:** YouTube; Reddit
- » **2006:** Twitter; SlideShare
- » **2007:** Tumblr
- » **2008:** 2008 election, also known as the "Facebook election"

>> **2009:** Chatroulette; Foursquare

>> **2010:** Instagram; Pinterest; Quora

>> **2011:** Snapchat; Google+; Twitch.tv

>> **2012:** Medium; Tinder

>> **2013:** Vine

>> **2014:** None

Many remember this social Internet revolution starting with AOL Instant Messenger (AIM). As kids, Millennials would rush home from a day of school to log into a chat room and exchange A/S/L (age/sex/location) information with another user. It was a world that Millennials became uniquely comfortable in, developing their own lingo (for example: brb [be right back], ttyl [talk to you later], lol [laughing out loud]) and etiquette (for example: *Always* post an away message when you're away from the computer for five minutes or more). AIM chat rooms were just the beginning.

Other platforms like Friendster, Myspace, and Thefacebook entered the scene. Many of the older Millennials remember when Facebook was "Thefacebook" and was exclusive to college students (you could only register with an .edu email account). Younger Millennials remember getting an account in middle school. In these early days of the social internet, adults were, mostly, nowhere to be found. Facebook was a virtual playground where you could add friends that you might otherwise have lost touch with. From Facebook, media consumption became more and more micro. Twitter launched, limiting users to express themselves in 140 characters or less. Then Instagram launched as a platform focused on photo sharing, condensed to a neat square shape. Snapchat and Periscope are only a couple of the more recent iterations. Whatever the new social platform, Millennials have evolved right alongside it, and it's shaped the way they live in some pretty major ways, both positively and negatively.

Examining social media's positive impact

One obvious plus about social media is how it helps the masses connect with one another while also arming them with tools to collaborate virtually. But that's not the only positive way social media has influenced the world and its users.

END OF THE EXPERT (CROWDSOURCING)

With the information firmly in the hands of the people, so ends the necessity of relying solely on the expert. Millennials have been able to contribute their own level of expertise on Wikipedia pages and review sites like Yelp and Amazon. This ability to get multiple insights and give input empowers Millennials to, at all times, make the most informed decisions. If they want to know the best place to stay in Belize, they can solicit information from online networks without paying a travel agent or worrying that the response is going to be tinged by personal interests. The crowd has supplanted the expert.

That's not to say that experts are unnecessary. We know that if you want someone to operate on your brain, you want a surgeon who is an expert in neurological science. If you want to read a worthy book about Millennials, you want to read the one written by a team of generational experts. ;-)

CONNECTING ACROSS PHYSICAL BARRIERS

It used to be that if you travelled away from your family or met interesting people abroad, you were restricted to basic forms of staying in touch: a very expensive phone call, an email, or — for the more romantic folks — a letter. Now, Millennials have a plethora of tools to stay connected with loved ones or interesting people who cross their paths. Through Facebook, Skype, FaceTime, WhatsApp, Snapchat, and countless other platforms and applications, Millennials have ways to stay connected and dialed in with the rest of the world. The virtual world has made the burden of physical barriers much easier to bear.

FINDING YOUR TRIBE

Is it a coincidence that in the last decade or so there's been a rising popularity in nerd culture? Probably not. Social media has made it easy to find your tribe. In the past, your tribe resembled some version of a John Hughes movie — the brains, the athletes, the princesses, the basket cases, the criminals, the burnouts, and so on. And in that world, the jocks and cheerleaders ruled the roost and it was harder for the dorkier among the bunch to find their people. But now, you can find fellow fantasy lovers, assemble Dungeons & Dragons players, bond over Magic the Gathering or Harry Potter tattoos, find a forum to dispute the pros and cons of David Tennant as Dr. Who and . . . well, you get the point. Maybe you're a vegan figure skater who enjoys collecting Dolly Parton vinyl records to listen to while bird watching. Weird? Some might say yes, but chances are you'll find a community online, and someone else who'll say, "Heck no, crank up 'Islands in the Stream'; there's a cardinal at my window."

ONLINE SOCIAL ACTIVISM

Detractors can be quick to denounce online activism as lazy "slacktivism," but there's no denying the amazing change it has helped create. From the Kony 2012 movement to the ALS Ice Bucket Challenge, and all the funds raised within crowd-funding platforms like Kickstarter and GoFundMe, Millennials have combined their desire to do some good in the world with their love of all things virtual, and they have managed to effect some amazing and positive change on the world. Rather than slacktivism, it's a new form of activism to create a current that every part of the masses can feel.

BLURRING OF THE PERSONAL AND THE PROFESSIONAL

Social media has helped blur the line between what is considered personal and what is considered strictly professional. Millennials will add not only friends to their Facebook feeds, but oftentimes colleagues, managers, and even clients. They've tapped into social media as an effective networking tool, and though some businesses have been slow to embrace anything other than LinkedIn (here's looking at you, finance industry), Millennials have bucked tradition and embraced it. By giving professional people access to who they are online, Millennials feel more free to be their authentic selves at work.

PAST TO PRESENT: HOW THIS HAS INFLUENCED MILLENNIALS IN THE WORKPLACE

To summarize all the gifts social media has given Millennials at work:

» They are masters of curating thoughts to make an informed decision.

» They have been able to find social circles that align with their interests and likely will create those values of inclusion and diversity at work.

» They believe that a collective voice online can move people enough to make a difference.

» They value authentic relationships, which is important to the current work-force but will be even more important to the future workforce.

Peering into the dark side of social media

As much as social media has served as an incredible tool to connect people and encourage sharing and collaboration, it's certainly not without its flaws or negative consequences.

HIGHLIGHT REELS VERSUS BEHIND THE SCENES

Social media gives you the ability to curate your persona to a crazy degree:

>> Only the best pictures go up on your feed.

>> For the most part, you're sharing your best news — promotions, vacations, weddings — and shushing up the bad.

>> You can Photoshop your images and apply filters to make you look your very best.

So, in that sense, people are always seeing the very best of you. But is it really you? Constant comparisons to other people have led to a high rate of anxiety and burnout in the Millennial generation. Constant comparison never did anyone too much good.

BULLY CULTURE PLUS THE LACK OF ACCOUNTABILITY

In many ways, the Internet is still the virtual version of the Wild Wild West. It's still this relatively new landscape that we're exploring as a culture and attempting to control. But the checks and balances of the legal system that help keep people safe and free of intimidation and harassment haven't caught up to the virtual world. Hiding behind avatars and screen names, online bullying has become a pervasive issue that has yet to be resolved. In the past, you could escape your bullies when you went home. But now, bullies are everywhere at all times. The consequences for Millennials — and even more so, post-Millennials — are shocking, and it's on managers like you and us to make changes and set the example.

VULNERABILITY PLUS THE FEAR OF FAILURE

The gift of technology is the speed at which everyone can now communicate. But that also leads to fear of the lag time. If you see a message like this on your phone:

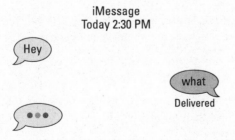

you will likely agonize over what the person is saying. A Millennial who sent an email and hasn't received a response for 48 hours may start to obsess over every period, exclamation point, and emoji in their last message. When who you are is what you post, and therefore what you write, you will take the time to meticulously craft your message. Some speculate that online personas are making Millennials and the generation after them fearful of failure, wary of coming off as vulnerable, and afraid of being less than perfect. How could you not if your entire world can be scrutinized and celebrated online?

STUNTED SOCIAL SKILLS

Millennials are criticized for being a generation that is lacking in interpersonal skills, and it's arguable that social media, in conjunction with texting as a favored form of communication, is to blame. Social graces require practice and face-to-face interaction. Growing up, many Millennials replaced in-person hang-outs with instant messaging, FaceTiming, or interacting via a collaborative game. Their social skills may not have had a chance to develop as well as, say, Xers or Boomers, and quite frankly the society they were raised in didn't force them into those situations. The good news is that Millennials are self-aware enough to know that face-to-face communication is not their strength; in fact, in a BridgeWorks survey, roughly 60 percent of Millennials said it's something they struggle with at work.

POLARIZED CONSUMPTION

By being able to curate who you follow and what you see in your news feed, social media has become an echo chamber of what you want to see. You don't often come across people with different perceptions than yours. What started out as a way to expand horizons and connect with others beyond physical boundaries has become a way to build virtual walls along ideological boundaries.

PAST TO PRESENT: HOW THIS HAS INFLUENCED MILLENNIALS IN THE WORKPLACE

To summarize all the negative ways that social media has impacted Millennials at work:

>> They are on edge, with potentially high anxiety, because they have to work at avoiding comparisons and have to monitor their online brand at all times.

>> Waiting is a virtue for this generation, who has received frequent communication in their personal lives, their entire life.

>> Social skills are being redefined because of social media, but that's not necessarily a great thing to other generations.

>> Millennials, for the most part, live in an echo chamber and aren't surrounded by people of different opinions as much as generations past were.

Checking Out the Messages that Mold Millennials

From a young age, Millennials were taught certain ways to behave. Pushing self-esteem, being part of a team, looking at the world as a whole instead of its different parts, and the effects of violence and the economy have all made Millennials into who they are today and how they work.

Gaining insight into the effects of the self-esteem movement

The self-esteem movement is directly responsible for what many see as some of the more unsavory traits of the Millennial generation, especially the older, leading edge Millennials. That seventh-place ribbon in the jump-rope contest (when there were only seven contestants)? A direct result of the self-esteem movement. Gold stars for a job well-done (or even just mediocre work)? Yup, the self-esteem movement strikes again.

So what was the self-esteem movement exactly? It was a theory pushed forward by psychologist Nathanial Branden, the author of the popular *Psychology of Self-Esteem,* published in 1969. At its core, the theory suggests that the self-esteem instilled in a child directly translates to success when he or she reaches adulthood. Accordingly, Branden instructed parents to raise children in a warm, encouraging atmosphere that would bolster the child's sense of self-worth. He recommended that this style of parenting be light on censure and punishment, and generous in conferring confidence through constant praise and validation. You might start to see where the idea for those participation awards came from.

A runaway success, selling over a million copies, Branden's book kicked off self-esteem mania in the country. From 1970 to 2000, thousands of articles were devoted to exploring the topic of self-esteem. Millennial kids reached their formative years at a time when the self-esteem movement had reached a fever pitch, and well-intentioned Boomer parents heaped validation, affection, and attention on their growing children.

In Figure 3-3, results from an Ngram Viewer, a search engine tool that tracks the usage of certain words and phrases over time, illustrate the sizable rise in popularity of the term self-esteem, peaking around the mid '90s.

WARNING

To gain an even more nuanced understanding of Millennials, take a closer look at Figure 3-3. You might notice that the popularity of the term "self-esteem" starts dipping after the mid '90s. While the reasons behind this shift are complex, what's important to take away is that older Millennials were more heavily subjected to the self-esteem movement efforts than younger Millennials. Older Millennials were also raised by older Boomers, who are generally more optimistic and idealistic than their younger generational counterparts.

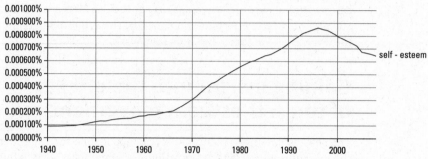

"Self-esteem." Google Books Ngram Viewer. (March, 2017). http://books.google.com/ngrams

FIGURE 3-3:
Self-esteem
graph.

The self-esteem movement shifted the way kids were raised — no longer was the parent-child relationship strictly authoritarian; it was more open and even. But this movement didn't just influence parenting style; it also influenced how children were educated. Teachers were told to sprinkle in positive feedback on all student work. They opted to focus on rewarding good behavior rather than punishing students when they got out of line. Rather than build in opportunities for competition, educators focused on teamwork, collaboration, and just plain feeling good. Grade inflation was yet another by-product of the efforts to raise student self-esteem. Ultimately, research emerged debunking much of the premise of Branden's best-selling book. But it was too late: A generation of Millennials — especially the older ones — had already been raised with the guidance of the self-esteem gurus.

Though it certainly had its failings, the self-esteem movement wasn't all bad. It created a highly collaborative generation that is only too willing to recognize the unique strengths that everyone brings. It helped Millennials embrace diversity. They focus on celebrating not just the best employee or the highest performer, but the team. They recognize that everyone brings something to the table, and everyone's voice matters. As leaders, Millennials are democratic and value different methods of motivation.

Understanding what it means to be raised by Boomer parents

To truly break into the Millennial mind, it's critical to look not only at what influenced them but at who. Their parents were obviously hugely influential in shaping the Millennial persona.

So let's take a look at Boomer parenting trends. Parenting can tend to take a pretty foreseeable pattern. While in many cases adult children love and respect their parents, they want to give their kids all the things they didn't have as children, and that includes not just tangible items but parenting styles. Because of this, there's a bit of a pendulum swing in how you were raised versus how you raise your children.

When you look at Baby Boomers, for the most part they were raised by conservative, strict parents who led their households more like a dictatorship than a democracy. There was a clear hierarchy in the house, usually with Dad being the top dog, Mom his close second, and the eldest child the next on the ladder of power and influence. But even the older brother or sister knew to do as he or she was told. It was more of a "don't speak unless spoken to" and "children are better seen and not heard" kind of time. After experiencing such a rigid upbringing, Boomers swore that their kids wouldn't experience the same. Instead, they vowed that their children would have more freedom to express themselves and explore their interests versus being put down a practical and professional path.

Messaging from Boomer parents to their Millennial kids looks like this:

» **"You are unique."** Boomers raised Millennials to believe that they were individuals. They told their kids that they were special, unique snowflakes, and that there was no one in the world quite like them. They wanted to make their children feel valued and important, and that their unique personality and skill set could change the world.

» **"You can do anything you put your mind to."** Baby Boomers grew up in a time when they witnessed and effected incredible change. They imbued their Millennial kids with the belief that if they tried hard enough, they could do the same. Boomers accomplished seemingly impossible social change when they were growing up. Why shouldn't their children be able to do the same, if not even better, feats?

» **"Never be afraid to speak up! Your opinion matters."** "Seen and not heard" was not something Boomers encouraged their children to be. They wanted their kids to speak up and share their opinions. Not only that, but because Millennials were so comfortable with new technology, they often turned to their kids as mini-consultants — whether the task was installing a new program on the home computer or sourcing the best-priced flights for a family vacation. Boomers appreciated, and in some cases relied on, their kids to speak up and share thoughts/opinions/ideas.

» **"Do something you love, and you'll never work a day in your life."** When they entered the workforce, Baby Boomers were fiercely competitive and did everything they could to get ahead and secure a promotion and the corner office. They worked incredibly long hours, missed more family events than they like to admit, and . . . for what? Boomers have encouraged their kids to do whatever is necessary to secure a job that matters and has meaning. They want their children to love what they do for a living, not just chase a corporate dream and someone else's definition of success.

>> **"If you ever need anything, I'm here for you."** When Boomers left their parents' homes, their old rooms were quickly converted into a home gym, office, or spare bedroom. Boomers have taken a completely different tack. When their kids left home, some parents preserved their rooms as almost mini shrines. The point is, they've made it clear to their kids that they're around for support, whether that be a place to stay, financial support of some kind, or advice. The kids may have flown the coop, but they're always welcome to boomerang back home. And before stereotyping Millennials as lazy for taking advantage of that, consider: 1) They have a close relationship with their parents and view them as constant allies, and 2) Many graduated into a recession with mountains of debt and no job prospects because employers either weren't hiring or sought people with at least five years of experience.

WARNING

As with all Millennial-isms, be careful not to shout all of these messages from the rooftops. Just because Boomers said them to their kids doesn't mean Millennials are proud that they did. For example, slandering Millennials as a generation of snowflakes will not go far toward reaching their demographic, if that is your intent — and we assume it is since you're reading this book.

Tracking the rise of the guidance counselor

The uptick in guidance counselors is inextricably linked to the spiking rate of violence that Millennials experienced (for more on violence during Millennial formative years, skim ahead in this chapter). In response to 9/11 and the school shootings that seemed to become ever-more-frequent as they got older, funding for guidance counselors rose substantially. These counselors were brought in to help children deal with the emotional trauma caused by these horrific events, or even just the threat that these could happen in their very school district, in their very school.

How did these counselors create safe spaces for Millennials? They spoke to them not as authoritarian figures, but as peers. They encouraged them to be open, to talk about their feelings and share their opinions and thoughts on the goings on about them. The messaging was "We're all equals. My opinion matters; your opinion matters. Everyone's voice should come to the table."

These guidance counselors are just another example of the deterioration of the "authority" figure. From school counselors and teachers to coaches and mentors, this generation is accustomed to speaking up and sharing their voices with others. The figures of authority in their lives have always been accessible and available for a conversation. Should we be surprised, then, that Millennials see no problem in reaching out to high-level management or CEOs? For them, it's only natural.

Getting behind the idea that there truly is no "I" in "team"

When Millennials were in their formative years, there was a perfect storm of messaging that drilled this idea: "Teamwork makes the dream work." Collaboration was held up as an ideal. Every adult in Millennials' lives encouraged them to put their heads together and tap into the power of the collective.

Collaboration in the classroom

In school, Millennials learned that the best results were achieved not when they did solo work, but when they were part of a team of collaborators. They grew accustomed to group projects, working on assignments that benefited from the melding of different strengths. After school, parents carted Millennial kids back and forth to various sports and clubs — be it basketball, soccer, volleyball, lacrosse, debate team, drama club, or whatever team activity was in season. They wanted their kids to learn to play well with others, and participating in team-based activities (however bad you were at dribbling or remembering lines) was yet another way to expose their kids to the group dynamic.

Collaboration with adults

But Millennials weren't just collaborating with other peers. They were learning to interact in this way with people in positions of authority as well. Every sphere of Millennial life functioned more like an open and encouraging democracy than a tiered authoritarian system (one that Boomers and Xers were more used to). At home, Millennials saw their family as a unit, a team where they were not the bottom of the barrel, but active contributors. At school, teachers went out of their way not to be strict disciplinarians, but to be approachable to every student. Guidance counselors asked children to speak up and share their ideas. Adults didn't want to belittle children or make them feel like they didn't matter. They wanted the next generation to feel confident in themselves, and pushed them to be bold, share their thoughts, and collaborate with the people around them, whether that be with their fellow second-grader or the teacher himself.

Collaboration with a virtual sphere

When social media debuted, it only made it easier for Millennials to extend their collaborative mindsets into the virtual world. Physical barriers were no longer an obstacle, because now even if they were sitting in a room at home by themselves, they were armed with the tools to collaborate virtually. Since the mid '90s, technology for collaborative work has only become more and more sophisticated. The youngest Millennials are so used to collaborating using FaceTime and Google Docs that, for them, it's almost as good as collaborating in person.

There are many people who value collaboration at work, but only to a point. At a certain level, a collaborative instinct can come across as needy, cowardly for fear of speaking independently, and inefficient. In one of the most negative ways, it can seem that collaboration equals groupthink. By definition, groupthink, in a sense, means that consensus is reached at the sacrifice of creativity and innovation. But creativity and innovation are positive qualities that Millennials are known for. Their collaboration is used to enhance creativity, not stifle it.

Parents, teachers, technology, pop culture, you name it — the tune was consistent: You are stronger together than you are alone. Here is an overview of some of the contributing factors that created this highly collaborative generation:

>> **The parenting:**

- Millennial kids were told they were an important, contributing member of the family and that they should speak up and share their opinions.

- Eldest child, baby of the family, girl, boy — it didn't matter. Parents told their kids that everyone's unique voice mattered when making family decisions.

- Boomer parents wanted their kids to "play nice" and enrolled them in sporting activities where the objective was less about winning, and more about being a part of the team (hence, the participation award trend).

>> **The schooling:**

- Millennial children grew up working on collective, group-based projects.

- They learned to lean on each other and found safety in the buddy system or latchkey (the supervised after-school program).

- Funding for after-school programs spiked in the mid '90s, further promoting group activities.

>> **The technology:**

- The Internet opened the world to collaborative gaming.

- From chat rooms to Facebook to Yelp, social media created a platform for "hanging out" with your friends, and crowdsourcing ideas and opinions.

- Online tools allowed for virtual collaboration so that you didn't have to be physically present to be able to tap into the power of collaboration.

>> **The headlines:**

- They say there is nothing quite as unifying as a common enemy, and the tragedy of 9/11 served as a unifying, rallying cry against the horrors and injustice of terrorism.

- The fear of school shootings encouraged students to stick together and not ostracize any member of the community.

- Captain Planet, Bill Nye, Fern Gully — programming encouraged kids to rally as a generation against climate change and promoted the idea that only by combining their voices could they make a difference.

>> **The pop culture:**

- Girl groups and boy bands exploded during their formative years, everything from Backstreet Boys to Spice Girls to Destiny's Child — groups were in.

- Group casting was trendy among popular TV shows: *Boy Meets World, Saved by the Bell, Friends, Seinfeld, The Real World.*

- Arguably the most famous hero of all time, Harry Potter, only became as such because of his team. He couldn't do it alone. Contrast his hero trope to the Katniss Everdeen, the heroine of *The Hunger Games,* who defines the next generation.

Past to present: How the effects of collaboration manifest in the workplace now

Millennials will

>> Desire collaborative, team-based projects

>> Feel no hesitation collaborating with leadership as well as colleagues

>> More easily accept diverse collaborators to the group

>> Be very open to mentorship programs, but will expect to contribute something themselves to the partnership

>> Possibly struggle making decisions without consulting the collective

>> Want to build consensus among the group

Globalization: Understanding a generation that knows no borders

Millennials came of age during the era of globalization. They are the most diverse generation the American workplace has seen thus far. The borders to the rest of the world opened up for them both literally and figuratively. Since 1990, the immigrant population in the United States has doubled, and the growth of the tech sector is just one of many reasons that immigration has spiked, bringing in skilled workers from all corners of the globe. Schools have also played their part in encouraging a more global-minded generation by increasing opportunities for international study as well as welcoming more international students. The number of international students in America has increased 72 percent since 2000, and the number of American students studying abroad has almost doubled in the same time frame.

Of course, one of the biggest contributors to globalization has been the Internet. It has made it easier to stay in touch, regardless of the miles and miles between you. It gave American Millennials direct access to people in India, China, Colombia, New Zealand, Tanzania — location was meaningless; as long as both parties could dial into the Internet, there could be contact and conversation (with assistance from an online translator). Millennials were also able to explore the physical world with the web. No library or expensive plane tickets were necessary to see Japanese temples. Instead they could just "Google it" — a phrase that would come to define an entire form of information gathering — and in seconds they'd have images, videos, books, and articles on the subject. There is no substitute for the real thing, of course, but the Internet has allowed for exposure to the rest of the world to a much higher degree than previous generations.

Because of globalization, Millennials are the generation that share the most cultural milestones across the world. They have experienced many of the same TV shows, movies, and pop stars. They've dealt with the unique challenge of growing up in a world where they needed to adapt to ever-evolving technology. Of course, each Millennial demographic will be highly influenced by the country they grew up in, but by and large, the influences that the Internet, the upgrade cycle, and social media have exerted on this generation are visible regardless of where they were born. To read more about Millennials around the world, see Chapter 11.

Past to present: How globalization has influenced Millennials in the workplace

Millennials will

>> Expect diversity in the workplace, not just in terms of nationality but in gender, race, religious affiliation, generation, thought, and so forth as well.

>> Be socially, economically, and culturally aware of international happenings. They may be especially sympathetic to particular causes.

>> Have a keen and underlying wanderlust; for many, business trips or even conference calls are not only part of the job, but also a way to satisfy cultural curiosity.

Feeling the impact of homeland violence

Before we even kick off this conversation, we have to get something out of the way: We are *not* saying that Millennials are the only generation impacted by violence. Traditionalists lived through the atrocities of World War II. Boomers served in Vietnam and witnessed violent protests, riots, and police violence at home. Gen Xers either participated in or watched the televised horrors of the Gulf Wars, and they experienced a loss of innocence as children became targets of violence through increased kidnappings. But while every generation has seen its share of violence, Millennials witnessed violence very close to home. We don't just mean on American soil. We also mean in the very place they thought was safest: the classroom.

Realizing that no one is untouchable: Terrorism

Forgive us for yet another disclaimer, but in this case we feel it's absolutely necessary. When we talk about terrorism during Millennials' formative years, the big event is obviously 9/11. It has unquestionably left a lasting mark on the Millennial psyche. That said, it doesn't matter what generation you belong to; when you watched the second plane hit the Twin Towers, your world changed in an instant. The tragedy of 9/11 touched every single one of us.

But consider this: Millennials witnessed these events as teenagers or young children. The adults of the world were beyond their impressionable years. They'd already had a chance to come to terms with the world around them and their own safety within it. For Millennials, still in the midst of growing up and figuring out who they were, this event was absolutely earth-shattering. Never in history had there been a terrorist attack, on such a massive scale, on U.S. soil. Millennials watched as the coverage came through television screens at school, and the weight of the silence and fear was palpable. All of us can remember where we were when 9/11 happened. Many Millennials can as well, but for them, it's a memory not only of where they were, but also of what it meant and who they became.

The attacks of 9/11 were an abrupt and devastating wake-up call. They left Millennials questioning their safety. The bubble of protection had burst. They realized that just because they lived in America, that did not mean that they were untouchable. Millennials internalized this messaging. Absolutely nothing was guaranteed. They decided to make the most of this moment and live for the now, because you never know what tomorrow will bring.

Living with violence in the classroom: School shootings

The 9/11 terrorist attacks penetrated the safety bubble on a large scale — America could no longer necessarily be considered a safe haven. But another trend during

Millennial formative years hit even closer than American soil — it happened in classrooms just like the one you sat in everyday growing up. School shootings showed Millennials that, truly, nothing was sacred — even institutions of learning.

The Columbine shootings kicked off a slew of violence directed at schools. Some of the more horrifying incidents include Virginia Tech and, toward the end of Millennials' formative years, the unthinkable incident at Sandy Hook Elementary school, where the bulk of the victims were children between six and seven years old. The number of school shootings since Columbine has reached the hundreds, sparking outrage and calls for more stringent gun control.

But shootings have not just been limited to schools. A troubling trend of mass shootings has spread across the states like a disease. Mass shootings have risen starkly since 2000, with the FBI reporting that from 2000 to 2006, there was an average of 6.4 mass shootings annually, while from 2007 to 2013 that number rose to an average of 16.4. The violence has become so prevalent that it almost feels like a normal part of the American experience, a terrifying but undeniable fact of life.

In response to all of this bloodshed and uncertainty, Millennials, despite the typical rhetoric, have become resilient. They've witnessed tough times, digested them with the help of parents, counselors, and even friends, and have come to understand the fragility and uncertainty that lies ahead for any generation. They're determined to make the best of the here and now and, in the face of change, roll with the punches as best they can.

TIP

Find ways to acknowledge Millennial's resiliency as a strength. Some can view it as a numb reaction to the world, while others question whether a tear-stained face paired with social media posts proves how resilient a generation is. What we know is that when polled, Old Millennials describe themselves as resilient less than Young Millennials do, so watch out for a resilient later half of the generation.

Feeling the weight of a constant stream of violence: News in your pocket

There's another important piece to look at when you consider the way Millennials have experienced violence, perhaps most relevant to younger Millennials. Older generations were able, to some degree, to disconnect from the news and all the atrocities flooding the media. To know what was going on in the world, you had to actively pick up a newspaper or turn on the TV to soak in the events of the day. For younger Millennials, the news is always there and always in their face (or in their pockets). Facebook feeds are filled with the latest episode of gun violence; AP mobile alerts wake you up to the news of the latest mass massacre or unthinkable acts perpetrated around the world. Maybe you somehow managed to avoid all the news sources that day. But wait . . . in come the floods of texts from friends: "Omg. Did you hear what happened?"

There is a dark side to being constantly connected: There is no escape. Millennials have been plugged into information from youth, and they have become used to being buffeted by news and information, and, unfortunately, much of it is quite sobering. As a result, there's a worry that — again, especially for the later Millennials — instead of galvanizing them to stand up and make change, they will become desensitized. It's just a daily part of life, another alert on your phone while you're ordering your coffee.

Past to present: How the effects of violence have influenced Millennials in the workplace

The way that Millennials experienced violence during their formative years has impacted their perceptions of the world:

>> They put a high premium on living for today, because tomorrow isn't guaranteed.

>> For Millennials, it's more important than ever to do something you love.

>> They hope to effect positive change on the world.

>> They're searching for meaning in everything they do.

Reeling from the economic roller coaster

When we think about Millennials and the economic roller coaster, the single most influential event has been the Great Recession. Examining the way that Millennials experienced this event, you can very clearly draw a line between the earlier Millennials (those who went to college before the recession) and the younger Millennials (those who entered college as the recession was in full swing). It was the difference between a childhood blissfully free of thinking about your or your family's financial situation and one where your parents might suddenly drop a shock at the dinner table: "Kids, we're so sorry, but we're in a sticky spot. We'll need to find a new home, and maybe dip into your college funds. If there were any other way out of this . . ." Obviously those are two drastically different experiences, and they have resulted in two shades of Millennials — the older, more optimistic cohort, and the younger, more pragmatic bunch.

The economy and older Millennials

The dot-com bust happened as many older Millennials were entering high school, 9/11 turned the global economy into turmoil as the eldest entered college, and then, just as Millennials were hitting their stride in the workplace, the recession sent them back home to live on their parents' couch. Youth unemployment continues to be an issue in the United States. Despite all this turbulence, older Millennials grew up in a time of relative prosperity. When they were kids and teenagers, their parents, for the most part, successfully weathered dips and fluctuations in the world economy. Even though many of these older Millennials graduated into a recession, they're still relatively optimistic about their futures and continue to approach their employment with a "reach for the stars" mentality.

The economy and younger Millennials

This segment was entering, attending, and leaving college as the Great Recession hit full force. Younger Millennials watched as the financial stability they had known earlier on was shaken to the very core. They saw older siblings boomerang back home to live with Mom and Dad because they couldn't afford to pay rent. They watched as parents were let go from jobs they'd devoted decades to or as friends' parents lost their homes. Financial stability changed from an expectation to a giant question mark. As a result of experiencing all this economic turmoil and uncertainty, they readjusted their goals and took on a decidedly practical lens. When considering college, they opted for an in-state school with a full scholarship rather than an expensive private institution far from home. They've become incredibly realistic as a generation, and when considering jobs, financial stability has been at the forefront of their minds.

ADULTESCENCE AND ADULTING

As a general rule, Millennials are reaching life's major milestones at later ages than Xers or Boomers. For many, pivotal "adult" events (getting married, buying a house, starting a family) have simply not been financially viable. Millennials are entering adulthood with record levels of student debt, and because they find themselves in some pretty tough financial straits, this generation has found itself left in a murky state of *adultescence*. This is a term demographers have coined to refer to a period of time after college but before major life events such as getting married, where major life events are put off because, in many cases, the finances are simply not there. The sluggish economy coupled with a generation who has notoriously close relationships with their parents created a perfect combination for a generation that has needed to, for financial reasons, put off the traditional steps of adulting.

Past to present: How the shifting economy has influenced Millennials in the workplace

The experiences of older Millennials have resulted in the following feelings and expectations:

>> A job with meaning and impact still ranks toward the top of their workplace expectations.

>> Now, however, they place importance on autonomy and work-life balance as they build their families.

>> They still have a sense of unbridled optimism about their futures when compared to their younger counterparts.

Younger Millennials are more likely to be characterized as follows:

>> They are more focused on taking practical steps to secure stability.

>> Financial stability ranks at the top of their workplace concerns.

>> They may have a more "get the job done" mentality, while Older Millennials may take a more "it's about the journey, not the destination" approach.

Exploring Millennial Values

The events and conditions that formed Millennial traits also led to a unique set of shared generational values. These values are central to the Millennial persona, and Millennials will apply these perceptions to every facet of the workplace. Table 3-2 examines four core values, where they come from, how those values might prove to be assets, and where they might cause some friction.

TABLE 3-2   **Shared Millennial Values**

Value	Where It Comes From	The Good News	The Bad News
Authenticity	Access to anyone and everything on the Internet and blurred lines between	Millennials aim to forge authentic relationships with their colleagues.	They may lean toward informality in the workplace that alienates or puts off other generations.
Efficiency	Ever-improving technology and processes that streamlined everything	They try to maximize efficiency in the workplace.	They may cut corners (like having a conversation) in favor of getting things done.

(continued)

TABLE 3-2 *(continued)*

Value	Where It Comes From	The Good News	The Bad News
Innovation	Disruptive inventions and ideas that weren't restricted to the upper echelons of society	Rather than accept the status quo, Millennials speak up to share new and innovative ideas.	They may challenge longstanding, vetted processes with little regard for those who put them in place.
Customization	Unprecedented choice online and retailers that allowed Millennials to pinpoint specific items, rather than taking on the whole	They take a unique angle and perspective on every project to ensure that an approach is always customized to find the right solution.	They may want to "customize" their workday and work set-up so it suits their needs, which may be challenging to accommodate.

Breaking the Mold: Rejecting Millennial Stereotypes

One of the major goals in trying to break into the Millennial mind by a scan of the major events and conditions is to try to understand them better and break down the disconnect between the Millennial persona and the harmful stereotypes. For a more robust look at Millennial stereotypes, you can flip to Chapter 20, but as an exercise, we want to debunk some of these more common Millennial stereotypes by using the understanding of the formative years. Here are some of the more common stereotypes:

>> **The entitlement stereotype**:

- *Where it comes from:* There's a perception that Millennials are so entitled that they feel they deserve to be promoted, and that they deserve the right to walk into the CEO's office without first having proven themselves worthy.

- *The kernel of truth:* Because of experiences like growing up in the time of the ever-increasing upgrade cycle, Millennials do have an expectation that they'll be able to move up the ladder at a fairly quick pace.

- *The debunking:* There's a difference between entitlement and expectation. Entitlement suggests a claim or a right, whereas expectation suggests a strong belief that a thing will happen. Millennials, because of their experiences as youth, do have an expectation that they will move up the ranks swiftly, but not because they have a claim or right to it, but simply because that's the way they've experienced the world, and they expect the workplace to operate in a similar way.

- ***Why it's dangerous:*** Entitlement equals a spoiled brat, and that's a harder thing to work through and look past. Expectations can be adjusted, based on the reality of the organization and what the Millennial can expect to see. It's the difference between, on the one hand, writing someone off as childish and, on the other, giving her a realistic timeline to operate off of.

» **The narcissistic stereotype:**

- ***Where it comes from:*** Millennials show up in an organization and want to flex that disruptive muscle. They want to change the way things have always been done, and they're confident that they have worthy ideas that should be implemented. This does not often lead to favorable opinions from other generations, who ask themselves, "How dare you think that you, a newbie, know more than the people with decades of experience who set up these systems in the first place?"

- ***The kernel of truth:*** Boomer parents did tell their Millennial kids that they were special. They were raised believing they have talents to contribute and a voice that should be heard.

- ***The debunking:*** Yes, Millennials do believe they have great ideas. Their belief may or may not be true, but they aren't narcissistic enough to believe that those ideas should always be acted upon. They are very willing to be coached through the rotten concepts and react favorably to a mentor who is willing to show them where they went wrong.

- ***Why it's dangerous:*** By writing off Millennials as narcissistic and self-involved, some decision-makers will be completely deaf to any and all ideas that come from this generation. They're missing out on new enthusiasm, fresh takes, and some truly golden nuggets of thought.

» **The lazy/no-work-ethic stereotype:**

- ***Where it comes from:*** "Are your work hours strictly 9 to 5?" "Can I have a two-hour break at lunch to get my yoga practice in?" These questions and others like them lead older generations to believe that Millennials just don't have the same work ethic as they do.

- ***The kernel of truth:*** The truth is, actually, that they don't. But that doesn't mean they don't work hard. Millennials just work *differently*.

- ***The debunking:*** Because of technology, Millennials can work from anywhere. They have integrated work and life so that they can be flexible in their work schedules but also make sure they get things done. Sure, they may get done at 11 p.m. from their couches at home, but they get done.

- ***Why it's dangerous:*** When managers cling too tightly to the idea that hard work can only be measured by long hours in the office, they risk losing a generation that works just as hard as the ones that came before them, albeit in a very different way.

» **The no-respect stereotype:**

- *Where it comes from:* When you're bold enough to send a personal email of introduction to the CEO on the first day, there seems to be no humility to speak of. The generations that have played by the rules of etiquette and respecting hierarchy are completely thrown off when a Millennial enters the scene and starts referring to your boss as Jane instead of Ms. Finch.

- *The kernel of truth:* Millennials are used to access to any and all information, as well as access to people in positions of authority. They don't see the world as a hierarchy, but more like the networked virtual world they grew up in. This can be off-putting when put into practice in the workplace.

- *The debunking:* Millennials do have great respect for leaders; they just show it in a different way. They want to connect with them and tap into the expertise and wisdom that these figures can offer. They may go about approaching them in the wrong way, but it's less a sign of disrespect than it is a sign of enthusiasm and eagerness to learn all there is to know.

- *Why it's dangerous:* Oftentimes, when people feel a lack of respect, they respond with terse-worded reprimands. If, indeed, that's what was happening, that response would be justified. But because it may more appropriately be viewed as enthusiasm, sharp shut-downs are tantamount to telling a Millennial her efforts/passion/energy isn't wanted.

» **The tech obsession stereotype:**

- *Where it comes from:* Selfies, Snapchat, constantly checking Facebook feeds, never having their smartphones farther than three feet away from them — the root of this stereotype isn't hard to identify, but some things are other than what they seem.

- *The kernel of truth:* Though arguably much of the world is dependent on technology, Millennials grew up with it. They may lean on it even more than generations past because they've never known a time without it.

- *The debunking:* Rather than saying "It's not true," the debunking here is more about saying "Is this really such a bad thing?" Oftentimes when they're on their phones in a meeting, they're actually sending an important and timely email. They may be on Facebook every now and again, but what you don't see are the times when they're working from home at 10 p.m.

- *Why it's dangerous:* Undoubtedly there will be Millennial employees who use technology as a distraction, not a productivity tool. But taking away the technology they use to improve their workflow, or placing firm social media restrictions without first asking questions and trying to understand their perspective, is sure to demotivate.

Chapter **4**

Discovering How Millennials Differ from Boomers and Gen Xers

Why do we have a chapter on Xers and Boomers in a book about managing Millennials? Great question!

» For Baby Boomer or Gen X readers, here's your opportunity to discover more about yourself and your generational peers.

» For those looking to satiate their curiosity about the other generations, here's your dose of Boomers and Xers.

» For those who want to be cross-generationally savvy, we want to give you the ability to don and remove any generational lens at will. In some ways, this can be your managerial superpower.

» Most importantly, this chapter is critical for those who understand that generations don't exisit in a vacuum. A full awareness of other generations makes you that much better at managing any one specific group, because you can see the intricacies of the cross-generational dynamics and manage accordingly.

This chapter explores the traits, values, and behaviors of today's working non-Millennials. It provides insights to help you manage these other generations, and avoid or smooth over the generational clashes that may arise when they work with Millennials. Beginning with Baby Boomers, we uncover what shaped them, how their traits and values show up at work, and why a subset of Boomers is called Generation Jones. Then we dive into an exploration of Generation Xers. Finally, we package all this information into an easy-access chart so that you'll never have to wonder what generation you belong to and how that compares to those around you.

Breaking into the Baby Boomer Mind

First things first — the Boomer generation is huge. Between 1946 and 1964, a baby was born every eight seconds. The result was, quite literally, a boom in babies and a boom in population. This generation's name could not be more accurate.

Getting the 411 on Boomers

To paint the most basic picture of this hard-working, once-long-haired, disruption-of-aging generation, the following sections examine the makeup of the Baby Boomer.

The numbers

Here's a look at the essential numbers that form a Baby Boomer:

>> **Birth years:** 1946–1964

>> **Formative years:** 1959–1983

>> **Population size:** 75 million (as of 2015)

The life stage

Lately, Baby Boomers have earned a new nickname: the club sandwich generation. Here's how that sandwich stacks up:

>> **Bread:** Taking care of aging parents.

>> **Meat:** Taking care of self.

>> **Toppings:** Taking care of kids. Forty percent of Millennials still receive some form of financial assistance from their parents (USA Today, 2015).

>> **Bread:** Taking care of grandkids.

REMEMBER

When it comes to Boomers' life stage, two key elements are noteworthy:

>> They may be on the verge of burnout but likely won't say anything.

>> They are entering their next life stage in a completely different way than generations past, just like every life stage they've touched.

The memories

Because Boomers' formative years stretch across a large chunk of time, their memories span from remembering the first color TV they watched *Happy Days* on to their parents' reactions when JFK was assassinated. We go into the signifance of these memories further in the next section, but if you are a Boomer, or manage one, these memories helped shape the employee you are or have:

>> Color TV was a commodity, and wow, was it spectacular.

>> At least one friend wanted to be an astronaut at some point.

>> Beatlemania was very real.

>> Pepsi was the soda of choice.

>> Parents were more classic authoritarian figures and definitely didn't talk about things that ventured into the list of taboo topics.

>> Parents definitely never cussed or showed any level of poor manners.

>> Boomers grew up under the dogma, "Children are to be seen and not heard."

>> A normal summer day meant being outside at sunrise and returning at sundown.

>> Oil crises of the '70s meant seeing "no gas" signs everywhere and long lines at gas stations.

>> Protests, riots, and sit-ins were frequently broadcast on TV.

>> For the first time, war was televised, and the country felt torn.

>> Long hair was in style for both boys and girls.

>> Hip-huggers and bell-bottoms were must-have fashion items.

>> B-sides could be good sides.

The stereotypes

Just like other generations, Boomers received their share of stereotypes when they first started working. Managers and colleagues had all kinds of preconceived notions about this generation. To name a few, Boomers were considered to be

>> Hippies

>> Lazy

>> Me, me, me

>> Stoners

>> Free loving, especially if they had long hair

But when Baby Boomers entered the workforce, they proved the naysayers wrong. Boomers went to work, cut their hair, and donned appropriate attire to become the image of polish and professionalism.

Exploring where Baby Boomers came from (and how it compares to Millennials)

To best understand the Baby Boomer generation (or any generation), it's critical to look at the events and conditions that shaped their generational identity. We're only too aware that you picked up this book up to learn how to manage Millennials, so as we go through each of these sections, we juxtapose the Boomer experience to the Millennial experience.

The parents

Boomers were raised by Traditionalist parents, many of whom had lived through the effects of the Great Depression and/or World War II. These events shaped Traditionalists into very specific kinds of parents. They were the type of parents who trusted the government, were loyal to neighbors and community, and communicated in a top-down command-and-control style. Boomers' Traditionalist parents ran a tight ship. Mom and dad were the bosses of the household. There was no room for discussion. You just did as you were told. When Boomers left home, went to college, and then entered the workplace, it meant that when the boss said "jump," they knew the right answer was "how high?" They're typically more comfortable within more hierarchical organizational structures.

Compared to Millennials: Dissatisfied with their Traditionalist parents' methods, Boomers did what most children do when it's their turn to parent. The pendulum swung to the other side, and Boomers decided to raise children in a new way.

You'll notice this pattern across the generations. As Boomers established their new families, they converted the household dictatorship into a democracy. Rather than the distant parent-child relationships they'd known as kids, Baby Boomers fostered close-friend relationships with their Millennial children, with open lines of communication and lots of positive reinforcement.

The news

As Baby Boomers entered their formative years, broadcast news transformed into a closer resemblance of local news today. The '60s and '70s saw news segments expand from 15 minutes to 30 minutes. Walter Cronkite became the most trusted man in news, and huddling around the television for the latest report became part of nightly traditions at home. Around the same time, *LIFE* magazine exposed stories and built upon the news on TV. This new media exposed the injustices of the time. It inspired Boomers to ask the important questions, protest, and fight back. The news covered a lot of the bad, but also a lot of the good. From footage of their positive efforts and the change they'd effected, Boomers saw the movements of the '60s and '70s make progress toward their goals. They made a difference and saw change, and developed a drive, optimism, and idealism that they still carry with them to this day.

Compared to Millennials: Walter Cronkite left his post long before Millennials began watching the news, and the style of the journalism they prefer has turned out to be quite different from Cronkite's earnest impartiality. Political satire evolved in the '70s with *Saturday Night Live's* weekend update and found its sweet spot with nightly shows like *The Daily Show* and *The Colbert Report.* These programs spoke to Millennials' desire for real (or absurdly fake) news with a comedic, sarcastic, and sometimes satirical twist. They also turned to social media platforms to consume peer-reported news and citizen journalism. Using social media as a news source (and "unfriending" anyone you disagree with) is partly responsible for the echo chamber that's led to so much division in the current political discourse.

The politics

As kids and teens, Boomers saw political tides shift and surge, and depending on their birth year, they were privy to vastly different political landscapes. While the first half of Baby Boomers freely idolized the likes of Gloria Steinem, MLK, and JFK, later Boomers (see the section "Meet Generation Jones" later in this chapter) were too young to appreciate these icons. Early Boomers were driven to action by the controversy of the Vietnam War, but later Boomers also missed this time of political activism and instead were blankly welcomed by post-war economic hardship.

Compared to Millennials: Millennials saw their share of political scandals. One of the first is the Clinton-Lewinsky scandal, but they can also recall the contentious Bush-Gore election of 2000. Millennials were in the midst of their formative years when the twin towers collapsed, and they felt the collective fear as the country asked itself, what next? On a more positive political note, they also saw the election of the first black president and the legalization of same-sex marriage, two pivotal moments in U.S. history.

The youth culture

In their youth, Boomers looked to their parents, but also said, "Mom, Dad, things need to change!" Their impetus for change stemmed from the wave of youth empowerment:

>> Advertising companies started targeting the youth demographic in the '50s and '60s.

>> Political leaders like JFK, Bobby Kennedy, Martin Luther King Jr., and Gloria Steinem all asked youth to join their causes and campaigns.

>> The motto was "Don't trust anyone over 30."

Now, they're a generation that is very young at heart.

Compared to Millennials: Frankly, the youth culture is quite similar. Millennials were also celebrated for their youth as their Boomer parents, ad companies, and the media paid special attention to their large demographic. This was particularly true during the aftermath of 9/11 and during the school shooting epidemic. Parents, teachers, counselors, and more adults encouraged Millennial children/teenagers to share their feelings and experiences.

The activism

In their youth, Boomers took to the streets to share their voices and fight for civil rights, women's rights, gay rights, and the anti-war movement. They believed that the collective could band together and stand up for what was right, and they did the best that they could as peacefully as possible. Boomer activists signed petitons, wrote their congressmen, and participated in marches and sit-ins, all in the spirit of peace and justice for all.

Compared to Millennials: Until recent years, widespread activism from the Millennial generation was fairly minimal. They may have protested the Iraq War or the War in Afghanistan in the early 2000s, or maybe played a role in Occupy Wall Street. More recently, footage of police violence against people of color, as well Donald Trump's election as 45th president of the United States, has motivated thousands of Millennials to remind America that Black Lives Matter. And that he is #notmypresident.

Meet Generation Jones

Baby Boomers are a huge generation, and their birth years span almost two decades. Because of this, to gain an even deeper understanding of the Boomer generation, it can be helpful to break them into separate subgroups: Early Boomers and Generation Jones. We use the term "Generation Jones" to refer to the second half of the Boomer birth years, those born between 1955 and 1964. This latter group's formative years occurred after the counterculture movement of the 1960s. They weren't witnesses to the electric and inspiring atmosphere that JFK, Martin Luther King Jr., and Gloria Steinem created for Early Boomers. Instead, their world was marked by competition, limited resources as fuel prices rose, and . . . disco. For these reasons and more, we call them Generation Jones. This Boomer subgroup was "jonesin'," yearning for something more while also trying to "keep up with the Joneses." Some key differences that set Gen Jones apart from Early Boomers include:

>> **Rising economy (Early Boomers) versus falling economy (Gen Jones):** The oil embargo of 1973 ushered in a seismic shift in American culture and economics. Gen Jonesers remember going to the gas station with their parents to wait in lines at gas stations for hours. Gen Jones grew up with a scarcity of resources, and this led them to develop a more competitive edge than those earlier Boomers. They knew they'd have to be scrappy and hussle for what they wanted. They're also more pragmatic, as a whole, and less optimistic and idealistic than Early Boomers.

>> **Large baby boom (Early Boomers) versus massive baby boom (Gen Jones):** You can't ignore Boomers' massive population size, but by and large, there are more Jonesers than Early Boomers. In school that meant that classrooms were at capacity. Athletic teams had way too many interested players, and the fight to be on the starting line-up was fierce. At school, there weren't enough desks to sit in or books to study from. It seemed like almost everything was in low supply and high demand. Securing a good job at work required proving yourself beyond everyone else.

>> **Stay-at-home moms (Early Boomers) versus. working moms (Gen Jones):** Though the working mom trend didn't take off until the '80s, when Gen Jones hit their formative years, women started surging into the workplace. Kids began spending more time unsupervised than generations past. The divorce rate also started to rise, making the youngest Gen Jonesers the very first batch of "latchkey kids," a phrase that is usually associated with Generation Xers.

Discovering Baby Boomer workplace traits and what they mean for managers

This section explores the traits that define Boomer employees. If you are a Boomer, you might read this and nod along. If you're a manager, you can use this information to manage your Baby Boomer employees and better understand how those employees interact with the Millennials in your charge. Collectively, Boomers are

>> Optimistic

>> Idealistic

>> Competitive

>> Wanting to put their stamp on the world

>> Young at heart

As a manager, it behooves you to know how those traits manifest at work. In the following sections, we cover some of the workplace situations that appeal to Boomers and how Millennials might perceive and respond to them.

Situation: The awards ceremony at the annual meeting

It's that time of year again, the annual staff meeting, when you get to celebrate just how valuable members of your team are. Maybe you have the meeting at the same location every year, or maybe it moves among a few favorite spots. Everyone enjoys getting together, playing golf, and learning actionable takeaways from keynote speakers and educational sessions. At the awards ceremony, you give a little speech about how great certain members of the team are and then invite them on stage to receive their trophy/plaque/fancy pen.

Why this works for Boomers: Boomers appreciate public recognition as it's how they've been able to feed their competitive spirit since they started working. Plaques and awards show everyone how well a Boomer is doing. They feel valued for their hard work.

Why it doesn't work for Millennials: Collaborative Millennials can also enjoy company meetings and events, but not if they're in the same location every year or there's no extra incentive to attend (an out-of-the-box company outing, a fantastic speaker, or an unusual space). They appreciate public recognition, but view a plaque as something that will collect dust.

Situation: The annual review session

You sit down for your annual review with Baby Boomer Basil and have everything ready to go and in writing. You and Basil have had ample time to prepare. You dive into the documentation during the session, complete with a rating system. You review all of the highs and lows of the previous year and take time to celebrate great work as needed. You give constructive criticism with kindness and structure — opportunities for growth are still opportunities, after all. You end the session on a high note, leaving Basil with a game plan for what he can accomplish in the next year and how you will support his efforts.

Why this works for Boomers (and Basil): Boomers were the masterminds behind the annual review. They wanted to know how they stacked up against their peers. It was also a great way to play to their competitiveness. Structure and formality during these sessions is a way to be respectful of Boomers' desire to stay professional. Ending the session on a high note gives this optimistic generation a wonderful silver lining.

Why this doesn't work for Millennials: For a Millennial, annual reviews are far too infrequent. Even if reviews happened every quarter, that would still be three months to cover in one session. Frequent, casual, and minimal structure is ideal. (Structure is still great, but not to the extent that Boomers prefer it.) If you don't find time for these regular meetings with your Millennial employees, they'll find ways to integrate it into conversation with you until they're satisfied.

Situation: The dress code

Your office upholds a standard of dress and formality. While you might not require employees to wear suits and ties, you show appreciation when your employees dress to impress. You allow for casual days, of course, and at times have fostered a culture that is business casual. As a manager, you believe that how you carry and present yourself at work — both in dress and communication — is a reflection of how much you value your job.

Why this works for Boomers: There was a time when Boomers valued the dress code immensely. "Dress for the job you want, not the job you have" was a motto to live and succeed by. Though they've changed expectations over time, they still have a level of respect for pressed pants and coats devoid of wrinkles.

Why this doesn't work for Millennials: Millennials don't see the value in a standard, impersonal dress code. In their minds, they're wondering how a suit helps them send better emails (actually, it's so uncomfortable that it might even impede the process!). They're all about work-life integration, and that preference applies to their dress preferences as well. Who says they can't be leaders while wearing a hoodie and Converse sneakers?

Situation: The face-to-face meeting

You want to connect with Laura, the Boomer you manage. You have a couple questions about a project she's working on and just want to get some key details to pass along in a meeting with other managers. To check-in with Laura, you approach her in one of two ways: phone or email. You don't email unless necessary or she says she prefers it. Instant messaging or texting is really just on a case-by-case basis.

Why this works for Boomers: More than any other generation currently at work, Boomers value face-to-face or phone converstions as the most efficient way of communicating. Why would you take three emails to say something that you could accomplish in one 30-second phone call?

Why this doesn't work for Millennials: It's no secret that the phone typically isn't the Millennial's favorite form of communication. (Yes, we know some love it; stop yelling at us!) But, in general, phone or face-to-face communication can seem intrusive. In their minds, email and instant messaging allow you to manage your time the way you want to manage it. They also see the value in taking their time to think about how they want to respond with the perfectly crafted message.

Situation: The continuing education and alumni network

One of your top Boomer employees, Benny, may retire in the next five to ten years. You see his potential and his passion to do more for the company. You ask him if he'd like to participate in a pilot leadership development program and whether he'd like to join the company's alumni network, a group of experienced employees who can serve as consultants on a part-time basis if they want to lessen their hours or "retire."

Why this works for Boomers: Too often, Boomers are seen as the generation that has learned everything they need or want to know and are set to retire in the very near future. Unfortunately, the longest-tenured employees can be the least engaged, and it's because they're no longer seen as assets with new ideas and a drive to continue making an impact. Asking Boomers whether they want to continue developing appeals both to their desire to do more and to their youthful spirit; they're not slowing down any time soon!

Why this doesn't work for Millennials: Gotcha! This one actually does work for Millennials. Continuing education for Boomers is something that doesn't usually happen because Millennials get so much of the leadership development training. Putting both Millennials and Baby Boomers in the same room is incredibly important for a fully engaged multigenerational workforce, and creates natural opportunities for mentorship and reverse-mentorship. It's a win-win. Do it!

Exploring Baby Boomer values and how they influence work style

Just as Boomers share traits across their own cohort, so too do they share common values. And while these may be shared by other generations, there are some key differences in Boomer values versus those of Millennials.

>> **Youthfulness:** Boomers are anything but slowing down, and they respect managers who acknowledge that.

   How this value collides with Millennials: In the greatest sense, it doesn't, as long as each cohort appreciates each other's youthful spirit.

>> **Novelty:** Contrary to stereotypes, Boomers seek the latest and greatest technology. If something new is happening at work, get the tech-savvy Boomers on board and the rest of the workforce will follow.

   How this value collides with Millennials: To the point around technology, this clash is one of the greatest. Millennials don't often view Boomers as eager to embrace new technology and dismiss them as not being tech-savvy. On the other hand, even though Boomers do appreciate the uses of tech in the workforce, they can grow frustrated by Millennials' brazen desire to make every process technology-focused.

>> **Luxury:** Of all generations (aside from Traditionalists), Boomers are in the most comfortable financial situation. Not only do they appreciate luxury, they can afford it.

   How this value collides with Millennials: While some Millennials appreciate luxury as well, tokens of how that luxury manifested for Boomers — for example, golf resorts, large suburban homes, and large vehicles — are going away. They lean toward the experiential versus expensive purchases (think trip to Cambodia versus new Cadillac).

>> **Professionalism:** Professional dress and etiquette indicate respect to a Boomer.

   How this value collides with Millennials: Professionalism can come across as being inauthentic to a Millennial. They value the blend of personal and professional lives in both their dress and their communication etiquette.

>> **Work ethic:** To show they were working hard, Boomers put in the hours, even if it meant working overtime, getting in early, or working weekends.

   How this value collides with Millennials: Millennials don't view long hours as necessarily indicative of success. Instead, results matter. As does the ability to work wherever and whenever to get the job done.

>> **Health:** To keep up with the Joneses, Boomers eat healthy and stay active.

How this value collides with Millennials: It doesn't! Health is a value that both generations can get behind, especially if that means having healthy food options at work and a fitness center in the building.

Breaking into the Gen X Mind

Generation X, also known as "the MTV Generation," "Latchkeys," and "Baby Busters," were born between 1965 and 1979. They make up a small band of 60 million, and because they're sandwiched between two mammoth generations (Boomers and Millennials), they're sometimes referred to as the forgotten middle child.

Getting the Scoop on Generation X

Xers, once known as being an apathetic, cynical, plaid-wearing, Nirvana-loving generation, have grown into roles as leaders in the workforce and devoted friends and parents at home. Just like with Boomers, time and experience have proved that while their generational identity and preferences have led them to work differently than generations before, they are still ambitious and committed to excelling in their professional lives. They've just done it their way. To give you the lowdown on what made Xers who they are, the next few sections will take a closer look at the intricacies of the Xer persona.

The numbers

Here's a look at the numbers behind Generation X:

>> **Birth years:** 1965–1979

>> **Formative years:** 1978-1998

>> **Population size:** 60 million (at their peak)

The life stage

>> Xers' current life stage can be best described as family focused, but trying to break through the gray ceiling.

- Xers want their kids to have the opposite of the latchkey experience. Efficiency at work is critical so they can go home precisely at leaving time and be present parents.

- With so many Baby Boomers in leadership positions (and not retiring any time soon), Xers are figuring out how to break through that gray ceiling into the leadership tier while also embracing their value of work-life balance to the fullest.

- Many Xers have made it to those coveted top-tier positions, and are leading in a classically Xer way — direct, honest, and highly supportive of the entrepreneurial spirit.

The memories

Xers' formative years were marked by a whole new world of media, as well as all the scandals that filled those hours of media consumption. Gen X kids fondly thought of the TV as their favorite babysitter and can remember watching Saturday morning cartoons while downing a sugary, very-not-good-for-you cereal. They can also remember all of the crime, intrigue, and corruption that the media covered nonstop. As you scan through these Xer memories, remember that these experiences shaped the Xer professionals in your office today:

» 24-hour news means there was always something to watch on TV.

» With parents divorced or working long hours, after-school time meant unsupervised afternoons at home and taking care of yourself.

» There was paralyzing fear and uncertainty around the AIDS epidemic.

» MTV actually played music videos. And everyone knows the moves to the *Thriller* dance.

» Everyone was glued to the TV watching OJ make a getaway in that white Bronco.

» Very seriously pondering this question — who shot J.R.?

» The hip-hop and grunge music scenes (and fashion) took off in popularity.

» Kids on the back of milk cartons made every parent and child worried about safety and the perils of stranger danger.

» The personal computer was a revolutionary new invention.

» Madonna was everything.

» Watching the tragedy of the Challenger explosion while at school was devastating.

>> Playing the latest video game on your Atari, Commodore 64, or NES systems was the best weekend ever.

>> The "War on Drugs" and "Just Say No" campaigns championed by First Lady Nancy Reagan pushed a strong message.

The stereotypes

Boomers received their fair share of stereotypes when they entered the workforce, and for Gen X, it was no different. They were dismissed as a bunch of "too cool for school" kids who cared more about their music and movies than they did about their career. Some of the many stereotypes you may have seen about Xers include:

>> Slackers

>> Apathetic

>> Cynical

>> Skaters

>> Dirty

>> A lost generation

Looking at where Xers came from (and comparing it to Millennials)

Here we zoom in on the more influential events and conditions that shaped Xers' generational identity. As with the Boomer section mentioned earlier, we go through each of these sections and compare the Xer experience to that of Millennials.

The politics

In Xers' minds, scandals = politics. This is what they learned growing up, because politicians were not to be trusted! When the oldest Gen Xers were in their formative years, Nixon famously said, "I am not a crook." When the youngest Gen Xers were in their formative years, Bill Clinton famously said, "I did not have sexual relations with that woman." Neither one of these men who held the highest seat of government in the country was telling the truth. Corruption, lies, and deceit were pervasive.

Compared to Millennials: It's true that the oldest Millennials can remember Clinton's famous words and remember the back-and-forth of George W. Bush's election and the turmoil in the wake of 9/11. In 2008, they saw the election of Barack Obama, who won the youth vote partially because of his platform for change and also because, in a groundbreaking strategy for a presidential candidate, he used social media to reach the masses. With Obama in office . . . scandals? Not so much. Progress for human rights? Yes.

The parents

Much like Boomers, Gen Xers had parents who preferred to parent from a distance. Traditionalists and Early Boomers parented in a more dictatorial way (though with large amounts of love). When their lovely children turned 18, they gave 'em a soft tap with their shoe and said, "Out you go! You're going to do great things, but please don't come home." And Gen Xers *really* didn't want to go home if they could help it. They were motivated to explore and accomplish things by saying, "I did this on my own."

Compared to Millennials: The difference is rather entertaining! Millennials had (have) a close bond with their parents and were told, "You can go away to college, but please know that you can always come back. We love you!" Later Boomer parents hovered over their children's lives and offered their support, insight, and resources to help ensure their kids' success.

The news

As previously mentioned, media exploded when Gen Xers grew up, bringing along shows like *Schoolhouse Rock!, The Cosby Show,* and *The Simpsons.* The news was not only nightly but also aired in the morning, afternoon, and all day. With CNN came 24-hour news and a constant unveiling of wrongdoings. With the curtain pulled back, Gen Xers witnessed every institution that their parents respected get called into question. Naturally, this made them skeptical.

Compared to Millennials: CNN was there, but so were multiple other 24-hour news networks: MSNBC, C-SPAN, Fox News Channel, and so on. Additionally, social media and widespread access to the Internet has made news all the more accessible and more easily filtered. Millennials aren't seeing just one news organization tear down institutions; they're seeing multiples. With so many voices thrown into the mix, Millennials are having an increasingly hard time knowing who to trust and avoiding the pitfalls of the echo chamber.

The after-school routine

Gen Xers had a pretty standard after-school routine . . . if you don't compare it to Boomers or Millennials. The generation of latchkey kids would saunter home after school, key on a string around their neck, and let themselves into an empty home (unless their siblings or pets were there, of course). After feeding Fido and grabbing a bowl of Apple Jacks for a snack, they'd sit in front of the TV to watch the latest music video or try to beat their latest Donkey Kong score. After working off their snack with some sweet dance moves, they'd maybe do their homework, play a game, pick up a book, finish chores, and prepare for their parents coming home just in time for a microwave dinner.

Compared to Millennials: Well, for starters, "latchkey" was the name of a supervised after-school program for Millennials. Their parents enrolled them in after-school activities so that there was never a second of downtime (especially unsupervised). Independence was locking the bedroom door and hoping your parents or younger siblings wouldn't bother you. Otherwise, adult supervision was pretty much omnipresent.

The youth culture

Gen Xers' youth was not so bright and bubbly as that of the Boomers before them or the Millennials after them. It was the first time that children were told, "You're not going to do as well as your parents." Even the magical world of Disney was decidedly bleak. The '70s and '80s saw a weak showing of animated films, and Disney laid off animators. Youth wasn't counterculture as much as it was alternative-culture. You weren't defined as much by what you cared about, but how much you didn't care. You stood out by what clique you belonged to at school and then went home by yourself to live your life, on your own and by your own rules.

Compared to Millennials: This is another stark comparison point. Millennials were told that they were going to change the world and accomplish wonderful things. Disney was in its prime — *Beauty and the Beast, Mulan, The Lion King,* and *Aladdin* were released, just to name a few of the hits. Millennials were, in general, empowered in their youth just like Boomers — though, admittedly, their parents and adults did most of the empowering.

Discovering Xer workplace traits and what they mean for managers

As a manager, it's critical to know Gen Xers' workplace traits because we have not-so-new news for you — Gen Xers are not like their predecessors or successors. If you are an Xer, maybe you'll start to feel like we're breaking into your mind. Or, in classic skeptical Xer fashion, you might remain unconvinced. Either way, it's important to understand these divergent traits and how they interplay with other generations at work.

- >> Skeptical
- >> Self-reliant
- >> Entrepreneurial
- >> Comfortable with change
- >> Independent
- >> Resourceful
- >> Highly adaptive

When these traits manifest at work, they can be your greatest asset. The following sections describe workplace situations that speak to Gen Xers as well as the Millennial take.

Situation: The prioritization of fewer meetings

You've noticed that Stephanie, a valuable asset to your team, has had weeks of back-to-back meetings. Though you notice she's been sharper than usual in her interactions with other employees, as the seasoned professional that she is, she takes it all in stride. You decide to enact a new policy for everyone (with Stephanie in mind): If you can accomplish a meeting in an email, do it, and limit meetings to 15 minutes unless going longer is absolutely necessary.

Why this works for Gen Xers: While most workers don't enjoy a day full of meetings, Xers especially loathe it. And if it then becomes a meeting about another meeting? Get ready for a disengaged Xer. When your culture proclaims that less is more with meetings, then you're watching out for Xers.

Why it doesn't work for Millennials: Less meetings can actually work for a lot of Millennials — with one caveat. Millennials appreciate efficient touch-bases to clarify progress on a project or to bounce ideas around. They may fear putting meetings on anyone's calendar if everyone seems opposed to them . . . but then you risk them wasting time fretting over whether they're on the wrong path.

Situation: The direct feedback session

You walk out of a meeting with Huck, a fellow Gen X manager. Before going your separate ways, you ask him to chat for five minutes. While getting a coffee, you tell him that you appreciated his comments in your recent meeting. You also tell him that the numbers he presented didn't appear well-vetted and ask him to be a bit more thorough next time. He thanks you, grabs his white chocolate mocha, and you walk back to your cubicles talking about the latest *Star Wars* film.

Why this works for Gen Xers: Giving feedback in the moment is exactly what Gen Xers are looking for — it gives them the impression that you as a manager aren't trying to hide anything or couch criticism. They appreciate honest and direct feedback at all times. Also, what Xer doesn't appreciate a *Star Wars* conversation?

Why it doesn't work for Millennials: Frequent feedback is fantastic, but completely candid comments about what went wrong in a public place can be, at times, jarring.

Situation: The "you own it" culture

Your mission is to show the people you manage that you support them. In that vein, you want to convey absolute trust. To show Mara, one of your Gen X reports, that you support her, you give her an individual project to run. You sit down and say, "I know that you want to excel in your career here. In order to excel, you own your career. This project will help build those skills that can take you to the next level"

Why this works for Gen Xers: This is a perfect method for independent and entrepreneurial Gen Xers. In order to show them respect, the best thing that you can do is leave them alone and refrain from hovering over their shoulders. In so doing, you become the opposite of a micromanager, which Gen Xers loathe.

Why it doesn't work for Millennials: In a sense, Millennials need a bit of micromanaging, at least while they're getting the hang of new projects and skills. While they appreciate the gift of additional responsibility from their managers, that doesn't mean they want to be left completely alone. To Millennials, being left to do their own thing might reflect your lack of investment in their careers and improvement.

Situation: The days off

You have a Gen Xer named Kel, who's been highly successful in his role. You ask him what he'd like as a reward and, to your surprise, he bravely asks for a day off. He explains that he's been spending a lot of time taking his kids to hockey practice and games, as well as soccer practice and games, and all he wants to do is take his partner out to dinner and relax for a day. With a smile, you say, "Of course, take a day off."

Why this works for Gen Xers: More than any other generation, Gen Xers value work-life balance. To them, the greatest gift is time off in any capacity. Money is great, too, but time off is an absolute treasure. Forget employee of the week. For Xers, time off trumps public recognition anyday.

Why it doesn't work for Millennials: Millennials (and Boomers) also value extra days off; Gen Xers are not alone in that. But if given the choice of a variety of benefits and rewards, they'll often opt for that group outing, travel incentive, or a gift card to their favorite restaurant.

Exploring Xer values and how they influence work style

While understanding Gen Xers' traits is important for all managers, perhaps exploring their values is even more beneficial. Below, we uncover some of Xers' strongest values and how they may collide with Millennials:

» **Transparency:** If you want to communicate successfully with the skeptical Xer generation, the best thing you can do is be as transparent as possible. If you're not, chances are they'll suspect that you're hiding something. As a generation, Gen Xers therefore communicate transparently.

  How this value collides with Millennials: While Millennials also value transparency, the directness (and borderline sharpness) it's sometimes accompanied with can be unwelcomed. To Millennials, authenticity and accessibility can be more valued than transparency in the form of blunt communication.

» **Work-life balance:** When Gen Xers were growing up, their parents were gone all the time. As they entered the workplace, they had a plan to change those standards. To them, efficiency and focus allow for the balance necessary to lead a productive work life and get them home on time. To an Xer, it's about quantity of time.

  How this value collides with Millennials: Do Millennials value balance? Of course! In their world, however, they value work-life integration more. With that value, they can spread their focus across a larger span of time to get the same amount done, but have more brain breaks in the meantime.

» **Trust:** The greatest gift you can give an Xer is trust. The greatest gift you can earn from them is *their* trust. Once this gift is exchanged, it indicates utmost respect, acceptance, and belief that both sides can accomplish anything to the best of their abilities at no cost to those around them.

  How this value collides with Millennials: With Xers, trust needs to be earned. This means that when first working with Gen Xers, they'll push back and ask a lot of questions to make sure you're worthy of their gift of trust. This initial incessant questioning can make Millennials feel unsure about themselves and like the Xer has little respect for their workplace contributions.

>> **Honesty:** Generation Xers have a very sensitive BS-o-meter and therefore do their best to never score high levels on another person's meter. They prefer communication and selling that keeps it real, cuts the unnecessary sugar-coating, and owns up to faults and weaknesses from the upfront.

How this value collides with Millennials: You may have heard the phrase "a spoonful of sugar makes the medicine go down." Honesty is a great quality — as long as it doesn't come at the cost of hurt. At times, the honest approach Gen Xers embrace can be so direct that it's hurtful. Millennials prefer their communication with a spoonful of positivity and, ocassionaly, praise.

>> **Self-reliance:** Growing up, Gen Xers learned how to do things on their own. They expect other people to be as independent and resourceful as they are. If they don't meet these expectations, they can seem needy.

How this value collides with Millennials: While Millennials have tech at their fingertips to seek answers and solutions to most challenges, they also value the ability to consult the team around them and crowd-source problems. This sense of collaborative information-seeking is different from their self-reliant Gen X colleagues.

Comparing Traits and Values Across Generations

As a generationally savvy manager, you'll get the most out of your awareness through a wholistic, full-pictured understanding of the generations. By learning how each of these interplays with the others, you'll be more apt to pinpoint a potential generational point of contention and stop it before it becomes a real issue. Refer to Figure 4-1 to cross-compare traits, values, and workplace perceptions and preferences for Baby Boomers, Gen Xers, and Millennials. Building a solid grasp of the "lay of the generational land" will empower you to build stronger teams that communicate more effectively and work together more efficiently.

	Baby Boomers	Gen Xers	Millennials
Traits	Youthful Optimistic Competitive Disciplined Nonconformist Idealistic	Skeptical Entrepreneurial Resourceful Independent Comfortable with change	Tech-savvy Searching for meaning Collaborative Realistic Integrated
Values	Novelty Work ethic Professionalism Luxury Youthfulness Health Individuality	Growth Transparency Work-life balance Family Trust Independence	Customization Choice Efficiency Tribal Integrity Speed Innovation
When it comes to:			
Formality	Put together but tie isn't necessary	Clean and pressed shirt with nice jeans	Why does it matter?
Communication style	Formal and politically correct	Immediate and to the point	Constant and collaborative
Work ethic	Driven Willing to take risks Want to make a difference	Efficient Self-reliant Seek work-life balance	Ambitious Multi-taskers Integrate work and life seamlessly
Career path	Management and employee share equal responsibility	The responsibility falls 100 percent on me	Parallel careers
Authority at work	Collegial — keep the leaders on your side	Skeptical — leadership must earn buy-in	Authentic — want direct access to leaders
Work-life balance	Keep my work and life separate	Work-life balance is a necessity	Desire to work flexibly without stigmas
Organizational structure	Process-oriented	Efficient	Collaborative
Rewards	Motivated by competition and recognition of hard work	The ultimate reward is personal freedom	Collaborative work that has an impact on the greater good
Goals	Career progression and monetary gains	Financial stability and dynamic career	Meaningful work that matches passion

FIGURE 4-1:
Comparing traits, values and clash points across the generations.

BridgeWorks. Minneapolis, MN. (October, 2016)

Chapter **5**

Managing through Your Generational Lens

H ere's the thing: It's not enough to only understand the Millennial whom you're managing. Yes, that's a huge piece of improving the manager–Millennial dynamic, but to be an effective manager, you need to take your own generational perspective into account and consider how it may skew your vision one way or another. Whether you're a Baby Boomer, a Gen Xer, or even a Millennial manager, your generational perspective is going to influence your management style — and the way you view the next generation. This exercise of looking inward and figuring out your own generational tendencies as a manager is a critical piece toward reaching pro status at managing the next generation.

In this chapter, we take a closer look at each of the generational management combos, uncovering both areas of strengths and the challenges that may crop up. First up is the Boomer manager of the Millennial employee. Next, we examine how Gen X manages Millennials. Lastly, we explore a hidden tricky relationship — the Millennial manager of a Millennial.

We use the analogy of a family to illustrate the differences and potential gaps between the generations. Trust us when we say we realize that this could get us in trouble. No one wants to be known as the "kid" at work or, perhaps even worse, the "grandma." This is an analogy. We're not actually calling Millennials annoying little siblings, nor are we claiming that Baby Boomers are finger-wagging parents. Our goal in using this analogy is to paint a picture of how we all manage from our unique generational position in our family tree . . . oops, we mean our unique generational position in the organizational structure.

WARNING

Though we are comparing these generations to family, here are some examples of what not to say to the generations in your workplace, unless you seriously want to make some people mad (not to mention increase your risk for claims of discrimination!):

>> You could be my parent!

>> You could be my kid!

>> Hey, gramps.

>> Even my little sister knows how to do that.

>> You don't know what I'm referencing?! Wow, I feel old.

>> You were born in *what* decade?

>> I have grandkids your age.

>> You're behaving like a child.

The Parent Trap: What Happens When Boomers Manage Millennials

Why is this section called "The Parent Trap"? Because we find that when Boomers manage Millennials, they can easily fall into the grooves of a parent/child relationship. We don't mean this in a condescending way, but rather recognize Boomers' natural ability to identify with the Millennials they manage because many of them have raised Millennials of their own. For Boomers, Millennials are not "agent unknown." They've been around them, and to some degree, they get how Millennials work. That said, this parent/child perception can have two very different outcomes. One is the Boomer manager becoming a Millennial's number-one champion. The other is the Boomer turning up his nose and digging in his heels with a "you're not *my* kid" sentiment that turns into a whole lot of stereotyping and typecasting.

Here are the two types of Boomer bosses:

>> **The champion Boomer boss:** When some Boomer managers see fresh-faced Millennials, they see nothing but potential. They are eager to teach them, coach them, and mentor them to ultimately see them "grow up" into successful counterparts and colleagues. This lights up many Boomer managers and is one of their incentives to go to work every day. Grooming the future of the workforce is a huge motivational factor, and they see their Millennial's success as a reflection of their own skill as a mentor and coach. It's a personal win for themselves. They know when to step in and when to step back, when to reward and when to reprimand. It doesn't mean the relationship is easy, but it can be the powerful bond that elicits some of the best work out of high-performing Millennials.

>> **The typecasting Boomer boss:** Unfortunately, we find the "typecasters" in numbers almost equal to "the champions." These are the managers who find themselves saying those annoying parental phrases like "when I was your age" or "kids these days . . ." Oftentimes, despite the fact that many of these typecasters are raising Millennials at home whom they adore, that love just doesn't translate to their Millennial at work. All too often, there are stories of Boomer managers who can't believe that their employee's parents are getting involved at work, yet they themselves are incredibly involved in their own child's career progression. As much as they connect with their own Millennial kids and their very Millennial tendencies, as soon as those traits and tendencies show up in the workplace in the form of their employees, those positives turn into giant negatives. Oftentimes these typecasters and naysayers are blind to the irony of the situation.

See the following table for a look at how to be a champion and how not to be a typecaster.

Tips on How to Be a Boomer Champion	Ways to Avoid Being a Boomer Typecaster
Encourage a two-way-street managerial relationship.	Don't engage in a power struggle.
Set rules and expectations, and then give them freedom to make mistakes.	Realize that every generation has pros and cons.
Don't be afraid to engage informally as well as formally.	Remember that some challenges are generational, while others are because an employee is new to the workforce.

Capitalizing on the unique Boomer/ Millennial alliance in managing

While this section is called "The Parent Trap," in many ways it could be called "The Parent Chance." Boomers and Millennials have a natural alliance, and the managers who can capitalize on that will be at a real advantage when it comes to getting the most out of their Millennial employees. So what makes these two generations a natural fit?

Natural optimists

Both Boomers and Millennials tend to be more optimistic than their Xer counterparts. Boomer managers can count on Millennials to believe anything is possible and rally around a new project or idea. They both like to celebrate big wins and lead with the desire to make a difference. In meetings, during brainstorm sessions, when assessing pie-in-the-sky ideas, these two generations connect over the possibilities. This degree of idealism that they share influences how Boomer managers affect Millennial employees' development and inspiration.

Easy, two-way mentorship

Whether it was their parents, coaches, pastors, or teachers, most Millennials grew up with a network of Boomers surrounding them. From Millennials teaching their Boomer friends how to use the latest technology to Boomers showing Millennials how to write a formal resume, communicating with each other is not new territory. A good number of Boomers have had some experience interacting with Millennials, and the two-way mentorship model could feel like a natural extension of what they already do.

Find your strength

Tap into your natural Boomer manager strengths by

>> Feeding into Millennial positivity and encouraging their ambitions

>> Opening the door for them to share their voices and ideas, while still imparting your own wisdom

>> Gently coaching them on the ins and outs of workplace etiquette

>> Sharing personal stories of where work has been and where it's going

Avoiding common mistakes

As anyone who has ever been a parent knows, it is all too easy to make a million little missteps until suddenly you look at your kids and think, "Who raised these monsters?" While no one is expected to be a perfect boss or parent, the following sections detail the top behaviors to avoid when it comes to Boomers managing Millennials.

Condescension

No matter how big the age gap is between you and your employee, it never justifies being condescending. Constantly touting how long you've been at your job or sighing at how woefully inexperienced your Millennials are is one of the fastest ways to lose their respect. Sure, you may have been working at your company longer than the Millennial has been alive, but smart managers realize that dismissing young professionals as "kids these days" gets you nowhere.

"It was so much harder for us"

This sentiment is where sayings like "I had to walk to school uphill both ways, barefoot in the snow, when I was growing up" come from. People love to think that they had it harder than the perceived cushy lifestyle of the Millennial generation. Boomers can be especially guilty of this. And sure, while you may not have had programs like Excel to calculate things for you, Millennials today are faced with new challenges that Boomers never had to worry about, like the pressure to bring your laptop home with you to work at all hours. Steer clear of this generational "one-upping" at all costs.

> "[My Boomer boss] is more 'get it done' and just gets it done, whereas I am more likely to [research first, and] Google it. Neither is wrong, but there is value in having both sides of the coin. Have only one and you're missing out. Hopefully subsequent generations have different skills, and that will be valuable." —*Kara F., Millennial and manager*

Prevent pitfalls

Avoid potential Boomer manager pitfalls by

- ⟫ Recognizing the different conditions Millennials grew up in
- ⟫ Focusing on the positive attributes Millennials bring to the workforce (instead of harping on the negatives)
- ⟫ Finding proactive ways to work on weaknesses, instead of dismissing them as generational failings
- ⟫ Finding the value and satisfaction in imparting your hard-earned knowledge to build talented next-generation leaders

The Annoying Little Sibling: Why Xers Struggle to Manage Millennials

On paper, it seems like Xers should have a pretty easy time managing Millennials. Both generations grew up around technology, both are relatively young, and both know the difference between an emoji, a meme, and a gif (or at least most of them do). In reality, we've found that these two generations have some of the biggest workplace clashes. The relationship between Gen X managers and their Millennial employees has been wrought with issues from the get-go, and while they are getting increasingly used to each other with every passing year, believe us when we say the struggle is real.

This conflict often manifests itself much like that between an older and younger sibling. There can be moments of friendship and even fun, but it can easily switch to squabbles and spats in an instant. In the workplace, though, squabbles and spats can be translated into tension and moments of deep frustration. Much like Boomers, the Gen X managers who can find a way to work with Millennials end up as champions, while the ones who succumb to the "annoying sibling" complex fall into the naysayer category. What do these two types of managers look like? Take a look:

>> **The champion Xer boss:** Here's a reference Xers should relate to: Opposites attract. Paula Abdul may have been referring to herself and an animated cat in her music video, but in this case, it applies to the workplace too. Rather than focusing on differences as negatives, the champion Xer boss figures out ways to transfigure them into positives. Take Xers' natural skepticism paired with Millennials' tendency toward optimism. This difference in mindset can either be cause for frustration or a chance for each person to bring what she does best. Millennials provide the fresh, new, unvetted, and sometimes crazy ideas, while Xers put their expertise to work by testing the idea's validity by asking tough questions.

>> **The typecasting Xer boss:** A major "tell" of the typecaster Gen X boss is refusing to meet in the middle. While Xers and Millennials may approach projects differently (hello, independence versus collaboration), there is a lot of gray area in between extremes for the two generations to meet. However, rather than looking for compromise, this Xer digs in and just says, "I'm the boss. Deal." This stalwart refusal to bend for Millennials often results in frustration that can teeter into the realm of resentment. It can shut a Millennial down completely, and it's not uncommon for a Millennial who is dealing with this type of Xer boss to either ask for a new manager or bow out of the company entirely.

The following table shows how to be a champion and how not to be a typecaster.

Tips on How to Be a Gen X Champion	Ways to Avoid Being a Gen X Typecaster
Reframe differences as positives.	Don't try to be "one of them" — it will come off as inauthentic.
Stay true to your Xer self (and let Millennials do the same).	Find ways to meet in the middle.
Find areas of commonality. (There are some!)	Avoid stereotyping Millennials before you even meet them.

Taking advantage of the natural alignments of Xers and Millennials

It's true. Gen Xers and Millennials can have a rough go of things. But it's not all bleak, bad news. There are lots of natural similarities that work in favor of this relationship. As anyone with a much older or younger sibling knows, while it can be challenging, it can also be just plain awesome. Here are some connections to capitalize on in a Gen X manager to Millennial employee relationship.

Transparency is best

Both Xers and Millennials appreciate full transparency from their leaders as well as the people they're working with. For Millennials this manifests as constant communication and feedback; for Xers that means knowing exactly where they stand and making sure any issues or areas that need improvement have been aired. Though each of these generations come at transparency in a different way, they both gravitate toward the basic tenet of always knowing where they stand.

Efficiency for the win

Though this leaning toward the efficient stems from different reasons, Xers and Millennials alike want to get work done in a fast and furious way. Don't get us wrong; they both want to do a good job — a great job in fact — but each generation appreciates taking the straightest line to their destination. For Xers this is true for an entire project, whereas Millennials may want to start off with a creative brainstorm session and then apply that efficiency to the actual "doing" part of a project. Either way, both generations love to find fast methods to get things done efficiently.

Find your strength

Tap into your natural Xer manager strengths by

>> Being transparent with your Millennial employees about where they stand in your mind and in the company as a whole

>> Connecting with them over new processes, technology, or anything that enables both them and you to do your job more efficiently

>> Showing them you value their input by soliciting their help finding tools and technology that will help do work better and faster

Navigating through the inevitable collisions

Older siblings everywhere know that younger ones can sometimes be the absolute pits. They get all the good stuff you had to fight so hard for without lifting a muscle, they are fawned over as the newest sparkly addition to the family, and they can be the most infuriating know-it-alls. We see some of this older-sibling-esque frustration in the dynamics between Xer managers, who think the following while working with their Millennial employees.

"Earn your OWN stripes"

Millennials are entering the workplace and shaking things up with abandon. Xers, who created great change in an albeit quieter way, look at these brash youngsters and think, "Are you kidding me?" Millennials are credited for being a techy generation, when Xers are the first generation to have had a personal computer and are the inventors behind a lot of today's biggest technological successes. Basically, Xers see Millennials lapping up the goods of all the Xers' hard-fought battles, and they think Millennials don't even know how good they have it.

Despite all of that, Millennials still find things to complain about, aren't loyal employees, and keep asking for more, more, more. A frustrated Xer manager may find herself thinking, "Why can't they just be grateful about how good they have it?"

> "My Millennial team members want to talk, ask questions, get clarity. My Gen Xers don't. The struggle is giving the same amount of time, direction, information, and leadership to my Gen X team members as I do my Millennials." — *Cathie S., Manager*

"Stop pestering me"

You know how younger siblings can be like shadows, following you around everywhere you go? Xer managers sometimes feel like they can't get rid of their Millennial employees. They show up for all of their office hours, they are constantly asking for feedback, and they don't seem to be able to do anything by themselves without a heavy dose of support and very explicit directions. Xers start feeling annoyed that so much of their resources are being drained by these needy Millennial hires. They feel like their resources are finite, and they can't continue to give up so much of their time. Unfortunately, this can result in an almost complete shutdown, where they shrug Millennials off and ask them to figure things out by themselves.

> "Coming from a different generation, it can be exhausting. I feel like [asking], 'Why? Why do you need this? I don't understand.' [But] part [of it] is recognizing that they do need [feedback] and making sure I deliver it in a way they need so we both are on a good operating situation." —*Julie A., Manager*

Prevent pitfalls

Avoid potential Xer manager pitfalls by

>> Understanding that Millennials are fighting their own battles (one of which is shrugging off all the negativity surrounding their generation)

>> Encouraging Millennials to do independent work and giving them a detailed road map to get them started

>> Stemming the tide of Millennial "neediness" by setting clear parameters about when you're available and when you're most definitely *not*

>> Communicating transparently without being brash

The Twin: Why Millennials Managing Millennials Is Not All Smooth Sailing

If differences in generational perspectives create hardships in the workplace, then surely a Millennial managing a fellow Millennial should be a pretty carefree working relationship, void of misalignments that commonly occur when a different generation manages a Millennial. In some ways, it's kind of a twin thing. They were raised in similar environments, listened to the same boy bands, shared awkward AIM screen names, and graduated from college into an anything-but-booming economic environment. Surely, they have each others' backs.

For the most part, they do. Though certainly not free from the normal working challenges that come along when any humans work together, there does appear to be some synchronicity between the Millennial manager and the Millennial employee. There isn't quite as big a gap to bridge in terms of communication, working preferences, perceptions around technology, and what work ethic looks like. The Millennial manager champion embraces his best Millennial traits and uses them as a connection point with his employee. Alternatively, the typecaster

Millennial manager rejects any blatant "Millennial–ness," which can result in friction and especially harsh feedback to her fellow Millennial reports. Check out the following descriptions for these two types of bosses:

>> **The champion Millennial boss:** Great Millennial managers make good use of the common ground. They're ready to give frequent feedback because they know that's what they would want. They entertain flexible work arrangements because flexibility is something they also value highly, and results are what really matter anyway. Opportunities to collaborate, both in the workplace and in team-building, are built into the day-to-day. The best of the Millennial champions aren't just interested in connecting with their direct reports but also actively invest in grooming their skills for the future. They don't let them coast just because they're fellow Millennials. Standards are kept high and assignments are challenging, but encouragement is free-flowing and the manager uses that shared common ground to develop and grow the employee.

>> **The typecaster Millennial boss:** The potentially less successful Millennial managers fall in line with the "I'm-not-a-Millennial" Millennials. Because it's been hammered into their heads so often, they, too, hold this idea that all Millennials are entitled brats, and they want to do everything they can to set themselves apart from the negative qualities that make up a Millennial. Because of this, when they see Millennial traits in those they manage, they laugh at the irony and are determined not to encourage these "failings." To put it a bit harshly, these bosses soak up the traits of the Boomer and Xer typecaster managers and turn them on one of their own.

Take a look at the following table for more on becoming a champion and avoiding being a typecaster.

Tips on How to Be a Millennial Champion	Ways to Avoid Being a Millennial Typecaster
Use shared ground as a point of connection.	Reassess your perception of the word "Millennial" and what that entails.
Be a Millennial advocate with the older generations.	Take a deep breath before reacting when a "classical Millennial" moment happens.
Hold them to a high standard of continuous improvement.	Own the positive Millennial qualities as a manager to lead by example.

Unleashing the power of the Millennial-Millennial relationship

Twins have a special relationship, and sometimes it's almost as if they can read each other's minds. We're not going to suggest Millennial managers can guess what their direct reports are thinking, but because they share the same generational perspective, they can easily put themselves in their direct report's shoes. Two areas where Millennial managers shine with fellow Millennials are coaching and balancing work-family life.

Skill coaching

What's a quick way to get a Millennial to disengage? Don't invest in growing his skills. Millennial managers know this more than anyone. They benefited from someone who pegged them as a high-potential future leader and are reaping the benefits. Not everyone can be a leader, but everyone should be invested in to see what his skills might grow into. These managers take the time to customize their training approaches to each of their employees, and they promote skill-building to show that they believe in their employee.

#Workfamily

The line between work and personal life is getting increasingly blurred. Millennial managers understand this concept and know that their people aren't going to want to engage in a strictly professional environment that doesn't promote authentic relationships with the people they spend 40+ hours a week with. They keep a keen watch on not just the day-to-day operational factors of the day, but also regularly feed the team-building goal.

Find your strength

Tap into your natural Millennial manager strengths by

>> Creating spaces for collaboration and teamwork

>> Being careful not to spill over into favoritism with your Millennial employees

>> Leading with the customization penchant to manage your Millennials for their distinct needs and preferences

>> Promoting positive conversations and understanding of Millennial employees among other managers

Easing challenges of managing someone in your own generation

Think about the twin relationship. Your twin (let's say identical twin in this case) is in many ways a reflection of who you are. Looking at your twin is like looking into a mirror. When typecaster Millennial managers look into this mirror, something strange happens. Instead of taking in the reflection, flaws and strengths alike, some sort of dysmorphia happens and all they're able to see is the negative, especially with the following sentiments.

Disassociation

"I'm not you" is essentially the sentiment here. The Millennial manager wants nothing to do with the Millennial qualities and is unwilling to do what she sees as indulging the worst of her generation's behavior. In an effort to balance things out, she can go too far in the opposite direction. She becomes inaccessible to her direct report and can feel cold and unfamiliar.

"I'm your age, but I'm your BOSS"

Another weird thing we see when Millennials manage others in their same age range is the need to prove, beyond a shadow of a doubt, that the manager is the *boss*, in *charge*, and the *leader*. The impetus for this is an attempt to establish authority in a relationship that might fall into a "Hey, you're around my age; we could be friends so I'll treat you like one" mentality. Preemptively fighting against this possibility, Millennials throw on the starchy "I'm your boss" shirt and effectively fend off any opportunity to build an authentic, strong relationship with their report. While this issue shows up with all generations, it can be even more prevalent for Millennials who are more likely to blend the lines between colleague and friend than other generations.

> "[My coworkers and I] are all in the same age range. I was on a team and promoted to lead people who were mostly my co-workers. [It's] my, 'friend versus manager challenge.'" —*Kelly O., Manager*

Prevent pitfalls

Avoid potential Millennial manager pitfalls by

>> Figuring out what Millennial traits are actually disruptive and communicating with/coaching your direct reports on how to improve

>> Demonstrating your authority not by coldly shutting off but by showing your expertise in coaching new skills and offering valuable feedback

>> Leading with humility first

>> Learning about those around you to inform the way you approach them as individuals

2

Navigating Potential Clash Points

IN THIS PART . . .

Anticipate and prepare for the most common generational clash points you are likely to encounter when managing Millennials.

Troubleshoot managerial issues quickly and effectively.

Capitalize on organizational structure to get the most out of your Millennials.

Build collaborative relationships that work for you *and* them.

Crack the code on effectively giving feedback to Millennials.

Discover ways to motivate in a way that truly resonates.

Find out how to deal with the blurred lines of workplace relationships and formality.

Chapter **6**

Adapting to Changes in Organizational Structure ... The World Is Flat

For decades, the traditional organizational model has played an invaluable role in creating law and order in the working world. This model places responsibility-heavy positions at the top with lower ranks trickling down, providing a fool-proof road map for accountability and responsibility and assigning everyone a position and rank within the organization. The traditional model has stood the test of time, left largely untouched as Traditionalists, Baby Boomers, and Gen Xers fought their way up the ranks and ascended into positions of influence and power. But for Millennials, a generation known for their proclivity to disrupt, the traditional hierarchical structure isn't sitting well. It looks and feels like a bunch of hoops they have to jump through. The perception is that this hierarchy creates barriers on the road to innovation and change. It's a model that many feel, rather than doing good, actually hampers creativity and stifles employees' abilities to contribute, share their ideas, and, at the end of the day, improve the bottom line.

As Millennials continue to make up a bigger and bigger segment of the employee pool, it's important for managers and leaders to understand the importance of their organizational structure as a tool in recruiting, retaining, and engaging the next generation. Inflexible adherence to the traditional model can damage buy-in and lead to disengagement and, consequently, lowered retention rates. This is not to say you have to throw the baby out with the bathwater. Understanding the why behind the new Millennial mindset toward work structure allows you to see through Millennials' eyes, understand their shifting perceptions, and adapt the workplace messaging so you don't alienate Millennials *or* their other generational counterparts.

In this chapter you explore the shift from a traditional hierarchical workplace structure to a more networked and interwoven model. You discover how to communicate the strengths that these two models bring to the table and how to capitalize on the pros of each while avoiding the challenges presented by the cons. We arm you with strategies to help use your organizational structure as a tool to recruit, retain, and engage Millennial employees. Finally, we review tactics for how to apply the Millennial lens to organizational structure even in unique — and sometimes inflexible — circumstances.

Transitioning from Hierarchy to Network

Ask anyone to sketch out what a typical organizational structure looks like, and odds are good that that person will draw you a traditional hierarchical model. (See Figure 6-1.) The layout of this wireframe is tiered, with power centralized at the top with the CEO and responsibility trickling down in layers from upper-level management to the bottom level, which may include administrative roles and internship positions. This is a classic structure, and though it has had some solid staying power, approaches to organizational structure are starting to shift. The top-down, command-control world that has been standard in the workforce is undergoing a makeover. Companies are testing flatter structures, where managerial titles are eliminated and corner offices exist only in movies and TV shows of the past. Millennials are embracing and, in fact, expecting a more networked, flatter world.

There have been many responses to this shift in perception of organizational structure — some successful, and some, well, not so much. In trying to appeal to the next-generation talent pool, some have completely done away with their old model in favor of a completely new, more-modern version. At The Nerdery, a digital strategy consulting agency headquartered in Minneapolis, every single employee bears the title of "Co-President," because of their strong belief in, as they term it, "distributed leadership" Internationally recognized organizations are also going the way of "the flatter the better." Zappos is famous for their holacracy structure, a move toward self-management that ditched titles, managers, and the hierarchy in general. It's proven to be a rocky transition because, as with any new concept, the kinks still need to be ironed out.

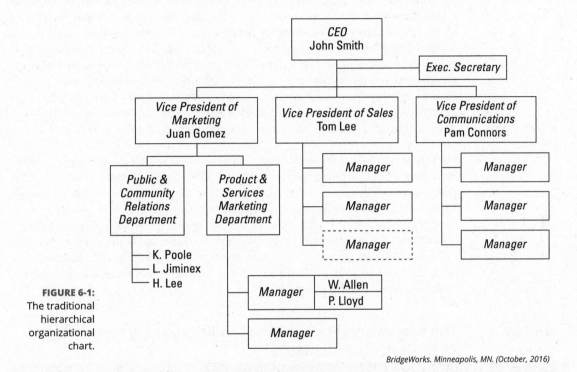

BridgeWorks. Minneapolis, MN. (October, 2016)

FIGURE 6-1: The traditional hierarchical organizational chart.

But Zappos is not alone in its move to bury the traditional hierarchical model. It's a trend that is gaining favor as more Millennials enter the workforce. And other small, regional companies are adopting elements of its model. These (sometimes abrupt) changes have not only alienated loyal Boomer and Xer employee bases, but can often lead to a feeling of chaos and overwhelming rejection of change. On the other hand, another equally foolhardy approach is to dismiss the networked version of the working world and stubbornly cling to the model that is currently in place.

> "[Since I've started working], it's been a top-down corporate setting. I think there's a lot of red tape that goes on and it can be really hard to get ideas heard and to feel like you're making a difference, to feel like your opinions are affecting the company. On the flipside, there's incentive and motivation to work up the corporate ladder."
> —Alexa S., Millennial

Can you guess how these scenarios end? Neither extreme is successful. Instead, aim for a happy medium that can be reached by understanding the pros and cons that each model brings to the table (see Table 6-1). Figure out how to capitalize on the clarity and efficiency of the hierarchy while leaving plenty of room for collaboration and accessibility that the network brings. There is no one-size-fits-all solution when assessing these two models. It's less a binary choice between one or the other, and more about tapping into elements from each that are implementable and make sense within your organization. For one organization, it may be keeping all job titles in place but eliminating the corner office to increase accessibility. For another company, you may do away with formal titles but offer a clear promotion path so employees understand their career growth options. It will be different for every company, but whatever the mix, the companies that have the best odds at effectively leading and managing the next generation talent pool are those that have taken the time to assess each of these models, and have envisioned and implemented a realistic compromise between the two — one that works.

Naysayers may be thinking, "Listen, I have no control over my company's structure. Why does this even matter if I can't affect the necessary change?" Valid point, dear reader, but as with many areas for improvement, a solution doesn't have to be of major proportions to be effective. One solution is a complete company restructure. This probably isn't a feasible option. Another that *is* more doable is tweaking your management style to reflect the more open, networked style that Millennials are expecting. This section presents strategies big and small to make organizational structure a tool you can use for increased success in leading the next generation of employees.

TABLE 6-1 **The Merits and Flaws of the Traditional and Network Organizational Structures**

	Pros	Cons
Traditional Organizational Structure	Clear chain of command and accountability	Bureaucracy slows change
	Explicit path to promotions	Stifles collaboration and innovation
	Efficient communication	Restricted flow of information
Network	Quick exchange of information	Unclear accountability
	Nimble implementation of change	Less control in crises
	Access to people across the organization	Confusion around promotion pathway and opportunities

Embracing the changing nature of the org chart

As you examine the two different models, you may be wondering why this shift is happening *now*. Every generation that enters the workplace brings its unique perspective to the working world and alters the way things have been done.

Millennials and the generation after them have grown up in a world that looks very different from generations past. When Millennials were in their formative years (see Chapter 2), the Internet arrived on the scene and changed the way we do everything. All of a sudden, Millennials had unprecedented access to information. They didn't have to rely on a parent or teacher to answer a question or satisfy their curiosity; they just used their dial-up to connect and — boom — the world was at their fingertips.

When Traditionalists and Boomers think of a company's internal structure, they see a traditional chart that clearly defines roles, ensures specific skill sets, and shows clear promotional pathways. But Millennials and even Gen Xers are leaning toward the network model that they see as fluid, efficient, instantaneous, and un-siloed, granting them instant access to almost everyone in the company. From their perspective, a traditional organizational chart is simply a set of hurdles to jump through. But for Boomers and Traditionalists, the network looks like a tangle of undefined roles. Who's in charge? What does career progression look like? How can there be any accountability? It's a logistical nightmare, and both sides think they're right. So how do you consolidate these fundamentally different views of how work should be structured?

> "I think having some hierarchy is good; you know where you stand and your role is defined. [Our organization] moved to a [flatter] team structure with mentors, [so] I'm still responsible for more decisions . . . but I like having the support [of a team] when I feel overwhelmed or don't have enough information to make a decision."
> —Clayton H., Millennial

The first step, as the saying goes, is admitting you have a problem. The problem in this case is inflexibility. Some readers may recall the fable of the oak and the reed. For those who don't, it's pretty straightforward. The oak tree was unbending and refused to change, relying on the strength it had acquired over years of growth and nurture. It stood tall in its convictions. The reed, on the other hand, was more pliable. It moved with the changing winds and bent this way or that depending on where the breeze was taking it. When a storm came along, guess who weathered it? Not the oak, which crashed and burned in a pretty magnificent fashion. The reed, which reacted instead of resisting the gale force winds, let itself be moved by the changing tides and made it through intact. Importantly, the reed did not become something other than what it was. It stayed true to its plant self. You may laugh, but the point stands. If you refuse to evolve and consider new ways of doing things because "the way things have always been done" has served you well, you are doing yourself and your company a disservice.

WARNING

We are not saying you should become something you're not. We've seen companies try to force Google-esque policies and organizational frameworks in what comes off as a somewhat desperate attempt to attract new talent. The thing is, if you start drastically changing things up, you're probably going to end up coming off as inauthentic and making new employees pretty unsatisfied with sudden shifts that don't fall in line with the company they've known. When considering any changes, use the following two questions as a screening tool:

>> Does this organizational structure shift resonate with our company's mission?

>> Is this proposed structure change more of an evolution or a revolution of our corporate culture? (**Hint:** Skew toward evolution.)

Explaining to Millennials the long-standing merits of the traditional structure

It may seem counter-intuitive, but one of the first steps in embracing the changing nature of the org chart is to look at the traditional org chart and see why it's worked for so long. There are many merits that have contributed to this model's longevity. You may take these strengths for granted, because you've witnessed the pros firsthand, but don't assume that your next generation of hires is going to innately understand why this model has stood the test of time and remains an incredibly effective model to this day. Remember that one of the best ways to gain Millennial buy-in is to explain the why behind the what. If you're dealing with Millennials who are pushing back against your adherence to the traditional structure and feeling frustrated by what they perceive is inflexibility within the organization, take the time to sit with them and explain the great value that the traditional model brings to the table.

Here are some examples of how to communicate these strengths in a way that will resonate with Millennials:

>> **Clear chain of command and accountability:** When it comes to explaining the what and the why, the traditional hierarchical org chart is a visual representation that eliminates guesswork and paints a clear picture of roles and responsibilities. There is no confusion as to who is in charge of what, or where the buck stops. You can draw a clear line between yourself and your manager, your manager and his or her boss, and so on. If you need to seek out someone for expertise, it's quite clear where to go and who to reach out to. In times of crisis, this clarity is extremely useful.

>> **Explicit path to promotions:** Millennials are a generation that inspires eye-rolling with their belief that after six weeks on the job, they're eligible for promotion. Often, they're not going to be eligible that quickly, and the org chart is a great way to soothe that frustration for both the Millennial and the manager alike. Rather than Millennials wondering when they are going to be promoted, regularly asking about it and consistently getting "no" for an answer, they will better understand the path to promotion and a road map for achieving that desired next tier of their career.

"I like touching base on goals . . . I think it's important to talk about [them]. [It] keeps me motivated to know my manager is thinking about [them as well]."
—*Michael S., Millennial*

>> **Efficient communication:** The thing about silos and specializations is they make it very clear who needs to know what piece of information. They eliminate the need for guesswork and prevent bombarding people with communications they don't necessarily need. They promote efficiency and clarity, two things that Millennials — the generation of 140 characters or less — most definitely appreciate.

Managing the generation who grew up tweeting the POTUS

Millennials have no qualms about taking their concerns straight to the top, even if that happens to be the President of the United States (POTUS). They perceive having direct access to leaders as perfectly natural.

WARNING

This section can be summed up as a giant warning sign to *not* immediately write off Millennials or their successors because they have different perceptions around the org chart and the working world. Yes, it's true that some of them may be inexperienced, but others have well over a decade of work experience under their belts. The key to softening your approach (rather than jumping in with harmful stereotypes and resentments) is to understand why their perceptions are different and to avoid some common mistakes managers make when trying to manage this generation.

Here are some standard *don'ts* to avoid:

>> **Don't mistake the desire to connect with authority figures for narcissism or entitlement.** Millennials were raised by parents who encouraged them to share their voices. They grew up in a world where they had unprecedented access to people in positions of power, and they're used to being able to access information at the touch of a button.

When they enter the workforce, the constraints of a traditional hierarchy can feel stifling. They perceive it as a major barrier to engagement. This is a generation that can tweet at the President, and you're telling them they can't have a conversation with the CEO? Stories of a Millennial hire being fired for walking into the boss's office for a casual chat are a dime a dozen.

» **Don't play the boss card (unless absolutely necessary).** Millennials rebel against the idea of a boss. They want someone they can work *with*, not *for*. This is one of the reasons the network model fits so snugly. It's a flat model that doesn't assign special rites or significance to one employee over another. Millennials want equality across the board. They want to collaborate and communicate with peers as well as leadership. They want access to you, they want access to the CEO, and they genuinely believe that everyone will be better off for it. In some cases, they're right. In some cases, they're not. Explain to them where the lines are in terms of how much access they can have, but avoid an authoritarian style when and where possible.

» **Don't view their input and opinions as cute.** For fear of being harsh, we had to put this "don't" to paper because so often Millennials feel belittled. Sure, they are the youngest in the workforce, but they grew up eating at the grown-ups' table. Every part of their lives involved adults seeking their input and opinion, so if they approach you, they're expecting a level of respect that generations in the past knew they didn't have the right to ask for. Millennials are running large organizations, and many have some remarkable ideas, but they're less likely to share them if they feel looked down on.

REMEMBER

If you're feeling frustrated by a Millennial's take on the workplace, consider where he is coming from. Take it on a case-by-case basis.

Understanding the upgrade cycle at work

When thinking about the transition from org chart to network, it's crucial to understand the way Millennials perceive change. They are not only receptive to change — considerably more so than generations before them — but they've also grown to expect it. This is, in large part, due to the way they experienced change growing up.

Consider what may, at first glance, seem like an unrelated example: the mobile phone. A Millennial's first memory of a mobile phone may be a clunky flip phone she borrowed from her mom. Then maybe she upgraded to a Blackberry or a pink Razr (if only those could be erased from our history). By the time many Millennials were graduating from college, those clunky flip phones had morphed into smartphones like Apple's iPhone. From then on, *planned obsolescence* became the status quo. What does that fancy term mean? Simply that the technology purchased had an end date in mind. Like eggs that go bad after a month or so in your fridge, Millennials became accustomed to the fact that within a couple years, their phones would need to be upgraded. And there you have it — the upgrade cycle.

WHAT TO DO WHEN YOUR TECHNOLOGY IS "SO 2013" (OR OUT-OF-DATE)

By now, leaders and managers know that trying to keep up with the demand for the latest and greatest technology is always a game of catch-up. By the time budgets are approved and infrastructure changes are implemented, the new computers, new phone system, new whatever-it-was is already out-of-date. Managers tell stories of new hires who, on their first day on the job, look at computers purchased a couple years ago and make comments like, "Wow, these are pretty dated. Any plans to upgrade these computers?" Word of advice: Don't sweat it. As Millennials get older, they'll understand all the reasons their work doesn't need the latest and greatest. Or, an alternate word of advice: Sweat it, but ask Millennials to help cool you down. If they're so eager for changes, maybe there are valid reasons. Ask them to put proposals together for new tech, whether it's apps, devices, or programs. You may be surprised by how resourceful they can be.

WHO DETERMINES EFFICIENCY? WHAT TO DO ABOUT PESTERING FOR THE LATEST APP OR SYSTEM

Millennials have a restorative nature about them — technology has always provided a tool, app, or system to make their lives more convenient. It's only natural for them to go to work and want to make systems or processes more efficient with simplistic (or complex) tech solutions. While the intent of their revolutionary mindset may be great, constant change can be frustrating. First, ask yourself these three questions:

- Will this process or system ultimately save the company time and/or dollars?

- Is there a budget for the system?

- Is there a training team/person to get everyone up and running on it?

If you can say "yes" to all three of the above, then ask yourself the following two questions:

- Will it cost the company more time to get everyone on board than not implementing it?

- Are you sure about your answer to the last question?

If you can say yes to all five questions, then don't implement a change. However if you can only say yes to the top three, it may be time to explore some changes.

But it didn't stop there. This upgrade cycle applied to other parts of their lives. Social media started as Friendster and blossomed into Snapchat. Facebook has been anything but static, undergoing upgrade after upgrade. The cycle of improvements has burned its way into the Millennial psyche, so it's no surprise that they expect the same from the working world. Why do Millennials expect promotions so readily? When you think about the upgrade cycle, is it any surprise?

TIP

Hopefully finding out about the root of "promotion entitlement" can help to overcome some of the frustration and skepticism that is often directed toward Millennials. Understanding that this expectation has been somewhat built into their DNA, try to work with them, determine goals, and, as always, set clear expectations to negate any preconceived notions about their role that they may be bringing with them.

Looking at Transparency in a Networked Structure

One of the values Millennials see in a networked organization structure is transparency. A network calls for a fluid exchange of information shared across the organization, whereas in a tiered hierarchy, it's pretty clear that all the information lies at the top and is trickled down as necessary to the other rungs of the ladder. In a network, information is accessible to anyone who takes the initiative to figure it out.

When you're assessing how to position your organizational structure, be it radically different from the traditional hierarchy or just a few tweaks here and there, one concept Millennials will be looking for is this idea of transparency. It is something you should aim to offer them, in ways big or small. Whether you do so by sending leadership meeting minutes to the entire company or communicating the big picture and organization-wide goals during one-on-ones with employees, you should try to weave a level of transparency into everything you do.

Millennials aren't the only ones who benefit from understanding the why. So why is transparency so darn important to the Millennial generation? What, exactly, does it mean to them? Here are some answers:

> » **Transparency means embracing a more democratic model of work.**
> He who holds the information holds the power, or so runs the conventional wisdom. Millennials grew up with Boomer parents who abandoned the dictatorial household of their childhood for a more democratic one, where every decision in the family was a group decision. Few conversations were off-limits. Additionally, the rise of the Internet gave Millennials access to information and power to influence more than ever before. A Millennial's world

was and is a level playing field where it doesn't matter if you're the 53-year-old CEO or a 13-year-old teenager; you have something to say because you have access to the same information.

» **Transparency means interconnectedness and seeing your part in the bigger picture.** Millennials are the generation infamous for asking one key question: "Why?" With earlier generations, if a boss told an employee to jump, the reply would always be, "How high?" But Millennials are flipping the switch, and instead of doing as they're told, they're asking, "Why?"

This is not because they're trying to be rude or impertinent (even though that's certainly how it can come across), but because one of the key things Millennials and the next generation yearn for is to be connected to the bigger picture. They want to understand how their contributions impact not just their boss or their direct teammates, but the organization as a whole. The act of being transparent, of taking the time to explain the why, is an easy, straightforward way to motivate a generation that thirsts for connection and impact.

» **Transparency means open communication and increased feedback opportunities.** Another by-product of a transparent model, from a Millennial's perspective, is that feedback can happen on a more regular basis. Instead of restricting feedback to the typical six-month or yearly review, there can be an open exchange of feedback — good or bad — that doesn't need to be neatly fit into a regularly scheduled performance review.

Nothing feels worse — for any generation, really — than to have a flaw or weakness pointed out months after you made the initial mistake. Millennials want real-time, immediate feedback as much as possible. This doesn't mean you need to be ready to comment on their every move at any given moment, but it does mean that as you examine your organizational structure, you should consider how embracing a transparent structure might naturally set up a more steady feedback system. You might consider implementing a weekly one-on-one with your employee or even a 5–10 minute daily check-in.

» **Transparency establishes a framework for more authentic interactions and builds trust.** Millennials grew up with parents blurring the line of the authority figure along with social media that provided a venue for making the private very public. Sharing what you're doing, what you're thinking, even what food you're eating, is a part of everyday life. Why would you try to hide who you are at work, when a simple Google search will reveal a great deal about who you are (on Facebook, anyway)?

To cling to the old model of the suit-wearing professional is to cling to the past. Just as honorifics like "Mr." and "Mrs." have melted away from popular use, in Millennials' minds, adherence to the "professional" is outmoded and outdated. Transparency means you can be your authentic self, communicate your ideas, and show that you aren't obscuring any information or have alternate plans or ideas.

ZAPPOS: A NETWORK AT WORK

An extreme example of how one organization embraced transparency is Zappos's *holacracy.* In this model, self-management reigns. Teams are swapped for "circles" and management is replaced by "lead links." It's a clever model that relies on everyone to put his best foot forward, embrace change passionately, and thrive in an environment that demands the most out of everyone. Some have praised this model. Others have shunned it. We have mixed feelings. Some organizations can benefit from borrowing elements of this model: embracing each "level" of employee, requiring universal account-ability, attempting to keep the workplace devoid of work politics, and accepting each individual. But beyond the perks, values, and shiny sparkle of something inventive are its flaws. Some employees feel so unclear about their path — as well as the company's — that they get disheartened and leave. Some need a little bit of structure to feel comfort-able (especially in a world of logistics and supply chains). Zappos can serve as a cautionary tale or a fairy tale depending on you, your workforce, and your product or service. Be sure of which one you want.

Using Your Adapted Organizational Structure to Recruit, Retain, and Engage

Many see organizational structure as just a foundational element of the work-place. You wouldn't advertise the fact that your company has a water cooler, so why would you use your organizational structure as a promotional tool? Obvi-ously, you're not going to be able to tap into the power of organizational structure as a tool if you're strictly adhering to the linear, hierarchical model. If, however, you can find a way to either restructure or, perhaps much more manageably, reexamine the way you interpret the org chart, informed with a next-generation lens, you'll have a powerful tool for recruiting, retaining, and engaging the upcoming talent pipeline.

A fresh take on the org structure can be used as a strategy tool for the following:

>> **Recruiting:** Adapting your view of organizational structure doesn't just have the potential to change the way you manage your employees on a day-to-day basis; it can be used to rethink your recruiting strategy. Organizational structure has massive implications on what an employee's work life looks like. Millennials ask themselves the following questions:

- Will I be able to interact with the well-established leaders that I have so much to learn from?

- Will I be able to expand beyond my role and learn from other departments as well?

- Are there venues for me to share my ideas (because I have quite a few)?

- Is there only one path to promotion, or can I skip a few steps if I can fully demonstrate my talent, ambition, and ability?

Knowing that these are the kinds of things that Millennials are looking for when scoping you out as a potential employer will help you highlight what you do in your organization to appeal to their desires.

» **Retaining:** Adapting a more networked model, being more transparent, and hearing new hires' and lower-level employees' voices are all things that create buy-in with Millennials. Yes, it's true that next-generation employees may want to be promoted quicker than is realistic. It's also true that they may want to share their ideas more than is necessarily appropriate. The trick is to accommodate these needs without being unrealistic about what is feasible for you.

» **Engaging:** Want to skyrocket Millennial engagement levels within your organization? The following actions have the potential to do just that:

- Provide access to leaders and people in positions of authority.

- Give Millennials opportunities to share their voice and communicate their ideas.

- Let Millennials know that their work has an impact on the company's global objectives.

"I so appreciate [this] about Millennials: their eagerness, and a level of engagement that is not just about satisfaction. The 'I believe in what I'm doing.'" —*Ann M., Manager*

Utilizing your brand story over brand reputation

A decade or so ago, you would find some version of this on the "About Us" page of every organization's website:

Established in 1903, our company has its roots firmly in the ground. With over a century of experience under our belts, and years to perfect our approach and messaging, we've stood the test of time and are a lean, mean, running machine — with the dues paid and the time invested to prove it!

Maybe this was written as a direct quote from the CEO, sometimes with a picture accompanying the copy. Likely, that picture featured a white-haired Traditionalist gentleman smiling — but not too broadly — into the camera, in an impeccably pressed suit. His image reinforced the text: "We have wisdom. We have experience. We are professional. We are the real deal." Though this approach may still resonate with some of the older generations, Millennials see it as a glaring red flag.

Experience is a great thing, of course. If your organization has been around for a while, there is no doubt that sacrifices were made, hard times weathered, expertise accumulated, and so on. But what other generations saw as a badge of honor is viewed quite differently by Millennials. Some words that may come to mind include "stagnant," "inflexible," "outdated," and "uncompromising."

Rather than trying to impress Millennials with senior leadership delivering formal speeches, take a different track. Showcase what it's like for an actual, real-life person to work for you. Don't try to impress them with numbers and titles, but rather produce a highlight reel that showcases the company culture, the atmosphere in the office and what that person's career progression looks like. This is an effective tool for both the Millennial prospective recruit and the one already within your walls.

TIP

You don't have to completely eliminate your history, because chances are it's fascinating, important, and even inspiring. Pair the new messaging alongside a more streamlined, modern take that honors your years of experience and history with story, not just fact.

Creating the perfect open-door policy

To retain and engage the next-generation employee, many leaders announce to their team, "I have an open door policy . . . if you ever have a question, please know that my door is always open." This is a great practice, but when that welcoming Gen X manager has to deal with a pack of Millennials in his office having breakfast, lunch, or an afternoon coffee, he's going to want to pull out his hair (and probably theirs as well). You don't have to be *always* accessible or have lunch with your Millennial colleagues every day to keep them engaged. Instead, try an easier option:

>> Monthly lunches or happy hours with four people who signed up in advance

>> Virtual Q&A platforms that are accessible to everyone and may feature a corresponding Twitter hashtag

>> Quarterly open forums where Millennials can share their ideas

>> Panel discussions composed of Millennials during your manager or executive meetings

"I have a rapport with [my managers] that I never shy away from saying things good [or] bad. They have an open-door policy, so I never feel like there is a hierarchy. They make me feel heard, and when something [is] bothering me, they [always] address it. They don't see me as an annoying Millennial." —*Lauren W., Millennial*

Inviting Millennial input from day one

Millennials want their voices to be heard even when they're at the bottom. When we say day one, we actually mean the first day of training. Little things can go a long way. They don't need to be giving input on the next mission-critical strategy. They just want to know that they've had the opportunity to present their thoughts and that their idea is being considered. They'll be fine with you having the final say.

Inviting Millennial input doesn't have to mean checking in with a Millennial before making all of your decisions. Sometimes it's the symbolic gestures that can make a lasting impact. One strategy a mid-sized architecture firm implemented is pretty simple: Breakfast with the president. About once a month, any employees who were hired that month are invited to a greasy spoon diner for breakfast with the firm's president. He comes prepared, knowing each of their names, where they came from, and what their new role is at the firm. The morning is laid back, as is the conversation, and even though in the grand scheme of things this is a relatively small gesture, it's one that has longstanding value.

Think about why this strategy is so successful, especially when considering effectiveness with the next generation. There is no attempt at pretention. There is no fancy restaurant or stiff-collared event that requires employees to be on their best behavior. The diner creates a casual atmosphere where employees can relax, be themselves, and connect with the "top dog" on a casual and conversational level. He shows an interest in learning about who they are and what they hope to contribute to the company. The gesture shows that they're not just another cog in the machine, but valued new additions to an organization that wants to get to know them on a personal level and invest in who they are. And no one — not even the president himself — is too good to sit and learn from them.

Common pitfalls to avoid when soliciting Millennial input include:

>> Being unclear that you're looking strictly for feedback, not final decisions

>> Forgetting to indicate the time and place that you're willing to hear ideas

>> Neglecting to instruct Millennials on the written and unwritten rules of giving input

>> Shutting down ideas instead of using them as teachable moments

Motivating through career progression without promotion

One of the major pitfalls of adapting a more networked structure rather than a hierarchical model is that the promotion pathway can become murky. All generations wanted a fast progression when they were young professionals, but for Millennials, fast change and progression have been a standard in every part of their lives leading into their first, second, or third jobs. When the route to *leveling-up* their careers becomes unclear, you may start to lose the attention of a generation known for wanting quick promotions. They're unwilling to feel stuck, even if an organization has promotion restrictions for valid reasons like required skills, experience, or pay.

Fortunately, a promotion isn't the only way to progress someone's career. Consider these alternatives:

>> **Pump up your rotational programs.** Few programs have been as popular with the next generation as rotational programs. They're such a logical solution to the promotion conundrum: Hire a top group of young talent and rotate them every six months or so to different teams and departments. The employees gain exposure and access to departments they might not otherwise experience, garner company knowledge and responsibility, and feel refreshed by the constant switch-ups. In the end, Millennials feel like they've

learned immensely, that they were trusted to take on new opportunities and projects, *and* they're likely to recommend the program to other talented recruits. Companies like General Mills, Deloitte, and Lockheed Martin succeed in recruiting top talent year after year because they've adopted the rotational program mindset: "I'll give you everything we've got for three years if you agree to give us the same thing."

» **Allocate time for creativity.** For decades, the youngest generation has been painted as the most entrepreneurial, but in reality, *every* generation is entrepreneurial. How so, you ask? Because, within each cohort, there is a pocket of people who have something to give beyond their job description. But Millennials feel especially at home because they've grown up packing every additional extracurricular into their days. If you can't promote a Millennial, at least give him the chance to show off his skills. Adopt something like 3M's long-successful 15 percent program wherein employees get 15 percent of their workweek to focus on non-job-related passion projects.

» **Give "extra-credit" assignments.** Assign additional responsibilities and projects that otherwise may not get done to the youngest generation. This may require some tact in the art of delegating, but turning over the reins of a project you have high expectations for to a Millennial can make her feel valued for her skills and energized to work hard. Ask her to organize an event, lead a team on a side project, or assist with your biggest project.

"We assembled a planning team to [celebrate our company's centennial anniversary] and decided to make a Millennial one of the chairs of the committee. [We] got a call from a planning committee member who thanked us. He thought his ideas would be dismissed, but [our Millennial] let him open up about his experiences and genuinely cared." —*Ann M., Manager*

WARNING

Some look at Millennials who want to move up the ranks quickly as entitled kids who need to "pay their dues." Manage these situations on a case-by-case basis. Some Millennials are perhaps unworthy of a promotion, but instead of firing or writing them off, view this as an opportunity to coach them through their ladder-climbing oversight. Others may actually have a valid argument for advancement and may prove themselves well-worthy of a quick promotion. All Millennials grew up on the upgrade cycle, which can make them hungry and enthusiastic, and there's nothing wrong with that. You just need to tap into their passion for promotion and help them see what is best for them as well as for the company.

Engaging alumni employees

Perhaps one of the most meaningful differences between the network and the top-down organization chart is one that is a bit more esoteric. The tiered pattern of the traditional org chart leaves little room for interpretation: Movement occurs (more or less) in one direction. There is a beginning and an end, a starting point and a peak. The crystallized pattern of the network lacks clarity in both, which is the secret weapon to defeating the war on losing talent and knowledge. Enter the alumni program, or, for the more comic-book-inclined, the Batman effect. This is a fairly new concept in the working world. Almost more than Millennials, Baby Boomers can be credited for the birth of work alumni programs.

Alumni programs in the beginning

Boomers are retiring differently than generations past and are often staying on as consultants for the companies they've devoted much of their working lives to. They are, in a sense, alumni. Creative HR departments have designed formal programs to retain their knowledgeable alumni so that when a problem arises, they can put out the bat signal for the Dark Knights (alumni) to save them from work troubles, confusion, and stress.

Alumni programs in the present

The same concept that's being used for Boomers can be refurbished for Millennials. Instead of shaking your head in frustration when a Millennial leaves after three years, smile and recite to yourself, "If you can't beat 'em, join 'em." Millennials may leave after three to five years, but that doesn't mean they can't still be of value to you and vice versa. If you accept them into your alumni network, they'll be on your periphery for rehire, you'll have the luxury of knowing their work background and skill sets, and you may even get access to their professional networks. Millennials, in turn, will be reassured knowing they can get back on your hiring radar without going through the motions. Everyone wins. Happy Millennials will be your greatest asset, whether they choose to leave your company or stay with it.

Dealing with Special Circumstances

It's understandable if you are toying with the idea of reassessing your organizational structure but feel hesitant. Frankly, it would be odd to have a mind free of doubt, especially if you work remotely or in an office so traditional that it has an uncanny way of transporting people back to 1960, or if your structure is so devoid of actual structure that an outsider can make no sense of it. You may be thinking, "Wow, yeah, shifting the organizational structure is a mighty brilliant concept, but. . . ."

Well, we unfortunately can't address all the "yeah, buts," but we can give you a trio of tactics to send the "yeah, buts" that tiptoe their way into your thoughts moonwalking right out the way they came:

>> Don't panic. Just because you don't have the perfect situation to adopt doesn't mean that you shouldn't try at all. Changing the organizational structure or process isn't supposed to be easy, but the fact that you're thinking about it is a good start.

>> Keep an open dialogue with your Millennial hires. Acknowledge any unusual or sticky situations that you're in and encourage them to bring their ideas to the table; they may have a perspective that no one else has. This may be one of the greatest gifts of the next-generation hires — and new hires of all generations.

>> To borrow the phrase from Sir Francis Bacon, knowledge is power. Research what others have done in your situation: What are your competitors doing? How have organizations like yours conquered these challenges? Why have any of them fallen short? What (or who) makes your situation different? Thorough planning and research will help your organizational world go 'round.

Put these tactics to use when considering the environment you work in and how to best form your organization model.

Managing Millennials remotely

Your situation:

You are one of those 21st-century workers who manages some, if not all, of your employee base remotely. You may also be managing digital nomads, unattached but eager to use the wonders of technology. While all generations can create, focus, and get results untethered to a certain geographical location, the youngest generation may face some challenges. Sure, these Millennials can build relationships via tech and electronically submit their work, but maybe you struggle as a manager because you lack opportunities to connect, scheduling informal check-ins is awkward, and soliciting input from them at the water cooler is truly physically impossible.

The challenges:

>> Millennials are wont to write an email rather than pick up the phone.

>> Few, if any, opportunities exist for impromptu run-ins, which can be critical to collaboration and innovation.

>> Authentic relationship-building can be a challenge.

>> There's a potential lack of trust. Can you really believe that someone is working his hours if you don't see him doing the work?

The strategies:

>> **Accept the realities.** Get comfortable with the reality that Millennials are more phone shy than other generations. Though some buck this trend, know that there are other creative ways to seek input and build relationships.

>> **Make a big effort for connection.** Budget time and dollars for team gatherings, whether virtually or in person. A Skype meeting once a week can get the energy and enthusiasm that you need from Millennials. Additionally, find a way to budget an annual event (most expenses paid) that brings everyone together for work and fun. Many startup cultures successfully build loyalty, trust, and one-on-one relationships by virtue of these kinds of events.

>> **Clarify how you see trust.** Set timing expectations. It's easy for a remote worker to adopt a highly flexible schedule if she isn't needed at the home desk/coffee shop every hour of the day. As a manager, be very clear about when and how you expect your employees to be available and prove that they're doing the work.

Working in an extremely traditional environment

Your situation:

You are leading the next generation in a law firm, a government agency, a financial institution, a medical office, or even a retail store, where your organizational structure may be quite rigid, sometimes for good reason. Adapting to a transparent network model is likely out of the question and almost laughable. Before you get a side stitch, know that although this may be your reality, you still need to find creative ways to adapt if you hope to attract and keep your next-generation hires.

The challenges:

>> Strict, controlled flow of information that can feel bureaucratic if you're not careful

>> Necessity for polished, professional attire

>> Disengagement as a result of authoritarian leadership styles

The strategies:

>> **Focus on small things.** Set up your own infrastructure for informal feedback. As a manager, invite ideas in one-on-one meetings with your reports. Make it

clear that you want to hear your Millennials' ideas, even though it's likely that many of those won't be implemented — for now at least. Champion their ideas with higher-ups.

>> **Take time to explain the why.** This is one of those cases where over-communication wins the day. To you, it may be obvious why the Millennial can't knock on the CEO's door, wear flip-flops to the office, or present a revolutionary idea to the leadership team. For the next generation, the reasons may be less clear, but they'll heed your words if you explain the reasoning behind them.

>> **Know when to let go.** Some people are drawn to rigid and structured environments, but they could be either few and far between or unsure if there is an open position that fits their skills. While you may have the drive to help Millennial hires mold to your environment, acknowledge when the molding causes you more energy than it's worth. Whether it's recognizing when to say goodbye to an outdated process or someone who's not a good fit, just embody Elsa's famous line and "Let it go."

Working in an extremely nontraditional environment

Your situation:

For you, it's difficult to find any traditional organizational structure in your company because you've adopted a highly networked model. You likely either work for — or patterned your work environment after — an ad agency, a newsroom, or the seedling of a tech startup. Working around the clock is possible because hours are crazy and unstructured, there is no obvious layer of management or leadership, and your company culture is either still in the process of being determined or so out there that it can be hard for people to wrap their heads around it. Chances are you work in this environment and love it . . . or you're struggling to find a way to focus in the perceived chaos.

The challenges:

>> No obvious route for career progression

>> Lack of clarity around "normal" work processes like pay raises, reviews, and job changes

>> Confusion around who is in charge and who is accountable for information and direction

>> Too much exchange of ideas (enter the overshare)

The strategies:

>> **Make sure Millennials know who to turn to.** One of the biggest pros of the hierarchy is that you know who to ask for what you need. When there are no silos and you're truly cross-functional, it can feel like trying to find a path in a deep fog (not in a sketchy, horror-film way) to those seeking assistance, information, or guidance. Make yourself accessible to help people find the path by either announcing your open-door policy or writing a thorough flow-chart of information sourcing.

>> **Make it visual.** As organizations reinvent what the standard org chart looks like, take the time to draw your own version of the org chart. Many organizations that have altered their structure have depicted their hierarchy in alternate but familiar patterns like a circle, matrix, or Charlotte-esque spider web. Whatever shape or blueprint yours takes, draw it out so that not only Millennials but all generations have an idea of how things work.

>> **Take accountability.** The next generation may be drawn to a networked environment where every person has the same amount of power, but they're ultimately looking for someone to take charge and, if necessary, take the blame. The more you take on — both good and bad — the more likable and respected you'll be as a leader or manager.

Chapter **7**

Encouraging and Facilitating Collaboration — Go Team!

One thing that's hard to dispute about the Millennial generation is that they're a collaborative bunch. Of course, individual preferences can dictate the level of collaboration they enjoy, but as a whole, Millennials take workplace collaboration to a whole new level. They gravitate to whiteboards like moths to a flame. If a new idea is on the table, their first inclination is to flesh it out as a group, right then and there. For them, working together trumps working alone — teamwork makes the dream work.

As a manager, you may be thinking, "Okay, a naturally collaborative group is the stuff that managerial dreams are made of, but I also need my employees to be capable of independent work." And you may be wondering whether Millennials' desire to work with each other extends to working with other generations too.

Over the course of this chapter, you'll discover how to wield the Millennial penchant for collaboration as the mighty tool that it is. We walk you through one of the biggest generational workplace clash points — the independent Gen Xers' work flow bumping up against the highly collaborative Millennials' — and give you tools for alleviating tension and encouraging comfortable collaboration. This chapter explores onboarding and training techniques that appeal to this Millennial collaborative tendency and reviews best practices for building a collaborative mentorship model. Lastly, we dive into what it means to have a truly open and collaborative work infrastructure, from the physical space to the virtual tools you use to making remote employees feel they are truly a part of the team (as a heads-up, "collaborative space" isn't synonymous with open square footage occupied by beanbag chairs and ping-pong tables).

Shifting Your Perspective on Collaboration

WARNING

First things first: We know, we know. Millennials and collaboration aren't like Prometheus gifting fire to the human race. Millennials didn't invent collaboration and bring it to the working world as their unique contribution to workplace functionality. Every generation wants to collaborate and sees the immense value in it, but there are two key things to remember. First, each generation has a different perception of what collaborative work looks like. Second, that perception is influenced by how that generation grew up, how they were taught to work together in school, and what was drilled into them during their first few years in the working world.

Boomers: Come together, right now

The Baby Boomer experience and resulting perception on collaboration is defined by a couple significant conditions from their past. The first? The many human rights movements of the '60s. Through these movements, the earlier Boomers saw the great power their generation could effect as a group. They learned the power of the collective and brought that with them into the workplace. They believe that if everyone collectively moves toward a shared mission, they'll accomplish great things. On the other hand, later Boomers grew up in a time when the Baby Boom effectively overwhelmed the country's infrastructure. They saw scarcity in the classrooms (desks, books, teachers), scarcity of jobs, and scarcity of opportunity. Their takeaway from this condition of fighting for resources is that to succeed, you need to have a competitive edge. Collaboration is well and good for these late Boomers, but in the back of their minds, whether working alone or in groups, they know they need to stand out from the crowd.

The resulting Boomer perception of collaboration is that teamwork coupled with independent work is best, but individual recognition is most motivating. Collaboration should be structured.

Gen Xers: Stop, collaborate, and listen

When Xers were growing up, the world looked very different. It was during their formative years that the divorce rate tripled and more women entered the workforce. Consequently, the term "latchkey kid" came to describe children who let themselves into their homes after school, zapped a Hot Pocket for dinner, devoured the latest music videos on MTV, and took care of themselves while their parents wrapped up the workday. This generation learned, from early on, how to take care of themselves. TV was their favorite babysitter, and even their video games — Pac-Man, Tetris, Frogger — reinforced the idea that it was just fine to do things solo. To be clear, this does not mean that Gen Xers are a bunch of recluses who don't like interacting with other human beings. They can collaborate when needed, but they're a generation that really subscribes to the idea that if you want something done right, you'd better do it yourself. And when they do collaborate, they want to do it in a hyper-efficient way.

The Gen X perception of collaboration is individual work first, teamwork only if necessary and truly beneficial.

> "I find [Millennials] very collaborative, and I think this can lead to other generations getting frustrated that things don't move fast enough. Because everyone needs to be heard when it comes to making a decision." —*Ann M., Manager*

Millennials: We belong together

Millennials, who grew up during the self-esteem movement, were bombarded with messages like "two heads are better than one," "there is no 'I' in team," and "you're better together than you are alone." Group projects were the norm and a frequent feature of their education. At home their parents encouraged a more democratic and collaborative family structure. Parents frequently solicited opinions and advice from their kids on all sorts of decisions, from small matters (like "What movie should we see this weekend?") to big ones ("What car should we buy?"). On top of that, technology created yet another way for Millennials to collaborate, whether that meant working together on homework over AIM or — especially for the next generation — FaceTiming to practice a group presentation. With the ultimate collaboration tool in their pockets, their phones, Millennials expect to be able to connect and collaborate whenever and wherever.

Millennials' perception of collaboration is team first, solo work later. To them, group wins feel just as good as, if not better than, individual wins. Collaboration should be informal.

> "It's more conducive to generate ideas and bounce them off of each other. It's more of a feeling of equality and everyone's ideas matter and can be put into practice." —*Alexa, S., Millennial*

Reconciling Differences: Independent Xers versus Collaborative Millennials

When you say "let's collaborate" and every generation comes to the table with a different idea of what that means, it's easy to see how things can get confusing — and frustrating — fast. Each generational combo can yield its own specific frustration. Boomers' proclivity for more meetings can bother Xers' need for fewer. While Millennials and Boomers have their own unique challenges around the formality factor of collaborative work, when it comes to working together (or alone) one clash comes up as almost iconic in its intensity: Xers versus Millennials, with the former strongly favoring solo work and the latter showing a stalwart preference for collaboration.

This Xer-versus-Millennial dynamic, and the reason it causes so much frustration, can be boiled down to one fine point: Millennials lead with their collaborative foot, and Gen Xers lead with their independent foot. Someone is bound to get stepped on. Add to that the managerial dynamic, often that of the Xer managing the Millennial, and you've got quite a puzzle on your hands.

REMEMBER

Both sides have good intentions. You've heard the concept of the golden rule, "Treat others the way you want to be treated" — likely as early as pre-K, when teachers were trying to stop you from swiping your fellow student's snack pack. While this saying imparts great wisdom in principle, especially for a group of mischievous toddlers, in the workplace the value of that golden rule crumbles when you're trying to manage or work with others. Xers assume that Millennials want to be managed the way that they, the Xers, like being managed. Millennials assume Xers want to collaborate the way they, the Millennials, like to collaborate. Good intentions, bad results. So as you attempt to take off your own generational lens and put on that of another, check out the following sections to view collaboration from both an Xer and Millennial standpoint.

Looking through Gen Xers' eyes

Independent Xers are fully of the mindset that if you want something to be done right, you need to be the one who does it. They're the kind of employees who, when given a project, say "Tell me what you want, when you want it, and how you want it. I'll take it back with me, work on it alone for a while, and bring it back to you later." In a nutshell, "Back off — I got this."

To Gen Xers, micromanaging is borderline insulting, because it suggests they're incapable of carrying out a project to completion independently. They prefer to create their own structure, because at the end of the day, they are the ones who understand their work flow best.

In Xers' minds, solo work is by far the most efficient way to complete a project, and check-ins along the way, while sometimes needed, are not integral to getting their work done on time and getting it done well. Teamwork and collaboration have their uses, but like a fine seasoning, they should be used sparingly.

Seeing Millennials' viewpoint

On the other hand, for Millennials, collaborative work is the quickest way to develop the best and most innovative work. Working with their peers and managers is a way to pull winning ideas from the collective. For them, it's almost presumptuous to believe that their own individual ideas are the best ones.

Millennials tackle projects with the belief that working collectively is a quick way to reveal inefficiencies and weaknesses — more eyes on a certain project means more varied perspectives and more ways of testing as you're creating. Why would you wait until something is fully baked to present it to others? Odds are good that you'll have missed something, and it seems like such a huge waste of time to backtrack and fix the problem after the fact. That's why they gravitate toward collaborative work, with many eyes on any given project, lots of clear structure, and multiple opportunities for feedback along the way. These constant check-ins during a project are one of the most obvious showcases of Millennials' collaborative nature.

> "The Millennials on my team are like, 'Hey I included this person because they have a great perspective.' They aren't territorial; they think that doing this will net the best results." —*Greta H., Millennial and Manager*

Finding the right ways to manage collaboration

Here are some tips for managing the Millennial collaborative spirit:

» **Don't get frustrated.** This may seem like a silly tip, but we've talked to many an Xer manager who can hardly mask the annoyance in his voice when talking about a super-collaborative Millennial employee. "Are they even capable of thinking for themselves?!" The answer is, of course, yes. They may just need a little help along the way — at least at first. Don't lead with frustration. Start by understanding the Millennial's perspective and go from there.

» **Explain the why.** Often the best strategy to encourage a Millennial to do anything is to explain the why. There will be moments when independent work is clearly the best way to approach a task. When that's the case, take a few extra minutes to explain that's the case.

» **Encourage independent work, even if it's not great at first.** Understand that odds are good that working independently is not a comfortable thought for your Millennial employees. They will fumble during their first try, fear failure that can lead to losing their reputation or job, and look to you as a guide. Help them through the process, gently pointing out where they can improve while simultaneously encouraging their wins.

» **Offer yourself as a resource.** What? Doesn't this negate the whole "work independently" thing? It's true that offering yourself as a resource makes you and your Millennial a mini team of two. But, especially during the first few projects, Millennials are going to feel like they're on an island. Let them know you're available as a resource and for support, within reason, as they work through their first few solo projects.

» **Preemptively schedule check-ins.** Many Millennials are intuitive enough to know when they're pestering instead of questioning. If you are one who's prone to a "less is more" mentality when it comes to the project touch-base and smile to mask clenched teeth when a Millennial knocks on your door, articulate your needs early and let them know the most appropriate time to check in. Take it upon yourself to create the check-in schedule. It will save you and that Millennial from playing the "I wonder if they're annoyed with me yet" game.

» **Decide where and when collaboration would be most useful.** All independent work makes a Millennial a dull boy (or girl). Sometimes teamwork is a good approach to a project or assignment. Find those opportunities to vary the work your Millennial reports are involved in. Remember that if all of your Millennials' work is independent, they'll find it draining and demotivating.

OLD MILLENNIALS AREN'T LIKE THE OTHER YOUNGLINGS

Chances are high that if you ask a Millennial to describe herself, she won't use the word "collaborative." In the eyes of many, the meaning of the word has become synonymous with "too dependent on group-think to function." While this entire chapter digs into the collaborative mindset of Millennials, we've found in our research that some specific nuances exist when comparing Old Millennials to the next generation of Young Millennials and Generation Edgers. In brief, here's what you need to know:

- **Old Millennials are more collaborative.** On the scale of who's collaborative, this segment is the most group-oriented of the generational cohort. In a BridgeWorks survey conducted in 2016, they were also the most likely to describe themselves as collaborative. They will be more likely to have the open brainstorm sessions.

- **Young Millennials are less collaborative.** This group knows the power of collaboration and seeks it out, but not as often as Old Millennials. Rather than desiring the opportunity to chat as a group, they want to sit together in a room with their peers, working silently.

- **Generation Edgers are also less collaborative.** Many of this generation have Gen X parents, and they've adopted their independent nature. They're more likely to see collaboration as a waste of time if it brings the focus too far from the goal. Their priority is to get the job done with as few check-ins as needed. Though this is a great shift in working style, there are concerns that they may not check in as often as needed as new hires. Keep your manager eyes peeled for this scenario and adjust as needed.

Understanding what Millennials really want when they ask to collaborate

When you think about Millennials and their desire to collaborate, what comes to mind? There are definitely those who paint quite the picture in their head. Xers may think that Millennials just want to sit around a campfire and hold hands, singing in unison and swaying back and forth. Others envision a room of Millennials sipping on IPAs and shouting out ideas during a brainstorm, with those thoughts all written in colorful dry-erase pens on a massive whiteboard. Yes, Millennials are a hyper-collaborative generation, but that has been a part of their cultural upbringing.

Once you deconstruct the pieces of the collaborative workplace pie, you'll find that, ultimately, all Millennials want is to work together on a project to reach a goal. Working collaboratively is not limited to having a brainstorm session with a huge team of their peers. Collaboration can be seen when they get feedback from a manager or a peer. It's a natural part of their mentor-mentee relationships. It occurs in-person and virtually.

Instead of writing them off as a needy, pack-minded bunch, think about what Millennials are really asking for when they ask to collaborate:

>> **Millennials want the best idea to come to the fore — even if it's not their own.** As much as this generation gets the title of "narcissist" slapped on their persona, they can be incredibly humble when it comes to the workplace. That love of the group brainstorm? It's because they know that the collective will almost always produce a better idea than the individual. They can bounce thoughts off one another, using one thought as a jumping-off point for another. Millennials truly want the best idea to win out, even if it's not one that they dreamed up.

>> **Millennials want constant feedback to know they're on the right track.** The whole "Millennials love feedback" thing is not because they're needy, but because they want to know that they're on the right path. It's a "Millennials love efficiency" thing. If you give them feedback, or if they solicit feedback from their coworkers or their team, they can then course-correct before it becomes a bigger problem.

>> **Millennials don't want a babysitter; they want a coach.** When they look for guidance and collaboration from their managers and leaders, they want a relationship that's more coach and less babysitter. A babysitter hovers and watches your every move, may talk down to you, and knows he is in charge. A coach, instead, grooms you. He doesn't scold you when you make a mistake but rather builds a path to refine your skills. It's about bettering your Millennial employees rather than punishing them or hawking over them.

>> **Millennials don't need to collaborate with you, but they want to collaborate with someone.** The onus doesn't always lie with you to be the one to work with them. You're busy; they get that. The pressure on you to be the collaborator can be easily alleviated by giving them a chance to collaborate with one other. Team up people who complement each other. Assign work in team-based projects when possible. Or simply assign Millennials a buddy they can check-in with if they need to run something by someone.

Helping Millennials do independent work

Millennials don't need help when it comes to collaboration. That piece they've got down pat. The struggle we find many managers wringing their hands over is getting their Millennial employees to do more independent work.

REMEMBER

It's not that Millennials are incapable of solo work, or even that they don't enjoy it. They're just used to a collaborative work style. The key is to support them in their independent endeavors, not get frustrated at their attempts to collaborate.

When encouraging Millennial independent work, be incredibly explicit about the first independent project you assign them. No detail is too small. A foolproof way to help Millennials as they embark on independent projects is to schedule a kickoff meeting with them to explain the assignment. Lay it all out. Assure them that you'll be there along the way to help them with any snags they may encounter.

Before those meetings, refer to this checklist. If you want Millennials to do their best independent work, you should be able to confidently say you have done each of the following bolded statements. A good way to test if you have, in fact, done all you need to do, you should have provided clear direction on each question following those statements as well before sending them on their way:

>> **I set crystal-clear expectations.**

- What is the desired outcome of the project?

- What should the final deliverable look like in terms of length, form, tone, font, style, production, and so forth?

>> **I provided a road map of the project.**

- What is the deadline?

- What milestones need to be checked off in the process?

- If the schedule gets derailed, how should it be readjusted?

>> **I described the frequency of check-ins and what a typical check-in meeting might look like.**

- Are you meeting once a week? Twice a month? Every other hour?

- How long do your check-ins last?

- Who puts them in the calendar and schedules follow-ups?

- Do you want the employee to prepare questions ahead of time?

- Did you include a directory of all the resources that may be needed?

- Are there online tools the employee can use to answer questions?

- What can you provide the employee with in advance to help with the project?

- Who is held accountable for note-taking, and how will those notes be captured?

>> **I told the employee who he can collaborate with besides me.**

- Is there another teammate the employee can turn to for support?

- Who in the workplace is best to turn to for what kinds of questions?

- Does the employee feel comfortable taking charge independently?

- Does he have a good idea of when to seek someone else's opinion instead of relying on his own?

The skeptical reader may be thinking this checklist seems like massive overkill and way too much work. We get that. Just keep in mind that you won't be doing this every single time. You're getting the Millennial primed to succeed at independent projects and laying the groundwork for successful solo work in the future. Though it may represent a heavy time investment upfront, you'll see major payoffs later on. And eventually, the Millennial may even run these project kickoff meetings with other Millennials for you.

Onboarding Millennials

When new employees join your ranks, getting them up to speed and ready for the task is a huge part of their manager's job. This process, known as *onboarding,* isn't a one-day or even a one-week task. Often, it can take several months before a new hire is fully onboarded, and collaboration can be key to a manager's success. Knowing that collaboration is a core part of the Millennial personality, you'd be wise to find ways to incorporate more team-based activities into your onboarding and training. Not only will Millennials like it more but it will also spread the responsibility around so it doesn't all land on you. First impressions go a long way, but you don't need to roll out the red carpet and crown them next generation all-stars to make them happy. Stick to these seven strategies of onboarding, and you'll appeal to the next generation's collaborative nature:

>> **Connect the dots to the bigger picture.** Take time during their first week to show Millennials how even when it seems like they're doing independent (and sometimes even menial) work, their efforts weave into the company's goals and benefit the team at large.

>> **Involve people from all levels and layers**. The more, the merrier. Though in many cases it's impossible to involve everyone in your company in the onboarding process, the more you involve (within reason), the better. Don't just introduce new hires to their managers, but also to colleagues from different departments, to the custodian, to accounting. They want to meet their team.

» **Introduce them to the higher-ups/leadership.** Introductions and, even better, conversations with leadership are more than what they seem. They are a way to show new hires that they matter, they have access to leadership, and that collaboration of some kind is possible with people at all levels.

» **Connect them to their peers.** Where is their team? Where are the people they'll be working with from day to day? With whom will they be able to collaborate? Show them. Make sure you introduce Millennials to the peers and potential collaborators they'll be working with on a regular basis.

» **Do something fun.** Millennials are embracing the idea of a #workfamily, integrating work with home, and bringing their authentic selves to the workplace. Do something outside of the ordinary lunch with colleagues on the first week. Do something fun that can spark friendships and bonds with their colleagues and provide a foundation of trust and understanding, which serves as a springboard for collaborative work. Activities can range from a friendly competition of office Olympics to happy hour at the local haunt to a scavenger hunt around the city.

AN ONBOARDING ADVENTURE: A CASE STUDY

While there are numerous creative ways to onboard Millennials in a fun way, one of the best examples we heard about included a scavenger hunt around the city, complete with cupcakes, selfies, conversations with leadership, and the element of surprise.

The scenario: A group of 20 next-generation hires all began at the same time. They received their onboarding agenda and thought they were heading to a compliance presentation. Yawn. (No offense if you're fond of compliance.)

The surprise: They sat down to listen to compliance, mentally trying to remember the lyrics to the new Rihanna song they just heard on the radio while maintaining composure in what was meant to be a very serious presentation. After the first ubiquitous company slide came a colorful one proclaiming, "Scavenger Hunt!".

The scavenging: Millennials were put into teams with their peers and given their first clue. Solving riddle after riddle, they were sent around the city to their managers' favorite cupcake shop, the local hotel where they had to take a selfie with the doorman, and a trendy café where senior leadership sipped lattes and awaited their questions. The first team who made it back won a group prize. All were treated to a nice evening meal.

The reaction: Not to blow it out of proportion, but one Millennial said, "This is why I chose to work here and why I'll stay. I love that there's such a focus on company bonding and fun, even in the onboarding process, here."

>> **Find out about their individual goals.** They want to know that, as their manager, you're not just treating them as employee #329, but as Rebecca. Get to know Rebecca: her goals, what she's interested in, what her passions are outside of work. Invest in her as a person and show that you're interested in working with her to build her career and help her become an important and contributing member of the company.

>> **Set expectations about feedback.** Millennials want feedback from you — probably more often than you're used to or even comfortable with. Be clear about expectations of feedback. Ask them what their ideal would be and build a structure around what works for the two of you.

Training Millennials

How do you train a generation that wants to do almost everything as a group? Obviously all-group all-the-time isn't feasible. In many cases, employees are not hired together like a graduating team of first-years, but individually. Therefore, we introduce seven strategies of training that appeal to that desire to collaborate with those around them and render your training more effective:

>> **Mix the formal with the informal.** Classroom-style training and/or clicking through e-Learning program after program isn't going to do the trick. Mix this type of training with more informal styles — say, a lunch and learn — with other employees in the same role or the role above theirs, who can fill them in on the organization's unwritten rules. Bonus: Cater in unique food from a local favorite restaurant.

>> **Keep training interactive and experiential.** Ditch the traditional training manual. Millennials will no doubt assign it the TL;DR (too long; didn't read) acronym. Build real-time, live practice training whenever possible. Contrary to popular belief, Millennials — and especially the next generation — actually favor in-person training. They live most of their lives in a virtual world and savor the opportunities to step outside of it where everyone can learn at a similar place and experience the edutainment together.

>> **Use team-based learning when possible.** Some organizations put groups of hires through Training 101 courses, where they "graduate" together as a team or present at milestones after a job rotation. This is a great way to build connections among new hires. Again, this won't always be possible — but when you can use team-based programs, you start building those invisible bonds that become natural venues for the Millennial collaboration that is so sought after.

>> **Keep *tweet-sized* top of mind.** Don't overload your new Millennial hire with all the information he could ever need on that first day or week. Space it out. Remember, Millennials are a generation used to consuming bits of information. When you make it bite-sized, they'll share the best of the information with their peers. Great training deserves to be discussed, even if it's in a list of "the ten things I learned in my training."

>> **Teach the basics.** Don't assume that the new hire will know all the professional ins and outs on day 1 — or day 500. Topics like formality of dress, how to write an email, and when it's okay to reach out to leadership (and when it's definitely not) should all be covered in your training. The written and unwritten rules change over time, and you have the opportunity to create a safe zone of honest conversation in trainings. Maybe something will come up that they can even work through together! (Subdue the "Kumbaya" groan if you feel it coming on.)

>> **Assign them a training buddy.** You're not going to want to be the one answering all the questions that will undoubtedly bubble up to the surface as they learn the details of their job. Give them a buddy to lean on who can help them along the way or serve as an extra support as they both navigate your training program together.

>> **Give them training options.** Most learning and development departments have a library of training they roll out to their workforces. This element of customization is especially appealing to the generation that masterfully filters through information. Much like choosing courses in college, Millennials will turn to each other to see who is going to what and when — get ready to see increased attendance and chatter if there's a fun list of trainings to choose from and attend.

REMEMBER

Effective training is about more than just teaching skills. It's teaching your employees the tools they need to succeed in your organization. Some of those are very concrete and tactical, like understanding who to call for purchase orders or how to use the printer. Others are more intangible and strategic, like building lines of communication among employees who want so badly to connect and collaborate with one another.

Mentoring Millennials and Vice Versa

It's no coincidence that there's been a renewed interest in mentorship programs right as Millennials have become a major presence in the working world. Why is that the case? Firstly, technology has changed the game, in more ways than one. It used to be that mentoring wasn't a collaborative sport, or at least not nearly as much as it is today. Your mentor was a wise sage: think Obi-Wan to Skywalker.

The mentee soaked up all the information from the wise mentor. Nowadays, young employees, many with less than a decade of work experience, are bringing digital expertise that make them valuable mentors to more senior employees (enter the era of reverse-mentorship). Secondly, Millennials are pretty savvy about where they could use some extra help. They're used to collaborating with people in positions of authority and know this access is the best (and maybe only) way to get the 411 on institutional knowledge and other must-know info that you just can't Google.

Millennials are clamoring for mentorship programs, and leaders are taking note. After all, these programs are a win-win. Not only do Millennials get more opportunities to make valuable contributions to the company, but they get access to someone who'll invest in their future and help them level-up their skills. This allows Millennials to have their voices heard, grow their range of proficiencies, and collaborate with high-level employees, all of which are key to Millennial retention. Mentorship programs touch so much more than Millennial collaboration. They have become essential to keeping attrition rate low and Millennials engaged.

Checking out the Millennial mentor and mentee roles

Millennials and the generation after them are entering the workplace with a wealth of knowledge about how to use technology and the Internet. Because they've grown up with this tech, they have a level of comfort exploring new systems and tech tools that is unparalleled, earning them the title of "digital natives." Though their love of technology can also lead to Millennial scorn, this skill isn't something to be scoffed at. They're frequently looked to for advice and sometimes even IT help from the older generations. Millennials' comfort and knowledge around technology is a real value add and something they bring to any mentor-mentee relationship. That one-way has quickly widened into a two-way street. Beyond technology, they may have innovative perspectives on processes or systems that could change. They may be eager to apply the latest technique they learned in school to their current role. At the right times, these perspectives can be powerful.

On the other hand, Millennials often get a bad wrap as know-it-alls who are so used to Googling everything that they feel they don't need to rely on anyone's wisdom or expertise, because the answer to any question lies at their fingertips. The good news? This is absolutely false. Millennials are only too aware of the limitations of their good friends Google and the Internet. The practical and real-world experience of other generations is a wealth of knowledge that they are incredibly eager to tap into. Millennials want to be mentored; they want access to authority; they are thirsty for knowledge.

"I have a bunch of mentors, not one person for everything. It's casual — half a dozen or dozen people I go to for a variety of different things. They're so incredibly valuable, when I'm around someone like that I shut my mouth and open my ears." —*Kara F., Millennial and Manager*

Establishing effective mentorship guidelines

As you're reading this, you may be thinking to yourself, "Awesome — check! We totally have a mentorship program. It says so on our website. Done and done." Wait a second, though. It's one thing to say you have a mentoring program, but another thing entirely to *actually* have one that people use and appreciate. When consulting with organizations, we frequently find that though leadership may think a mentorship program is in place, there are so few guidelines or such slight assistance in developing those mentorship relationships that employees don't even try. They have no idea how or where to start. If you want to create a productive and celebrated mentorship program, you have it in you!

WARNING

Without easily accessible guidelines and training, your mentorship program is in all likelihood lacking. It doesn't matter what your website copy says or what you say to new employees. A handful of examples of successful mentor–mentee relationships does not a successful program make. Having some sort of structure is crucial, and for Millennials, the more prescriptive, the better. Your mentors may want more freedom to define the relationship, because they'll likely be the ones with the fuller plates, so it's not a bad idea to allow them to have some level of autonomy in setting the specifications for what that relationship looks like.

To ensure that the right people are matched up and that both are getting what they want out of the pairing, ask potential mentors and mentees to answer these questions:

>> What is your desired outcome?

>> What type of skills are you trying to improve?

>> Do you have a personality or gender preference?

>> What is the weekly or monthly time commitment you are willing to put in?

>> How often do you want to meet?

>> How often do you have access to the other? (For example, are Fridays the only good day? Do you never work in the office at the same time?)

>> What is the preferred structure of the meeting (agenda-driven and formal, free-flow and informal, themed each time, long- or short-term goals, and so on)?

>> Is there a company-prescribed model that each mentor/mentee can follow or use as a jumping-off point?

>> When will you know that the learning has been accomplished and that it's time to move on to another mentor/mentee?

Use the information gathered to be sure the right mentors are paired with the right mentees and to create guidelines that will work for everyone involved.

Be as unambiguous as possible about the time allowance and access that Millennials will have to their mentor. Think about the kind of access they've had with their parents. It was basically all the time and any time. In the workplace, this type of access is improbable if not impossible. By setting clear expectations at the top of each relationship, and then later at the top of each meeting, you avoid overloading your mentor with the eager, info-hungry, and sometimes overbearing Millennial mentee.

As nice as it would be for mentors and mentees to naturally gravitate toward you, don't hold your breath waiting for this to happen. A best practice is to inquire of every new hire whether she's interested in a mentor and then utilize a member of the HR team to actively place this new hire with the appropriate mentor.

"I think it's important to have an advocate for you in your career; someone higher up who can stand in your court, vouch for you, and pass on knowledge that they've acquired in their years in the working world. It's tough because sometimes I find networking a bit awkward. If you're going to have a mentor, it has to be with someone you click with — natural, relaxed, and someone you can trust."
—Alexa S., Millennial

Harnessing the power of reverse mentorship

When pairing your mentors with mentees, be sure to consider what each party would like to learn more about. Use that information to build successful partnerships that even Sherlock and Watson would be proud of. There is much to be gained by opening the relationship to a two-way model of learning, rather than the more authoritarian "I'll-tell-you-what's-what" style of the past:

>> **Learning-hungry older gens will add to their skills repertoire and feel quite valued in the process.** Just because an employee has been around for years and years, has a wall of career accolades, and is incredibly proficient in his role doesn't mean he has bid adieu to learning anything new. Too often, companies stop investing in these types of employees because they

incorrectly assume that they've learned everything they want to learn. Cue the disengagement. In fact, older Millennials usually are the most eager to learn new skills and will seek roles outside of the company to get the education if they aren't offered the opportunity at work.

>> **Millennials will feel empowered and less likely to seek a new environment to work in.** Millennials may be known as the generation with the shortest work tenures, but that doesn't mean they'll necessarily be that way. Many Millennials choose to stay in an organization when they know the impact they have and when their voices are being heard by their peers and leadership. When they join a symbiotic mentor-mentee relationship, they witness firsthand the impact they're having on an individual and, consequently, the organization as a whole. This could be the magic tonic to retaining Millennial employees.

Building a Collaborative Infrastructure

When thinking about building a collaborative workplace, you can consider interpersonal relationships and communication styles between managers and employees. Next are the Workplace 2.0 considerations: physical working space, tech tools that encourage collaborative work, and managing to balance collaboration with remote learning.

The changing physical office space

In response to this hyper-collaborative new generation of employees, the physical working space has shifted as well. Office cubicles have been replaced by open rooms with pods, lounge areas, and plants. Whiteboards have been painted onto large walls, affording Millennials spaces to brainstorm at will. Rooms with plush couches and mood lighting invite employees to come in, sit down, get comfortable, and innovate or meditate. In some extreme cases, tree houses have actually been designed for the office (we think that one's a bit excessive).

The light side of these developments and changes is revolutionary and positive. Millennials see closed doors and corner offices as an extra barrier they need to break down to pursue their goal of collaboration. Many prefer the access and opportunities for impromptu collaboration that open workspaces afford them.

The dark side of these developments is how unproductive and unwelcome some feel in these environments. Baby Boomers may bristle at an email announcement that they're going to lose the four walls they worked 30 years to achieve. Gen Xers could run in the other direction once they find out that they're losing the solace of a private space. All that darkness aside, many can see the benefits of open space for its encouragement of conversation and transparency.

Building your dream space

To build the best environment of flexibility for your office, take appropriate steps to make sure that the space matches trends for your workforce. When in doubt about what to do, ask your staff! They'll like the ability to contribute to a dream and feel a sense of pride when they see their ideas materialized in a new space.

Defeating the nightmares to achieve your dream

We know that there are numerous constraints to building the dream. If you confront any of the following, don't fret! There are some simple solutions:

Conundrum: What if I can't knock down walls?

If you have offices that aren't going anywhere anytime soon, leave doors open as much as possible to promote that feeling of collaboration. Open windows and shades to allow for as much natural light as possible. Don't underestimate the power of greenery — it gives the vibe of open, natural environments. Or consider turning one of those walled rooms into a meditation room or a lounge area to serve as an alternate room for working with a quality vibe. Don't worry, people who want to make that change will eagerly assign themselves to the task force to get it done well and get it done cheaply. (Hello, IKEA!)

Conundrum: If I have a collaborative work space, how do I signal that I need to work without interruption?

>> Use headphones as a sign that you're busy (headphones on means "I'm not available").

>> Adopt the stoplight method. Create red-yellow-green signs for employee desks that signify their availability. Red means "no distractions at all, please," yellow means "you can interrupt only if necessary," and green means "I'm available for any and all inquiries!"

>> Give everyone a chalkboard and chalk. Then, people can write their own modern version of an AOL "away message." Depending on their current working state, they can indicate whether they want to be bothered or not. For example, the chalkboard could read, "Acceptable interruptions today are client questions. Tomorrow, I'll accept cat video interruptions."

>> Appoint flex offices as refuge rooms. Many companies are taking to the idea of a "refuge room" where people can find an environment they need to get work done. This way, it's like a haven.

Don't alienate generations that don't want a collaborative workspace. You may have heard the horror stories about companies that completely did away with all walls and corner offices in a misguided attempt to appeal to next-generation hires. Guess what happened? Those Boomers and even Xers who worked so hard to get to the corner office . . . well, that tangible reward and acknowledgement of their hard work was all ripped away, somewhat brusquely, from them to make room for the next generation. Don't fall into that trap or you'll see a mass exodus of the older generations that have been so loyal and fought so hard to get where they are in the organization today. Find a way to meet in the middle. Offer some open collaborative spaces but leave room for closed-door offices as well. Exactly where you land on the spectrum from traditional closed-door offices to completely open-office spaces filled with beanbag chairs will depend entirely on your company culture, but the important thing is to keep all generations in mind when deciding where you stand.

"We are looking at partitions and movable work environments to create an environment conducive for the day you have." —*Ann M., Manager*

THE EXCEPTION TO THE RULE: THE CASE FOR THE ANTI-COLLABORATIVE MILLENNIAL

The unspoken elephant in the collaboration room is the debate of: "Isn't this just the difference between extroverts and introverts?" That question is a valid one, because while this entire chapter digs into the collaborative mindset of Millennials, we've found in our research some specific circumstances where collaboration nation is just not where Millennials want to live. Some exceptions to the rule include:

Extrovert versus introvert: Many introverts need their quiet space at work more than extroverts. They'll wear their headphones as part of their work uniform and sign up to use flex spaces more often than their peers.

The "engineer's focus": Engineering is not the only career that requires extreme focus, but we've found that engineers, and people who think similarly, are sometimes the most averse to an open work environment. If you have a staff that values focus and grows irritated by distractions, they're not going to thrive in an open room of desks.

The multi-generational office: Do not, we repeat, *do not,* change your environment for one generation. It will likely backfire, and then your staff won't carry the same respect they once had for their environment or their job. Millennials are sensitive to changes made for them; don't let them bear the brunt of shame for a changed environment that works for the minority.

Utilizing instant messaging as a key workplace tool

Technology offers a wealth of tools to help expand upon and improve how your employees collaborate. Email changed the game when it entered the scene, and it cut down on unnecessary meetings. A new method of collaboration was introduced — the virtual way. Millennials, perhaps infamous for their love of email (over phone anyway), are embracing another way to collaborate in the workplace — instant messaging (IM).

Say "IM" to some managers, and you might induce some eye-rolling. *Childish. Frivolous. Unnecessary. Silly. Inefficient.* These are just a few of the many words that bubble up when we ask managers to describe instant messaging within their workforce. Instead of seeing the value that instant messaging can bring to day-to-day tasks, this platform is written off as a Millennial tool for chatting or sending memes to one another in the office.

While, yes, instant-messaging tools are used for strengthening interpersonal relationships at work, the effect also extends far beyond that. Millennials use IM platforms as a way to quickly and efficiently communicate ideas. Much like Xers saw email as a desperately needed and blessed way to cut down on meetings, Millennials view IM as a desperately needed and blessed way to cut down on emails. They use it as a way to improve the work flow of the day, and, in many cases, it works.

The problem is we see managers rebelling against the idea of these IM platforms and laying judgment on Millennials who choose to use them as a main communication tool. We totally understand the frustration around this topic. Managers can barely keep from coming unhinged when they tell us the typical "Millennial-on-IM" story that goes something like this:

> "We all sit in pods in our office, and Ron was at his desk while I was sitting right across from him. He had a question about a project, and instead of just taking off his headphones and asking me directly — thus saving time — he IM'd me. It was the simplest of messages. Why, I mean *why* couldn't he just stop what he was doing and take two seconds to ask me directly? He does this all the time, and so do his peers. For the life of me . . . I just don't get it."

At face value, it does seem like Ron was being lazy (and maybe averting yet another face-to-face encounter that he's not super fond of). But if we look at this through Ron's eyes (and those of many Millennials), it's likely he was just trying to be polite and respectful of her time. He'd probably be the first to agree that he'd pinged his manager with a simple, straightforward message. The reason he didn't just get up and go talk to her in person is that he didn't want to interrupt her workflow. To him, it might have seemed presumptuous to interject with such a small query. In his mind, sending her an IM was a way for him to ask his question without demanding an immediate response (or clogging up her email inbox). It was a way to be conscientious of her time. She could finish up the task at hand, and get to his IM when she'd wrapped up her email, thought, project, or whatever it was she was working on. It was a move made out of consideration, not out of laziness or a lack of respect.

TIP

Despite the frustrations of other generations, IM can be the most efficient and effective way to have quick conversations at work. Recently, there has been much research published about how interruptions, however small, can be incredibly disruptive to the workday. Some suggest that it can take upwards of 20 minutes to regain focus. IMs are a way to skirt the issue, to ask without disrupting workflow or burying a co-worker in unnecessary emails. If you have an IM system, embrace it! Refrain from monitoring it so closely that everyone feels like they're being watched for response time and content. Millennials use IM tools to increase productivity and to communicate in a smart, thoughtful way. And yes, it is possible that Millennials will also turn to IMing as a fun outlet to communicate with their peers, and that's a really beautiful thing because they'll be building relationships that are critical to a happy workplace.

Collaborating from afar

Remote workers are becoming more commonplace as technological advances make it easy to work from home, or anywhere really. Whether they're working from home or from a coffee shop or wherever the case might be, they're still a part of your team and they still want to feel like they're a piece of the overall pie. You've probably heard the phrase "out of sight, out of mind." When your employees aren't showing up at the office day after day, this becomes a very real danger. The onus falls on the manager to implement guidelines that ensure remote Millennial employees feel as if they matter, they're being invested in, and that even though they're not in the office, their contributions are still an important point of collaboration for the team.

Think about what you do for the Millennials who are in the office. How often do you meet with them? Look at everything from the casual morning hello to the feedback you may give them after a presentation or a project. Try to mimic this behavior with your remote worker, plus an extra 20 percent to make up for what's lost in translation. Try to check in with them every morning for a quick hello. Solicit their ideas and opinions about meetings they dial in for. If at all possible, create opportunities for them to come into the office and interact with their peers and managers.

» **Revising your review strategy**

» **Managing feedback up and down the ladder**

» **Troubleshooting the most common feedback challenges**

Chapter **8**

Supercharging Your Feedback Loop . . . Gold Stars Abound!

N o matter your level of leadership, if you're not able to deliver meaningful and constructive feedback to your employees, you're simply not doing your job. Deft delivery of feedback is arguably among the top most important managerial skills to have. It's how you refine your employees, giving them the input they need to accomplish their goals and meet the organization's expectations. Without a proper feedback loop, you're at risk of company stagnation and employee disengagement. At its worst, infrequent feedback or poor delivery can lead to employees running for the exit sign. At its best, a manager who can curate feedback for employees is grooming skills, improving morale, positively affecting the bottom line, and building a pipeline of next-generation talent.

Back in the day, feedback was boiled down to a "no news is good news" mantra, and an annual review was your one chance to get development insight. Nowadays, with new generations in the workplace bringing different expectations and perceptions, that model has become woefully outdated. Now leaders, managers, and employees are required to give feedback regularly, in formal and informal environments, and in a way that caters to each employee's unique individual needs.

In this chapter, we show you how to present good and bad news to next-generation employees in a way that resonates. We also discuss how every element matters: the time, place, frequency, style, written delivery, and verbal delivery.

Giving Feedback in the Instantaneous Age

Instant gratification nation. That's a term that's been used to describe the Millennials and the generation after them. Growing up in a world where technology peeled open the world, Millennials were raised with unprecedented access to information at ever-quickening speeds. Slow dial-up Internet transformed into super-fast, fiber-optic web surfing. Anyone can download or stream a song on a whim, Amazon Prime delivers goods faster than ever before, and Google is always around to answer any and every question that pops into your head. So, how will Millennials expect to receive feedback?

While you chew on the preceding question, it should become clear that your method and style of delivering feedback to Millennials should undergo some substantial customization. The once-a-year thing just isn't going to cut it, nor will the super-formal, boss to employee "let-*me*-tell-you-what-*you*-did-wrong" approach of the past. The instantaneous age has groomed Millennials to expect the feedback they receive to have some form of these three pieces: speed, frequency, and transparency.

Speed: I can't wait a year for feedback

Technology has given the workplace many gifts, and a prominent one, perhaps above all, is speed. For Millennials who were raised on rapidly changing technology — so rapid that their emotional intelligence can barely keep up with it — quick-fire communication is a necessity. If it takes under five minutes to read through three lists of the best Bluetooth headphones, and another minute and a half to post your own review, why can't in-person reviews be just as fast? While annual feedback used to make employees thrive, the world has become too fast for that process to be as effective. Luckily, a solution lies in the midst. Some managers employ a daily three-minute one-on-one. Others deliver feedback via text or IM. Still others use what kayak.com has dubbed the five-word performance review. Whatever your method, when possible, deliver feedback as soon as you can (ASAYC). No matter what. ASAYC likely has varied specs in the fine-print for every leader, so expectations need to be set earlier rather than later.

Frequency: I want to be kept in the loop

It's not just about how quickly you deliver information, but also how often. Regular feedback, whether good or bad, lets your Millennial employees know whether they are on the right track. If yes, awesome. They can keep soldiering on without having that pesky voice in the back of their heads, questioning whether they're doing things correctly. If not, they have the opportunity to ask some questions and change their approach before investing too much time. Either way it's a win-win. With frequent micro check-ins, you have a constant pulse about where your employees are at and how they're feeling, and they get the benefit of knowing exactly where they stand and how they're doing. Exactly how often is often enough will depend on your organization and, frankly, your Millennial. But simple things like checking in every morning or sending a weekly email can go a long way.

> "I am a big proponent of frequent reviews — not [formal] reviews, but getting feedback continuously as it happens. We have a very structured, formal review process. I understand why that happens . . . but when you have more frequent contact, there should be no surprises. Getting instant feedback is optimal."
> —*Lia D., Millennial*

Transparency: I want the whole truth

Managers often have to learn the art of delivering feedback that couches, cushions, structures, and/or positions criticism. While this attention to feedback detail makes a nice written paragraph on a page, it does little to tell a Millennial that you're giving them constructive feedback they need to hear. Growing up in an instant era made them accustomed to instant feedback, and one of the gifts of instant is the lack of time to finesse your words. Adopting speedy and frequent feedback methods will naturally lend itself to a transparent dialogue that communicates trust. When you provide a mostly unfiltered piece of feedback, you're saying to a Millennial: "I'm telling it like it is because that's all that I have time for!" This transparency (as long as it isn't clear to the point of rude) delivers an authentic message that Millennials need, and want, to hear.

Avoiding potential drawbacks of the instant feedback style

Too much of a good thing is always possible. When adopting this new style of feedback, you may all of a sudden find yourself sucked into the vortex of an inescapable feedback loop with your Millennial employees that keeps you from getting anything done. Setting clear expectations about when, how often, and how long your check-ins may be is crucial to keeping your resources from being drained and your Millennials happy. Additionally, there *will* be times when pausing to let the dust settle before launching into a critique will be the smartest approach.

As you embrace the instantaneous feedback method, remember that

>> **Millennials are humans, not robots.** Speedy delivery of feedback doesn't mean blunt delivery of feedback. If they just gave a bad presentation, don't catch them on the way out the door with ideas for doing better next time. They're probably feeling the sting, and it's probably a case of "too soon." Remember to consider when instant is a good thing and when letting the clock tick for a bit is best.

>> **Time to reflect is still important, especially for younger employees.** Millennials love all things instant, and they may struggle to realize that reflection is crucial to having a productive feedback session. Encourage them to take some time, write a handful of reflections on the project/meeting/task, and then come back together for a quick debrief.

>> **Documentation may be needed.** No one likes it, but it's necessary in today's work environment. It can serve as a great record of celebration and also the necessary steps to take if you have to let someone go. Try to keep some of your check-ins informal, but make sure to take some notes afterwards so that you have documentation for your files.

TIP

Take a "celebrate, then deliberate" approach with Millennials. *Celebrate* wins in the moment (with messaging customized for the length, size, and breadth of the project or task), and then *deliberate* — meet with necessary people one-on-one and give direct feedback, negative and positive. If you don't take enough time to celebrate wins with Millennials (not just point out the shortcomings), you'll sow resentment and they'll become more and more likely to leave your organization.

REMEMBER

It's not all about the Millennial. You need to take care of yourself and your work flow too. Try to find a speed and frequency of delivering feedback that takes care of your Millennials without sacrificing your work or well-being.

Rethinking the Review Session

When Baby Boomers entered the workforce, they entered into stiff competition with millions of peers to try and get ahead. In order to better understand how they stacked up with others, Boomers collectively created the annual feedback process. At the time, this yearly review was considered revolutionary. Fast forward 20 years and you had Gen Xers growing weary of the style and infrequency of the yearly evaluation. It felt too formal, too delayed and, in a way, insincere. Xers had different objectives and priorities from their Boomer predecessors. The old model wasn't working for them, so they shook things up by asking for more regular and transparent feedback.

Enter Millennials. They're the first generation in the workforce that grew up with the Internet. It has shaped who they are and what they expect, and they're bringing those new expectations into the working world. To stay competitive, companies have to adapt and adopt a progressive feedback structure. The ones leading the pack are those whose leaders recognize that their talent development strategies need to evolve with the changing demographics of their workforce. Successful feedback and reviews are absolutely critical. Oftentimes an employee's exit can be traced back to a poor review session with his manager. If you're not rethinking your review session to appeal to Millennials' unique needs, you're going to slowly (or quickly) see your turnover numbers creep up.

Don't be afraid to examine your current review structure and ask questions. Your review policy should be a living, breathing, evolving thing. Has it been touched in the last ten years? Five years? Past year? Do your managers give both formal and informal feedback? Is there flexibility in feedback frequency, or is the rate static? Do you customize your approach based on the generation and/or the individual's preference? Are you staying abreast of what your competitors, as well as the best-of-the-best, are doing? If you answer "no" to any of these questions, read on!

WARNING

Like everything else in this book, if you make a 180-degree shift in the way things used to be done, you're going to face an unhappy flood of Xer and Boomer employees. Make sure you're giving people a few options. Maybe your Xers don't want a weekly check-in and once a month serves them just fine. Don't ever assume; take the time to ask. And always remember that change is hard, and in the workplace, if you're trying to retain *all* generations, evolution trumps revolution.

Knowing what works for Millennials

When strategizing about how to deliver feedback to Millennials, don't spend sleepless nights daunted by how much you need to change. Yes, Millennials are wired a bit differently, but at the end of the day, they're just people. To make things easier for you and more valuable for them, it's helpful to get a handle on understanding what works for them. Chances are you've got a pretty good grasp of how to communicate with Baby Boomer and Gen X employees, but start thinking (or asking!) about what works for Millennials before you sit down for a review.

Ask them to self-evaluate before they pontificate

One of the first steps to make a review session work for Millennials is to give them time to think and evaluate first. This practice is not uncommon to Millennials — they've likely been doing it from elementary school all the way through their MBA programs — but that doesn't mean they do it without prompting. Sitting down and listing all the things you've done right and wrong isn't necessarily a fun task for any generation, but it certainly is worthwhile. Prior to an informal or formal review session, ask Millennials to reflect on their performance.

"I usually ask what they think first, versus me just telling them. Ninety percent of the time they hit on things I would hit on and also give me insight into things I wouldn't think of. We talk about what we can change together. It creates friendship over an authoritative model." —*John S., Millennial manager*

Ask yourself if you know what to say and what not to say

While it may seem obvious, do your best to think before you speak. Consider phrases/words/thoughts commonly used in the workplace that should be avoided and replace them with something more savory.

Don't Say	Do Say
Three months ago . . .	Last week or a couple hours ago . . .
Why do you need so much feedback?	How much feedback do you prefer?
What could you have done differently?	What did you do well and what would you change?
Back in my day . . .	What has worked for me may or may not work for you . . .
Let's talk about your weaknesses . . .	Let's focus on your strengths . . .

Ask them

Yup. That is it. Just plain ask them how they like their feedback. In all likelihood they have lots of thoughts on the topic. This book is full of tools and techniques to help you manage and retain the Millennial generation, and hopefully you're downloading some useful and implementable strategies. But you can't forget that, though they belong to the Millennial generation, each employee is an individual. Take the time to have a conversation with them about how they prefer to receive feedback. Come to the meeting prepared with a proposed review session and format. Ask them for their thoughts, amend as necessary, and go from there. If you're feeling adventurous, ask them if they need anything different from you as a mentor.

Differentiating between formal and informal feedback

Feedback sessions lie on a moving scale of formality, where all levels are equally important, but knowing when and how to go about each one . . . well, that requires a dash of experience with a pinch of emotional intelligence. That said, Millennials show a marked preference for the informal end of that scale. They're an inherently informal generation because they grew up in an environment that allowed for constant and candid communication. Facebook, Twitter, and Instagram all allow Millennials to give feedback on people's lives with a thumbs up/heart icon/emoji or comment. An acquaintance might post a recent picture of a vacation in Spain, and the response might be "Whoa, Jordan, those bullfighters are impressive. Looks fun!" Even if they've only spoken to Jordan a handful of times, they're comfortable commenting (in a way, giving him feedback). They're so accustomed to constantly giving and delivering feedback via these informal platforms that, to a Millennial, informal is the new normal, to the point that very formal feedback can stir up anxiety and feel a bit uncomfortable.

In stark contrast, other generations grew up in an environment when the norm was being left alone to fend for yourself unless something was going terribly wrong. In the workplace, older employees wait for the formal review process and use it as a scale to track progress over time. In this format, you condense a half year or year's worth of comments into a couple-hour time block. The window for feedback is typically opened for that brief period of time before being shut again for all but the most immediate and/or pressing needs. politically correct language and documentation are standard, as well as professional attire and thorough preparation for every single review session.

There's clearly quite a difference between the formal standard that Xers and Boomers are accustomed to and the more informal check-in that Millennials hunger for. In all likelihood, all your employees — whether they're 25 or 68 — prefer a healthy mix of the two (with Millennials tipping the balance in favor of the informal). To make sure that you deliver, you must first understand what differentiates the formal from the informal.

Formal feedback looks like this:

>> The review is often scheduled months in advance.

>> Pre-work is a prerequisite.

>> The review room is organized in a specific way (for example, the manager deliberately sits across from the employee).

>> The review always takes place in person.

>> It lasts for a set period of time, typically one to two hours.

>> Criticism is carefully couched, using phrases like, "This is an area of opportunity."

>> Professionalism and polish in communication and dress are expected.

>> The review is meticulously documented.

>> Communication is (mostly) one-directional.

>> Extended periods of time lapse between sessions.

Informal feedback, on the other hand, looks more like this:

>> Feedback is delivered instantly or within a couple hours or days.

>> Little or no pre-work is required.

>> A public place or open office is often preferable to a closed-door office.

>> Virtual communication is an acceptable alternative to meeting in person.

>> Time frames are short and flexible, typically 5–15 minutes.

>> The style of communication is casual and open — direct, but not abrasive.

>> There are no expectations regarding decorum or dress.

>> Documentation is scant, aside from determining next steps.

>> Communication is two-directional.

>> Flexibility is key in finding time that works, which may often be determined on the fly.

REMEMBER

Each individual may prefer feedback that is particular to his career and lifestyle, so what works for one person won't necessarily work for another. It will take a bit more work upfront, but make sure to curate your approach based on the needs of the individual.

Determining the right frequency

It's no secret that Millennials want constant feedback. Of course they do — they've grown up in an instant world and know that the sooner they learn something needs fixing, the sooner they'll be able to fix it. The work environment, however, isn't necessarily designed to accommodate that model, at least not at the present. HR policies, overscheduling, and lack of resources can all get in the way of instant communication and evaluation. As a manager, you work with the tools at your disposal. Keep the lines of communication open with both your higher-ups and your direct reports. To ensure that you're determining the right frequency — one that works for you, your employee, and your organization — follow these three steps:

1. **Ask.**

    Get a gauge of how often the Millennials you're managing want your thoughts. You will find that it varies from person to person, and you'll save valuable time that might be lost in making assumptions.

2. **Research.**

   Seek insight from fellow leaders about what works for them. How often do they meet with their teams, and how rigid or flexible is that schedule? You can even take it a step further and track what trends and best-in-class examples are being referenced in the news and apply those concepts to your own practice.

3. **Act.**

   After asking and researching, set a plan into action. Pilot a feedback timeline for a month and then review until you find what works.

The following are signs that the frequency may be too high:

>> When you meet with your direct report, you have trouble coming up with a review topic, whether the feedback is good or bad.

>> You spend all the review session talking about your personal lives.

>> Your own work is suffering.

>> The Millennial keeps cancelling your sessions.

>> There's not enough time between your conversations to see positive changes in performance.

>> You're bored.

>> They're bored.

TIP

At most, stick with a default frequency of once a week. Younger generations will favor informal feedback in the moment, but in many cases that just may not be practical. Instead, as a base, schedule one-on-ones regularly for 15–30 minutes. Set a time and a location, and make it a habit. That way you and your reports will grow accustomed to these check-ins. It's up to both of you to assess and readjust the necessary frequency from there.

Mastering the compliment sandwich (hold the cheese)

Some time ago, in a land of corporate masterminds, a brilliant and deceptively simple idea emerged from its cocoon: the compliment sandwich. Here's how it works:

>> **The slice of bread:** A specific, positive assessment on a recent accomplishment

>> **The cheese:** A nice, vague compliment; for example, "People seem to like you"

>> **The meat or black bean patty:** All the things that really need work because, whoa, have you missed the mark

>> **The lettuce:** One more quick criticism that is minor but matters for future reference

>> **The slice of bread:** But, really, overall you're doing pretty well here

Sure, there are flaws to this method, but the intent here is spot-on. Most people will freeze up if your review opens with everything that they've done wrong. A compliment to kick things off creates a pleasant, nonconfrontational environment for the meeting, and closing with positive feedback lets the employee leave feeling motivated (rather than wondering if he'll ever be able to do anything right). Millennials want nice thick slices of bread on their sandwich — more so than other generations — because they've been fed positivity and encouragement their entire lives. This is in direct juxtaposition to Gen Xers, who are known for a "hold the bread, extra meat" mentality. They favor an honest, direct, transparent, and anti-fluff feedback model where "area of opportunity" is a cringe-worthy phrase that is better substituted with what you actually mean, "weakness." That's them, though, and that mindset doesn't always work well for Millennials.

TIP

Though Millennials want that compliment sandwich, you must tread carefully because they are allergic to inauthenticity. The worst thing that can happen is that the sandwich turns into an overcooked, inedible mess that's full of falsities. Too often, people take the compliment sandwich approach without understanding that it's really easy to read through the vague compliment cheese. If this is paired with a specific criticism of work, the next generation will naturally assume that all you're doing is trying to get to the bad stuff. So make sure your compliments are valid, or hold the cheese. You could also consider throwing out the sandwich all together and adopting one of these alternate approaches:

>> **Stop, continue, grow.** Meet with a Millennial on a regular basis and discuss two or three processes/behaviors to stop doing, two or three to continue, and two or three that can be improved upon. This allows for all ingredients of the sandwich but lays it out in a more transparent way — an open-faced sandwich, if you will.

>> **Cheers, perseveres, and keep clears.** Cheer the Millennial for a job well done, outline the areas she needs to keep pushing through (or persevere), and lay out the things or behaviors she should steer clear of going forward.

>> **The good, the bad, and the ugly.** Highlight the wins; point out the areas that have been, simply put, rather bad; and then pinpoint the areas that start as ugly ducklings but can turn into swans with just a bit of growth and change.

TIP

A little humor goes a long way with Millennials. If you've got some tough feedback to give, of course, give it the gravity that it requires, but if you come in with a doom-and-gloom attitude, you'll scare the wits out of them. Crack a joke or two, or share a story about how something went wrong in the past that's now a bit humorous in hindsight.

Avoiding the "participation trophy" mindset

Millennials have earned the dubious honor of being labeled the "trophy generation." Maybe you've thought to yourself, said out loud, or overheard someone else say, "I just can't deal with this 'everyone gets a trophy' thing! Why do the Millennials I manage expect praise for just doing their job?!" As is usually the case, there is more to this whole participation trophy thing than meets the eye.

How Millennials feel about the rewards for trying

To let you in on a not-so-secret secret, Millennials didn't ask for any of the trophies or certificates that they received. Most Millennials were raised by Boomer parents who gave them out because the self-esteem movement was in full storm. The feel-good rewards for effort prevalent in the 1980s through 2000s were a reaction to the earlier feel-not-so-good era of command-and-control parenting styles.

Today, Millennials are none too happy to be referred to as the trophy generation because even though they probably did get a certificate for "best character" at the senior-year award ceremony and/or a basketball ribbon that read "participant," they're not proud of it. They may even deny that the trophies and ribbons impacted them because they are only too well aware of how ridiculous they were (it's been an incessant source of scorn, teasing, and mockery since they entered the working world). Though they may deny it, these participation awards did impact Millennials . . . but that doesn't necessarily have to be a bad thing.

Give them accomplishment (not participation) recognition

Millennials don't expect a trophy after completing every assignment, but they do want recognition of their efforts and praise for a successful finish. They do understand rejection; many of them learned what that felt like when they graduated into a recession economy. They're wary of underperforming and are looking for the encouragement that was the status quo of their youth. The praise doesn't have to come in the mindset of, "You tried really hard; here's a ribbon." Acknowledge that Millennials need more encouragement, but do it authentically. To them, a "no news is good news" mentality likely won't fly.

BOOMER PARENTS VERSUS GEN X PARENTS

The participation trophy phenomenon is a direct result of how Millennials were raised. Boomers embraced the self-esteem movement and wanted their kids to feel valued and supported. As we look at younger Millennials and the generation after them, you can see the impact that different parenting styles is having on their generational personas. The majority of older Millennials were raised by Baby Boomers, whereas the majority of the tail-end Millennials and their successors are being raised by Gen Xers. Parenting styles differ based on which generation is doing the raising, as well as the time period the children are growing up in. These differences in parental mindsets have shaped clear distinctions between Old Millennials, Young Millennials, and the next generation.

The dark side of the participation award

No one ever thinks about the flipside of this participation trophy thing. When everyone gets a trophy, the winners actually end up losing. By watering down the meaning of the award, it makes the win feel that much less satisfying. Millennials want that win, and they want it to mean something. If you praise them always, even when what they're doing sucks, you're doing them and yourself a disservice.

> "Acknowledging — [whether] in an email or meeting — work that people are doing . . . is enough for me to feel acknowledged and get positive feedback in my mind." —*Michael S., Millennial*

Ditching the "but I had to figure it out on my own" mindset

You may remember a time when, upon receiving tough feedback, you took it and figured out, on your own, how to improve your performance. While that may work in an authoritarian-leaning work environment or for a very independent generation like Gen Xers, the next-generation worker has different expectations. Millennials grew up with coaches, teachers, and counselors who consistently helped them grow and change for the better, constantly offering techniques and skills to help them confront challenges. If they lost the tennis match, their parents didn't say, "Well, you lost; now go figure out what you can do to be better." Instead, they said, "Well, that's too bad. What do you think you could've done differently to win? Here's what I would suggest. We can work on your backhand over the weekend. Now let's go get some pizza."

Like it or not, as a manager, the onus is on you to help set Millennials on a course for improvement. When Millennials look at their careers, they don't see themselves as solo players but as part of a team, and you're their coach. Instead of delivering feedback with the expectation that they will figure it out on their own, ditch the "do-it-yourself" mindset and come prepared to help them figure it out.

Here are some ways to help Millennials help themselves:

>> When delivering feedback on areas of improvement, present them with a framework restricted by deadlines and to-do lists.

>> Check in on the framework regularly so that you (and your Millennial employee) can track progress over time.

>> Be clear about what you want changed, how you want it changed, and when you want it changed by.

>> Give them a list of resources other than yourself, including websites, training tools, and other employees.

>> Offer small carrots along the way that they can "unlock" as rewards for improved performance, for example, a $5 gift card to their favorite coffee shop.

>> Avoid sticks (harsh punishment). Millennials will not react favorably, and you'll end up demotivating them.

>> Whenever you deliver tough news or commentary on performance, follow it up with a proposed plan of improvement.

You may be thinking that this sounds like a lot of hand holding or is even a counterproductive (and time consuming) way to get the most out of your employees. While those thoughts are not entirely unwarranted, adopting structured, prescriptive styles of feedback delivery that can be measured over time will help you set Millennials on a fast-track to independent and excellent work. The more time you invest upfront, the more streamlined and hands-off you can be with them in the future. For now, a structured plan of improvement is one of the easier processes to adopt to prevent a Millennial asking (or singing), "Should I stay or should I go?"

"I find that [Millennials] are all about continuous improvement and excellence. Not just feedback about the past but coaching around how they can get better. People think [feedback] is past tense, but I think it's important to collaborate with them about what excellence looks like in the future." —*Ann M., Manager*

What are the best of the best doing?

Since annual reviews grew in popularity in the 1960s and 1970s, there have been standout companies and CEOs that have served as forward-thinking examples for others to model their own reviews on. Now, even those progressive companies are changing their ways. When it comes to feedback and reviews, there's no one-size-fits-all approach. As a leader, you can sift through the best-in-class examples to uncover and adopt either general overhauls or specific changes that make sense within your performance evaluation process.

General feedback considerations

Before overhauling everything about your feedback model, you may want to examine the most basics elements that, when shifted, appeal more to the Millennial demographic. While these shifts may be large (eliminating the annual review that you have 30 years of records for in an HR basement), it may be the most seamless shift you can make.

>> **The death of the annual review:** Though in many environments a case can still be made for the formal, annual feedback process, some large organizations are finding that it's too time consuming and just doesn't deliver the desired results. There are no sacred cows in the workplace of the future. Ask yourself whether your company is properly using the annual review and — more importantly — whether it's still the best use of time. There may be some micro versions that accomplish the same thing without stirring up such a big to-do.

>> **The 360 approach:** It's no longer enough for feedback to go in one direction — it needs to come from all positions in the company. Your manager is not the only person who may have constructive comments, and for Millennials, the more feedback from the more people, the better (within reason of course). Work is affected by everyone, not just one person. Many organizations have approached this more holistic, democratic approach to soliciting and receiving feedback.

Specific feedback considerations

If you're feeling creative, innovative, and bold about embracing changes to your feedback methods, then adopting versions of these examples may be best for you and your company. The companies below adopted unique feedback models to deliver specific results, and most are reaping the rewards. Maybe you'll read these and it will spark a unique idea of your own.

>> **Kayak.com's five-word performance review:** The process is simple. You meet in an informal environment like a coffee shop or restaurant. Either the manager or employee can request feedback that boils down to five words (two negative, two positive, and one of your choosing). You go over the words together and then decide what to do from there.

>> **GE's switch from "rank and yank" to "PD@GE":** When GE was under CEO Jack Welch's reign, it was famous for substantially growing in business, serving as an example for Six Sigma, and setting a precedent for the "rank and yank" or "vitality curve" model that placed employees on a bell curve. If you were in the lowest 10 percent, you were fired. Over time, that model has changed drastically into the more-current version, which reviews employees using an app that constantly grades their priorities as either "continue doing" or "consider changing."

>> **Pixar's "Plussing":** Pixar is becoming feedback famous for adopting a simple method: Any word of feedback requires constructive criticism. If you're going to deliver a criticism, it has to be followed by a "plus," an idea or suggestion that will help improve the original idea.

The reality is that the feedback and review process has to work for you and your team. Determine a plan that makes sense for your organization, and don't be afraid of testing it. When considering a new review method or technique, take these steps:

1. **Do the research.**
2. **Poll those you're leading and managing to see what works for them and what they feel is lacking.**
3. **Propose a vision for what could work and get insight from others.**
4. **Decide on a course of action and test it over a set period of time.**
5. **Reevaluate and course-correct (if necessary).**

WARNING

Many large, big-name organizations are adopting all kinds of fancy apps to make instant feedback less complicated and more painless, but it's just not that easy. One particular app allows employees (younger ones, let's be real) to send emojis throughout the day that express how they're feeling about work. A novel concept, but chances are high that if you present this new app to a room full of next-generation employees, they're going to sigh, roll their eyes, and put on a smile to please the leaders who are trying just a bit too hard to reach them. Flashy and new doesn't always mean best-in-class. Consider all angles before implementing drastic change.

Realizing that Feedback Is a Two-Way Street

The organizational structure has been flipped, spun three times, and pushed through a reinvention machine right along with the communication ladder. There is no one way to move around in an organization, move up the ladder, or get the job done. Feedback and communication are also multidirectional as the world shifts to accommodate a more networked model of work. Communication doesn't just flow from the top down; it can flow upwards, sideways, horizontally, or any which way. Instead of accepting a chain of command, Millennials push for a multi-directional model. The model is now a free-flowing structure rather than the linear start-stop of the past. Do you have feedback for your Millennial employees? Yes, of course you do. And you can be fairly certain that they have thoughts they'd like to share with you too. Rather than shutting off the possibility of a symbiotic back-and-forth relationship, open your eyes to the feedback model that Millennials are hungering for — no longer a one-way street, but a two-way highway of information.

> "I expect the unexpected because they're coming to [work] from all walks of life and have different intentions. Just always be ready. Millennials aren't afraid to give feedback." —*Nate P., Manager*

Ignoring your inner voice ("But in my day, I never gave my manager feedback!")

Back in the day, freely giving your opinion to anyone in a senior level could be quickly followed by a not-so-pleasant conversation of "this is just how things work around here" or "please pack up your things and go." Logically, it's still a bit unsettling when a younger generation challenges authority confidently and candidly, either in person or virtually. But Millennials grew up in a world that invited them to regularly question the status quo — disruption and innovative ideation were rewarded from a young age with gold stars and high grades. Social media gave them a platform to communicate with the President of the United States or the CEO of a local organization as easily as they would connect with their best friend.

Before getting too frustrated by this mindset around authority, understand that the reason Millennials want to give their manager feedback is because they want to perform to the best of their abilities. Some of that may come down to not what they do *for you* as a leader, but what you do as a leader *for them*. With the best intentions, they hope that by providing feedback to you, you can become a better manager to them, which will in turn make them a better employee and ultimately have a positive impact on the company and the bottom line. This two-way communication, though substantially divergent from practices of the past, can be a powerful gift if both sides approach it thoughtfully and respectfully.

Soliciting valuable input

Creating an environment that doesn't shut down, but rather encourages, mutually beneficial feedback and feed-forth is only the first step. Next is ensuring that the two-way communication is productive. While vague questions like "How can I be better?" or "What are three things I can do to change?" are well-intentioned, they're too broad to elicit valuable feedback. One of two things can happen: The floodgates are opened (see the next section), or unhelpful and vague comments dominate the conversation.

To ensure that you're receiving the most helpful feedback as a leader, create some structure around how you like to receive feedback. One idea is to create an input form with a clear structure. This will make the Millennials' job manageable and straightforward, and it will shield you from the flood of unwanted, unproductive, or way-too-candid feedback that you may receive otherwise. It could be as simple as asking, via email, for five specific pieces of feedback regarding your involvement with recent projects or initiatives. Or you could ask for three highlights about what went well in the past months and three lowlights about where they wish things had gone differently. If you prefer an even more structured approach, you can present employees with a feedback form after a project or a time period for annual/semi-annual reviews (see Figure 8-1).

FIGURE 8-1:
Form for employees to give their managers feedback.

Manager Feedback Form

Date:

Project or time period:

What went well/how I felt supported by my manager:

What could have been improved (both self and manager):

Next steps:

BridgeWorks. Minneapolis, MN. (October, 2016)

How to stop (or at least control) the floodgates

Asking Millennials for input is an excellent move in the right direction, but there is the risk that once you crack open that window, the feedback won't stop, lines will be crossed, or opinions will start coming out of turn. To ensure you have control over the feedback gates, take a creative and intentional approach when you solicit a Millennial's opinion. You may not be a manager who wants the constant drip–drip–drip of feedback, and that's totally fine. Communicate your expectations, and don't be afraid to be prescriptive in designating clear places and times for that feedback to be delivered. Consider the following options:

>> **Hold a Millennial open forum.** Many leaders have taken it upon themselves to create a venue for a group of Millennials to give feedback together. You could host an off-site meeting every year with employees under 40 to hear, directly from the source, whether the trends that others say about Millennials are true for your company too. This forum can also be run by an outside consultant if you feel like your staff won't open up to your own organization's senior leaders.

>> **Upgrade the anonymous tip box.** Sometimes employees have feedback that is more global and that you may have little power over. Instead of an anonymous suggestion box that may attract the ever-so-lovely "I hate your shoes" type of commentary, designate a wall in your office as the suggestion board (we're talking big white-board wall). They'll be less likely to give useless or over-critical feedback and instead will be thoughtful about what they recommend. This new process may get off to a slow start — it's public, after all — but you can lead the way and empower them by kicking it off with a few ideas of your own.

>> **Set clear boundaries.** You have no way of knowing how your employees will react before you seek their insight, so set expectations as clearly as you can about what's acceptable feedback and what is crossing a line. If you feel like a Millennial steps over the boundary, be honest about it. Every moment is a coaching moment.

>> **Ask for proof.** When you ask for feedback on your performance as a manager, the intention is not to make yourself a target for any and all comments, either hurtful or positive. If they're giving you feedback, ask them for examples to back up their statements. "You never take the time to check-in with me" is far less valuable than "in the past month, we have only had one 15-minute check-in." By asking for examples, they'll need to think and be deliberate about the kinds of comments they give you, rather than just go through a laundry list that may be half based in reality and half a reflection of perception and nothing more.

Acting More Like a Coach Than a Boss

Millennials usually don't leave a bad job or company; they leave a bad manager. In those situations, it's likely that the manager was acting too much like a stereotypical "boss" character — driving employees too hard, blaming others when things went wrong, and seeking a workhorse to do his bidding and earn company dollars year after year. Okay, this may be the worst depiction of a boss, but it can ring true to anyone who's felt like she's had one who's too tough.

In today's work world, these bosses will lose the popularity contest with all generations, especially Millennials, because this generation grew up with coaches who knew how to give tough feedback, helpful encouragement, and, yes, also a few trophies. To them, an ideal leader is constructive, acts like a role model, and rallies you to push a boulder up a hill versus a boss who criticizes how you're pushing.

Imagine the best coach you've ever had, whether it was in tennis, basketball, or on the debate team. Coaches are mentors and guides whose intent is to make you stronger and better than you were before. Assume this mindset, and you'll be a better leader to Millennials without even knowing it. They're seeking a coach at work who can behave authentically, listen like a trusted confidant, and push like Coach Taylor (a reference for you *Friday Night Lights* fans).

> "I come prepared, my talking points ready to go. I always give examples and then get ready to explain myself because they'll come back with questions. I'm not afraid to say 'That's a good question and I need to research [the answer].' I also want to hear about your life and kids and dog; it's about balance, not just being a boss."
> —Nate P., Manager

Common Feedback Troubleshooting

If you've ever struggled giving a Millennial feedback, you're not alone. It's hard. There is no one way to do it, and it doesn't always get easier with the more people you've led or managed; however, one thing is true. Whatever you're feeling, you're not alone. Others have felt your pain, your strife, and your desire to be better. A Millennial is just as much of an employee as someone from any other generation though, so there's no getting around this. Here's a brief guide on how to navigate the ins and outs of feedback with Millennials.

Delivering tough feedback

No matter the generation, level, or age, delivering tough feedback is rarely a fun process. It can lead to a defensive attitude, a reluctance to change, or even a desire to leave. But everyone deserves the opportunity to identify and improve on sore spots, and you're entitled to the opportunity to improve your team and fix problem areas. The way Xers prefer to receive difficult feedback (they most likely want you to rip off the Band-Aid as quickly as possible) doesn't necessarily work best for Millennials.

The challenge

When you deliver tough feedback to Millennials, you worry that they're worrying. You may be nervous that they're starting to think too hard about what they need to do differently. Chances are that what you thought was a helpful conversation became one of their worst work moments ever.

Possible cause

Millennials were raised in the self-esteem movement and weren't given the tools for handling criticism at a young age. While other generations learned how to let it roll off their backs or deal with it and move on, younger generations internalize the feedback, all while merging their personal lives with their professional lives.

The remedy

If they're internalizing your feedback, it typically means they care . . . a lot. They likely view you as someone whom they want to impress. Maybe they view you as their confidant and coach. It may not seem like it in the moment, but this is actually good, so here's how you can move past the discomfort:

>> Get comfortable knowing that the situation may get tense or awkward.

>> Don't waste time getting to the tough feedback.

>> Deliver your critiques in an appropriate time frame, the sooner the better.

>> Provide a structured road map to improve.

>> Follow up with next steps.

>> Be a voice of encouragement along the way.

What to do if a Millennial cries

It's most managers' and leaders' worst nightmare — what happens if a Millennial starts blubbering, you panic, and you don't have tissues to provide for them? Okay, not all Millennials cry, that's an overexaggerated depiction of what truly transpires. But it's more likely to happen with this generation, especially in their earlier years at work. You better start prepping now if you haven't already.

The challenge

Millennials can sometimes internalize evaluations and react defensively or sensitively, occasionally resulting in watery eyes, drops of tears, or a minor breakdown. This outcome can prevent a productive review session if what you intended as helpful words of change were instead heard as scathing criticism.

Possible cause

Millennials grew up in an environment that asked them to be vulnerable and open with their feelings, whereas other generations learned early on how to control their emotions and keep their poker faces intact. Additionally, Millennials may be taking feedback personally, not just professionally, and a comment about their work may be heard as a comment about them as a person.

The remedy

While it may be distracting, confusing, and even a bit frustrating, you can take these simple steps if a Millennial is crying:

>> Don't automatically get frustrated.

>> Don't draw too much attention to the tears.

>> Continue with your thought.

>> Ask if there's anything the Millennial wants to say.

>> Welcome the option to talk later.

>> Don't respond with pity or condescension.

>> Offer a small packet of tissues with printed turtles or other small, adorable creatures (just kidding).

What if Mom and Dad get involved?

Millennials have a close bond with their parents and view them as trusted allies and quite possibly even friends. Sometimes this relationship can go a bit too far if the doting parents become meddlesome in the work environment. It started when Millennials were young, and it's very different than the way their parents were raised.

Millennials are growing up and becoming more independent from their parents — especially older Millennials who have been in the workforce for well over a decade. Luckily, that means fewer calls from Mom and Dad. But when it comes to younger Millennials and even the generation after them, their folks may still be around for support — much to the chagrin of managers.

The challenge

Millennials' parents may overstep and contact a work environment to discuss a feedback session gone wrong, amongst many other things. It comes across as unprofessional, annoying, and inappropriate.

Possible cause

In many cases, your Millennial employees may not know that their parents are calling. They likely discussed the situation with their parents, asked for advice, and may be seeking a solution, but the parents took it upon themselves to help solve the problem for them. Your Millennial employee likely didn't set his parents on you like a pack of Rottweilers.

The remedy

Consider some damage control and prevention before griping about meddlesome Boomer parents.

>> Thank the parents for their interest, but let them know you need to speak directly to their Millennial child regarding anything work-related.

>> Ask the Millennial about the incident.

>> Explain to the Millennial why his parents' involvement can actually be hurtful, not helpful, to his career.

>> Confront it and move on.

>> Don't hold the incident against the Millennial or use it as a reason to think poorly about him.

>> Use the close parent-child relationship in a positive way to boost your company's employer status. Consider creating an environment that welcomes parents to the office in a "bring your parents to work" day. This can be a great marketing strategy.

I think my Millennial is about to quit . . .

If Millennials leave an organization, it can likely be traced to the last time that they received feedback. You don't want that last review session to be the ultimate reason that a Millennial decided to leave the organization.

The challenge

A Millennial receives a firm review, and rather than planning how to change her behaviors or work, she starts plotting her exit to find a workplace she feels will be more conducive to her growth and career improvement (or hurt her feelings less).

Possible cause

If Millennials receive critical feedback without a clear structure of how to improve, they'll feel deflated instead of motivated. If weaknesses are focused on more than strengths, Millennials may be wondering whether they do anything right. *What are my contributions? Why am I even here?* While other generations wouldn't have dreamed about leaving their job without finding another one, Millennials believe that it's worth it if they don't have to sacrifice more of their life in a job that makes them unhappy.

The remedy

Move quickly and swiftly if you want your Millennial to stay.

>> Schedule an informal meeting.

>> Have an honest check-in and provide the option of a follow-up check-in.

>> Give the Millennial the opportunity to give you feedback.

>> Ask whether a clear structure is in place for the Millennial's growth and improvement (if not, put one into action).

>> If things aren't going well for you or the Millennial, consider that it may be time for the Millennial to leave.

Chapter 9

Motivating Millennials — Generation "Why?"

"What gets you out of bed in the morning?" It may sound simple, but garnering this information about what motivates each person is vital to understanding how to work with and retain employees.

Put the question out there and you get a whole spectrum of responses from individual to individual, as can be expected, but there are resounding similarities across the generations: connecting with great colleagues, challenging work, feeding the dog (and themselves), paying the bills, funding a vacation, and so on. Everyone, no matter the generation, wants fruitful, meaningful work — any manager or leader would agree to that. If, however, you want to level-up your managing skills, you need to understand not only the similarities but also the important differences among what motivates each generation. By understanding these nuances, you can collect the right tools to properly light a fire under your direct reports, regardless of what generation they belong to.

The thing is, managers have been working side by side with Boomers and Xers for quite some time and have already honed their spidey sense for the best tips and strategies to bolster motivation among these two groups. Millennials, on the other hand, especially the younger Millennial hires, are a bit more of an agent unknown.

Managers are discovering that they need some extra help to better understand the complexity of a generation that is motivated so differently from generations past. This chapter sheds light on how to reward and inspire Millennials. It explores why meaning is so important to Millennials and why you should reexamine the value of the dollar and shift to creative nonmonetary rewards. We'll give you an idea of what those rewards look like and explore how #squadgoals isn't just for the Kardashian clan. Finally, you'll discover how to tap into strategies for building a strong community of friends and colleagues within your walls and retaining a generation that is notoriously slippery.

Managing for Meaning

One common complaint from managers about Millennials is, "Why is it that what motivated me isn't motivating them?" To fully understand the answer to this question, you have to travel back in time to see how the other generations were raised. By looking at the stark differences that have wired the Millennial mindset, you can see why this generation is so hungry for meaning, above almost all else, in their work.

WARNING

Millennials are always going to hunt for a job in which they are making a difference, but the way it's manifested can take a variety of forms. They can be making a positive impact on people's lives, animals' lives, or the community at large. It can be as big as contributing to the fight against climate change or as small as paying forward a cup of joe. Whatever the case may be, Millennials *need* to know: Do I make a difference in my work? Do I matter? Because if that answer is no, it's going to be nigh impossible for them to get out of bed in the morning.

Looking back across generations

Once upon a time, the Traditionalist generation raised their Baby Boomer children with one goal in mind: to achieve the American Dream. In pursuit of this goal, many Baby Boomers followed the traditional path of college, job, marriage, money, house, and family — hopefully, with a bit of fun along the way. For them, working hard was a badge of honor, and Baby Boomers put in the hours, effort, and made sacrifices to earn the respect and success they aspired to. They worked themselves to the bone, fought hard for their wins, and didn't have the time or luxury to redefine what work looked like. They competed with millions of their peers to land and keep a job, and understood the harsh reality that if they didn't get a paycheck, they wouldn't eat — and neither would their family.

Some Baby Boomers achieved the level of success they so desired, but at what cost? They missed out on watching their kids grow up and abandoned personal hobbies and interests in exchange for more hours at the office. Yet, when the Great Recession hit, many Boomers saw their company loyalty repaid with layoffs and financial ruin.

Having experienced the dark side of the American Dream, Boomers naturally wanted to raise their Millennial children with a lighter mindset. They taught their kids that the paycheck didn't matter as much as using their time and talents wisely: "If you're going to work as long and hard as I have, you better do something that matters to you." If Millennials had a nickel for every time they heard that sentence, they'd be a wealthy (and debt-free!) generation.

This messaging from their parents is one part of the equation that led to meaning-hungry Millennials. The other part is what they witnessed happening in the world around them. Millennials saw institution after institution crumble. They experienced homeland violence in the form of a deluge of school shootings and the horrific terror attacks of 9/11. They watched Al Gore's *Inconvenient Truth* as preteens, to be only further haunted by a series of inconvenient and, frankly, disturbing truths as revealed by *The Daily Show* or *VICE* news. Their Boomer parents encouraged them with sentiments like, "You can be part of the solution. You can help make our world a better place." The message struck a chord, and it has been part of the Millennial psyche ever since. For Millennials, if they aren't actively contributing and impacting the organization or the world in a positive way, they aren't doing anything at all.

Picture for a moment a 28-year-old professional named Albus. He's intelligent, driven, creative, and ambitious. He has switched jobs multiple times in his career because recruiters have been knocking down his door (or direct messaging his LinkedIn profile) to capture his brilliance for their organization. Being so sought after and successful, you'd think that young Albie would feel great about his current situation. But what you don't hear or see is his expressed dismay at happy hour with his friends — he's confused. He confides to his friends, "I'm grateful for all this opportunity. But I just don't know if what I'm doing matters . . . I'm not sure I can work much longer in a job that does so little for the world." None of his roles have connected him to the bigger picture or left him feeling like he's made any societal impact. So for now, he continues to chase the dream of using his talents in a way that leaves the world a better place than he found it.

Connecting the dots for Millennials

For every naysayer who believes Millennials aren't unique because they want to have a meaningful job, you're right. Millennials are not unique in this regard. Young Boomers were a generation of activists driven to make the world a better place, and Gen Xers wanted to disprove their apathetic label as a misnomer and positively affect peoples' lives. Here are the two critical slivers of difference:

>> Other generations didn't, and still don't, need others to affirm how they're making a difference. Millennials struggle to see their footprints if they don't see the end results and the tangible way their work contributed to it.

>> While other generations were willing to wait to ascend into positions where power, influence, and money could effect the change they wanted to see in the world, Millennials want to make a difference from day one.

To ensure that you're keeping Millennial workers engaged and motivated, help them connect the dots. Show them how their job and its associated tasks positively impact you, your company, and the community. There are countless ways to approach this. Depending on your organization, your chosen approach will depend on budget, workforce, and industry. Luckily, you have options no matter what kind of work environment you manage in. Try one of these proven methods of connecting the dots for Millennials:

>> **The physical connection:** One large organization implemented a program called "Line of Sight." Its intent was to connect each employee's work to the mission. On a large wall in the company's headquarters, you can find your role in the organization and connect, via the web of other departments, until you reach the top where you'll find the company's mission displayed prominently. You're literally a cog in the machine — but unlike the negative connotations of this idiom, without you and others like you, the machine falls apart. It's a quick and effective way to impart meaning to any role.

>> **The family connection:** When the job is hands-on and laborious — think warehouse and facility work — connecting workers to a lofty human purpose can feel like a bit of a challenge. One organization found that even if they connected the product in the warehouse to the end consumer's positive experience, the messaging wasn't resonating with their employees. It was too anonymous and ineffective. They decided, instead, to make it personal. Each employee was asked to share a picture of his loved one and then fill in the blank, "I work hard so that _____." By connecting the mission to their loved ones, employees were able to see an end goal that was worth working for.

» **The individual connection:** To capture just how purposeful everyone's job is, accounting firm KPMG launched the "Higher Purpose Initiative." They asked the employees themselves to connect the dots. The firm asked each employee to contribute to their *10,000 Stories Challenge* that demonstrated how each person found meaning in work. After accumulating an impressive 42,000 stories and realizing that the exercise was a runaway success, KPMG went one step further. They created internal posters and external advertisements showcasing what had been shared. The results wove a story of engagement and increased loyalty and pride in the organization that resulted in them jumping 17 spots on the *Fortune* 100 list of Best Places to Work For.

"Anything I can do to help with other people's tasks and support [them] — that's where I find meaning in my work." —*Michelle S., Millennial*

» **The peer connection:** Sometimes, connecting the dots doesn't require a formal program. Instead, it calls for a culture that invites others to share when they're doing something meaningful or working alongside someone else who is. If your industry doesn't have straightforward connections to the bigger purpose, focus instead on creating a culture that is so inviting that it becomes the driver in and of itself. Build a network of peers and colleagues who can lean on one another, encourage friendships, and create an environment where working for the betterment of the team becomes the main goal at hand.

"[When] you spend the majority of your life at your job, it's more than just that. You [should] enjoy your days. [My coworkers and I] do group outings and pot lucks and have more of a social aspect to the workplace . . . It feels more like a family." —*Bethany B., Millennial*

What if the job isn't particularly meaningful?

Some careers have meaning built into the job description: nonprofits, community service, social work . . . your job of "connecting the dots" is essentially done for you. Other times — namely in industries like manufacturing or food service — it's just not that straightforward. Sometimes, it may seem like "it's just a job." Or, "this is just something to do to the pay my bills and help the company's bottom line." Many times, that way of thinking sells the work anyone is doing short. Regardless of position, title, or industry, a job can be connected to a meaningful purpose easily. The most important step for you as a manager is to connect the dots of the work to the purpose beyond the dollar sign, and that task of connection can be easy for you. We've created a simple flowchart for managers who need some assistance connecting the dots. The end result could still prove challenging, but maybe answering these brief questions will shed light on an opportunity for connecting the dots that you haven't seen before. (See Figure 9-1.)

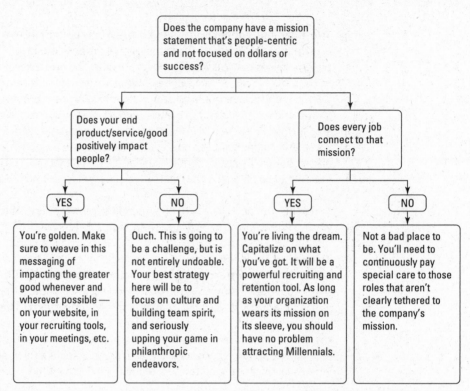

FIGURE 9-1: Helping you connect the work to a purpose.

Does the company have a mission statement that's people-centric and not focused on dollars or success?

Does your end product/service/good positively impact people?

Does every job connect to that mission?

YES — You're golden. Make sure to weave in this messaging of impacting the greater good whenever and wherever possible — on your website, in your recruiting tools, in your meetings, etc.

NO — Ouch. This is going to be a challenge, but is not entirely undoable. Your best strategy here will be to focus on culture and building team spirit, and seriously upping your game in philanthropic endeavors.

YES — You're living the dream. Capitalize on what you've got. It will be a powerful recruiting and retention tool. As long as your organization wears its mission on its sleeve, you should have no problem attracting Millennials.

NO — Not a bad place to be. You'll need to continuously pay special care to those roles that aren't clearly tethered to the company's mission.

BridgeWorks. Minneapolis, MN. (October, 2016)

Engaging in philanthropy

There is no quicker way to inject meaning into your organization than to become heavy participants in philanthropic endeavors. Truthfully, in the corporate world, embracing a robust giving stratagem is a solid plan no matter the organization (or the mission). From a PR standpoint, the past 30 years haven't been kind to corporate America. The media, including news outlets and Hollywood, have taken down the business world in a major way. Next-generation would-be employees are wary of "corporate greed" and loathe the possibility that they may have to "sell their soul" or "work for the man" to pay off their college loans.

To counter these negative stereotypes and fold in another layer of significance, you should make engaging in philanthropy a major objective. Step one is to establish these programs and make sure to include a few that really speak to Millennials. Step two is to yell it from the rooftops. If no one (specifically job-searching Millennials) knows you're actively participating in these programs, you might as well not be.

There are different ways to tap into philanthropy, but to get you started, try the following:

>> **Volunteering:** Is this one a bit obvious? Yes, a little. Is it incredibly important? Absolutely. You should be putting substantial effort into nurturing these programs. Offer a day of the year, fully paid, to engage in a volunteering opportunity of the employee's choosing. Better yet, as a fun company outing, sponsor volunteer events as a way to bring co-workers and departments together. You might even consider hosting special trips that employees need to apply for, and fly the selected few out to an exciting and international destination to do their voluntourism. (How's that for a good carrot?) Whatever your company's budget, you can find volunteering solutions that work for you and appeal to Millennials.

REMEMBER

Millennials are a "pics or it didn't happen" generation. They want an active hand in the philanthropic process, and the more experiential and share-worthy the event, the better. Focus on collaborative and active events. That way they'll continue to build relationships with their colleagues, have something fun and interesting to share, and, through that sharing, hopefully attract others to your company.

>> **Active giving:** The idea of active giving is a slight tweak to your volunteering efforts. Millennials are a generation that have embraced health and wellness trends like social running events (think the Color Run or the Warrior Dash) and gamified fitness. Why not combine this healthy mindset with a philanthropic objective? You'll be simultaneously speaking to their desire to stay fit as well as their need to build community with a workplace of like-minded peers. Form a workplace team to participate in a charity 5K, or implement a push-up challenge that raises money for a local school. The opportunities are only limited by your imagination (and your fitness level!).

>> **Corporate giving:** There are countless ways that you can enroll in a corporate giving program, and if you haven't already, you should. Understand that Millennials will lose trust for your company if you don't. (Check out *Charity and Philanthropy For Dummies* by Karl T. Muth, Michael T. S. Lindenmayer, and John Kluge, also published by Wiley, to find out more about all the ways your company can donate.) Give your next-generation employees some say in where corporate dollars go — ask for their opinions and advice, put it to a company-wide vote, or invite them to control an entire portion of corporate budget.

>> **Paycheck donations:** This concept isn't new, but it's a great way for all employees to feel like they are giving back. For each check that your employees get, ask whether they want to donate a percentage or dollar amount to a selection of charities. Giving them the ability to choose is critical, because some may hold more value in your Millennials' eyes.

"One of the most rewarding parts of my job is to be on the sidelines, [watching] folks get out in the community and give back resources, money, and talent. There is no way our brand would be as strong as it is today without the entrance of Millennials; [they] challenged us to integrate doing good with doing work." —*Ann M., Manager*

WARNING

Your company's philanthropic efforts can function as one of your strongest marketing tools or as a deal breaker. Be transparent about what and who you're donating to, because if it's kept a secret only to be discovered later by some resourceful reporters, you'll lose trust —and not just from your Millennials. On the flip side, you could sway an unsure candidate to choose your organization over another by giving to an organization that shares her values.

Compensating the Noncompensation Generation

Millennials are a generation saddled with debt, which — to the untrained eye — might make them seem like the group most eager to chase the paycheck. Alas, fair reader, we wish the Millennial motivation strategy was as easy as offering a regular pay increase. The truth of the matter is much more complex.

Finding out why compensation isn't enough

Millennials want to pay off their debt, but that alone isn't going to be enough to stay in one job for the paycheck. Why, you ask? Here are the top reasons:

>> **Their parents are hanging around as an invisible safety net.** You may have heard the term "Boomerang kids." It's no accident that "Boomer" is in the phrase. Is their kid's job unsatisfying? Do they need some extra time to find their "forever career"? Boomer parents are letting Millennials move home, often rent free, to give them the support and freedom to quit their jobs, do some soul-searching, recalibrate, and re-career so they can find the role that will be most fulfilling in the future.

>> **The future is far from guaranteed.** The events of 9/11 occurred in the middle of Millennials' preteen and teen years: It hit them where it counts and left a lasting impact on an otherwise optimistic generation. They learned firsthand that you never know what tomorrow will bring, so you better love and make the most of what you're doing right now.

>> **Money promises nothing.** Millennials watched their parents, their friends' parents, even their teachers and counselors lose homes and retirement accounts during the Great Recession. Sure, making money is one of their goals, but they're well aware that it can be easily snatched away with the next economic downturn, no matter how hard you've worked or how carefully you've saved. Interpersonal relationships, experiences, and even career skills are impervious to the economy's whims, and in Millennials' eyes, much more worthwhile investments.

While Millennials aren't as motivated by money as they are by meaning, general feelings of goodwill won't pay the bills. A smart compensation strategy can be the deciding factor in whether a Millennial chooses to stay or leave your organization. Women in particular are more likely to leave if they feel they aren't being fairly compensated, especially in relation to their male peers. Compensate smart, but don't make it such a high priority that all other motivation factors and rewards are forgotten. When you need to talk salary, do so tactfully and mindfully with help from the next section.

Compensation: The dollars and cents conversation

The term "compensation" is more all-encompassing to Millennials than just paper and coin. When recruiting, or during the interview process, show them that you take a multi-tiered approach to compensation. It's not just a transactional relationship where you send them paychecks for their time; it's more complex and nuanced. It's about investing in their development, building a culture of community and teamwork, and even providing support for their general health and well-being.

> » **Phrase that won't work with a Millennial:** "It's going to be tough work at first, but you'll see, it'll be so worthwhile when you start realizing how much money you're going to make!"

> » **Phrase that will work with a Millennial:** "We value our employees and invest in them not only with our compensation structure, but also with training opportunities and wellness programs, because we believe in developing well-rounded individuals."

Compensation: The fairness conversation

Access to the Internet is synonymous with access to the truth (faulty journalism aside), which means that pay inequalities based on race, gender, status, and so forth are common knowledge. The youngest of the next generation in particular expect you to come clean about how you compensate. Additionally, they're looking for a structure that values their individual needs; they value the ability to customize everything, and compensation is no exception.

> » **Phrase that won't work with a Millennial:** "We believe in treating everyone fairly, so everyone has the same compensation structure."

> » **Phrase that will work with a Millennial:** "We are transparent and fair about our compensation structure. That's why we tell you the process that goes into it and invite your opinion when necessary (for example, if you're earning commission on top of a base salary)."

Compensation: The comparison conversation

In the past, sharing and comparing information about salaries would have been absolutely unthinkable and considered a major breach of propriety. Older generations can be completely taken aback when they see that Millennials are comfortable talking about many things not traditionally PC in the workplace, and that includes their salaries. It isn't uncommon for them to chat about what they took home last week or their latest commission check. They grew up grading each other's homework in class, so it only makes sense that compensation has the potential to go public as well. You won't be able to control what they're saying to one another, but you can help turn the tide of the conversation.

>> **Phrase that won't work with a Millennial:** "I can't believe you are comparing your salary with others. What they are making has nothing to do with you."

>> **Phrase that will work with a Millennial:** "Many behind-the-scenes factors go into calculating individual compensation structures. Let's focus on how we can help you achieve your goals."

COMPENSATING LIKE A BOSS

Compensation is so much more than meets the eye. To pay like a pro, don't view compensation myopically, but open your eyes to the "total rewards" structure. Think about how to reach Millennials beyond just throwing more money at them (which is likely to be a foolhardy approach anyway). Build in commission options, additional perks, and training opportunities, all filtered through the Millennial lens:

- Benefits are part of the compensation package, and Millennials will expect a robust benefits package that includes a wellness focus.

   Give wellness programs the attention they deserve. They're highly sought after by the Millennial generation.

- Millennials value salary over high commission structures.

   For example, a 70/30 commission structure is better than a 30/70 one.

- Flexibility in how, where, and when they work can be enormously motivating.

- Pump up the perks. Little, seemingly insignificant perks can go a long way.

- Get creative with your compensation. Everyone offers the gym discount, but maybe your organization is the only one to offer participation in a yearly triathlon or yoga retreat.

What is it with YOLO?

Thanks to rapper/singer/songwriter Drake, the next generation has adopted a popular motto that captures the essence of how they're living their lives: YOLO, or "you only live once." The mentality is not a new one — "tomorrow isn't guaranteed," "carpe diem," and "live in the moment" are all iterations of the same mindset — but Millennials have taken the message to heart. Naturally, this may lead to some genuine frustration from other generations that have invested a lot of time and care into carving out a successful and comfortable future for themselves, often sacrificing comfort in the present moment in order to play the longevity game. Millennial behavior can seem erratic — as if they're wearing YOLO blinders — that leave them with a shortsighted mindset that results in impulsive decision-making.

Some common frustrations about Millennials that can be explained by YOLO include:

» Leaving a job without having another one lined up

» Leaving a high-paying job for one they enjoy more, but pays less

» Changing career paths only a couple years into trying one path

» Spending instead of saving

» Renting instead of owning

» Prioritizing hobbies and personal endeavors over work

WHERE YOLO COMES FROM

The Great Recession taught Millennials that corporations can't be trusted, buying a home isn't always the best decision, and saving may lead to losing. Add to that all the tragedies Millennials witnessed growing up — from 9/11 to movie theater shootings to the Boston Marathon bombings — and we have a generation that wants to live for today.

Rather than griping about why this mindset is counterproductive, celebrate how passionate it makes Millennials in the moment. While it may be a loss for some organizations as employees leave money and prestige for a meaningful career, others will tap into the enthusiasm Millennials bring to the day-to-day and the tasks at hand.

Rewarding Millennials

Past rewards structures were designed for employees who valued longevity and time above all else: pay increases and additional PTO (paid time off) aligned with the time spent with a company. Anniversaries were rewarded with cake and selecting a gift item from the company's anniversary catalog. Though some companies still offer similar rewards programs, they may need to consider reinventing these programs in the next 5–20 years. That's not to say that those who take pride in the time they've spent with an organization shouldn't be honored and recognized for their loyalty — they absolutely should. But you should also take the time to reward employees who've done an incredible job for the company within three short years. The workforce shift from seniority to meritocracy is too crucial to ignore, and there are absolutely ways to reward both preferences.

Making the most of the almighty dollar

TIP

Just because Millennials are motivated by many things beyond the dollar doesn't mean that money is unimportant or that they want to be paid in feelings tokens. Using monetary compensation as a reward can be energizing — if executed correctly:

>> **Commission:** Compensation structures are so industry- and position-specific that they deserve their own book, but throw on a generational monocle and you'll see this: Millennials, in general, prefer the reliability of salary balanced with commission rather than the unpredictability of commission balanced with salary. The economy has been too volatile for Millennials to risk steady income or pay rooted in the whims of others.

GOODBYE FANCY PEN, HELLO SABBATICAL

You may be surprised to hear that the generation that received a whole display-case worth of trophies growing up isn't looking for the same kind of rewards in the workplace. Plaques for good performance will be shoved into some dark corner of their closet along with the other stuff they don't know what to do with. The recognition they're looking for lies less in the tangible and more in the experiential. Can they take a sabbatical so they can cross "backpack through Southeast Asia" off their bucket list? Maybe they are given more freedom to work from home. Either way, ditch the tangible stuff. Well intentioned as it may be, odds are it'll end up in the trash someday.

THE SALARY VERSUS COMMISSION DEBATE

For Millennials, life outside of work matters too much to be subject to the weekly stress of unlocking enough commission to make rent. Unlimited commission, balanced out with a lower salary, is much less motivating than a decent salary with some commission, giving them the flexibility to rely on salary if necessary. It buys them the peace of mind to enjoy their family, friends, and hobbies outside of work, without worrying about making ends meet. Some industries, like finance, have had to completely overturn their compensation structures. Under the stress of knowing that the majority of their income was reliant on commission, Millennials fled to other industries or to progressive firms that understood that for the next generation, financial peace of mind in the here and now trumps the competitive commission model of the past.

» **Salary increases:** Millennials expect more than the standard pay increase year after year. If they feel a bigger bump isn't in their future, they'll look elsewhere. For them, it's not about seniority; it's about meritocracy. Debt, "adulting" (purchasing a home or starting a family), and saving are still top of mind for Millennials. A decent raise could mean the last student loan payment or putting down an offer on a house.

» **Bonuses:** For decades, bonuses have been a motivational tactic and rewards marvel. Regardless of the occasion, few will turn up their noses to an extra chunk of money (if you do know those people, please, introduce us — they sound like fascinating case studies). However, take heed when giving Millennials a bonus and be sure to offer them choices. For example: Give them the option to choose cash or an experience (concert tickets, a trip, and so on).

"I feel like a monetary [reward] is the practical approach. If I want to use [it] for something fun or adventurous, then I can choose what that would be, but if I need to pay the bills, I can [do that as well]." —*Alexa S., Millennial*

Rewarding the individual versus the team

Carrots and sticks are the age-old ultimatum when it comes to motivating your team. While the stick method is the mother of all fear-based incentives, maybe subjecting your workforce to potentially terrifying ultimatums a la *Law and Order* isn't the best way to go. Instead, dangle a delicious and rewarding carrot that depends on group effort. Millennials will be more incentivized if they know their hard work will benefit both them *and* their teammates. While this next generation takes pride in individual accomplishment, they are more driven by team wins. Motivate and reward the team with some clever tactics:

>> **Make it visual.** When a team can visualize a reward, it's easy for everyone to get on board. For example, if your team is attempting to reach a sales goal, put sticky notes on a wall in a creative pattern; as you make sales, employees can take turns peeling the sticky notes away.

>> **Include surprise rewards.** As a manager or leader, giving an unexpected reward can be the greatest way to motivate your people. For example, if you adopt the sticky-notes method mentioned in the preceding bullet, hide secret surprises underneath some of the notes. They can be as simple as a frozen yogurt outing or as big as a $100 bonus for each employee — either way, they're bound to put a smile on your employees' faces (and a pep in their motivation step).

>> **Attach it to emotions.** Sure, that sale brought in so many dollars for the company. But what if you knew that, in turn, that money helped pay someone's salary, who could then finally pay off his car loans? *That* gives a Millennial that lovely warm fuzzy feeling. Make the bottom line more human, and you'll give your team more reason to push forward.

Finding nonmonetary rewards that motivate

The struggle to find the perfect reward can be boiled down to one question: What will motivate beyond money? For many Millennials, cold, hard cash doesn't even come close to the top of their perks list. Instead, consider the following three categories of rewards, in order.

Category One: Career growth

The life-stage of a twenty-something demands focus on professional growth and ambition. Sure, not *all* Millennials demand more work or responsibility — but the top recruits and future leaders do. Many are at a stage where they may be wondering, "If I can't learn or move up quickly, why am I here?" and they're turning to you to understand that. If it takes too long to gain purchase or the process is so bureaucratic that all they see are obstacles, they're going to be less inclined to stay motivated. Reward stellar work with a new title, responsibility, or level in the organization. Keep them on the career trajectory. (See Chapter 7.) A smattering of options for career growth includes:

- » Promotion to a new position

- » Rotation to a different department

- » Access to an esteemed mentor

- » Placement on an important project

- » Appointment to leading an Employee Resource Group

> "[Our organization has] a lot of different groups that people identify with — Asian Americans, LGBTQ — so I see a lot of Millennials getting involved in those groups [and] championing them. [They're] setting the culture . . . it gives them purpose and [dictates] how they feel when they come in everyday."
> —Greta H., Manager

- » The green light on a passion project

Category Two: Autonomy

Millennials have a drive to control their workload and their schedule. Much like Gen Xers, they have an entrepreneurial bug and seek freedom to explore their endeavors and passions devoid of micromanagement and skepticism of their work ethic. If a Millennial does something well, reward him with more autonomy and trust. Do your best to hand over the reins and provide support as needed. In our research, we've found that autonomy is critical across the board for the next generation, and especially for older Millennials.

Category Three: Fun

To state the obvious, every generation wants to have fun at work. It's not like someone wakes up in the morning, looks in the mirror, and says, "Today will be different. Today, I'm not going to have fun. Really looking forward to it." That would be bizarre and, frankly, very sad. But Millennials may be more apt to associate fun with work and are interested in creating experiences with co-workers — inside and outside the office. Using good times as a reward not only shows that you care about their hard work but also motivates them to become an even more integral part of your organization. Here's a smattering of options for fun:

- » Participate in a group fitness class or boot camp.

- » Invite a group to a local concert.

- » Get nosebleed seats at a local sporting event.

- » Host a friendly competition in the workplace.

>> Take a team out to the newest lunch spot.

>> Have a YouTube video and drinks break.

>> Instagram your trip to the local fro-yo joint.

>> Invite your team to go on a scavenger hunt around the city.

>> Venture to a food or drink festival.

>> Set the calendar for beer o'clocks.

>> Pay for a classic happy hour.

Giving Millennials shareable work moments

Millennials have grown up in a #YOLO society with countless social networks to tend to. From posting updates from your latest hike to liking your friend's five-course dining experience, leaving a digital footprint is ingrained in this generation. One side effect of this lifestyle is that Millennials are always on the hunt for the coolest, most daring, most share-worthy experience. The Great Recession made very clear the low value of goods and placed high value on experiences; Millennials learned early that an amazing experience will be emotionally rewarding long after the luxury of a new car wears off. The next generation looks to leaders to understand their desire for fun and experience — and the two go hand in hand. Create a sharable work moment by taking the following steps:

1. **Brainstorm a list of group events that cater to your team's interests, hobbies, and passions.**

   Is your team interested in sports? Do they love trivia? Use what you know (or ask, if you don't) to come up with recreational options.

   WARNING

   Understanding your team's passions is a great starting point, but don't forget to take into consideration their lives outside of work as well. For example, if the majority of your team is composed of parents, they might not find your evening wine tasting rewarding when they have kids to pick up and spouses to assist.

2. **Narrow down that list with restrictions and limitations.**

   Take into consideration budget, number of participants, location, timing, and so on. It may seem obvious, but making sure the event is in line with company standards — and that your team can actually attend — is rather important.

When thinking about activities, take into consideration what your company can and will pay for, but also keep in mind what your team would like as well. Skimping on a reward is not only a dirty trick; it puts unintended pressure on your team to pretend it was worth their time. Too much extravagance, on the other hand, can make your team feel as if you're putting on airs. In addition, make sure your event fits into your team's schedules. If you know your team is likely to have a bunch of personal commitments throughout the workweek, try to make your event's end time flexible; those who need to head out early can do so without feeling guilty.

3. **Make it sharable.**

The good news: If you've crafted the experience to fit your team, you're halfway there. They'll appreciate the time and effort you've put into make it picture perfect. The second half comes down to the little things that will take your event from "meh" to must-share. Take, for example, happy hours. They're a dime a dozen. But happy hours where attendees are taught how to craft their own cocktails by a mixologist? Shareable (and dang fun). Try to add a twist that can take your event from awesome to #awesome.

Helping Millennials find their squad

"There is no 'I' in team" and "two heads are better than one" are mottos Millennials grew up rolling their eyes at for their sheer level of insistence. They knows the ins and outs of group-think, team projects, and peer networks. And guess what? They very much rely on their peers in the workplace today. At work, they have a mindset of: "If I'm going to be spending eight to ten hours with these people every day, why wouldn't I want them to be good friends?" Millennials don't want a hard divide between their personal and professional lives — they want to be their whole and authentic selves at work and at home, so their friends should be present in both spheres as well.

Millennials may love surrounding themselves with like-minded peers, but that doesn't necessarily mean they all have the gift of initiating and developing relationships. Hop into an elevator with a Millennial and you won't be greeted with sparkling conversation or an instant friendship — instead, you'll find a laser-focus on the phone and a muttered, "Have a good night" as she rushes out the door. All that is to say that Millennials respond well to structured networking and social events to help initiate work friendships.

Giving 'em a buddy

All Millennials can benefit from a coach or, in the case of work, a Mr. Miyagi (a la *The Karate Kid*), a Han Solo (a la *Star Wars*), or a Frenchie (a la *Grease*). They want a colleague to take them under their wing. Providing them this champion or buddy at work gives them a point of contact for questions that may not be necessary to direct to their manager. It gives them the inside scoop into the written and unwritten rules of the workplace, and, as a bonus, their work buddy could become their actual buddy. If you want to develop a program around this concept, ask for peer-match volunteers and have them design the system. You may be surprised by what you get.

TIP

Whether the buddy system is formal or informal, keep a good pulse on close work friendships because they could lead to a thoughtful reward. Imagine a 26-year-old phenomenal employee named Maya, who is part of a rotational program: For three years, she spends six months in one location before moving on to the next. Each six-month stint means new people, new work, and new friends. When the three years are complete and you want to celebrate all her hard work, ask Maya if she wants any of her past colleagues at the celebration and then fly them out for the big party. It may seem slightly excessive and over the top, but this is just the kind of reward that sets you apart from everyone else.

"We have a new-hire organization that lets you meet people across the company. It provides great networking and you can also meet people your age and experience level to make friends. These types of programs are great to help our generation [blend] into the workplace." —*Lia D., Millennial*

Offering up office extracurriculars

Aside from fun non-work-related experiences, consider work responsibilities and tasks as a way to get Millennials together and reward the group. Give them big responsibilities to show off their skills:

>> Ask them to run a meeting or all-hands meeting with a theme to give them a little taste of leading.

>> Create a task force of Millennials to solve generational challenges in the company.

>> Host an all-company cook-off for employees to show off their culinary talents.

>> Bring the philanthropy within your walls. Can your employees help with professional development for underprivileged kids? Or you could put on a silent auction, with all proceeds going to a local charity.

>> Offer them the chance to mentor a brand-new hire. It'll give them an opportunity to show off some leaderships skills and maybe even make a new work buddy.

Chapter 10

Dropping Workplace Formalities: Let's Be Friends

Seasoned employees feeling frustration toward the new kids on the block is not a new phenomenon. Traditionalists wrote off Boomers as hippies, Boomers denounced Xers as apathetic slackers, and just about everyone thinks Millennials are entitled narcissists who expect to be rewarded for just showing up.

When a Millennial, experienced or not, joins a team, questions mired in this frustration inevitably bubble up: Are you going to work as hard as I did? Why do you think you can work flexible hours? Are you incapable of putting down your phone? Why don't you show some effort and dress professionally?

The root of the problem here is pretty straightforward: Change is hard. Each generation brings different perceptions around what the work ethic looks like, the lines that should be drawn between workplace colleagues, and how to communicate effectively.

With so many preferences in the mix, trying to understand the correct workplace etiquette to employ can feel like an uphill battle. What seems appropriate to one generation (Millennials) can be seen as disrespectful to another generation (Gen Xers and/or Baby Boomers). In this chapter we take a closer look at the shifting nature of workplace professionalism, from workplace attire, flexible schedules, and working relationships to social media usage, to help you unpack — and hopefully find a way to be at peace with — why Millennials would rather head to a café midday for a latte and some off-site work than partake of the break room's Keurig selection and finish working at their desk.

Distinguishing Between Formality at Work and Work Ethic

For decades, the close relationship between formality and work ethic has gone largely unchallenged. It has been a truth, almost universally acknowledged, that someone with a great work ethic surely exhibits all the outward signs of professionalism and proper workplace etiquette. As each generation has entered the workforce, it has fashioned its own version of what that work ethic and formality look like.

Checking out work-ethic mindset through the ages

For Baby Boomers, imagine the Mad Men–type work environment of the '60s and '70s: An eager, entry-level twenty-something respected all rules around dress, communication, and the clock. This respect, along with some extra hours and a solid work performance, meant that employee got ahead and avoided getting fired. The immaculate suits; long hours in the office; and flawless, perfectly formatted meeting agendas were all badges of a good employee with an impeccable work ethic.

Now imagine the Working Girl–type professional environment of the '80s and '90s: An ambitious, no-nonsense, power-suit-wearing college grad built trust and respect by knowing when and how to bend the rules. The new hire mastered the blurred line between casual and formal dress and earned respect through an efficient work style that resulted in getting more work done in a shorter amount of time.

Millennials have their own take on formality and work ethic. Simply put, they've tossed the formula that says formality = work ethic out the window. For Millennials, defined work hours, strict dress codes, and communication pleasantries are all good and well, but not essential to doing their job or even excelling at it. The three-piece suit and alphabetized memos can be easily replaced with jeans and instant messaging the boss, without sacrificing quality of work or determination to succeed.

> At [my company], there was a [mentality of] 'This is the way we do things here, your appearance and your presentations need to be buttoned-up.' It was a big shift when we started to implement changes to be more open to Millennials' work styles and more casual dress." —*Susan K., Manager*

For a snapshot of how formality has shifted through the generations, see Table 10-1.

TABLE 10-1 ## Views on Formality through the Decades

issue	1960s and 1970s	1980s and 1990s	2000s and 2010s
What hard work looks like	Long hours Arriving early and leaving late Working weekends Never saying "no" Always willing to lend a hand	Fewer hours, working more efficiently Arriving right on time and leaving right on time Late nights only if necessary Work hard, play hard Prioritizing for the sake of balance	Working anywhere, anytime Results — not hours — prove the level of work Innovative processes reap the most rewards Work hard, play always
What to wear	What you wear reflects how much you care about your job "Dress for the job you want, not the job you have" IBM Blue suits	Professional attire is a necessary evil Bend the rules (will wear the suit but not the tie); shoulder pads and popped-collar polo shirts Business casual	What you wear has no influence on your work Dress for the day, not the job Jeans and Converse sneakers
Personal life versus professional life	*Work-life separation:* Who you are at work is not who you are at home	*Work-life balance:* Get all the work done first, then engage in light chatting at the water cooler	*Work-life integration:* What you see is what you get; who you are at work is who you are at home

REMEMBER

There is no golden generation. Every generation will have those bad eggs who don't work as hard as they should, but they will also have the overachievers who make everyone else look bad. The general attitudes toward balance and integration should serve as a summary to help you understand the complexities. That way you can weed out the difference between a just plain bad Millennial employee from one who shows promise but just happens to view work differently than you.

THE NEED FOR AUTHENTICITY

A side effect of work-life integration is that anything appearing to be "put-on" or false can be met with hesitation, and even skepticism. Formal attire and communication can read as inauthentic to Millennials. Can you trust a suit? Can you trust politically correct conversation? Maybe. But maybe not. They can be read as a lack of transparency, and may lead Millennials to wonder what you're trying to hide. Just analyze the celebrities, role models, and bosses that Millennials respect the most — they're the ones who seem like they have nothing to hide. They're vulnerable, make mistakes, and admit to their own shortcomings. Look no further than Millennials' obsession with Jennifer Lawrence as an example: Her shameless demeanor in interviews, her undeniable charisma, her fearlessness in just being herself — cursing, tripping, and being almost too candid, all on camera — and her vulnerable interviews in magazines are devoid of any pretense. This desire for authenticity seeps beyond celebrity and into nearly every Millennial work-place expectation.

Unpacking the impact of dress code

Gone are the days when people had great expectations to "dress for the job you want and not the job you have." Sure, there are times you need to dress to impress, but what exactly does everyday "professional dress" look like now?

Certain industries have their own rigid expectations and guidelines (for example, finance and law still enforce rather strict dress codes that, in comparison, make Silicon Valley workers look like hipster peasants) but for the majority of the work-place, dress codes have shifted from business formal to business casual to casual.

The need to dress it down

Many Millennials ask, "Why does it matter what I wear? I can do just as well (and maybe better) if I wear what I want!" Why the sudden shift with Millennials? Well, for most of Millennials' lives, what was once defined by formality is now, instead, opting to reflect the latest trend and/or become markedly *not* formal:

» CEOs can, and do, wear shower shoes on camera (looking at you, young Mark Zuckerberg).

» Fine-dining servers wear jeans, plaid shirts, and suspenders if they're fancy.

» Your "Sunday best" can describe your favorite jersey.

>> The whole notion of dressing up for a flight has been tossed out the window in favor of what can only be described as dressed-up PJs.

>> The athleisure (workout clothes worn in other settings) market has skyrocketed . . . Millennials are choosing stretchy over starchy.

>> What you sweat in costs more than what you impress in (yoga pants cost more than slacks).

In addition to this list, remember that Millennials grew up in a time when the news exposed countless industries, institutions, and people as corrupt or deceptive. Dressing down is arguably a reaction to that — it eliminates any potential for falsity. Informal-wear means more than just personal comfort; it's an appeal to authenticity. The perception is that you're not putting on airs, and you're not pretending you're something you're not. Who you are at home is who you are at work. You bring your authentic self to the workplace.

Sorry, Zuckerberg, your hoodie isn't trending

You know that quintessential Silicon Valley image of a Millennial? The one that assumes all Millennials wear the hipster uniform of hoodie and skinny jeans, drink IPAs on tap all day, spend hours playing foosball in the breakroom, and occasionally sit down to brainstorm or partake in a frenetic coding session? That representation captures only the tiniest slice of the Millennial generation.

First of all, the vast majority of companies don't (and can't) foster a Silicon Valley culture, and second, many Millennials don't actually want to work in that environment. The tech/start-up world may seem glamorous on the surface, but it can be incredibly draining, requiring long and demanding hours from its employees. Obviously, not all Millennials are suited to that type of work. It's not a pervasive generational desire to work at start-ups or even the more established Googles or Ubers or Facebooks of the world. What *is* a universal trend across this generation, though, is a strong preference for freedom in the workplace to dress in a way that suits their personality and lifestyle, whether that be a nice summer dress, the trendiest new wear, or simple jeans and a tee.

WARNING

The next generation isn't going to give a round of applause to managers who allow casual Fridays. Though even this one day of casual dress is a large change for many organizations, it can give them a taste of what could be, and they'll wonder why you can't just extend this to every day. Dress matters less for success than it ever has before, and, arguably, clothes that make you happy and allow you to breathe may actually improve performance.

Setting a Millennial-friendly dress code

Don't think that because Millennials prefer informal dress, the best course of action is to throw out all your company standards and give them free reign to show up in their ripped denim and graphic tees. Instead, consider how you can move the needle and adapt what you already do in a way that doesn't sacrifice your company's culture. Don't be afraid to challenge the status quo of your dress policy in as objective and unbiased a way as possible. Gather a team of leaders to assess the options. But watch for the following two characters who will inevitably show up. If you can identify them beforehand, it's probably even best to try and avoid sending invites for this conversation, because they're not going to be valuable additions to the group:

The hater: He's not even listening to the conversation. He's annoyed that you're even considering "kowtowing" to these Millennial upstarts, and his goal at the meeting is to remain rigid and unbending, no matter how sound the logic may be. He's obviously not going to be super helpful.

The groupie: She loves Millennials and thinks they're the best thing to happen to your organization since email. Just like the naysayer, she'll be blindly willing to change whatever it takes to accommodate the next generation hires. Her perspective, far from unbiased, will only serve to further annoy those who may be more skeptical.

With your team of open-minded leaders assembled, ask yourselves these questions: Is a dress code absolutely necessary to get the job done? When was the last time it changed? Have you invited your employees' opinions about it? How much time and money would it take to change the dress code? Are there certain times when formality might be more appropriate than others?

Even if you have zero pull in your organization as far as being able to change policy around dress, don't fret. There are some things you can do to manage your own assumptions around dress code and also bend the rules to make the workplace slightly more accommodating for your Millennial direct-reports:

>> **Don't make assumptions in interviews.** Just because some Millennials may seem underdressed, that doesn't necessarily mean they're not serious about the job. Don't let the few wrinkles in the pants, missing jacket, and tattoo sleeve distract you from the potentially brilliant mind that lies beneath. Listen, bias-free, to what she's saying. It's a far better indicator of future performance than what she's wearing. Of course, if you work at a firm with a very rigid dress code and casual wear is not welcome, consider telling candidates this before the interview so they can show up dressed appropriately.

>> **Set expectations early.** The worst mistake you can make is getting frustrated by an unprofessionally dressed Millennial when you didn't articulate your preference in the first place. Believe it or not, growing up idolizing start-up culture does not an easy task of "acting professionally" make. Communicate expectations around dress clearly upfront. Because you know what they say about making assumptions.

>> **Allow for flexibility where possible.** If you express how you expect your staff to dress, good for you for your clarity! If you can, try to embrace a "dress for your day" culture where your employees dress for the day that lies ahead. Are there meetings with the higher-ups on the calendar? Is it an all-email kind of day? Ask Millennials to dress up or down depending on the situation; that way they can add some dress-down days where it makes sense, without sacrificing all decorum.

>> **Separate client code from office code.** If you happen to manage Millennials in a client-centric organization, then opt for a "dress for your client" code. Articulate the differences between what's okay with the client versus what's okay in the office. You should consider that more and more of your clients are Millennials themselves and may even appreciate a dressed-down version of the client meeting.

MUCH ADO ABOUT TATTOOS

Millennials are getting inked en masse. One in three of them report having permanent body art. While members of other generations who took the plunge and got tattoos ensured that they were hidden, Millennials are sporting them publically and proudly as markers of their individualism. A generation that loves customization, they've now taken to customizing their own skin with designs that are emblematic of who they are and what they believe in. All the hullabaloo about tattoos being unprofessional falls on deaf ears, because ink or no ink, Millennials don't see it as a barrier to how they do their jobs.

If tattoos are just not going to fly in your environment, ask yourselves: Is it because they're inappropriate? Distracting? If so, why, and is there any room to change that perception? Unless your young employees have tattooed "bug off" across their foreheads or lude/offensive images on their hands, in most cases, the tattoo shouldn't be an issue. Don't write off the tatted candidate just because you can't see past the tattoos. Simply ask Millennials to cover up the ink that's causing a stink, and explain that, *for now,* it's what would be best for the situation, the times, and the company. It's likely that in a few short years, as Millennials ascend up the ladder, more and more Fortune 100 companies will have heavily tatted CEOs.

Most companies that get voted as "top places to work" buck corporate trends. Typically, the ones on these lists have accomplished the difficult task of dismissing outdated professional norms without ruffling the feathers of older employees. They also understand that "looking the part" is critical to the organization's brand and legacy. Before you put up the wall that resists change, step into a land of pure imagination and think of ways you can bring the look your company requires into the modern era. For example, if you ask employees to wear ties, might a skinny tie suffice? Or one with a fun print? If nice shoes are on the "must-wear" list, maybe retro sneakers can fit the bill . . . at least sometimes. . . .

WARNING

Avoid gender-specific guidelines because they're simply no longer relevant and will serve as a giant red flag to candidates. The next generation expects and demands equality in all matters of diversity, and enforcing gender-specific dress codes will deter them from your company. Opt for gender-neutral guidelines. You should also be cognizant of and sensitive to other matters of diversity like culture and religion (not to mention, it's the law!).

Turning off the clock: The impact of work hours

When Boomers entered the workforce, work was a destination. All meetings, calls, and daily tasks *had* to be done in the office because it's where all the workplace tools and trappings were kept. It was also the only place to show your manager just how dedicated you were by arriving early and staying late.

Due in large part to technology's seemingly limitless ripple effects, work nowadays is more about a state of mind than a designated physical space. The capability to work from anywhere, anytime, means that you're not restricted to the bounds of a 9 to 5 workday. Cue the debates about the merits of Millennials leaving early, staying late, requesting too much time off, and wanting to leave in the middle of the day to go for a run or to get their hair dyed blue.

For Millennials, it makes sense to weave work in with the personal. If you're a night owl and that's when you do your best thinking, why wouldn't you save a difficult assignment for late evening and take care of some errands in the morning? The end result will be better work, and isn't that the goal? In their minds, sticking staunchly to a set schedule isn't nearly as good a measure of an employee's drive and ambition as delivering exemplary results and innovative new ideas.

"Tell me what I need to do to be successful and then let me figure out how to get it done. That might mean I work at 8 and I leave at 3:30 for yoga . . . trust me to know when I can't leave at 3:30. It's not about butt in seat anymore, it's about the work you're delivering and working for the life you want to lead." —*Greta H., Millennial and Manager*

Testing out the flex schedule

This is what the next generation *hears* when a boss says, "We run the schedule this way because that's the way it's always been done, and at this point it'd be impossible to change":

>> No, you can't defer some of your duties to off-work hours.

>> No, we can't build a schedule that accommodates your other interests.

>> No, we'd rather you don't leave during the day for any reason other than a doctor's appointment or a pressing family emergency.

>> No, we don't believe you're working hard if we can't physically see you typing away at the office.

>> No, our culture doesn't allow for much flexibility; sorry if that makes you feel uncomfortable.

>> No, we aren't interested in considering you as a person versus a worker bee.

Summary? A lot of no's that can feel like a big slap in the face. Millennials start to feel like a resource that's being squeezed and forced into an inflexible model rather than flesh and blood human beings with needs that should be taken into account on a case-by-case basis. The answer is not to scrap all policy and revert all the no's to yes's, but it should serve as a wake-up call.

This equation is wrong:

Need for flexibility = lazy, entitled, bad worker

This equation is much closer to the truth:

Need for flexibility = different work ethic

If you feel like this only confirms what you've suspected, that it's yet another example of Millennial entitlement — this time around flexibility — believe us when we say we understand where you're coming from. But hear us out. There's a difference between going home to goof off and going home to pour yourself, full force, into a project you're passionate about. If you want to find out which of the two is the case, try your hand at a little experiment: You may find the results are truly excellent work (with even more hours put in than if they'd restricted themselves to only the standard work schedule).

Follow these steps to test a flexible work schedule:

1. **Clearly define your expectations of "office hours," times when you wold like your Millennial(s) to work from the office. From there, you can decide together the "flex" part of the schedule.**

2. Hear out the objections, and invite ideas from Millennials if they have constructive solutions.

3. Make time and effort to try these solutions, with a "yes, and if" approach ("Yes, let's try this new arrangement, and if results aren't meeting expectations, we can revise our approach").

4. Review the results.

"When I have new team members, I have a 'getting to know you' meeting. I have a worksheet with two columns, one being personal and the other professional. I [also] communicate [that] I don't need to know if you have a doctor's appointment, just go. Just get your work done, I don't care. That is the level setting." —Greta H., Millennial and manager

5. Come together to debrief the experiment and then decide to adapt, adopt, or cancel it.

Checking your gut reaction

Before reacting unfavorably on impulse to a request for workplace flexibility, make sure you're actually hearing the Millennial's request. What does that look like? Say, for example, that you manage a stellar Millennial who is itching for a more fluid schedule. During a one-on-one meeting, your conversation goes something like one of the following two scenarios.

Scenario #1: The shutdown

You: "So, any questions for me before we end the meeting?"

Stellar Millennial: "I do have one — just curious — is everyone expected to be here until 5 every day?"

The question can lead to logical reactions: Are you saying you don't want to be here until 5? Do you think you don't have to work as hard? Do you want to work fewer hours? Needless to say, you feel a little frustrated. And rightly so. You put your boss hat on and give this sterile response:

You: "That is the expectation that we went over when you started, yes."

What did you accomplish? Complete shutdown. The Millennial likely feels embarrassed for bringing it up and confused as to why you wouldn't even hear her out on what may have been a perfectly reasonable request. After all, she's proven her work ethic and value to the company. Shouldn't her stellar performance be taken into consideration?

FLEXIBILITY FOR NON-EXEMPT WORKERS

Managing Millennials who are either hourly employees or unionized adds layers of complexity to the work-ethic discussion. Flexibility is not a friend to rules, so you likely have fewer opportunities to bend. It's unfortunate but true. However, putting on a creativity hat to help you view the situation from different angles can turn these obstacles into opportunities:

Angle A: The resource repository

If you manage employees on the floor of a factory, rather than giving them breaks without resources, consider giving them tools to make the most of break times. One small-scale factory encouraged break times for book clubs or hobby time. They even went so far as to offer education sessions from the company so employees could choose to find more ways to add value to the organization.

Angle B: Empower to get power

Another company, after growing tired of people complaining about schedules, created a task force to solve the issue. The managers asked front-line workers to make decisions for the whole company and, in turn, found a great solution that increased engagement and buy-in.

Angle C: If *Shark Tank* had a union sister

One organization's top manager told her employees that management sets aside a certain amount of budget for process innovation. If an employee had a good-enough idea to change a process that might help run work more efficiently, he could propose the idea and have at it. Rules, compliance, and bargaining didn't have to prevent flexibility; they could just as easily open the door to more creative flexible arrangements.

Scenario #2: The attentive manager

> *You:* "So, any questions for me before we end the meeting?"
>
> *Stellar Millennial:* "I do have one — just curious — is everyone expected to be here until 5 every day?"

Before freezing up and pondering all the reasons behind the question, you take a step back and inquire into why the question was asked in the first place.

You: "Good question but before I answer, I'm curious; why do you ask?"

Stellar Millennial: "I understand that a lot of people work that way here, but I feel like I'd be able to get more done if I could leave around 3 and work from a coffee shop. I'd be available via phone or email and could return to the office if there were any issues. Would that be okay?"

You: "Thanks for understanding our work environment. I'd love to give you that flexibility — let me check with the team first. If all are okay with it, then we'll have biweekly check-ins to make sure everything is getting done to your regular quality."

What did you accomplish? A few different, really positive things. First, you showed that you're willing to listen to that Millennial as an individual, with his own track record of performance. Second, you demonstrated a flexibility in management style, showing that you're willing to work with him to find middle ground that works for both parties. Nothing was promised, and no ground was given up. You simply listened to a reasonable request with a reasonable (and satisfying) answer.

Allowing yourself to reimagine work schedules

Many things are not as they appear at face value, and the same follows for seemingly frustrating requests for flexible scheduling. If any of the following flex schedule frustrations arise, please pause and allow yourself to rethink and cuddle up to the idea of a different working style:

>> **A Millennial requests extra time off.**

Worth reimagining because . . .

Past generations never had the luxury of asking for an extra week off during their first decade of work. Millennials have seen the effects of burnout in their parents, relatives, and friends and have read articles about countries with progressive work policies where employees spend less time working and more time vacationing. The result? Not just more fun pics on their Instagram account, but better work when they return. The next generation has seen the proven value of mental breaks; they're an opportunity to increase productivity and creativity. If time is money, time off is an investment. For both you and them.

"I value [flexibility] and want to do things after work and not worry about working weekends all the time. I think it's important to have time to yourself to rejuvenate and revitalize. [If] you burn out, you can't add value to the company, [so] in the end, it's counterproductive." —*Alexa S., Millennial*

» A Millennial asks for additional and alternative work duties before completing her day's to-do list.

Worth reimagining because . . .

The greatest plight for any hard worker is to feel useless. If Millennials are at risk of feeling like their skills aren't being utilized, they may turn to ad-hoc projects to feel motivated. The generation raised on an overloaded schedule of extracurricular activities can feel most comfortable when set on a variety of tasks and projects.

» A Millennial arrives late/leaves early.

Worth reimagining because . . .

When a Millennial gets to work an hour past the typical start time, chances are she's not trying to show you how disrespectful she is. Millennials show respect in the work they produce and the way they treat their employers and co-workers. They've adopted the concept of ROWE — results-oriented work environment — and taken it to heart. Before jumping to assumptions, just ask what they were up to. Maybe they had a networking breakfast, or perhaps they wanted to beat traffic and get in a few more work hours at their favorite café. Either way, if the work is getting done, is there any reason to stand on principle just to prove a point?

"I left my corporate job because I was not able to drop my daughter off at school. My husband and I both work and I'm proud of being a working mom but I needed to be able to pick her up and pick up my computer later too. Flexibility is important for employees in the long run." —Kara F., Millennial and manager

TIP

At a large medical device company, a manager had two Millennials who pushed to have some autonomy over where and when they worked. Open to new ideas, the manager gave each Millennial two weeks to try out his inventive way of getting things done. While Millennial One worked from a café two days a week and came into the office from 8 to 4:15 on other days, Millennial Two found respite in her home office for three days and came to the office from 9 to 6 the other two days. After two weeks, the manager regrouped with the pair and looked at results. Millennial One got more done in the two weeks and Millennial Two got less done. Reaching a compromise, the manager decided to allow all her reports one flexible day per week to work wherever he or she chose, and an 8:30–4:30 schedule the other days. If ever results weren't being met, they would be dealt with on an individual basis.

WARNING

Silicon Valley is heralded for policies that allow people to take unlimited vacation. Companies boast about cultures that let you work from wherever, whenever. While that may be beneficial to some Millennials, to others, it's crippling. Complete flexibility leads to a workforce where everyone is bound by the proverbial golden handcuffs — they sure are pretty and appealing, but you're chained. You may run the risk of vacation shame: people taking less vacation for fear of taking advantage of the system. In 2016, Alamo Rent A Car released their annual family vacation survey findings. Surveying 1,500 adults nationwide, they found that guilt over taking days off was widespread, with Millennials the most likely generation to feel bad about using their rightful vacation days.

Working hard or hardly working

Of all the stereotypes that exist about the next generation, and there are many, one of the most prevalent and most inaccurate is that Millennials are lazy and lack work ethic. Just because someone fails to conduct himself formally doesn't mean that he is unwilling or unable to work hard. Asking for an updated dress code, flexible schedule, or extra vacation day does not lack of ambition make. To be sure that you don't write off Millennials as lazy, try the following:

>> **Don't lead with negative preconceptions.** Understand that most Millennials do want to work very hard and give you their all. Try not to assume that just because they're working differently, they aren't putting in solid effort.

>> **Put yourself into a Millennial mindset.** Taking off your generational lens and seeing the world through another's is easier said than done, but it may be the key to relating to and connecting with Millennials.

>> **Provide flexibility in whatever way you can — whether it's dress, work hours, or workplace.** Millennials are driven to work even harder when they're given the parameters in which they prefer to work. Minor changes you make can create a major impact with the next generation. A few minor fixes you can try:

- Focus on results, not hours or rules.

- Adopt the phrase "I'm flexible" into your vernacular.

- Share your story of work ethic and invite them to share theirs.

- Explain why certain rules or expectations are in place.

"The informal hierarchy and flexibility of schedule are what sold me. I know a lot of people have chosen to work [at my organization] because of the flexibility [and] they've sacrificed pay [for it]." —*Lauren W., Millennial*

>> **If you've tried the preceding three bullets but are still unsure, trust your intuition.** If you're reviewing these tactics and still can't find the answer you're looking for, ask yourself whether you've maybe hired a bad employee. If you're still unsure, maybe your struggles are really more about motivation and feedback, which you can read up on in Chapters 8 and 9.

Millennials have their own heavy lifting to do. It's not the manager's responsibility to cater to the younger demographics without expecting anything from them in return. To help Millennials meet you halfway, ask them on a scale of 1 to 10 how comfortable they are with the standard work expectations and rules. Then ask them for suggestions about what you can do to help make that number higher. Offer mentorship and guidance to those who are seeking to change but explain that first they should:

>> Understand the work schedule policies and why they're in place.

>> Talk through workplace expectations with a manager.

>> Prepare an action plan and present it to their manager if they still feel strongly that a change is important.

Maybe it isn't such a bad idea that Millennials push for fewer hours spent in the office. Studies and reports have shown that the biggest regret of older people is how much they worked. The United States consistently rates lower on the scale of overall satisfaction with life as the country with fewer vacation days, longer work weeks, and less paid maternity/paternity leave. Perhaps the hustle isn't so great, and just maybe Americans as a whole should stop taking pride in how busy we all are. Yes, there are countless other factors to consider like the economy, standard of living, and so on, but working fewer hours may be worth considering or at least discussing with your younger co-workers.

Drawing the Fine Line Between Manager and Friend

In a hierarchical workforce dominated by Traditionalists, Baby Boomers, and Generation Xers, relationships between manager and direct report were incredibly clear: They were professional, the roles of power were explicit, and a solid distinction between work and home life left no confusion about what was inappropriate to share at work and/or at home. The traditional organization chart led a helping hand in defining the boundaries of that relationship.

As Millennials have entered the workforce, they've blurred all the lines that were previously commonplace and remained, mostly, unchallenged. Now, their cohort seeks colleagues that moonlight as friends. They hope for a manager who can either exist within or, at least, loop the perimeter of that friendship circle.

If you can get onboard with this pretty momentous shift in the manager-employee relationship, you'll be a step ahead of other managers in the retention game. Your employees will be more likely to trust you and feel even more incentivized to work hard for you.

WARNING

Drawing a line between manager and friend requires two things: your clarity on what kind of relationship you are comfortable with, and a willingness to clearly articulate if and when the line is crossed.

Telling Millennials when it's just TMI!

Remember the taboo topics of conversation? The ones that would send any mother and/or father into a tizzy if they were brought up at the Thanksgiving dinner table with gram and gramps listening in? If you don't, congrats on your psychedelic childhood surrounded by hippies who freely spoke about the three major taboos: money, sex, and politics. Today, the next generation is not only willing to speak about those tabooed topics freely but will also gladly bring up all kinds of heretofore completely outrageous stuff to discuss in the workplace — their crazy weekends, the recreational drugs they may or may not have tried that one time, the latest messages from their Tinder dates, and so on . . . the list is long. To Boomers and Gen Xers who are unaccustomed to their level of oversharing, the first time it's heard can be quite the shock.

Take a look at Jay, an exemplary Gen X manager. His rapport with Millennial colleagues is impressive — they value his candor, sense of humor, and motivation to team development. Jay values their positivity, their ambition, and that they unironically laugh at his dad jokes. They all worked well together and were a top department in the company. Then one Monday morning, Nick, an eager 26-year-old, walked in and plopped into his chair. He was — in a matter of words — worse for wear. When Jay inquired about his disposition, Nick sighed, "Oh, man, I am so off today. I'm really hungover." That line between manager and friend? Consider it crossed.

TIP

When, or if, you are in a situation wherein you feel like Jay, take a step back and think about what you could have done differently to set a clearer boundary of what's acceptable and what's not. Then rest the situation that very moment — find a private place to make it clear when the line was crossed and why. Use the moment as a coaching opportunity to explain how you interpreted the exchange and how a senior partner or client might view it. Then, if you can, find a way to laugh about it because having a too-much-information moment can be thoroughly entertaining for everyone involved. It's not the end of the world if it happens a couple times; it's a problem when oversharing becomes chronic.

"I once went to a concert and told [my manager] I was going. I went, didn't get home until 3 in the morning [and] called in sick. My manager called me in. That's when I started to learn boundaries." —*Sokun B., Millennial*

Navigating social media

Every generation favors social media, but Millennials were the first to use it. Believe it or not, to a Millennial, making a relationship "Facebook official" is a big deal when it comes to work relationships, because they're sharing a big part of their personal lives. So, if they send you a friend request or try to follow you on Twitter, it's a sign of flattery, not a misguided step to pry into your private world. That said, if you don't want them in that world, that's okay! If you, like many Xers, want your social media connections to extend no further than LinkedIn, then take the appropriate steps to set expectations:

1. **Determine what is on and off limits to you in the social realm.**

2. **Set your privacy settings on your accounts (purposefully or just in case).**

3. **Wait until they attempt to connect with you rather than putting the kibosh on it from the beginning.**

    For example, instead of saying, "I prefer not to be friends with any of my colleagues on social media" on Day 1, wait until you're sent a request and then kindly say, "I saw your request. Just so you know, as a general rule, I only connect on LinkedIn just so I treat everyone equally."

REMEMBER

If a Millennial is giving you access to her private life whether on social media or in person, you will probably learn things about her you never knew before. No, that doesn't mean you're going to hear in-depth stories about crazy weekends, but you will hear an earful about trips to the apple orchard, their Disney-themed parties (shouldn't that theme be reserved for kids?), and even what their friends are saying in negotiations at other companies. Instead of adopting concern at this exposure, use it as a point to connect with them. If something is questionable to their character in your organization, that's worth discussing. Otherwise, Millennials are self-aware enough to know that they're giving managers and leaders access to their political opinions on just about everything, even marijuana legalization, and will hopefully refrain from anything that's not company-appropriate.

Explaining work social events to Millennials

As Millennials get to know their colleagues, walls come down. It's a lovely showcase of their comfort if they do the same with you, their manager, but it's not so lovely when they keep those walls down at the company holiday party or client networking event. Without a voice of condescension, let them in on your work social event dos and don'ts. First, if they exist, outline any company policies around social events ahead of time so the expectations are clear and set. Second, be the mentor you always wanted. For example, say:

> "Word of advice at client events: Keep it to two drinks. You don't wanna be *that* guy/girl."

Or:

> "Something I wish I would have known when I was your age is that if your manager or leader invites you to happy hour, they genuinely want to see you there. It looks good to your colleagues and leadership if you show up to get to know everyone."

Placing boundaries where needed

As the organizational structure has flipped and turned (see Chapter 6 for the whole story), so have the rules of hierarchy. No longer is the senior leadership team untouchable or unapproachable; the opposite is now the expectation for Millennials. The President of the United States is on Twitter, after all; the leader who was once the most inaccessible is now just 140 characters away. You may have heard stories of Millennials emailing the CEO or popping into the senior VP's office for a "quick chat," and while these examples may seem outlandish, they're happening on a regular basis. While some leaders find this kind of behavior charming or impressive, they're usually in the minority. If you have Millennials charging to the top when they should be embracing more prudent behavior, explanations are in order.

For starters, explain why boundaries are needed:

» **Describe the difference between ambition and desperation.** Millennials likely think they're taking the right approach, an impressive one in fact, without knowing that they're rubbing you the wrong way.

» **Coach them on how to approach leadership.** To a Millennial, senior leaders aren't scary; they're just people. An audible scoff could be heard from them if people create a fear cloud when leadership passes by in the office halls. They won't automatically respect boundaries, so help them find an alternate path to be heard at the top — even if it's just a path through your voice as a messenger.

Making yourself accessible is a helpful strategy:

>> **Open the door.** The physical act of opening the door is less important than communicating your willingness to hear thoughts and ideas from all levels. Maybe you can attend a new-hire orientation just to answer anyone's questions. Maybe you can move your corner office to the middle of the floor in an open cubicle. No matter how you do it, make it known that you're open to input.

>> **Step up your social presence.** The next generation does not need to see you face to face to get their opinions across. An intranet or company Twitter account can open the conversation to change.

Channeling Your Inner Emily Post: Communication Etiquette

Unlike Baby Boomers and Gen Xers, Millennials weren't drilled on the ins and outs of etiquette while they were growing up: They're less likely to hold a door open for a stranger, shake your hand upon meeting, or refer to you as Mr. or Ms. so-and-so. It's not that Millennials are uncivil or rude; they just didn't learn the so-called rules of propriety because they weren't necessary in the society they grew up in. When they go to work, they may need basic training in etiquette and unwritten rules — a "Manners at Work Boot Camp," if you will. Rather than feeding a fire of frustration, prepare to train them on some basics:

>> Phone call dos and don'ts

>> The proper way to write an email

>> Phrases or slang to avoid

>> When to send a thank-you card

>> Turn around/response times

>> Times to hug versus times to shake hands

>> Requests for time off

>> What to prioritize during the day

Accepting the habit of multitasking and its side effects

Growing up in an era of technology at their fingertips wired the next generation's brain differently than generations past — their ability to multitask is unlike any of their predecessors.

We know that the act of multitasking is neurologically impossible, but switch tasking is not. When we say "multitasking," we're referring to the speed at which the younger generations are able to switch between devices and tasks at lightning speed.

Millennials are on a mission to work hard to accomplish the day's tasks in due time but will pause to stretch their mind with a reading break, their body with a quick basketball game, or their social world with a ten-minute skim through the latest on Instagram and/or Snapchat. These mind and body breaks could make you draw conclusions about their unprofessionalism, but keep in mind that what may look like unprofessionalism to one generation is just another using their brain as it's wired.

Consider the following habits, side effects, and likely truths you may encounter, along with some handy coaching cues.

The habit: Taking BYOD (bring your own device) too literally at meetings — phones and computers up and on.

The side effect: As Millennials (and they're not the only generation) check their phone or computer during a meeting, their colleagues and leaders feel frustrated. The Millennial appears distracted by personal or professional matters and disinterested in the conversation.

The likely truth: Yes, it's true that seeing the latest Snapchat story update is absolutely not important, but there is a laundry list of reasons why they may be checking their phone. If it's a text update, recall that Millennials' phone etiquette relies on fast responses because a delayed text response is rude, and that text may be from a fellow co-worker. Maybe they're checking for an email that hasn't yet come from a client or reading through documents to be extra prepared for the meeting.

The moment to coach: Checking a phone or computer in a meeting *is* distracting to the person speaking — if you say that it isn't, you're well accustomed to the habit by now. If necessary, make it a tech-free meeting or kindly ask them to close the computer and turn off the phone before every meeting.

The habit: Scrolling through social media while working.

The side effect: A surrounding colleague and/or manager assumes that the habitual Millennial is using company dollars to work on his personal life.

The likely truth: What may look like distractions to one person can be the exact activity needed to stay focused for others. When Millennials were teens, Friendster, MySpace, YouTube, Facebook, and Twitter came out in rapid succession. Checking them became a daily activity and pastime from a young age. Rather than view their occasional checking of Facebook as a misuse of company time, consider it an occasional, much-needed mental break.

The moment to coach: The best way to manage it is to establish trust. Say something like, "At company XYZ, we trust you. We trust that you aren't updating a Facebook page all day but know that you might check it occasionally, but not at the cost of your work or your team."

REMEMBER

There is a high probability that Millennials checking their social media are doing it for business purposes. They're scanning the company Facebook page or scoping out what the competition is saying on Twitter. Try to assume first that they're on social media for business reasons and second for personal ones.

The habit: Wearing headphones all day.

The side effect: Putting off an air of "I don't want human contact or conversation at work" and making other generations feel disrespectfully tuned out.

The likely truth: While this could be seen as disinterest in human contact at work, it may be the most productive way to get things done. Via tech like Zunes, MP3s, Discmans, and iPods, Millennials have carried music around in their pockets since adolescence. While they survived CHEM 401 classes in college thanks to Pandora's study playlists, today they're tuning into Spotify's focus playlists to get their work done. Their headphones are a sign that they're getting down to business.

The moment to coach: It may be necessary to adopt a headphone policy: Headphones on signifies a "please don't interrupt my work" work mode. However, if it's urgent, send an instant message or email to have a necessary conversation.

Understanding (and accepting) why Millennials won't pick up the phone

Millennials are notorious for their fear of phone calls and refusal to check their voicemail. While it may be easy to make fun of this perceived lack of communication skill, they're already in on the joke. Many are aware of their awkward demeanor on a phone call and longingly look at the ease with which their Gen X and Boomer colleagues pick up the phone and converse. Join in on the fun and acknowledge all the reasons Millennials aren't naturally skilled at picking up the phone:

> "[Millennials] are easy with chat and email, because they are technical and digital communicators; it's nice to have a digital message trail. Phone is probably the hardest [way to communicate]." —*Kelly O., Manager*

>> **Instant Messenger:** Millennials chatted with their friends after school on AOL and MSN Messenger (if you want to have a bit o' fun, ask your Millennial colleagues what their screen names were).

>> **Online dating:** Blind dates are essentially a fable for today's singles, and meeting someone in a bar or at church — once common ways of meeting partners — is now an adorable meet-cute story among Millennial friends. If meeting a partner — arguably one of the most primal things humans do — entails online conversation prior to meeting, then you can imagine that building rapport quickly in person doesn't come naturally.

>> **Small-talk shield:** Millennials grew up protected — the world was scary, and to stay safe, they were warned not to speak to anyone they didn't know. It has led to Millennials being a little weak on small-talk skills. For a fun social experiment, watch two strangers in their seventies meet versus two strangers in their twenties. The pair in their seventies pair will likely find some commonplace conversation and make nice, while the Millennials will introduce themselves, have a quick convo, and then resort to their phones. One way is not better than another, but they certainly are different.

Some Millennials prefer the phone — they find texting tedious and emailing slow. Older Millennials didn't even get their first cellphone until after graduating from college. Young Millennials and their successors prefer FaceTime to texting and phone calls. Don't stereotype too easily — one Millennial is not necessarily like another.

Just as you wouldn't make fun of a 70-year-old CEO who doesn't know how to use Snapchat, so too should you not make fun of a 28-year-old Millennial who gets anxiety every time she answers the phone. The worlds they grew up in were different, and they each have their own communication strengths and weaknesses.

> "[Millennials'] natural tendency is to do most things electronically versus sitting down and talking, especially over the phone. I wouldn't say it's difficult, it's just their tendency to start with texting, emailing, or IMing." —*Julie A., Manager*

Figuring out who needs to adjust

In nearly every situation, asking one generation to change everything for another doesn't work — adjustment needs to happen in every generation. Knowing who needs to adjust and when to do so can be tricky, but you can use Table 10-2 as a starting place.

TABLE 10-2 **Common Formality Issues and Adjustment Recommendations**

Issue	When the Manager Needs to Adjust	When the Millennial Needs to Adjust
Work ethic	The 8–5 schedule is producing results but not happy employees. Creative ways to find efficiency are possible.	The 8–5 schedule is necessary for clients and colleagues because being close to the phone/computer/client/patient is the only way to achieve results.
Dress etiquette	Your dress code feels antiquated or others in the industry are adapting their dress code. Or when blue jeans Fridays aren't even motivating anymore. Or when you ask your staff what they prefer and the majority responds that they want casual attire.	Clients expect a certain type of dress from you in order to do their business. Senior leaders have expectations, and moving up and around the organization demands their approval. Certain events require special dress.
Flexible hours	Focusing on results rather than the rules will usually produce superior work.	Their work is suffering in a results-oriented environment, and they need to just put in the hours as asked of them.
Communication etiquette	When communication isn't up to your standard but work is still getting done as asked, expectations may need to shift.	If behaviors consistently read as rude, inappropriate, or apathetic.

3

Accommodating Individual Differences Among the Millennial Masses

IN THIS PART . . .

Find out about all the Millennials that no one else talks about.

Get a gauge of who Millennials are around the globe and understand how to approach managing them in your respective region.

Get a peek into Millennial personas and segments — the hipsters, the martyrs, and more.

Explore how life stage impacts Millennials at different stages.

Discover how critical generational cuspers are to the generational conversation.

Understand how white-collar Millennials differ from blue-collar Millennials.

See how Millennials with science and art majors are different at work.

Chapter **11**

Managing Millennials 'Round the World

There's a stat in the working world that has been tossed around with abandon, and there's no doubt as to why — the stakes are high. What is that stat? By the year 2025, Millennials will comprise 75 percent of the labor market (Deloitte). Yes, *75 percent.* Some may think it a jaw-dropping number because it means only a quarter of the workforce will then be composed of generations other than Millennials. We understand these jaw-droppers. As the fraction of Millennials in the working world swells globally, there should be no doubt about the pressing need to understand not only Millennials in the United States, but also the intricacies of the global Millennial population. As organizations continue to expand their influence to global markets, a U.S.-centric approach will simply no longer suffice. Maybe you are one of those organizations.

In this chapter, we explore generational theory through a global lens. We give you insight into the Millennial traits and trends that remain constant around the globe, as well as some key differences in major regions. We'd be kidding ourselves (and fooling you) if we said we could try to describe all global Millennials in one chapter, so instead, we explore Millennial traits by region and leave you with tools to help apply generational theory on a more micro, country-specific level. In many cases, it's about knowing what not to do, how to avoid making assumptions, and how to ask the right questions that will elicit illustrative information about how your Millennials want to be managed, regardless of where they hail from.

We'll come clean with you. We are generational experts, not culture experts, and when you're considering cultures around the world, trying to understand the intricacies of different cultures on every continent is setting a pretty high bar. As this chapter is meant to serve as a brief introduction to global generations, we fully acknowledge a margin of error, so we ask that you, as our reader, do the same.

Viewing Generational Theory through a Global Lens

When you consider applying generational theory on a global scale, the natural question is . . . how? If the core of generational theory, as covered extensively in Chapter 2, relies on how events and conditions during formative years shape a generation, then surely each country will have its own unique set of influential events, be they big political, economic, social, or cultural ones. Naturally, it must follow that each country will have its own unique set of generations. To some degree, this rings true. But to break down each country's generations would be lunacy, and minute cultural nuances would run amuck. Thankfully, larger patterns of generational traits have been found by region:

>> North America (United States and Canada)

>> Latin America (Central and South America)

>> Western Europe

>> Central and Eastern Europe

>> Middle East

>> Africa

>> Asia-Pacific

As we mention previously, regions and countries have unique qualifiers that differentiate them from the rest of the world's generations. But Millennials in particular, who have had access to the Internet and shared cultural milestones via their computer screens, share quite a few traits and values (we discuss this topic in more detail in the next section).

Keeping these regions in mind, we start by answering a simple question: Are Millennials everywhere known by the same (or a similar) moniker? Turns out, the answer is yes and no. In much of the Western world, "Millennials" tends to be first name of choice, and in all areas that it isn't, "Generation Y" wins. There is a degree of variance when you look into Asia and South America. In China, they refer to Millennials more commonly as Post-'80s and Post-'90s. If you really want to find out what generations are called around the world, because you're just that interested, take a look at Table 11-1 for a small sample of not just what Millennials are called, but what all generations alive today are named across the globe.

We chose to show you these countries because of the role their Millennials play in the global economy, but there are *so* many more populations who have a large impact as well. All we're saying is that we know this is a small sample. That important preamble of perspective in place, read on.

TABLE 11-1   ## Generational Monikers Around the Globe

United States	India	China	Russia	Brazil	United Kingdom
Traditionalists	Freedom Fighters	Post-'30s/ Post-'40s	Silent Generation	Traditionalists	Silent Generation
Baby Boomers	Free Generation	Post-'50s/ Post-'60s	Sputnik Generation	Baby Boomers	Baby Boomers
Generation Xers	Generation X/ Generation E	Post-'60s/ Post-'70s	Gen X/The Last Soviet Generation	Generation Xers	Thatcher's Children
Millennials/ Generation Y	Generation Y	Post-'80s/ Post-'90s/ Little Emperors	Generation Y/ Generation Pu	Millennials/ Generation Y	Millennials/ Generation Y

TIP

We feel the need to note that some of these names are more common in the media vernacular than the social vernacular. If you're ever talking to Millennials in a country outside of the United States, we suggest addressing them as Generation Y.

Aside from each generation's global moniker, another important piece to understanding the global generational pie is population sizes. If you think the sheer number of Millennials in the states is overwhelming, exploring the global Millennial numbers may come as a bit of a shock.

Here are some patterns to note: In China, Millennials are a smaller population because of the one-child policy. In India, the Millennial population is booming. In Europe and Japan, the population of Millennials is drastically smaller than that of other generations. It's tough not to throw out more numbers when they can paint a picture so well, so put on your math-lete hat and puzzle through these generational stats from around the globe:

>> Globally, Millennials are three times more likely to be unemployed than older working-age people. (*Global Employment Trends for Youth,* 2013)

>> Millennials are the European Union's minority population. (Pew Research Center, 2015)

>> By 2020, half of India's population will be younger than 25 years old. (Society for Human Resource Management, 2009)

>> More than 26 percent of Japan's population is 65 or older. (Statistics Bureau, Japan)

After looking at all these differing population trends, you may be wondering how difficult it is to draw conclusions from so many variances. Lucky for you (and for us), experts have found connections among many of the variances in the Millennial population. Isn't it wonderful that humans out there dedicate themselves to demographic and sociological research?

REMEMBER

Generational differences is one lens of diversity. Around the globe, many other diversity lenses impact the workforce and are talked about more often, from gender diversity to racial diversity to psychological diversity.

Implications of globalization, the Internet, and technology

Globalization has peeled open the world in a very real way. In recent history, major game-changers have arrived on the scene, melting away the barriers that kept populations isolated from both a physical standpoint and a communication standpoint. The Internet has opened the world to unprecedented access to information; affordable intercontinental travel has made globe-trotting and job-trotting an achievable dream; and as physical and virtual restraints have become things of the past, companies are increasingly expanding into diverse markets the world over. While generations before witnessed the expansion to a global economy and know what it means to *not* have access and easy travel, Millennials have never known a world without it. Millennials, who have always been early adapters, have experienced an increasingly small and diverse world through technological innovation:

>> **Information technology — shared cultural experiences:** Millennials from almost every country have grown up comfortable with phones in their pockets. They've been able to watch firsthand, first from a computer and then

from their smartphones, as news happened worldwide, whether that be 9/11, the Arab Spring, the 7/7 London Bombings, or the tsunami in Japan. Shared exposure to, and experience of, these events and conditions have brought Millennials around the world much closer to one another than generations past. In a sense, they have actually come of age together.

» **Communication technology — expanded social circles:** As technology improved, so did Millennials' social networks and communication tools. With email, text, Facebook, Twitter, Skype, WhatsApp, and FaceTime, communicating with Millennials on the other side of the planet can happen with the touch of a button. Immersed in diverse worldviews and opinions, Millennials are not only more exposed to other cultures, they've made co-workers and friends with people from other countries. In many ways, it's part of the reason that so many Millennials want to work abroad at some point in their career. A global survey conducted by J Walter Thompson Intelligence even found young people reporting that 25 percent of their friends are a plane ride away. It sounds so posh, but it's like modern day pen pals opting for electronic mail versus good ol' pen and paper.

» **Transport technology — fulfilling cultural curiosity:** Despite 9/11 and the ensuing panic around flying (at least in the United States), Millennials have made travel an essential part of their lives. From study abroad to backpacking trips to work-abroad programs, Millennials have taken advantage of the state of transport to see the world and experience new cultures. Simple things like lessening study restrictions and the adoption of the euro have made this especially easier in some parts of the world. Today, the Millennial generation seeks jobs and careers in other countries partly out of necessity and partly out of baseline want.

"I think the Internet makes it easy for us to see the whole world, get news efficiently, make friends overseas; it's totally changed our life model."
—*Millennial, from China*

With more access has come a higher cultural awareness and more common ground across Millennials, which has led to the expectation of open and diverse work-places in the sense of generations and culture. Especially with younger Millennials and going into the next generation, this inclusion is an expectation in many parts of the world, whereas other generations saw a time when it wasn't.

There is no doubt that technology has evolved — and continues to evolve — at a blinding pace. Today, iPhones are rather common, but when they first debuted in 2007, they were considered a luxury item. Of course, there are places around the world where technology is still considered a luxury and isn't easily accessible, if at all. Even though the United Nations sadly reported in 2012 that more people on earth have access to cellphones than toilets, that doesn't mean more technology equates to more opportunity. Millennials in these locales may share fewer traits with Millennials with tech access. The same applies for places with restricted Internet or media, such as China. With government regulations in play, Chinese Millennials have access to a completely different online world, including different social media networks.

A universal event and condition that shaped Millennials outside of technology was the global recession. Certain parts of the world, especially countries like Greece, Spain, and Italy, are still recovering where Millennial unemployment remains so high that they either emigrate for work opportunities or have decided that a life centered on balance is more important than aspirations for professional success.

Noting some regional differences

Millennials around the world have many similarities, but there is no doubt that they're also incredibly heterogeneous, and it would be silly to pretend otherwise. Each region of the United States has its own set of events and conditions that uniquely shape a segment of its generations. So, naturally, broadening the scope to the entire world means that each continent, each region, each country has its own set of events and conditions that separate them from the standard definition of a generation. (Or, for the sake of this book, the standard definition of a Millennial.)

Different world events have had different impacts on Millennials: For example, when we interview Japanese Millennials, they mention the March 2011 earthquake, tsunami, and ensuing nuclear scare as the most relevant events in their lives. Their perspectives on work are therefore shaped differently because of their culture and their formative events and conditions. In our interviews with managers of Japanese Millennial teams, we hear quite often that they can behave drastically different in the workplace from Millennials in the United States, the United Kingdom, Russia, and Brazil. For example, these managers tell us that Japanese Millennials perceive and respond to authority more than their peers in other countries. Western Millennials generally view authority figures as equals: They feel comfortable pushing back, questioning their superiors, and driving change. Japanese Millennials, on the other hand, are extremely respectful of authority figures. They rarely push back and are quick to handle the task at hand as directed. There also are far fewer of them in their country, but that can get us on a tangential (however incredibly fascinating) sect of information.

Since the early 2000s, companies and research houses — including our own — have focused on Millennials in BRIC/BRICS (Brazil, Russia, India, China/South Africa) countries because of their respective country's potential for economic growth. As different factors, including the largely influential impacts of a global recession, have changed that trajectory, we still focus attention on those regions. However, we are aware that they are not alone and that dedication to Millennials in other regions and countries is equally as important. Other samplings of how

both BRICS and non–BRICS events and conditions have impacted Millennial identities in different regions/countries around the world include the following:

» **German Millennials:** The fall of the Berlin wall significantly impacted the
young people there. German Millennials overwhelmingly approve of the
direction their country is going, and with the largest economy in Europe, they
place financial performance as the greatest indicator of success. Germany is
an interesting case study, as there is still a large disparity in employment and
income between East and West, and the majority of Germany's young
population resides in West Germany. When you examine outliers in what
motivates Millennials and what they want from leaders, Eastern Germany still
answers in line with Eastern Europe versus Western Europe.

» **Chinese Millennials:** China's one-child policy, put in place in 1980, created an
environment of high expectations for only-child Millennials. They also received a
lot of attention, both good and bad. Important to note for this generation is how
the emergence of technology differently affected Post-'80s from Post-'90s
Millennials in China, because one group had the optimism of a booming economy
paired with the simplicity of not everyone having a cellphone. Post-'90s, on the
other hand, were tethered to technology from the earliest of their formative years
and have only seen one side of the economic boom — the prosperous one.

» **Russian Millennials:** Referred to as Generation Pu, Russian Millennials were the
first generation to grow up in the post-Soviet world. Because Russia is no longer
seen as the power it once was, many Russian Millennials have a negative outlook
on Russia's economy, but Millennials don't know a world when they were in that
position of power. Their formative years have been dominated by Putin's position
in government that has valued the Russian individual, so this generation can in
turn be a bit more risk averse than other generations.

» **Indian Millennials:** Unlike their generational predecessors, Indian Millennials
only know a time when their economy was rapidly increasing due to the
economic liberalization in 1991. As a result, Indian Millennials are fiercely
ambitious and competitive, seeking value in more extrinsic factors versus
intrinsic ones that past generations so valued. At work, this manifests in a
generation seeking rapid career progression. Additionally, a large portion of
those who want to succeed are women but their participation in the workplace is declining, thus making their office demographics starkly different than
other countries.

» **Brazilian Millennials:** These South American Millennials grew up in a time
when Brazil was under the lead of the first democratically elected president
since 1960 and experiencing a period of economic stabilization and growth.
This gave them a well-founded optimism growing up, but it's also worth
acknowledging that their economy hasn't remained stable and is shrinking
again, which will have a large impact on the youngest Millennials and the next
generation.

Looking at Global Millennials' Uniting Trends and Key Differentiators

There are two sides to understanding Millennials from a global perspective. One is to have a firm grasp of the similarities between Millennials as they show up across the globe. The other is to use that base of similarities to then explore and understand the differentiators that truly distinguish one region's Millennials from another's.

Overall, we've found many similarities between Millennials all over the world in terms of ideals, goals, and perceptions. For example, globally, Millennials describe themselves as tolerant, authentic, curious about the world, positive, and flexible. We are noticing substantial differences, however, around behaviors in the workplace, acceptance of hierarchy, and innovative capabilities.

Similarities in Millennials across the globe

Here are some of the main similarities among Millennials around the world:

>> **Technology is key** to advancing in the world. Millennials expect to have access to the latest and greatest tools in order to accomplish their jobs in the most efficient and effective manner. They've also all had access to social media and its ensuing social norms, even if the platforms used vary throughout the globe. Social is as social does, one might say.

>> **They're looking to be leaders**, but for different reasons. Millennials around the globe are all young professionals; that is, they're seeking advancement in their careers and will leave an organization if there aren't opportunities to advance. However, in a report by Universum, it is clear that in Eastern Europe, Millennials want to enter managerial roles because they offer higher earnings. In the Middle East, the appeal is in the power to make decisions. In North America, it's a close race between higher earnings and more opportunities to influence the company.

From their own leaders, they also want different things. Western European, North American, and African Millennials want someone who will empower them. (We like to think of this as the coach versus manager mentality.) Asia-Pacific and Middle Eastern Millennials want someone who is a technical expert in their field. (We like to think of this manager as Mr. Miyagi from *The Karate Kid*.) Latin American Millennials want someone who is a good role model. (We also like to think of this person as Mr. Miyagi.)

>> **They want work-life balance,** with emphasis on enough leisure time for their personal lives. There is a mentality across the globe that work is not worth giving up your personal life. Millennials are looking to have access to flexible work policies so they can better balance work and life. Fun fact: When

asked if they would give up a well-paid job with prestige for better work-life balance, Millennials in every country outside of Eastern Europe said yes. Needless to say, balance is important.

» **The loyalty challenge is universal.** Across the board, Millennials are less likely to stay with one organization for more than five years, let alone for the rest of their professional lives. People in almost every region expect to retire around the age of 60 or earlier, partially because there are retirement laws in some countries. More exposure to more opportunity naturally leads to seeking and taking more of those opportunities.

» **They see business as a way to have a positive impact on society.** Business is not just a means to an end, or a way to pay your bills, but a way to make an impact on the world. Business ethics and social consciousness are top of mind for Millennials worldwide. They are strongly connected to a sense of purpose, and when they feel their values align with their organization's, they are more likely to stay.

» **The economy is top of mind,** whether positive or negative. Youth unemployment is still relatively high worldwide, and the Great Recession, while a North American event, affected Millennials across the globe. On the other hand, Millennials worldwide believe they have it better than their parents and hold an optimistic outlook on the economy. However, there is a difference between emerging markets where they are nearly twice as optimistic their lives will be better off than their parents than Millennials in mature markets.

» **They want a team-based culture.** Teamwork, collaboration, a sense of community . . . these are not pluses in the workplace, but an expectation for international Millennials. Workplaces with cohesive, team-oriented cultures are attractive to Millennials.

"[I prefer working] collaboratively, because all the people that work at the company make the company. Everyone puts in their point of view . . . and this way, the final result is normally much better than when you work independently." —*Marcos E., Millennial from Brazil*

As you see in this section, Millennials have similar traits, but when it comes to why or how, the differences that lay beneath the similarities may tell you more about a particular region.

Distinguishing Millennial features by region

Though there are similarities that unite Millennials around the globe more than any generation in the past, it should come as no surprise that depending on where you grew up, there are distinguishing features. Here are some of the more salient Millennial features/trends broken down per region of Millennial. We've highlighted the most significant tidbits for you in an attempt to avoid too much repetition or crossover:

>> **North American Millennials**

- Consider work-life balance a top priority

- Seek leadership positions so they can influence organizations

- Desire managers who empower them

- Place a high value on flexible work arrangements

- Strongly value team-based environments

>> **Central and South American Millennials**

- Believe that job titles matter

- Feel business should contribute more to society

- Think that individuals (not government) have the biggest ability to influence society

- Appreciate challenging work because it means learning new things

- Are enthusiastic about leadership opportunities

- Worry about not realizing their career goals

>> **Middle Eastern Millennials**

- Care about innovation

- Agree that it's better to have no job than a job you hate

- Worry about getting stuck in their careers

- Fear that they won't find a job that matches their personal passion

>> **Western European Millennials**

- Care about innovation

- Agree that it's better to have no job than a job you hate

- Strongly value workplace relationships

- Feel that getting stuck in their careers would be abysmal

>> **Central/Eastern European Millennials**

- Care about innovation

- Agree that it's better to have no job than a job you hate

- Seek leadership positions as a way to increase future earnings

- Want managers who offer technical expertise

- Place value on securing high-paying jobs

>> **African Millennials**

- Seek leadership positions as a way to provide mentorship to others and increase opportunities

- Place a high value on work as a way to better society

>> **Asian-Pacific Millennials**

- Show more deference to the traditional hierarchical workplace model

- *Note:* Country to country, there are obvious differences in traits for each of these regions. Per a recent Universum study, one of the regions that shows the most stark differences is Asia-Pacific. Chinese Millennials, Japanese Millennials, and Indian Millennials all vary pretty significantly in their traits and workplace expectations. It's much too simplistic to assume their traits as a whole region. Yes, we just want to make this even more complicated for you.

TIP

We've got a bit of a catch-22 here. When talking about Millennials from a particular region or Millennials as a global whole, don't underwrite the cultural significance of where they're from and how they grew up. At the same time, don't rely solely on culture or region to predict Millennials' traits or box them in. Avoid pinning Millennial behaviors and traits on culture or generations alone. As hard as it may be, it's crucial to think about both aspects simultaneously. Sometimes, as a fast and easy solution, people may try to lump all Millennials from one region together. But that can be wrong. Just as we cover in other places of this book, any step you can take to avoid stereotyping is the best possible strategy for you and everyone else.

Tapping into the Power of Generational Theory Around the Globe

You may still be thinking to yourself: Okay, this information is useful, if a bit too — pardon the pun — *global* to be applied specifically. If you're a manager who is working specifically with Colombian Millennials, you may want to hone in on who they are, what makes them tick, and how you can be the best manager to that specific demographic.

Becoming a generational expert

How do I become a better manager to my specific demographic? Become a mini generational expert yourself! A good place to start, and forgive us for stating the obvious, is an Internet search of Millennials in your region or country. Google is such a wonderful tool (no, this is not product placement). From there, you may be tipped off to some of the relevant influencers and key trends. That's a good place to start, but then, much more importantly, come the interactions with Millennials themselves. As you're building up your docket of how to understand the Millennials you're managing, we recommend the following steps:

1. **Google them.**

   Go down a wormhole of generational surveys, reports, and articles about Millennials in your region or in the region that you manage.

2. **Interview other managers about Millennials.**

   Chances are the more managers you interview (or have casual lunch with wherein questions about Millennials are posed), the more likely you will be to form conclusions about Millennials in your region.

3. **Interview your Millennials.**

   Get a gauge of how different they are from what you've read. In a sense, the Google search can serve as your control and everything else can serve as your comparison to test a hypothesis. But not in a creepy, lab experiment kind of way. It doesn't need to be formal. Just grab a cup of coffee with some Millennials on your team or make it a habit to ask some questions of them at the beginning or end of your meetings. The tidbits you learn directly from them add up, and soon you'll notice trends that will help you manage.

If you've hit the panic button for drafting interview questions for Millennials, we've got your back. See the following section if you don't believe us.

Honing the fine art of asking questions

Whether you're a human resources professional seeking to develop the best practices for working with Millennials across various markets or a manager working with remote employees across the globe, the best way to tap into generational theory to better understand Millennials is through asking them questions. You can start with the overarching Millennial trends seen as constant the world over, and then see where the specific region you're working with may start to have Millennials with divergent viewpoints.

TIP

Try to take notes of the types of answers you receive from Millennials to these questions. If you'd rather not write them down in the moment, go back and jot them down later. This way, as patterns start to emerge, you'll be able to mark the trend. And beware the focus-group-of-one trap. Just because one person has completely variant views, that doesn't mean he is representative of all Millennials. Imagine this as your exploration into the world of generational research. We may be biased, but we think it's super fun and fascinating.

Here's a sampling of the types of questions you may ask. Some may work for you; others may not. The key is to be an attentive listener and keep tuned in for patterns. And don't forget that to get the best answers, start with softball questions and lead into hardball ones. Best of all, Millennials, who seek to have their voices heard, will appreciate you taking the time to learn a bit more about them. We like to call this a win-win situation.

>> **Checking in on the overarching Millennial trends:**

- Would you describe yourself as collaborative? Why or why not?

- What motivates you?

- How do you prefer to receive feedback?

- How often do you like to receive feedback?

- What are some stereotypes about your generation?

- What's something you wish your manager knew about how you like to work?

- Describe your ideal working relationship with a manager.

- What does hard work look like to you?

- Describe what work-life balance means to you.

- Do you prefer a hierarchical working structure, or are you more keen on a flatter model? Why?

>> **Examining Millennial patterns specific to country/region:**

- How was growing up in (country/region) different for you than it was for your parents?

- How has the political and social climate changed over the years?

- What were the big events and conditions you experienced growing up in (country/region)? Tech? Political? Social? Pop culture?

- Do you associate more with being a member of (country/region), or more with being a global citizen?

- Are you connected with Millennials from other regions and countries? How do you stay connected?

- How do you feel growing up in (country/region) was different or distinctive from other parts of the world?

- How do you feel your culture and upbringing shaped the way you approach work today?

- What differences do you notice between yourself and your contemporaries from other countries/regions?

- Are there noticeable differences in how you approach work?

TIP

When possible, avoid asking "yes" or "no" questions. They prevent a thorough and creative answer that will give you more insight into who that Millennial is that you're interviewing. Also, if you're asking country/region-specific questions about events and conditions, try to start with easier questions, like who their favorite musician was growing up.

Chapter **12**

Adapting Your Management Style to Different Millennial Personas

You won't be shocked when we tell you that Millennials aren't 100 percent homogenous. No generation is! Though Millennials share many traits, values, and preferences, there are obviously differences, big and small, within their cohort.

Imagine this: You're running a focus group made up of Millennials. Ten of them are gathered to talk about what they like to eat on vacation, and much to your surprise, they couldn't be more different from one other. After an hour, you've discovered that not only do they have different food preferences (my gosh, they *don't* all like kale, sushi, and craft beer?), but they also prefer different environments and brands. After running ten of these focus groups, you start noticing patterns in their attitudes and preferences. There does seem to be a "type" who opts for the the healthy organic foods and specialty beers. Others have more classic preferences and scout out the local McDonalds or Subway when on vacation. Then there's the kind of Millennial who seems to dislike the whole premise of the focus group, rejecting the term "Millennial" entirely. What you've discovered is Millennial personas.

A persona is a character description that represents a group of people who have similar tastes, goals, and general behaviors. In the following chapter, we're going to take you through some of the more common Millennial personas that show up in the workplace. We'll explore the challenges that arise from working with different Millennial personas and then give you some solutions for effectively managing those challenges. It's an even more granular approach to the generations topic that will take you to the next level of generational awareness.

REMEMBER

It would be impossible to fit all Millennial personas into one chapter, so naturally we'll be leaving some of them out. We've focused on the most common Millennial personas you're likely to encounter, namely the Needy Millennial, the Hipster Millennial, the Hidden Millennial, the "I'm-Not-a-Millennial" Millennial, and the Millennial Martyr.

Coping with the Needy Millennial

Perhaps you've had the experience of managing Millennials who are so dedicated to doing something flawlessly that it appears they can't do anything by themselves. They ask numerous questions and prefer to be shown every single step in the process before they attempt it. While to some this may feel like hand-holding and, dare we say, needy, the Millennials in question are simply attempting to avoid making a mistake. This Needy Millennial persona can be more properly understood if we explore it bit by bit.

A portrait of a Needy Millennial

Let's pretend that you manage an ambitious Millennial named Gunther. In his initial interviews, you valued how prepared he was, from his knowledge of the company, to his new ideas for the role, to the list of questions he came prepared with. Right away, you knew that Gunther would be a dedicated, hard worker.

Fast-forward a couple months, and you're starting to grow agitated every time Gunther comes near your desk to ask a question — he asks a *lot* of questions. Just last week, you assigned him a project and he checked in not one, not three, but *six* times to pose a query or ask you to review his work. You've started to think that he can't complete an assignment on his own, and you hear murmurs that others agree. When Gunther asks, "Did you get my email?" his colleague Whitney responds through clenched teeth, "Yes, I got it, but haven't yet had time to respond." If you have one more 10-minute meeting that turns into 20 minutes because Gunther needs step-by-step instruction on the correct way to do something, you may just start pinching yourself to control your anger. You want to remain a great manager and groom Gunther to be all that he can be, but your patience is wearing thin and he's burning through hours of your own productivity.

Breakdown of the Needy Millennial

Whew. Gunther sounds a wee bit exhausting to manage. His Needy Millennial persona showcases that he

>> Asks a lot of questions, all the time

>> Wants constant feedback

>> Checks in too often on tasks that don't require it

>> Impatiently pesters others who are working on their own schedule or list of priorities

>> Wants to know the ins and outs of all the information he receives

>> Needs validation of his work and decision-making before sending it along

What makes a Needy Millennial tough to manage

Though these Millennials may be needy, they're also anxious to do right by their team and the company. While you might already see that, that won't stop you from feeling annoyed when you have to provide hand-holding on every single task and project. Your time slips by when you dedicate hours to grooming a Needy Millennial instead of completing items on your own to-do list. Instead of feeling like a manager, you begin to feel like the thing that you loathe — a micromanager.

Why Needy Millennials can be great

While it's so easy to get frustrated with a Millennial who pesters, questions, and checks in on a regular basis, instead try to think more along these lines:

>> Wow, this is one of the of the most engaged employees I've ever managed.

>> Well, at least I never need to wonder where he's at.

>> He probably won't keep any secrets or go rogue!

Surviving the Needy Millennial

While your predicament with a Needy Millennial may seem dire, we can sympathize. And in so sympathizing, we offer the following (don't worry, we don't think you're needy):

>> **Clearly communicate boundaries.** Set expectations early on with each project or scenario. Articulate when you want to check in and for how long. Explain when you *are* okay with being approached with questions and when you're *not*.

>> **Stop the behavior as soon as you see it.** The earlier you can call out actions and behaviors that appear needy, the better. Don't let them get used to certain behaviors, because if you address them later on, they'll be confused and even a bit perturbed. These Millennials may not even know that they're coming across as needy.

>> **Acknowledge that sometimes, you will need to hold their hand.** Unlike Generation Xers, Millennials sometimes need a bit of micromanaging. Not in a breathing-down-your-neck, watching-for-everything kind of way, but in a will-give-specific-instruction-at-all-times kind of way. To a Millennial, giving specific instruction or answering a laundry list of questions isn't micromanaging, it's ensuring that everything is running smoothly.

"[Some Millennials may be] a little more needy; they're inexperienced and I do feel like they don't tend to take things a step further proactively. If you give direction, they take it amazingly and do what you told them to but there is a lack of [follow-through]." — *Greta H., Millennial and manager*

>> **Praise them when they do something solo.** Some behavioral psychologist out there is smiling. It's not just about correcting the bad behavior but also about reinforcing the good. When a Needy Millennial does manage to do something on her own, recognize it. We find that this specific type of Millennial tends to be super sensitive to positive praise, which can be a powerful tool.

>> **Create a safe space for failure (within reason).** Failure, or doing something wrong, is a Needy Millennial's kryptonite. On low-risk projects, give them free reign, and if they fail or mess something up, let them know it's not the end of the world, but coach them on how they can improve next time around. Once they've conquered their fear, they'll feel more confident tackling the next project without constant supervision.

>> **Delegate their needs.** You are not the only resource for a needy Millennial, so delegate their coaching, championing, and instructing to other members of your team. Chances are the more exposure to people in the organization, the better for you *and* the Needy Millennial.

Hangin' in There with the Hipster Millennial

This Millennial persona is the one that other generations love to hate. It's who the media depicts in nearly all of its headlined articles, like "Why Millennials hate fabric softener" and "Top gifts this season: The best beard gadgets for your Millennial nephew" or "Thanks to Millennials, home-brewing is the new book club." While we can laugh at the lanky, bearded, and tattooed models used in every Millennial ad campaign, there's a reason those ads exist. They do actually appeal to a specific type of Millennial, and we wouldn't be surprised if as a manager, you've come across one or two of these Hipster Millennials during your career.

A portrait of a Hipster Millennial

While we don't know the Millennial population that you manage, we imagine that you might know someone like Delilah. When you hired her, you thought, "Wow, you look just like my daughter's friends who all live in the city and wax poetic about their love of local beers." She wears thick-rimmed glasses; has a vast collection of skinny jeans in shades of mustard, black, and maroon; and usually pairs those skinny jeans with a flannel button-down, a cropped sweatshirt, or an oversized sweater. She has a few visible tattoos, her favorite being an outline of her home state of Minnesota on her inner forearm. Her hair changes color and length more times in a year than yours has over a decade. You saw her Spotify playlist once (because she *always* wears headphones at work) and when you remarked that you didn't know a single artist, she suppressed a smirk, "I'm not surprised. They're all pretty up-and-coming to the scene." This makes you feel even cooler as you stroll toward your minivan at the end of the day.

Delilah is the epitome of work-life integration: She demands flexible hours for her art showing of papier mache antelopes or her band practice (she plays the banjo). She tried to host a taste-test of her home-brewed kombucha at lunch, and on more than one occasion she's attempted to convince people of the power of being a fruitarian. Delilah rebels against corporate staples like dress codes, strict schedules, and continuing to follow a process just because that's how it's always been done. While you appreciate her ideating mind and proclivity for disruption, you've grown wary of asking for her opinion because she usually assumes her ideas are best while quoting David Foster Wallace or Dave Eggers.

Breakdown of the Hipster Millennial

Wow, this Millennial is certainly uniquely challenging because, well, she is so unique. While Delilah appears to be a super hipster, she may have a lot in common with her hipster persona peers because she

>> Believes her ideas are the best and most innovative

>> Craves only unique ways of doing things at work

>> Opposes anything that reflects corporate professionalism

>> Has a tendency to dress down even when intending to dress up

>> Is a diligent worker, but demands a flexible schedule

>> Has visible tattoos

What makes a Hipster Millennial tough to manage

In brief, Hipster Millennials pride themselves on their unique qualities and their one-of-a-kind approach to all things in life. That is an inherent Millennial trait, just for the record, but it's exaggerated in the hipster mindset. This makes them a population of Millennials who want to brand themselves by their unique qualities when sometimes what they need to do is, simply put, get in line like everyone else. They also take work-life integration to a level unlike other Millennials because they so want to buck the traditional norms of work life.

Why Hipster Millennials can be great

We admit that we're biased in this department because the writers of this book have shades of the Hipster Millennial within us. If you manage a Hipster Millennial, think of her not as a cliché, and instead embrace the strengths she brings to your organization:

>> At least she's always honest about her opinions and willing to share them.

> "I appreciate that if [the Millennials I've worked with] are given a chance to contribute, [I] find that they are very in tune to the pulse of the organization and they can give you very valuable feedback." — *Jayson M., Manager*

>> She has such interesting, out-of-the-box ideas and approaches to the way she gets her work done.

>> She embraces integration as the new model of work-life balance; generations that follow will expect a similar set-up.

>> She does more than her job description, is always striving to improve, and never settles for good when she sees an opportunity to be great.

Handling the Hipster Millennial

Before grabbing your hair in a tight fist and readying yourself to pull, read through these tips to find whether there's any unique approach you haven't tried to reach the unicorn Millennials. In all seriousness, they usually have great ideas that just need to be fielded and vetted in the right way and in the appropriate environment.

>> **Coach them on how to present ideas.** As a segment, the Hipster Millennials pride themselves on sharing unique, out-there ideas — and that's not a bad thing! But their presentation could leave something to be desired (read: they share ideas with apparently little regard for why things are done a certain way). Coach them on how to present ideas in a way that everyone can hear without feeling disrespected, hurt, or offended in any way.

>> **Find authentic shared interests.** This group defines themselves by their interests — whether that's music, theater, dance (yes, they like the arts), food, beer, or something nostalgic. If you can find an authentic connection with them in that area, it will help build a manager-employee relationship in the personal sphere that can then extend to the professional sphere.

>> **Try to focus on results.** We know this tip is a tale as old as time, but it's especially important with this Millennial persona. They'll have unique ways of approaching the workday and getting things done. You might not agree with all of their methods, but if it's not disruptive to the rest of the team, don't step in just because it's not the way you would do it. If they're meeting their goals, let them choose their own path, even if it befuddles you.

>> **Embrace the weird.** Okay, stay with us on this one. Hipsters have their quirks, but that can also be a sign of creativity. We recommend embracing those quirks and inviting them to ideation sessions. You never know what they may come up with!

Finding a Way to Deal with the Hidden Millennial

In the exploration of Millennial personas, you'll likely come across a whole swath of research about Millennials who work from coffee shops, aren't married, live in the city, regularly use social media, stay in a company for only two to three years, and seek to change everything the moment they start their jobs. While this research can be helpful in studying Millennials, it disregards a whole group of Millennials waiting to be found and understood. They are everything the typical Millennial picture is not. They hope to stay in a job for at least a decade or two, are not tech-savvy (tech-comfortable at best), favor strict hierarchy in the workplace, and are already married with kids and living in the suburbs by the time they turn 23. How do you find this Hidden Millennial? The truth is they're not actually all that hidden. They're just not covered by the media, so you may be surprised to find they're Millennials and scratching your head about how to manage them.

A portrait of a Hidden Millennial

You've always liked Derek because he seems unique in his peer group. In the distribution center you manage, he gets along best with those who don't belong to his generation. He said in his interview that he's in it for the long haul, and from the way he works, that still seems true five years later! He proves his work ethic by his record of no late clock-ins and no early clock-outs — he's perfectly on time every single day. When you asked him if he could support a new position or a change in the near future, he seemed to get nervous and assured you that he is comfortable and happy with the way things are. He responds really well to clear direction but sometimes gets flustered when you advise him to come up with his own ideas or creatively problem-solve — it seems pretty obvious that he prefers a manager who leads with a hierarchical nature. In the past couple months, you tried to bond with him about your kid's experiences using social media only to find that Derek not only doesn't have a social media account, but has never used one.

Breakdown of the Hidden Millennial

While Derek possesses a lot of great qualities, he can be a tricky one to read. You know he's of the Hidden Millennial cohort because he

>> Thrives in an environment that typically struggles to recruit and retain Millennials

>> Aims to stay with a company for longer than the norm

>> Prefers an authoritative hand in management

>> Doesn't have a social media account (I mean, c'mon, even you have a Facebook account!)

What makes a Hidden Millennial tough to manage

The most difficult move to conquer in Hidden Millennial chess is the sheer unpredictable nature of their motives. Most other Millennials, the ones written about throughout this book as well as the ones written about in this chapter, are a bit easier to pin down and figure out because *so much* is written about them on a regular basis. The unseen challenge to managing this cohort is that while they may seem like a blessing because they don't embody the traits that you've come to define Millennials by, they despise being called out as a member of their cohort and have very different expectations at work. For example, while you've come to appreciate the innovative nature of Millennials and created programs just for them, you may find that everything that worked for every other Millennial doesn't work for the hidden ones. They could possibly be the most slippery Millennial persona of them all.

Why Hidden Millennials can be great

Who doesn't love a person who is complex, unique, and different from the trend? The days when being an outsider was a negative are behind us. Chances are that you, or fellow leaders and managers like you, have a soft spot for these Millennials who do everything differently because their hidden nature has a lot of benefits for you to think about:

>> They can be predictable and lower maintenance as they stick to a schedule and a prescribed set of to-dos more than other Millennials.

>> They may serve as a natural bridge-builder between Millennials and Traditionalists or those who've been working in one environment for a long time.

>> Special treatment could be the opposite of motivating to this group, and that may take some of the pressure off your shoulders.

Dealing with the Hidden Millennial

Just because few resources talk about this entire hidden cohort doesn't mean you have to hide in the dark with them. Make your Millennial management expertise obvious by stepping into the light and adopting some of these management strategies:

>> **Don't assume that all Hidden Millennials are alike.** In the example with Derek, we couldn't even capture the most exaggerated version of the Hidden Millennial because they come in so many forms. Some Hidden Millennials have a lot of traits, and others have few. Take it in stride and learn to manage them one by one.

>> **Don't assume that they're robotic.** A common misconception about Hidden Millennials is that their aversion to work-life integration means they don't want to build personal connections at work. In most scenarios, this is a false assumption, as most assumptions are. They're game to build the relationship but just prefer more structured interactions that don't take away from their workday.

>> **Apply traditional Millennial management methods in doses.** Just because they're hidden doesn't mean they lack *all* the Millennial traits and behaviors that you're used to. In most scenarios, they may show these traits in slightly different ways or to a smaller degree. With that in mind, apply the methods spoken about throughout this book in small doses and take note of what works and what doesn't.

TIP

Millennials who manage Hidden Millennials may have the most difficult time with them. Millennial managers may be used to building instant connections with employees near their own age and then suddenly find themselves struggling to manage this group. Or, perchance, they've become so confident in managing their own generation that when the approach backfires with Hidden Millennials, their entire style is called into question. If you're a Millennial manager reading this, try tweaking your style using some of the tips mentioned earlier. And don't let your experience with a Hidden Millennial completely derail your style that works with others.

Dealing with Denial in the "I'm-Not-a-Millennial" Millennial

This Millennial persona has become all too common. Their uniting thread? Because they're actually good employees, they don't think that they belong to the Millennial generation. They are the "I'm-Not-a-Millennial" Millennials. You can file them next to jumbo shrimp, paid volunteers, and other oxymorons. Their reasoning is this: Millennials embody all the stereotypes that others generations love to hate. In an effort to combat the idea that they're narcissistic, lazy, impatient, rude, and entitled, these "I'm-Not-a-Millennial" Millennials say either, "Oh, I'm *not* a Millennial, trust me." Or, "Ugh, I'm not *that* kind of Millennial; I hate labels." The funny thing is that they usually tend to embody many of the traits and values that positively define Millennials.

A portrait of the "I'm-Not-a-Millennial" Millennial

Trista has always been a good worker, but she has also always been the person who comes to mind when you read an article about Millennials or hear a presentation about them. One of her best qualities is her ability to connect with everyone at the office, and you've noticed how she leads by developing personal relationships with people. You've had to have more than one meeting with her about taking on too much as she constantly volunteers for projects but then struggles when she begins to lose the balance she seeks. When you share some information with her that you read in a very helpful chapter in this book (wink, yes that's some blatant self-promotion), she scoffs and says, "Um. I'm *not* a Millennial. I don't believe in that kind of stuff anyway. Isn't it just more about life stage?" Taken aback, you think about how not to say what you're thinking: "But, Trista, books like this and articles similar to this have helped me know how to manage you."

Breakdown of the "I'm-Not-a-Millennial" Millennial

Oh Trista, Trista, Trista. We'll be honest with you — this is by far the most common type of Millennial we come across and the most difficult because they reject generational theory (at first). Trista fits so perfectly with her segment because she

» Is incredibly hard-working but demands flexibility

» Has a knack for building close bonds with her co-workers without knowing that it's an inherently Millennial way of leading

» Believes she is unique — which is the most Millennial thing to think because the entire generation was raised by a sea of Boomers who told them, "You are so special and unlike any other person in this world"

» Doesn't believe she shares anything in common with the Millennial masses

» Thinks that what defines a Millennial is being a bad, entitled employee

What makes an "I'm-Not-a-Millennial" Millennial tough to manage

To put it simply, they turn a blind eye to the truth. They're unwilling to accept that they have some of the most powerful and beneficial Millennial traits and behaviors and are representing their generation to great advantage! By rejecting the topic of generations, they lose the generational perspective that could help them build stronger connections across generations and also better manage their manager, who likely belongs to a different generation. They see the topic of generations as the easy way out, a way to stereotype and put people into a box (a box that they don't see themselves belonging in). They could be toxic among their own generational peers because they look down on anyone who has the traits they've deemed to be Millennial-specific.

Why "I'm-Not-a-Millennial" Millennials can be great

While they may refuse to see what the mirror (or the HR file) says about their Millennial qualities, this segment has some excellent qualities. Instead of getting frustrated by their perceived lack of self-awareness, train your brain to know that

>> They are one of the best representations of the Millennial generation without realizing it.

>> They often embody the best qualities of Millennials (hard-working, relational, creative) and leave the less appealing ones behind (entitled, lazy, narcissistic).

>> They'll reflect someday on their past and acknowledge who they really are.

>> They can be won over to the topic once you show them it's not about pointing out flaws and weaknesses, but creating a better understanding of who we are at work and why.

Working with the denial of the "I'm-Not-a-Millennial" Millennial

While they can be challenging (especially as they might ruffle some of the other Millennial employees' feathers), it *is* possible to manage these Millennials in a way that works for both you and them. Here are some strategies to manage this Millennial persona, and maybe even win them over:

>> **Express your love for Millennials.** We don't know where you're at on a scale of "Don't make me work with Millennials, *please"* to "If I could only work with Millennials, I'd be the happiest of all happy people." Regardless of where you lie on that scale, take time to vocally express the things you appreciate about Millennials in front of the "I'm-Not-a-Millennial" Millennials. They probably only notice the negatives and need a manager like you to point out the good stuff.

>> **Resist the urge to point out their Millennial qualities.** We find that especially after reading a book like this one, managers are likely to say things like "Wow! What you just did/said was *so* Millennial!" While you think you are being astute, this persona may not appreciate the sentiment. While the truth will be obvious and even a good thing in your eyes, for them it might feel like a way to strip them of their hard-earned reputation of being an excellent employee. A sure way to turn off their willingness to connect is to poke fun and announce all the Millennial things about them. Bite your tongue as best you can, and maybe when they start to realize it themselves, you all can have a fun sitcom moment of realization and laughter.

"I don't pay attention to the incessant stereotyping of Millennials in the media and in corporate America: 'They only want to text and don't actually want to have a conversation; they lack motivation and drive; they're entitled and not loyal.' In my experience, I've found Millennials to be the exact opposite. Perhaps it's a leadership issue versus a Millennial issue." — *Cathie S., Manager*

>> **Help them find their Millennial selves.** Groan, could this sound cheesier? The real goal is to give these Millennials the tools, resources, dialogues, trainings, and conversations to help them turn all of their "I'm not *that* Millennial" defenses to "I *am* a Millennial!" celebrations.

Preventing the Demise of the Millennial Martyr

Millennial Martyrs often get lost in the shuffle of work-life. They're probably too busy to notice just how crazed they are and feel too guilty to call attention to it even if they are aware.

REMEMBER

Before exploring this segment any further, we need to point out that every generation has this segment of folks; it just manifests in different ways. These people are martyrs for the job. Some may call them workaholics. Others may call them incredibly dedicated, married to the job, or the "most annoying colleague who just wants to make me look bad." This persona isn't new, of course, but the manifestation does shape-shift across generations.

A portrait of the Martyr Millennial

Assume that you manage a Millennial martyr named Katherine. From day one, she has impressed you with her work ethic and passion for the job. Unlike others of her own generation, she seems motivated to work hard not only for the reward but for her career, her reputation, and the welfare of her team. However, the number of hours she puts into the job both at the office and at home are a bit extreme. On more than one occasion, you've had to pull her aside to either stop boasting about working 80-hour workweeks or neglecting to sleep just because she wanted to take on more work. You've noticed her making judgmental comments and expressing disappointment in her colleagues who don't take their work computer home on the weekends.

In two years, the only vacation she has taken was a family vacation to Mexico, during which she Instagrammed the latest version of *Harvard Business Review* sitting on her beach towel, and she answered one too many emails while away. After speaking with her about her vacations, she said that she feels guilty if she's disconnected from work.

When new employees start, she proudly describes her love for the company and dedication by stating that she hasn't missed a day even in the worst weather conditions or when she's been hacking up a lung. Katherine cares so much about her job that, at times, she seems physically and mentally depleted while also making others feel like they're not doing enough.

Breakdown of the Martyr Millennial

What a worker bee that Katherine is, even though the phrase "working to death" may bridge on a bit too literal. She belongs to the colony of Millennial Martyrs because she

» Works 24/7 and is therefore almost always "on"

» Feels guilty taking vacation

» Takes pride in showing up for work even when she shouldn't

» Is incredibly passionate about her work

» Feels the need to take on more for the team

» Doesn't believe in shutting off after hours

Why the Martyr Millennial is tough to manage

While this Millennial continually churns out excellent work, she is constantly at risk of burning out herself and others in the process. Members of this segment typically place undue stress on their colleagues when they're really just holding themselves to standards that are too high. As a manager, you may want to help them see value in toning down the stress they put on themselves, but they may not hear it as often as they should. The funny contradiction that these Millennials may not see is that the more they work and try to help their team, the more they add pressure to their mindset that they may not be doing enough.

Why Martyr Millennials can be great

This segment is unique in that a sea of Martyr Millennials isn't great. Millennial women are burning out in their 20s in growing numbers. Millennials have a high rate of anxiety and depression, and overworking themselves isn't a helpful antidote to that. All of that said, they are obviously productivity masters, and we have to acknowledge the great things about them:

>> They are incredibly ambitious and driven by wins.

>> They bring passion to all the work they do.

>> In extreme circumstances and seasons where people really do need to put in extra hours, they will be there to help.

>> They're willing to give it their all at all times.

>> Because of all the extra hours and effort they put in, they tend to be very good at their jobs (until they burn themselves out, that is).

Stopping yourself from getting sucked into the Millennial Martyrdom

One of the biggest challenges in managing the Millennial Martyr is that he's likely one of your most valued employees. It's highly possible that he puts out more work, gets more praise, and offers more ideas than his other Millennial peers. But, maybe there's a way he can put out the same high-quality work with fewer hours, less sickness, fewer panic attacks, and without exerting undue pressure on others. There is a way! Here are some ideas as to how to achieve that dream:

TIP

>> **Set an example around vacation policies.** Do you have a great vacation policy? Do you allow one week off a year? Two weeks? Three? Whatever it is, as a manager, *take those vacation days and disconnect.* Everyone should have colleagues to rely on who can take on the workload in their absence. If you take the vacations, then others will follow, including the Martyr Millennial. Also, anytime a martyr connects while on vacation, make it clear that you don't see it as a positive.

Some companies have taken this vacation policy following so seriously that they block people from emails when they're away, with one company we've heard of going so far as to change people's passwords while they're on vacation. Sure, that may incite rage and panic in some, but it sets a precedent. When you vacation, you vacation. You're expected to take the time off because you're equally expected to return to work fully refreshed and ready to take on the challenges you're assigned.

>> **Don't praise their martyrdom.** The most flammable fuel for the fire is the 100-proof bottle of praising the martyr. You can praise their work, but *don't* praise the process. This process is what can make the martyrs boastful of how incredible they are (and no one wants to work with that). The less they get rewarded for the way they get work done and the more they see others

praised for their own processes sends a message: "You set your own boundaries, and you're expected to follow them with great results." It also sends a message of what you praise: Does it celebrate being a successful busy bee? Or does it celebrate working until you drop as an overworked drone?

» **Teach them the value of prioritization and delegating.** Prioritizing and delegating go hand in hand, but don't expect these folks to come by either skill naturally. If they're spending extreme hours at work or struggle to ask for help or delegate, then demand that they do in order to get more opportunities and more rewards. Remind them that allowing others to take on their responsibilities passes along an ownership and pride in work.

"When I first started here 5 years ago, I overworked. The last couple years . . . I feel I have a better work-life balance and leave work when I leave the office."
— *Sakun B., Millennial*

Chapter **13**

Making Adjustments for Ages and Life Stages

O n your journey to Millennial management expertise, a few inevitable questions are bound to crop up. Questions like, "Is what I'm learning generational or something else?" "Are these patterns really generational or just life stage?" "What if you're born on a birth-year cutoff and don't align specifically with one generation?" We'll be honest with you . . . we've also had similar doubts.

Or, maybe you manage a band of what seem like Millennial misfits. No matter how much you learn, you just can't seem to make sense of all their unique qualities. When you think about the Millennials that report to you, do any of the following sound familiar?

>> They don't really act like Millennials, but they're not quite like Gen Xers either.

>> They're in their early careers but look nothing like early-career Millennials did ten years ago.

>> They are DINKs (dual income, no kids), HENRYs (high earners, not rich yet), or some other new acronym that doesn't align with traditional life stages.

>> They're approaching parenting in a completely new way, with different demands and expectations.

If any of the above struck a chord, then you're delving into the rough and complex terrain of Millennials 3.0. In this chapter, we help you decode certain nuances of the Millennial generation. We introduce you to the in-betweeners or "cuspers" who serve as a bridge between generations and don't necessarily identify with one generation or another. Then we explore the differences between Millennials and Millennial cuspers by looking both at those who cusp with Gen X as well as those who cusp with Gen Edge. We take some page-space to discuss the boundaries between Young Millennials and Old Millennials. And finally, we dig into what happens when Millennials enter the next stage of life — whether that's adopting the DINKy lifestyle or becoming a Millennial parent — and how to manage them successfully regardless of which road they take.

Meeting Cusper, the Friendly Ghost

Just like the delightful childhood movie ghost Casper, cuspers are invisible phantoms to some and helpful, appreciated friends to others. While cuspers may sometimes feel forgotten in any conversation, workshop, or employee resource group centered around generations, the truth is that they play a pivotal role in ensuring seamless communication across generations. Cuspers are natural translators because they often speak the language of two generations. Sometimes we even call them generationally bilingual!

How to identify a cusper

A couple of methods can be used to identify a cusper:

>> **Birth year:** This is usually the main mark of a cusper. Check out the following table for a rough estimate of cusper birth years.

Birth Year	Cusper
Born 1976–1982	Gen X/Millennial cusper
Born 1992–1998	Millennial/Gen Edge cusper

>> **Birth order:** A less cut-and-dried method of discovering whether someone is a cusper entails examining birth order. Youngest siblings who were relatively close in age to influential older siblings have a high chance of skewing more in their older siblings' direction. Say, Alexis's older brother Sean is born in the Gen X years, and Alexis just makes the Millennial cutoff; she will very likely identify with Gen Xer traits.

The reverse can also be true. For example, an Xer/Millennial cusper whose siblings are all younger than her may have grown up watching more *Full House* and less MTV. That doesn't mean all youngest/oldest siblings are cuspers, but birth order can have an impact.

REMEMBER

Many people you manage may feel like cuspers across all generations. For example, someone may hear about cuspers and think, "Gosh, well, I think I'm part Boomer, part Millennial. Am I a cusper?" Technically, the answer is no. But this topic is fluid! People can assign themselves to whatever definition fits them best and flow in whichever direction they like.

The power of being a cusper

Cuspers play an incredible role in this thing called life. They came into the world as a natural bridge. At work, they are great mediators. But they may struggle to understand why so many others don't value multiple perspectives the way that they do. They may find themselves translating spoken and unspoken sentiments at work all the time.

> "I consider myself a cusper. I was not born and raised with social media; it came around the middle of college. I have the best of both worlds; I'm comfortable with it but not tied to it." — *Kara F., Manager and Millennial*

TIP

Cuspers oftentimes need to be shown how to harness their powers. Because we've seen too many cuspers dampen their cusper flame, here are a few tips to give fuel to their fire:

1. **Own it.**

   They need to identify where they fall on the cusper scale. Are they 20 percent Xer and 80 percent Millennial? Rather than scoffing at applying the generational lens to their work, encourage them to find their place. It will likely be a good, "just right" fit once they discover where they lie.

2. **Discuss it.**

   This one is simple. Cuspers can feel more comfortable after spotting and discussing the gift of cusper-ness in others. Connecting cuspers to bond over their shared experiences and how it impacts their working style can be a good way to empower them in their role as natural mediators.

3. **Live it.**

   Once they've identified and feel comfortable with their place in the cusper spectrum, coach them to act on their cusper instincts. They often see things that others can't, but it's best to encourage them to speak up when they do.

Introducing the Xer/Millennial: The Oregon Trail Generation

Ask Gen X/Millennial cuspers whether they identify as Millennials, and you'll likely get a resounding, "No!" Though they may technically be Millennials (or very young Xers), they believe they don't share any traits with those young, pesky professionals. To spot Gen X/Millennial cuspers, ask them to play the game of "Too old" and "Too young." The more yesses, the higher the score, and therefore the more likely they are Gen X/Millennial cuspers:

>> Were you too old for Backstreet Boys but too young for Run DMC?

>> Were you too young to see all the effects of the AIDS epidemic but too old to know a *Real World* without Pedro?

>> Were you out of college for the Obama vote but too young to vote for George W. Bush Sr.?

>> Were you too old to watch 9/11 unfold in middle or high school but too young to really know how impactful the fall of the Berlin Wall was?

>> Were you too old to learn every move to Beyoncé's "Single Ladies" but too young to know every move to Michael Jackson's "Thriller"?

>> Were you too old for smartphones in college but too young for an email-free college experience?

>> Were you the first generation to play Oregon Trail ?

This last question gets to the heart of why Xer/Millennial cuspers are sometimes referred to as the Oregon Trail generation (and what makes them unique). They were in school at the exciting time when technology first started becoming "a thing" and infiltrating classrooms. These cuspers can remember when their school got Apple II computers, on which they could play the very basic (but still thrilling) early edition of The Oregon Trail game. Reference it to any Xer/Millennial cusper and they'll laugh about attempts to avoid typhoid fever or dreaded snake bites. The most important takeaway, though, is not the nostalgic memories the game inspires, but the fact that these cuspers grew up in the space between transformative technological innovations. As kids and early teens, they witnessed the switch from no Internet to dial-up, and from computers being things reserved for NASA scientists to owning a personal Dell at home. They were taught the Dewey Decimal system, but later breathed sighs of relief when they could just Ask Jeeves. Their childhoods were mostly technology-free, but in their teen years and young-adulthood they explored the virtual world with gusto. They are the Oregon Trail generation.

Exploring events and conditions

Cusper birth years span about 6 years rather than the usual 15–20 year span for the generations. The following is a list of influential events that shaped Xer/Millennial cuspers:

>> Coverage of the Los Angeles riots escalated after the beating of Rodney King by police officers.

>> The World Trade Center was bombed in 1993.

>> Pedro made history as an HIV-positive man on *The Real World,* and his marriage to Sean Sasser was the first public gay marriage on television.

>> The Columbine shootings happened when many of these cuspers were in high school.

>> The O. J. Simpson trial was a big deal, and everyone watched.

>> Princess Diana's death by paparazzi was sad, tragic, and extensively covered on the news.

>> Animated series for adults started up just as these cuspers became teens — *The Simpsons, South Park,* and the like.

Aside from these events, here are some conditions of the time that were highly influential as well:

>> Coming of age when technology began its steep innovation increase — these cuspers were in the crux of their formative years when the world went from analog to digital.

>> Graduating into an economy rich with job opportunities.

>> Being raised by optimistic and idealistic Boomer parents.

Recognizing workplace traits

These cuspers share traits with the Gen Xers and Millennials on either side of them. As a whole, this generation at work tends to be

>> **Interdependent:** Millennials are known as a collaborative generation because they were raised in the self-esteem movement. This band of cuspers takes to it in a unique way, however, because they're the last group that may have had actual latchkey kids in their classes (as opposed to a supervised after-school program). They adopt a healthy blend of working together and working alone.

>> **Honestly sensitive:** While these Cuspers aren't as brutally honest as Gen Xers, they do tend to have an honest edge that comes out more often than Millennials as a whole. If Xers are an axe and Millennials are a butter knife, then Xer/Millennial cuspers are the scalpel.

>> **Optimistic opportunists:** When they were growing up, adults said, "You can be anything you want to be." They graduated from college believing in the power of their abilities and easily found jobs. It wasn't uncommon to get a *paid* job that matched their skillset and degree path after graduation. They still tend to be optimistic about career possibilities.

Cuspers may shake their heads at being labeled optimistic about the economy, and we know they were not free from suffering financial strain during the recession. However, compare their experience to Millennials who graduated during the peak of the recession when jobs were scarce and paid opportunities were as rare as Willy Wonka's golden ticket. Those different economic environments matter, and Gen X/Millennial cuspers graduated into a much more thriving job economy than the Millennials after them.

Understanding key differences

While Xer/Millennial cuspers may sometimes look like Millennials, talk like Millennials, and smell like Millennials (gross, why do you know what they smell like?) remember that they are not all the same. As you read through this book and juggle with all the tips to manage Millennials more effectively, pay attention to those who may be cuspers and don't quite align with what you know about Millennials. Keep these considerations in mind:

>> **They're not necessarily tech mavens.** Can they figure out the latest and greatest technology innovations? Absolutely. But that doesn't come as innately as it does to, say, the Millennial cohort or Millennial/Gen Edge cuspers.

>> **Their first jobs were good jobs.** As mentioned earlier, they had good fortune when they graduated from college. Even more than Millennials as a whole, they had the ability to find a job rather easily upon graduation because entry-level positions were aplenty.

>> **They went from analog to digital.** Gen X/Millennial cuspers not only know what a card catalog is, they used it in their elementary-school libraries. In middle school, they went to a computer lab with Apple computers that may have required some coding skills to use. They are the ones who saw the transformation from "old-school" methods to "new-school" technology.

>> **They were the last group to graduate from college social media–free.** To any Millennial, this is so unbelievable to think about . . . an education, college party, or friendship circle *without social media?!* Unreal. This may seem like an

irrelevant point, but the exposure (or lack thereof) to social media creates pretty stark divides in generational behaviors and traits.

>> **They were the self-esteem movement guinea pigs.** Though the popularity of raising children with high self-esteem began to rise in the '70s, it didn't fully take off until the early to mid 1990s. Parents, coaches, and teachers at this time all banded together to reward more based on effort and intention than on results. Later generations, the younger Millennials and Gen Edgers, began to question rewards given not for winning, but for participation alone.

Snagging management tips

If you're scratching your head thinking, "This is way too much to keep track of: tips for Millennials *and* Gen X/Millennial cuspers *and* Millennial/Gen Edge cuspers *and* Old Millennials and Young Millennials?!" we hear you, and hopefully this book will serve as a handy reference point for you when needed. However, if you have a card catalog of a brain (see what we did there?), then file these tips away when it comes to the Oregon Trail generation:

>> **Keep it honest, even if it feels brash at times.** Just like Gen Xers who prefer brutal honesty, Xer/Millennial cuspers prefer that you keep it real. Because of the self-esteem movement, they may also expect positive feedback on their work, but from a manager, they also appreciate someone who tells it like it is.

>> **Do not, under any circumstances, call them Millennials.** Don't lump them into that cohort, and don't lump them in with Gen Xers either. It's insulting not only to them but to the Millennials as well.

>> **Use them to your advantage.** As we point out in multiple ways throughout this book, the divide between Gen Xers and Millennials can be vast, and the clashes abound. But tapping into this group of cuspers who understand both the generations surrounding them can be just what the doctor ordered when it comes to closing the gaps or, at the very least, narrowing them. Ask them questions, have them lead teams that involve both generations, or just seek their advice. These Gen X/Millennial cuspers are often an untapped resource.

Getting a Glimpse of the Millennial/Gen Edger: The Snapchat Generation

On the other end of the Millennial cusper spectrum is the group sandwiched between the digitally innate and the digitally savvy. It's easy for managers to look at new college grads and lump them into the Millennial cohort, but doing so will give you a false (or heavily Photoshopped) image of this group. Just as we suggest with the Oregon Trail cuspers, play a game of "too young" and "too old." Remember, the more yesses, the higher the score, and therefore the more likely they are Millennial/Gen Edge cuspers:

>> Were you too young for N*SYNC but too old for One Direction — maybe you were more into Hilary Duff?

>> Were you too young to remember the events of 9/11 but too old to live-stream national tragedies on your phone in middle school?

>> Were you too young to experience a mostly smartphone-free high school but too old to have WiFi limitations at home as a kid?

>> Were you too young to fall in love with *Bananas in Pyjamas* but too old to fall in love with *Dora the Explorer?*

>> Were you too young to remember the launch of Facebook but too old to view it as obsolete?

>> Were you too young to rely exclusively on a mailed letter to find out if you were accepted into college but too old to have hand-selected your college roommate via social media?

>> Were you and your friends among the first users on Snapchat?

While there are many important influencers that give these Millennial/Gen Edge cuspers their identity, their use of technology and social media is really what divides them from the Millennial bunch. For example, while Millennials may pride themselves on their know-how of social media, the Millennial/Edger cuspers are social media mavens. They're too young to remember a time when it wasn't a daily staple in their lives. That said, they *do* remember (unlike Gen Edge) the game-changer that was the introduction of the smartphone. So, yes, they're techy and cool, but just not *as* techy and cool as Generation Edge.

Exploring events and conditions

REMEMBER

As a generation that grew up in a post-analog era and entered work in a post-recession economy, they share some stark memories about their formative years:

>> President Obama, the first African-American president, took office.

>> Sandy Hook and the Boston Marathon bombings stirred fear across the nation.

>> Police violence against men and women of color became a focal point in the news.

- The iconic Michael Jackson died.
- Hurricane Katrina wreaked havoc.
- The H1N1 virus, known as the Swine Flu, becomes a global pandemic.
- Pluto was determined to no longer be a planet.
- *Kony 2012* debuts on YouTube.

Conditions that impacted this generation include the following:

- They were raised less by optimistic Boomers and more by skeptical Xers or pragmatic Generation Jonesers who raised them to focus more on the practical rather than the aspirational. (Learn more about Generation Jones in Chapter 4.)
- The release of the first iPhone around their awkward teenage years was followed by new/better/faster/smarter phones every ensuing year.
- Gun violence and mass shootings grew more prevalent during their formative years, with Virginia Tech, Sandy Hook, and the Aurora movie theater shooting among the many tragic incidences.
- The momentous shift to on-demand (think Netflix, Amazon Prime, and Lyft) gave them the ability to watch, shop, and travel at their own leisure.

Recognizing workplace traits

While this young group of cuspers is often stereotyped as the group who can't communicate in person, we have found that the Millennial/Edgers keep proving everyone wrong. They tend to share the following traits:

- **No-nonsense:** Being raised by Gen X parents gave this cusper group an edge that serves them well at work. They are less interested in filling chunks of time with cat videos and more eager to focus, get to work an hour before everyone else, work hard and efficiently, and leave earlier than everyone else.
- **Eager for first:** With this group of cuspers we see the competitive spirit start to emerge (though Gen Edgers carry a more concentrated form of this competitive trait). For Millennial/Gen Edge cuspers, the competition level in high school was stiff, and they've had their LinkedIn profiles set-up and perfectly polished since before they received their high school diplomas. Competitive, but still collaborative and team-minded, they're a fantastic addition to any project.

Understanding key differences

Prevent yourself from making the Millennial management faux pas of giving Snapchat cuspers the same treatment as Millennials. See the following for the key differences between the two (don't worry — we're looking at similarities too):

>> **Upgrades are boring.** A generation that only knows a time when upgrades were constant isn't energized by them in the same way that older Millennials may be, and they don't seek to disrupt everything at work the way that Millennials do.

>> **Questions can be directed to Google.** While Gen Edgers are even more well-known for their resourcefulness, you have to give credit to Snapchat cuspers who have the ability to filter any and all information in such a way that it stuns older generations. At work, they know to figure things out on their own before asking questions. (Of course, this comes with its own issues as well.)

>> **"Kumbaya" meets "just do it."** Millennials' collaborative natures and self-esteem movement rubbed off on these cuspers, but at the same time, they were raised by the notoriously honest and sometimes brutal Gen Xers and competitive Gen Jonesers. Snapchat cuspers enjoy teamwork, but want their team to win.

>> **Social media is a second language.** They grew up playing outside with their neighbors just like Millennials but were also Instagramming and posting statuses in middle school. Their social media comfort level is high, and their utilization showcases that, but they're not as close to being social-media savvy as the generation after them.

Snagging management tips

As these cuspers become more prevalent in the workplace, their traits will become more recognizable. Managing them requires a balanced approach that, like any other generation, demands someone who can focus on the individual while also understanding them from a generational perspective. If you want a head start in managing these cuspers, take heed of these tips:

>> **Communicate as efficiently as possible.** Every generation values efficiency! For these Snapchatters, focused and no-frills communication speaks exactly to what they need.

>> **Reward true winners.** The competitive nature of this cohort isn't going away any time soon, and it'll behoove managers and leaders to find a way to reward winning the competition. In that sense, create a measurement of how well they're doing in comparison to others, but be careful not to create a cut-throat environment.

>> **Use them to your advantage.** If you read the previous section on Xer/Millennial cuspers, this tip may look very familiar to you. But it applies here as well. As Gen Edge starts to enter the workforce in droves, this group of cuspers will be critical to helping you get a head start in managing Gen Edge (or, at the very least, understanding what on earth all those emojis actually mean).

Modifying Your Style for Old Millennials versus Young Millennials

Have you ever managed Millennials and thought, "Wow, one of these things is not like the other!"? If so, welcome to the club of Millennial segmentation. We took it upon ourselves to *divide* Millennials into two respective groups that share many traits and qualities but are separated by a few key events and conditions. To do this, we'll look at the older Millennials and juxtapose their experiences to the younger Millennials.

You may be rolling your eyes at the use of the word "old" here. Yes, we realize that even the oldest Millennials have still not hit their 40th birthdays and by no one's definition are actually old. However, because it's the simplest and most straight-forward way to divide these two groups, we're going to run with it. We're only using "old" as a relative term. With that out of the way, we define Old Millennials as those born roughly between 1980 and 1987. Young Millennials are those born from 1988 through 1995.

The Millennial generation can be segmented many times over, so this is by no means the one and only way to divide this massive generation. Cool your jets if this is stressing you out or causing an inner monologue of frustration!

The things that divide them

Let's start with the obvious division — life stage. Old Millennials are tending to their growing families and settling into careers as leaders or soon-to-be leaders. Young Millennials are only just breaking into the workforce and/or thinking about starting families of their own.

When we look beyond life stage, the two major factors that distinguish these groups from one another are 1) the evolution of technology and 2) the Great Recession.

With technology, Old Millennials witnessed the slow start, then exponentially increasing rate of change. Young Millennials began their formative years right as that rate of change picked up and innovation after innovation hit the marketplace. For Young Millennials, touchscreen cellphones were the norm, not the exception, in high school. While Old Millennials remember a time when you had to have a dot edu email address to get on Facebook, for their younger successors, Facebook is mostly passé and something that their family members frequent. Instead, they turn to the still mostly-grandma-free Snapchat or Instagram for their social media fixes. Older Millennials have expectations around disruption and innovation, and Younger Millennials have expectations around staying current.

Perhaps the biggest difference between these two subgroups is their experience with the Great Recession. Old Millennials graduated college before the U.S. economy took a steep downturn. While they were in school, they received the rosy and idealistic messaging from parents and teachers that they could reach for the stars and do whatever they wanted. After college, they easily found jobs and kicked off their careers. Though like everyone else, they were dealt financial and professional blows in the aftermath of 2009, they retained that optimistic messaging they'd received during their schooling.

On the other hand, Young Millennials were entering, attending, and leaving college as the Great Recession hit full force. They graduated into an economy that wasn't hiring experienced workers, let alone freshly minted college grads. They were either in high school applying to colleges or in college and planning for their careers when they got the blanket message of: "Good luck, paid internships don't exist and entry-level jobs require five years of experience; oh, and get humble because you may have to live with Mom and Dad while you try to figure out this thing called life." Despite their idealistic upbringing by Boomer parents, Young Millennials weren't spared the bleak realities of entering the working world saddled with crippling college debt and no job opportunities in sight. Consequently, this latter half of Millennials tend to be more realistic and financially conscious than the collaborative and optimistic Old Millennials.

The ties that bind

As a whole, they're all still Millennials. For the most part, they were raised by Boomers, albeit differently aged Boomers. They all know what it's like to live in a world where everything from technology to social media platforms is constantly being upgraded. They transitioned from tapes, CDs, and MP3s. They rocked out to boy bands. They played Oregon Trail, whether it was the first edition or the fifth. They have strong affiliations to team iPhone or team Android. They enjoy collaborative work environments, and flexibility in their working lives. They want jobs that matter, and strive to make a difference in the world.

Old and Young Millennials are not so different that they're unrecognizable, so don't make the mistake of thinking that they're diametrically opposed! All in all, the commonalities outweigh the differences.

The different managerial approaches

TIP

For the most part, stick to what we've told you in this book so far about Millennials. We've worked to make sure that the tips and content encompass all Millennials. However, we want to give you the keys to making yourself a top manager. So, read this section in context of the rest of this book but keep in mind some key differences between Old and Young Millennials:

>> Old Millennials tend to be more collaborative employees and leaders.

>> Old Millennials are more likely to be motivated by autonomy rather than financial incentives.

>> Old Millennials tend to be a bit more optimistic about all the possibilities.

>> Young Millennials are more realistic with themselves and the world.

>> Young Millennials adopt a different tech comfort and use.

>> Young Millennials prefer to focus at work all day and get the work done before playing — outside of work. Old Millennials, however, prefer to work, then play, then work, and repeat this pattern, alternating throughout the day.

"When I was 23, I was so gung ho! I would do everything that I could to fix the world; not that I don't feel that way now — I'm doing good work — but being out of college you want to do a good job and know that you are not going to fail. But compared to a 34-year-old, your priorities shift." — *Sokun B., Millennial*

TIP

Some Millennials are sensitive to the terms "old" and "young," but we use them in this book because they're simpler to understand than the alternatives. If you want to use an alternative, we also prefer early and late Millennials *or* Early Millennials and Recessionists.

Meeting Millennial Parents

Just like generations past, Millennials are getting busy making babies. Unlike generations past, more mothers and fathers are sharing the work at home and at the office. While you may be shaking your head in doubt that Millennials actually are settling down, have no fear, because they are. Currently, more than half of Millennials are parents, and according to a study by marketing platform Crowd-tap, 80 percent of Millennials will have children in the next decade. We know, it's very anti-everything the media says about them. But the media tends to prefer the sexy stories, and choosing to have a beautiful family just isn't as sexy as going paddle boarding for a cause on a lake and then stopping at the latest brewery tap-house for a drink, upset that your rent has increased so much that you're contemplating moving into a tiny house you'd build yourself. With a new wave of parenting comes a new wave of societal pressures and expectations for both fathers and mothers:

>> **Foods must be organic and ideally include kale.** The pressure is on for organic, all-natural, homemade, and practically homegrown baby food for a six-month-old. If parenting wasn't hard enough before, now parents have the added burden of feeding them a perfect diet. This is making an already tough job nearly impossible. Try adding a career to the mix, and parents are even more overwhelmed.

>> **Everyone knows!** Neighborhood support and gossip have always existed. Now, however, access to social media makes the exposure more prevalent than ever before. On the plus side, it provides a crowd of information to use as resources, but on the other hand, it showcases all the beautiful and, well, not-always-beautiful sides of parenting.

>> **Have it all, but not in a flashy way.** As every generation before them, Millennial parents are having to decide what it means to really "have it all," and when workloads are split and the pressure is on to throw a Pinterest-perfect birthday party, working outside the home becomes increasingly difficult.

As you continue to manage Millennials, you're going to have more who are married and more who have children. Thinking about how to manage these changes and a new generation of working parents doesn't have to be stressful. Instead, it can be an adventure that you chart together and one in which you may even be able to share some of your own wisdom if you are a parent yourself. However, while some things about being a working parent are absolutely evergreen, some challenges are new for this generation.

What does the new working mom look like?

How wonderful is it that the world now is less June Cleaver and more Claire Huxtable? Working mothers have had to chart an unknown and obstacle-ridden path for decades, and now Millennials are clearing their own way.

What she looks like

To get an understanding of how this working mom is different from generations past, consider the following:

>> **She is sharing.** Both partners in a relationship share the roles more evenly in parenting now but, by and large, women (if studying a male-female relationship) are more likely to say that they will make career sacrifices for their families. See Figure 13-1 from Pew Research Center.

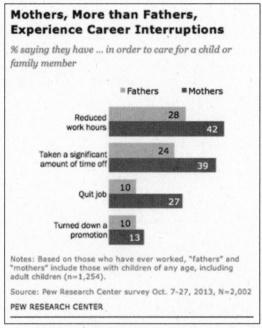

Mothers, More than Fathers, Experience Career Interruptions

% saying they have ... in order to care for a child or family member

■ Fathers ■ Mothers

	Fathers	Mothers
Reduced work hours	28	42
Taken a significant amount of time off	24	39
Quit job	10	27
Turned down a promotion	10	13

Notes: Based on those who have ever worked, "fathers" and "mothers" include those with children of any age, including adult children (n=1,254).

Source: Pew Research Center survey Oct. 7-27, 2013, N=2,002

PEW RESEARCH CENTER

FIGURE 13-1: Career interruptions: mothers versus fathers.

"Women More Than Men Adjust Their Careers for Family Life" Pew Research Center, Washington, DC (September, 2015) http://www. pewresearch.org/fact-tank/2015/10/01/women-more-than-men-adjust-their-careers-for-family-life/ ft_15-09-0_workchildren_1/

>> **She is networked.** About 90 percent of Millennial moms find social media helpful in their parenting process, using blogs, crowdsourcing, and Facebook pages as a way to stay up-to-date on the latest trends, tips, and advice for Millennial mothers (Crowdtap, 2016).

"We have so much access to tech now. From daycares that have cameras where you can check in, to teachers who respond via text or email, and there's so much out there for working moms." — *Michelle S., Millennial*

>> **She is not as common as you'd think.** Progress continues to be made with a higher number of women returning to work after having a child, and there are fewer hiring discrepancies for working moms in big roles. However, the great strides that women have been taking are starting to take a dip. As of 1990, the United States boasted having one of the world's highest employment rates for women. However, according to data from the Organization for Economic Cooperation and Development, after rates consistently climbed for more than 60 years, the percentage of women (ages 25 to 54) at work has been declining as of late, falling from 74 percent in 1999 to 69 percent today. While it's hardly a steep drop, it is worth noting. Lack of flexibility and the ability to work from home are making qualified and successful women feel like parenthood and working don't mix.

>> **She is ambitious but concerned.** According to a Pew Research Center study in 2015, 58 percent of Millennial moms are concerned about how their parenthood will impact their careers. Check out Figure 13-2. Will the DINKy (Dual Income No Kids) peer of hers get the job instead because she has more flexibility and fewer time constraints?

Working Mothers and Career Advancement

% with children under age 18 who say being a working mother/father makes it ... to advance in job or career

	Harder	Easier	No difference
Working mothers	51	2	46
Working fathers	16	10	72

Notes: Based on adults who are working or have ever worked and have children younger than 18 (n=528). Voluntary responses of "Depends" and "Don't know/Refused" not shown.

Source: Pew Research Center survey Oct. 7-27, 2013, N=2,002

PEW RESEARCH CENTER

FIGURE 13-2: Working mothers and career advancement.

"On Pay Gap, Millennial Women Near Parity — For Now" Pew Research Center, Washington, DC (December, 2013) http://www.pewsocialtrends.org/2013/12/11/on-pay-gap-millennial-women-near-parity-for-now/sdt-gender-and-work-12-2013-5-01/

How you can best manage her

As a manager, you have a unique ability to make a big difference for the women that you manage. Your Millennial-mom employees are looking to you for guidance, resources, and tools to make the most out of their careers while also being the rock-star mom they know they can be deep inside. Consider simple things that you can do to better connect with her:

>> Take a genuine interest in her personal life.

>> Give her as much freedom and flexibility as possible.

>> Don't be afraid to talk about it.

>> Support her. If you don't know how, ask.

>> Don't make assumptions about what she will or won't do after she has a baby (or two or three).

>> Ask questions. Be sure to ask Millennial dads the same ones.

Meet the Millennial dad: #RedefiningMasculinity

In recent years, very pro-woman and pro-man movements have coincided with gender-equality initiatives and the movement to redefine what it means to "be a man." On one hand, this has put Millennial men in a place of confusion — when the labor economy changed to a service economy, the physical strength and resulting demeanor that had played a heavy hand in other men's successes no longer mattered. Millennial men continue to find their footing but in the meantime are becoming fathers who aim to act a little less like their own fathers.

What he looks like

Much like Millennial moms, Millennial dads are finding their niches online with blogs like Fatherly and groups of friends. To get an idea of what he looks like, here are a few clues:

>> **He splits his time.** In many Millennials' households, Mom managed the house and Dad managed the finances. He came home late to dinner on the table and children who were already showered and fed, ready to be tucked in for the night. These kind of traditional gender roles are still prevalent, but the outside world is tremoring with mindsets that embrace all kinds of changes. He is spending five more hours a week with his kid compared to dads in 1995, says a report in *The Atlantic*.

>> **He's resourceful.** When a younger dad is trying to understand how to do something or figure out the way to fix that thing that broke that no one can fix, he can always go back to his toolbox, where he was told to find a solution. And if he can't find a solution there, then he needs to build it.

"I think sometimes it's all about being busy. Workplaces put so much emphasis on hours worked that there is less home time." — *Bethany B., Millennial*

>> **He's stuck in a changing world.** While lots of things have changed on the home front and dads are now washing dishes and painting their daughter's toenails, the workplace has somewhat lagged behind when it comes to serving them. Typically, managers are still more likely to understand if a woman asks for a flex schedule or needs to take time off to take a kid to a doctor appointment. Dads can often feel stuck between a rock (their spouse/kids) and a hard place (their boss).

How you can best manage him

As you strive to balance managing both Millennial moms and dads, keep in mind these tips for the dads specifically:

>> Assume that they're fighting for flexibility just like mom.

>> Don't take their loyalty for granted.

>> Don't downplay how hard fatherhood is.

>> Be an example. (This is especially for you dad managers reading this book.)

Adapting the workplace for a new brand of parent

Regardless of whether you are a mom or dad in any kind of relationship, single or coupled, and regardless of your generation, being a parent is tough. Being a full-time worker and a full-time parent can be even harder, but you know that. To adapt to this younger generation of parents, heed this advice:

>> **Have a standard parental leave, not maternal and/or paternal.** This kind of policy implementation may be "above your paygrade," but we would be remiss not to include it in our book. As paternal leave becomes more normal, recognize that focusing on one parent's gender in the relationship is non-inclusive to every relationship and doesn't serve anyone well. There's a reason that we look to other countries like Norway and Denmark, who give ample

time to recover after having a child. The Department of Labor reported in the United States that more than 25 percent of women return to work after only two weeks. Maybe that's too fast. And perhaps, oh perhaps, parental leave will assist in those changes.

>> **Review flexibility policies.** If your flexibility expectations are set, then they're set! Just allow *yourself* the flexibility to reexamine them on a regular basis to ensure that you're providing a work environment that works for everyone.

WARNING

As much as parents in the workplace need flexibility, don't forget that their needs do not trump those of others who may not have children. This is an easy trap to fall into, especially if you are a parent yourself. It can feel perfectly acceptable to grant flexibility to an employee with a sick kid at home but scoff at the person who wants to work from home because he is having renovations done on his cool downtown condo. Fair is fair.

>> **Celebrate parenthood, don't ignore it.** It wasn't too long ago that women had to hide their pregnancies and keep them secret for fear of getting fired or treated differently. As a manager, celebrate new mothers and fathers for the changes in their lives, and take a genuine interest in so far as they want to discuss those lives.

DINKs: Motivating the Dual Income No Kids Subset

At the risk of giving a history lesson about the American dream, we suggest you think about how you've seen it change over time. How are your grandparents' stories different from your own? How have motivations changed over time? While achieving the American dream used to look like getting married, owning a beautiful home with a white picket fence, and having lots of children's mouths to feed, now it can look like some version of that *or* the equally accepted tiny home or apartment dwelling, with no additional mouths to feed.

REMEMBER

The media loves to paint Millennials as averse to marriage, averse to children, and averse to owning a home. Though there are more who align with these ideals in their generation, it is by no means the majority! Here's a more accurate view:

>> **The marriage dream:** Most Millennials want to get married but not at the age of generations past — for example, in 1960, the average bride was around 20 and the groom was around 23. Now, the average age of the bride is around 26 and the groom is around 29 (Pew Research, 2011). Some Millennials choose to

delay marriage either because it's too expensive or, in their eyes, unnecessary. Domestic partnerships and long periods of dating are more commonplace than ever before.

>> **The house dream:** Many Millennials seek new digs for their lives and lifestyles, which is probably why they are outpacing Generation Xers now as first-time homebuyers. It turns out that the majority of Millennials want to own a home, but what they plan to put in it — or, more accurately, who they plan to put in it — is slightly different than generations past.

>> **The kid dream:** While the majority of Millennials either already do or will have kids within the next decade, couples who dwell together, dine together, and see their futures together may envision those futures without wee babes. And that means their motivation is different. For couples of yore, the motivation was more simple — you don't work, your family doesn't eat. Now, that's changing.

As a manager, you've likely seen other generations of DINKs, so be sure that you can manage Millennial DINKs in a way that works for them. Here are our do's and don'ts:

>> **Don't make them work after hours because their responsibilities seem lighter.** Everyone has responsibilities outside of work. Granted, taking care of children is taxing and unpredictable, so there are different levels of implied flexibility. Be careful not to make it seem like the Millennial who doesn't have the same kind of responsibilities has more freedom to take on more and should, because that's what was done in the past.

>> **Don't pressure the DINKs into the non-DINKy lifestyle.** Millennials who are DINKs have likely heard plenty of adults in their lives ask them when that's going to change. Or, they've had adults say things like, "Well, that's just your generation's way of doing things, isn't it?" Don't call attention to their choices as something that will change in the near future.

>> **Do recognize that they are likely motivated by finances in a unique way.** Many DINKs are targeted by financial institutions because of their accrued and shared wealth, and chances are those you manage are happy to have more disposable income. They're also likely paying off student loans, among other debts, so they love having a higher bucket of income.

>> **Do acknowledge their thirst for freedom.** Millennial DINKs are a lovely image of the devourer of the experience economy. They take spontaneous trips, pick up and move to have a dream career, and excitedly take on new hobbies and responsibilities outside of work. As a manager, acknowledging those freedoms as having equal value/importance as those of a Millennial with children will go far to motivate Millennials.

GREETINGS FROM THE BASEMENT

Millennials got a terrible reputation when they graduated from college and moved in with Mom and Dad. Many saw them as privileged, lazy, and spoiled kids who just didn't want to pay for Internet, food, or a roof over their head. Many in other generations had, and some still have, an air of judgment about Millennials' decisions to do this. While others would have first sawed off their own arm before moving back in with Mom and Dad, Millennials saw it differently:

- Many graduated into a recession economy and couldn't find a steady, decent-paying job to cover their bills and student loans. Living with Mom and Dad helped get them enough money to start out on their own.

- They have a good relationship with their parents, so moving back in with Mom and Dad wasn't torturous.

- They weren't proud to live with their parents. It's not as if Millennials skipped home and felt like living with their parents was a factoid that every first date wants to hear. If you've had to move back home, you know how embarrassing it can be.

As Millennials have gotten older and the economy has improved, they've found another reason to move back in with Mom and Dad — to (eventually) get the home they've always wanted. Down payments require more than almost all couples have saved, so moving in with their parents for now allows them to keep that dream alive.

Remember: It's not an act of childish behavior or the inability to cut the cord with Mom and Dad; it's an act of financial savvy and maturity to make a sacrifice and live with the 'rents so they can then live completely independently.

Chapter **14**

Tailoring Your Millennial Management Style to Different Work Settings

Bear with us as we walk you through a somewhat wacky analogy — namely that of selling shoes. We'll start with this: The word "recruiting" is essentially another word for "selling," and "retaining" is essentially another word for "keeping a loyal customer." You want the right person to buy the right shoe. As a manager in whatever field or industry you're in, you're probably reading this book with an eye on creating a working environment that is attractive and desirable to the right Millennial. Just like there's an infinite number of potential products to sell, there are many types of work settings, and some are much easier to market. Think of those sleek Nike kicks with customizable colors, state-of-the-art cushioning, and, of course, the essential swoosh. They may not be great for your plantar fasciitis, but they're oh-so-stylish — these are the Apple of the working world. Others, not so much — think of the plain white New Balances that practically every dad ever has owned. They don't have much pizzazz, but they're dang durable. These would probably equate to a job in waste management. Though at face value, the New Balances may not have the same chances of being purchased as the Nikes, things are not always as they appear. The same is true of the working world. The key, just like marketing a solid shoe, is to own up to your faults and shout your strengths from the rooftops. You may not be the right fit or style for everyone, but you're someone's, and the important thing is to find the *right* match. And once you find that perfect match, you'll want to do everything in your power to keep that person.

Each industry and type of role has its own set of features that can be marketed to the Millennial generation. Just as there are nuances among Millennials, there are nuances from industry to industry. In the spirit of using the best tools to attract and retain the right Millennial talent, in this chapter, we take you through three dichotomous industries and fields. First, we compare and contrast Silicon Valley (technology) with Wall Street (finance). Then we examine white collar versus blue collar, and how managers can attract and retain Millennials in both fields. Finally, we look at roles in the arts versus those in the sciences and how managers can capitalize on the strengths of either one, while minimizing (but still being transparent about) weaknesses.

As we go through each of these couplings, we address how each really speaks to (or misses the mark on) Millennial traits and workplace clash points. As a reminder, those clash points are as follows:

>> Organizational structure

>> Collaboration

>> Feedback

>> Motivation

>> Formality

WARNING

Don't take these examples too literally. We're trying to get at a variety of *types* of jobs, and in doing so have had to lump many roles together. Wall Street (finance) is a huge umbrella of many different kinds of roles and specializations, but we think you'll find value in the overarching management tips embedded within each section.

Managing in Silicon Valley versus Wall Street

When you look at Silicon Valley (tech) and Wall Street (finance), there's a major connecting thread: To succeed in either of these industries, you have to work hard. Really hard. Hours are grueling, and expectations are high. In many cases there's a high-risk/high-reward mentality that creates an atmosphere of uncertainty, but the right employees thrive on it. The Millennials who are drawn to both of these industries will likely be seeking a high-paced, industrious world where their ambition and hunger will be in good company. The talent pool for both industries consists of highly educated individuals looking to put their technical skills to good use. Though there's certainly a degree of overlap between the two, most everyone would agree that you get something distinctly different from Wall Street than you do from Silicon Valley. Each of these industries has pieces that appeal to Millennials, as well as areas that present a bit of a challenge.

Viewing Silicon Valley

Check out the industry profile through a Millennial lens:

>> The rank and file as well as the leadership of Silicon Valley skews younger than in the world of finance. Millennials looking to join your industry will feel you have more of a finger on the pulse of recent trends and the up-and-coming innovative efforts with both your product and the way you structure the organization.

>> Many organizations within the tech industry are quite new and aren't long-standing financial institutions. This lack of established tradition or set of stringent rules gives employees a lot more room to have their voices heard and make a tangible impact on the company.

>> Disruption is built into what's expected. The space for Millennials to innovate is baked into the tech industry as a whole. Silicon Valley is looking for creativity and bright minds that will take the status quo, flip it on its head, and make something unexpected and unprecedented out of the mundane.

Clash-point considerations for recruiting and retaining Millennials in this type of environment include the following:

>> **Organizational structure:** The tech industry is one that has embraced the more networked structure that Millennials so crave. That transparency, authenticity, and flattening of the typical hierarchical model is something that speaks to Millennials' souls. Embed phrases like "opportunities to have your voice heard," "access to leadership," and "transparent and efficient exchange of information" within your marketing materials.

>> **Workplace formality:** Why? Because there is none! Silicon Valley focuses on the product or service rather than what their employees are wearing from day to day. Look no further than one of the most high-powered CEOs of our century, Mark Zuckerberg. The lack of stuffy workplace rules like what to wear or how to formally address your higher-ups is a huge selling point with Millennials.

DON'T TRY TO GOOGLE IT

You aren't Google. And you shouldn't try to be. Sometimes when managers read strategies for recruiting Millennials, they think, "Okay, this is great for companies like Google, but our company, and even our industry, is nothing like that. Ping-pong tournaments and napping pods just aren't realistic." We couldn't agree more. You don't need to become Google to attract Millennials; you need to own and sell *your* unique strengths.

If you're trying to attract the type of talent that thrives at Google, you may find that they're all sorts of wrong for your company and your culture. Not only that, but Millennials may feel like they've been catfished. If you sell yourself as a Google-esque place and your new hires find it's nothing of the sort, you're going to have a major problem. It's important that when attracting talent, you don't try to be someone else. You want to ensure not only that you're a right fit for them, but that they're the right fit for you.

REMEMBER

There's obviously a big difference between a start-up that's been operating for under a year and a large, well-established corporation like Microsoft. Don't sell yourself as a giant Google or a budding newbie if you aren't. Each type has something that appeals to Millennials — for example, in a Microsoft, there will probably be more opportunities for career progression and moving up the corporate ladder, not to mention a much higher degree of job security. But in a start-up, you find less bureaucracy and more opportunities to effect immediate change and have your voice heard. Sell to your strengths.

Weighing in on Wall Street

Here's a look at how Millennials view the Wall Street industry:

>> This is a well-established industry, with decades of tradition built with a "this is the way things have always been done" mentality. You have vetted methods to accomplish certain tasks and employees who take pride in institutional knowledge. This is both good and bad.

>> Though innovation is still valued, this is an industry where experience means a whole lot. Employees with years of experience are sought after for their knowledge in weathering challenges. Though Millennials may struggle with the message of staying within the lines, they'll appreciate opportunities to connect with and learn valuable skills from older mentors with heaps of institutional knowledge.

>> Silicon Valley isn't exactly winning the battle when it comes to diversity, but the finance industry is woefully behind in the game. Especially when you look at leadership, this field is staffed by what may best be described as "pale, male, and stale." (No offense intended, but it's a quick quip to get at what we mean.)

>> Tradition matters. The clientele skew older here, and it's no secret that Traditionalists (as their name implies) love to stand on ceremony. Longevity is a way to buy confidence with clients. No one wants to trust his money to a fledgling company that's only been around for a handful of years.

Here are a couple clash-point considerations for recruiting and retaining Millennials in this kind of work environment:

>> **Meaning:** This one may come as a surprise at first. With the finance industry maligned in every newspaper headline, it may take a leap of faith to see how meaning would be an area of strength to push with Millennials, especially when everyone's chasing commission and a competitive salary (for more on this, see the nearby sidebar, "Focus on finance: Up recruiting, debunk stereotypes"). But the thing about working in the finance world is you can see the impact you're having in your clients' lives. It's direct and all-encompassing: growing their investments. Helping them plan for retirement. Providing calm in some of the most stressful conversations. These things are not to be discounted. You can so easily connect the dots for meaning-hungry Millennials, and you absolutely should.

"I have witnessed a Millennial [financial manager] have a team lunch and bring them coffee. The effort of noticing [their work] goes a long way, but it doesn't always happen in the quantity [Millennials] prefer." —Lori D., Manager

>> **Collaboration:** Old habits die hard, and for years and years finance leaders have been incentivizing their employees by encouraging competition within the ranks. Hyper-collaborative Millennials aren't going to love this type of messaging. Think about how you can set up more collaborative sales goals so your organization is more team-minded, instead of pitting individuals against each other. Another collaboration hitch you may run into is managers thinking something along the lines of, "Yea, but no one helped *me* when I was coming up." Work with the idea of reverse-mentoring to encourage experienced employees to pair with newbies so that both parties get something out of the exercise.

TIP

There's no question that a turnoff when recruiting Millennials will be your industry's adherence to tradition and formality. The finance world will probably never be the type of place where jeans and hoodies are considered acceptable attire (or at least not in the foreseeable future). That shouldn't stop you from thinking of ways you might move the needle to accommodate the Millennial desire for some degree of informality in dress and communication. Think about how and when you can shift toward the more casual. If someone is spending the day cold-calling clients, why is a suit so necessary? Find those areas where it makes sense to implement small tweaks to the rules.

FOCUS ON FINANCE: UP RECRUITING, DEBUNK STEREOTYPES

It could be said that Wall Street, and the financial industry as a whole, has a bit of a PR problem. When you look at how the media portrays those in the public sector, it's not surprising that Millennials remember only the negative associations. Gordon Gecko's "greed is good" slogan or scenes of the antics and corruption from *The Wolf of Wall Street* may flash through their minds. Hollywood depictions aside, many Millennials blame those in the financial sector for the 2009 recession. Occupy Wall Street and The Great Recession have made the next generation extremely mistrustful of people who manage money, and the stereotypes don't end there either. There's also the idea that people working in the finance industry are focused on swindling clients and doing whatever it takes to pull in a high commission, regardless of its effect on the client. All of these elements do not make for an industry that Millennials are keen to join.

Stereotypical descriptions surrounding the finance industry include:

- Greedy

- Corrupt

- Sales heavy (think cold-calling and used-car salesman)

- Outdated technology

- Stuffy

- Older, white men

- Self-serving

- Untrustworthy

- Dishonest

When you think about stereotypes from a generational perspective, it's obvious how harmful they can be to the conversation. The industry is buckling under the weight of these crushing misconceptions that are keeping you from finding the best next-gen talent. Reversing these stereotypes is the first step toward winning over a generation that has been, thus far, skeptical of your industry — and you may find that once you've won them over and they're on your side, they will share their newfound knowledge with their peers and be your biggest advocates.

Strategies for debunking stereotypes of the financial industry include:

- **Client first, commission second.** Emphasize the fact that your employees enrich the lives of their clients. They are there, firsthand, to witness the difference they effect on people's lives. It's impactful, it's inspirational, and it's prime Millennial motivation.

- **Relationships rule the roost.** Kill the cold-call misconception by replacing it with this truth — the world of finance is about fostering strong connections and relationships.

- **Shout it from the rooftops.** Make sure you're proactively sending this kind of messaging out there in as many ways as possible — be it in your marketing materials, during your campus visits, in your online presence, or through your social-media strategy.

Adjusting for Blue Collar versus White Collar

In the case of blue collar versus white collar, we have two potentially disparate types of work. White-collar workers are depicted as spending "normal" 9–5 work hours in an office or cubicle, whereas blue-collar workers may hold a graveyard shift and are typically on location, either in their specified field or an industrial location. White collar typically requires higher education, whereas blue collar requires more physical labor and technical skills. White-collar workers may be compensated with a salary, whereas blue-collar workers may be paid hourly and belong to a union.

Though blue-collar jobs have more than their fair share of Millennial employees, the Millennials in these roles don't feel like the generational conversation applies to them — and for good reason. Much of the Millennial-workplace talk, research conducted by large research houses, and media that talks about that research focuses on white-collar positions. Though white-collar jobs therefore seem like an easier sell, don't discount the value of blue-collar jobs to the Millennial generation. Millennials and the next generation are eyeing trade roles as a way to succeed, find stability, avoid debt, and bypass sitting behind a desk for hours on end, day after day.

Wearing a white collar

Here's a look at white-collar jobs as seen through a Millennial lens:

>> Depending on the job, there can be a high degree of flexibility in rules and regulations. It's possible to accommodate work-life integration, allowing Millennials to fit in doctor's appointments or midday workouts.

» Earning potential, as well as career progression, has no cap. Even if you've reached the limit within a certain organization, job-hopping around other white-collar roles means that Millennials can constantly seek to level-up their careers.

» The office setting allows for providing some of the little perks and benefits that are small but important pieces in Millennial retention: building opportunities for collaboration, providing catered goodies, and so on.

» Salaried roles mean there can be a focus on a results-oriented approach that frees Millennial employees from feeling as if they're being micro-managed. It lets them accomplish tasks in their own way on their own time, as long as they're meeting predetermined goals.

Clash-point considerations for recruiting and retaining Millennials in these kinds of roles include the following:

» **Meaning:** This can be a challenge within some white-collar jobs, especially for more entry-level positions. If, as a young Millennial employee, you're answering the phone and redirecting calls all day, it can be hard to feel how you connect to the company's bigger picture. Really take the time to connect the dots for employees whose roles may be distant from your company's bigger picture.

» **Feedback:** A great win within white-collar jobs is that oftentimes there's a well-established feedback loop within the company's structure. Millennials, who've been groomed from a young age to expect a constant stream of feedback, respond very well to opportunities to get constant commentary on their work, as well as chances to learn from mentors who've had more time at your organization and can teach them a thing or two. Constant commentary in these environments is most ideal when it comes from every level within the organization.

WARNING

More so than in blue-collar positions, the stereotype of "needy" or "entitled" hangs above white-collar Millennials. Those who've just arrived already want to fast-track their way to the top or want a face-to-face meeting with the CEO, thinking their ideas are brilliant enough to warrant her time. This may stem from the more lax rules and formality that come with typically white-collar roles, but don't chalk up Millennials' eagerness to entitlement. It's true that if you give them an inch they'll likely want another, but it doesn't have to be a negative experience for everyone involved. Tell them where you stand while being open to their ideas.

Going with a blue collar

Here's what blue collar means to a Millennial:

- Both managers and employees feel ignored, that the Millennial topic doesn't apply to them.

- Inflexible rules are pretty much the status quo within blue-collar jobs, and for very good reason. Oftentimes, the safety of both employees and clients/consumers is at risk, and staying true to rigid safety and scheduling standards is imperative to accident prevention. Other times, it may seem like change is impossible because every person is preoccupied with following every single rule.

- Manual labor is, as the phrase suggests, hard work. It can be physically straining on the body, with risk for injury and burnout. Workers must be on their guard the entire shift and are often subjected to elements beyond their control: working floor conditions, weather, and so forth.

- Within blue-collar roles, time often means money. Employees are compensated on an hourly basis, which means if they aren't there, they aren't making money. Compensation increases are incremental at best, and this can be a major challenge in wooing Millennial candidates.

- Oftentimes, higher education is not necessary for blue-collar roles. This can actually be wielded as a major draw, especially when you consider the generation after Millennials. Gen Edgers saw Millennials become hamstrung by mountains of student debt and are giving a curious eye to careers that don't necessarily require diplomas and all the financial hardships they entail.

Clash-point considerations for recruiting and retaining Millennials in these jobs are as follows:

- **Organizational structure:** Because rigidity and adherence to rules is baked into the way a lot of blue-collar jobs function, it should come as no surprise that the traditional hierarchy has not only stood the test of time, but is almost necessary in this kind of environment. Because the structure is very much power and influence at the top, trickling down to the bottom (where, typically, the newest employees reside), there's the chance that some of these Millennials will feel disconnected from leadership and start to see themselves as a peon, a number, a worker with no face and no name. Make an effort to connect lower-level employees with the upper tier of your company. Have managers/owners show up, walk the floor, make contact with the workers, and show not only that they're accessible but also that they care.

"[I like my hourly employees to know that] I'd rather prepare them for another employer than have them leave because they weren't happy. [It's about] understanding what they are looking to get out of the experience, and each person is different." —*Jayson M., Manager*

>> **Collaboration:** Working in a factory setting, focusing on one technical function day in and day out, can be lonely and isolated. Blue-collar managers should really put effort into building a team dynamic that encourages collaboration among workers. That may be through team-building opportunities offsite, resources for them to have a book club on their breaks, or meetings that encourage employees to speak up, come together, and share best practices. Opening up these moments for collaboration may seem like catering to Millennials, but they can instead be a retention tool that shows individual workers how their job impacts everyone and how their influence can promote working together to improve and streamline operations. You may be surprised by what emerges through encouraged collaboration.

INDUSTRIAL REVOLUTION 2.0: ROBOTICS AND THE LOSS OF BLUE-COLLAR JOBS

The Jetsons and *Ex Machina* are fictional depictions of the future, but they're not totally off base — a lot of blue-collar jobs are disappearing because of tech innovations. Artificial intelligence and automation have started influencing industries like trucking, manufacturing, and even white-collar roles like customer service and sales. These advancements may replace jobs and are also broadening the knowledge gap so that vocational and trade schools are struggling to keep up.

All that sounds rather apocalyptic, we know. But before you raise the white flag or start searching for a new job, here are some things to ponder about the future of robotics:

- Not *all* jobs will be replaced. Some skills — plumbing, carpentry, electric work, even housekeeping and landscaping — are too unstructured and amorphous for a bot to handle. A human hand will be needed (and much appreciated). Imagine a bot trying to unclog your toilet . . .

- There is and will be room for humans to work alongside and above automated machinery and processes. Human error will decrease, but until a time when machinery can be its own surgeon, humans will be needed to repair and debug machines. And as tech advances, so will training and schooling, even if it'll be a challenge. This a great place to market continuous developmental training to potential new hires.

- In the end, robots can't replace human interactions and relationships. They can come close (like, scary close), but they'll never fully replicate the full spectrum of human emotions, actions, and thoughts — at least not in the near future. Be sure to emphasize the importance of working relationships, whether or not you work with AI or automation now or in the future.

TIP

We're going to get real with you — the inflexibility of working hours is going to be your absolute biggest challenge when it comes to recruiting and retaining Millennials. Around the globe, Millennials cite flexibility and work-life balance as a top concern, and they're cautious about joining an industry where this isn't even a possibility. Rather than trying to diminish this fact, own it, and focus on what you can offer. Your hours may not be flexible and there may be no working from home, but there are tangible results of your efforts and the ability to leave work at work (none of that after-hours stuff). You can also market your culture and an environment that is really committed to their employees' well-being. This is a more powerful tool than you may realize.

Adjusting Your Style in the Arts versus the Sciences

For Millennials, the question of the arts or the sciences is one they can remember from their high-school and college years. Would they go the practical route and pursue a career in the sciences? Or would they put their efforts toward earning a diploma in the liberal arts, with majors like English or history? Boomer parents encouraged them to pursue whatever degree spoke to their heart, and degrees in the humanities were wildly popular during most of Millennials' college years (but dropped off steadily after the Great Recession). So, what do these two disparate career tracks have to offer? Creativity versus rigidity? Uncertainty versus job security? The truth is, as usual, the answers are much more complex. Though at first glance, it may seem like careers in the arts would be much more successful in speaking to the typical Millennial, there are more than enough marketable qualities within the sciences to appeal to Millennials, and perhaps even more so to the next generation. The following table gives some examples of careers that fall under the arts and sciences headings, respectively.

Arts	Sciences
Journalist	Research scientist
Marketing specialist	Doctor
Communications coordinator	Engineer
Management consultant	Mathematician
Graphic designer	Statistician

Stirring passions in the arts field

Take a look at how Millennials view the arts field:

>> A creative mind is a requirement, and creativity, by definition, requires innovation and originality, freeing the reins for Millennials' brainstorm-loving minds to roam free and push boundaries.

>> These roles can sometimes be dismissed as fluff and therefore can be among the first to get chopped when recession or downturn strikes. Job stability may not be a marketable trait with art fields, but for Millennials pursuing their passion, it may be worth the risk. (Also, as the workplace values talent more and more, these once fluffy roles will be so no more.)

>> A career in the arts world usually means more exposure to diversity, especially gender diversity, as fields like marketing tend to attract more women than, say, the sciences.

Clash-point considerations for recruiting and retaining Millennials in the arts include the following:

>> **Feedback:** Millennials are constantly looking for feedback, but when it comes to something as subjective as the arts and as personal as their own work, critiquing them can be a challenge. If you're a manager who's also in a creative role, take time to understand their thought process, review their concepts and iterations with a keen eye, and appreciate what they've done. If you're a manager who's in a different field, do your best to be as specific as you can, acknowledge what you don't know, and allow room for questions and pushback.

>> **Work-life integration:** Typically, roles in the arts crack the doors wide open for work-life integration. After all, trying to be inspired while sitting in the confines of a cubicle can be quite a challenge. Don't miss the opportunity to market this flexibility frequently and fervently! Millennials and flexibility go together like funnel cakes and Ferris wheels.

WARNING

There can be a dark side to the bounty of flexibility that creative jobs allow for. When you're each off doing your own thing, it can be hard to keep alignment within a project. As managers, don't let flexibility turn your team of full-time employees into what might as well be contract workers. There are times when it's important to come together — physically, not just virtually — and see the whites of each others' eyes. Appeal to the Millennial collaborative spirit by calling the troops together on a regular basis so your team doesn't start to feel disjointed.

Being mindful of the science field

Check out the science field through a Millennial's eye:

>> They say that business is part art, part science, and you'd be surprised which is which. Just because roles in science may be more linear doesn't mean that there isn't a great degree of creativity involved. New Millennial recruits will be looking for managers who encourage that creativity.

>> Science fields are rooted in facts, numbers, and research. They offer a level of certainty that Millennials enjoy, so when uncertainty comes into play, they can feel lost. Providing mentorship and guidance around things like career progression, work-life balance, and finding comfort in the unknowns will help them find their way.

>> Because jobs in the sciences have been traditionally marketed to boys (though we're starting to see a shift in the tides), there may be a tendency for some of these fields to feel like a bit of a Boys Club. For a generation that demands diversity, this doesn't sit well and could ignite some apprehension for young women entering the professional field.

>> Science careers are often viewed as more stable and higher earning, even for entry-level positions. The trade-off? More rigidity around rules like dress code, lab safety, and so on. Many Millennials will seek to change some of those rules; for example, Millennial physicians would like to change the stigma that all docs are burnt out because of being overworked and drowned in paperwork.

Consider the following clash points for recruiting and retaining Millennials in the sciences:

>> **Motivation:** Some fields within the sciences are more motivating, at least on the surface, than others. If you're a doctor interacting with patients every day, you see the impact of your work firsthand on a day-to-day basis. If you're a statistician, not so much. These Millennials may be more science-minded and focused on cold, hard facts, but that doesn't mean their motivation won't ebb if they're not connected to the company's bigger purpose. Explain the meaning behind their job. For example, a large pharmaceutical company has embedded part of their credo to put people first into every part of their culture. They end their meetings with it; they have it in every building's entrance. It's a daily reminder to connect the dots.

>> **Formality:** Where and when possible, don't be afraid to loosen up your rules and alter the "old school" way of doing things. Though the Millennials you attract may have a greater preference for order than those in the arts field, they'd still probably like to wear jeans and a graphic T-shirt under their lab coats.

TIP

The one problem with becoming an expert in a specific field is not being able to diversify your skills. On one hand, the type of Millennials you're attracting to these roles will know that's a part of the package. But unlike previous generations, they're still hungry to learn new skills that make them more well-rounded and can serve as a value-add to what they do/know. Think about creative ways that you can expose them to different experiences within the science field, even if they don't have the necessary qualifications. Encouraging a training, meeting, or mentor relationship that embraces the arts is a perfect counter to their day-to-day.

4

Gearing Up for the Coming Changes

Forecast future trends in the workplace as they relate to the generations.

Prepare yourself to manage the leadership of tomorrow.

Get a glimpse into the generation after Millennials: Gen Edge (also known as Gen Z).

Anticipate Millennial trouble spots that will arise in the next decade.

Build a workplace today that will last through the tides of change.

> » **Helping Millennial leaders capitalize on strengths and minimize weaknesses**
>
> » **Foreseeing potential Millennial leadership clash points**
>
> » **Prepping for the dynamics of managing up, down, and across**

Chapter **15**

Paving the Way for Millennial Leadership

opefully, you didn't need to suppress a snort when you read this chapter's title (and if you did, you may want to spend a bit of time in Chapter 3). Like it or not, Millennials are on their way to leadership positions, if not already there. Some of you may be scratching your heads at how to work with the Millennial leaders you already have, while others may be having a panic-inducing realization that Millennials are already gracing leadership positions with their presence.

Every great leader embodies indispensable factors: exemplary listening skills, empathy, conviction, honesty, and the ability to inspire. These leaders can be found across every generation and have loyal groups of employees who brag to their friends about their stellar boss, basking in their friends' jealousy. These leaders also likely have their own generational brand of managing, because each generation has made its mark on leadership. Now it's Millennials' turn to participate in this trend of change. (There's a trophy at the end, right?) Just as there are hundreds of ways to tie a knot, there are various approaches to leading well, and Millennials are already crafting their own brand (or knot, if you will) of inspirational leadership and management.

This chapter examines the present and forecasts the future of what may be when Millennials take the leadership throne. Well, "throne" is a very anti-Millennial view of leadership, so we'll opt for "leadership position" or "leadership beanbag chair" instead. By predicting future areas of collision, you'll gain insight into areas you can focus on now to build a strong pipeline of young leaders and managers. Then we take a closer look at the Millennial leadership persona: What will their strengths be? In what areas will they do just so-so? What areas of leadership are they most likely to struggle with? Toward the end, we examine every potential generational combo of Millennial leader to direct report.

Grooming the Leaders to Be

First things first. This chapter is *not* just about forecasting. Millennial leadership is not a thing of the distant future, because many of them are in leadership roles *right now.* Older Millennials have almost a decade and a half of work experience and are already cutting their leadership teeth. Younger Millennials, and even Generation Edgers in some cases, aren't too far from becoming corporate captains. For the skeptics out there, this is far from too soon to start having this conversation. On the contrary, the time is more than already upon you. And if that isn't enough motivation for you, what about thinking about how this will benefit *you*? Fostering leadership among Millennials will not only safeguard your organization's future but it will make you an even better leader in the process.

Knocking down mental blocks

The skeptics, however, must be addressed, and regardless of how primed or willing you think you are for this conversation about Millennial leadership, you may have some hidden mental barriers. Before you can tackle the tactical by grooming the leaders-to-be, make sure you acknowledge these sometimes conscious, sometimes subconscious, mental blocks. Then grab your Thor hammer and tear down the mental blocks.

The lack-of-loyalty block

Many current managers land on this one incredibly defeatist question — *Why bother?* They think to themselves, "These Millennials are just going to leave in a couple years anyway. Why bother investing time and money into developing their skills?" This way of thinking is the equivalent of cutting off your nose to spite your face. Research shows that Millennial attrition rates can be tied to lack of leadership training and promotion opportunities.

Remove the mental block: Simply showing your Millennials that you're considering them as potential future leaders can serve as a retention tool in and of itself. Invest in them early and they'll be more likely to stay. Millennials are more loyal than you think — just ask some of them.

> "[To me, loyalty means] not that you have to stay forever, but while you're there, you're doing your job well and treating [your co-workers with respect]." —*Bethany B., Millennial*

The "it's not fair" block

The generational conversation has taken off in the last couple decades, and the benefactors have been, for the most part, the younger generation. Everyone has sought answers to the questions about this young and confusing generation (looking at you, reader). Because of that, Millennials are the first generation to receive the full benefits of their managers/mentors/leaders tapping into generational awareness as a training tool. Boomers and Gen Xers, by and large, had to try and navigate misunderstandings without the added benefit of a generational lens. It's natural to feel some frustration that Millennials "have it easy," but it's no reason to begrudge Millennials this added help. Millennials are optimistic that young professional-hood can be different, so they're vying for leadership positions at an early age and departing businesses when they're unhappy; perhaps that's a great precedent to set for following generations.

> "When you think about who's in leadership now, Xers are feeling resentful that Boomers stayed on longer than thought. Xers didn't have a chance to step into [leadership roles], and now they're starting to open up. I feel it's set organizations up for underlying competition and Xers not wanting to see Millennials succeed." —*Ann M., Manager*

Remove the mental block: It's because of generations before them crying foul or demanding people to stand up for themselves that Millennials are charting a new path. See this as progress instead of unfair advancement and share the story of how difficult it was for you without turning into too much of a martyr. It could turn into a mentoring or coaching moment worthy of *Friday Night Lights 2: At the Office*.

The entitlement block

Overcoming the entitlement mental block can be hard. These eager-beaver Millennials keep asking for more promotions, more opportunities, more comfortable office furniture, more flexibility, more kombucha in the break room, more, more, more. Sometimes, when you encounter these kinds of zealous personalities, the gut reaction is to push them away. The entitlement sensor goes off and, all of a sudden, giving them your best advice and attention feels more like gratifying a spoiled child than grooming your best talent.

LEADERSHIP BOOT CAMP: WHY THE NEXT GENERATION NEEDS EXTRA HELP DEVELOPING SKILLS

It turns out that all of the structured play planned for the last few decades of school-children may have had some unexpected consequences. A study by the University of Colorado and University of Denver produced research that suggests that highly regulated play is interfering with development of some of the most vital skills necessary for high executive functioning. By having their play regulated and watched over, children are being stripped of the freedom to daydream, set their own goals, or even allow natural leaders to rise to the top of the pack. The implication behind this research is important for you in one major way: Millennials may need a bit more help developing leadership skills. While it would be easy to resent their need for "hand-holding," remember that different childhoods create different batches of employees, complete with pros and cons. Millennials will need more structured onboarding to the leadership path.

Remove the mental block: Don't be afraid to set expectations about what's realistic and what may feel more like overreaching, but also understand that Millennials' unbridled enthusiasm can be used as a resource to fuel hard work and hone skills, rather than just a reflection of entitlement and narcissism.

The "they're just kids" block

Millennials, especially the older ones, have been in the workforce for a respectable chunk of time. They're not newbies; they're not youngsters; they're not kids (in fact, many of them *have* kids). Even the younger Millennials shouldn't be written off as "kids," but future leaders in the making. We actually suggest striking this word from your vocabulary altogether — what generation has ever liked being called "kids?" People tend to underestimate the standing of the Millennial employee, picturing the brand-new college grad rather than the more accurate experienced contributor.

Remove the mental block: Instead of viewing Millennials as the youngest generation, just view them as their generation. As they get older, they'll still be Millennials and showcase similar traits and values, so view them as their generation now.

The fear-of-change block

Change, in most settings, is uncomfortable. When a young generation is giddy and waiting in the leadership wings, their energy and ambition can read as disruptive and even threatening. Though Millennials have a tendency to enter the workforce full of ideas and anxious to find new ways of doing things, they likely aren't plotting how to prove how worthless you are. They need your leadership to help them lead.

Remove the mental block: Change translates to progress, and the most progressive organizations are the ones ahead of the pack. Play to Millennials' strengths as well as your own to make the transition seamless.

Where to focus now

Make no mistake, the time is now. Or better yet, yesterday. Baby Boomers are starting to retire or pursue encore careers. Seasoned Gen X leaders are stepping up to fill the posts Boomer leaders are leaving behind, and Millennials are being bumped up to fill the roles that those Gen Xers just vacated (sometimes sooner than is comfortable). In addition to that, there simply aren't enough Gen Xers to fulfill the roles that Boomers will vacate, so either roles will shift in the workplace or, the more likely scenario, Millennials will fill the holes that Boomers are leaving behind. If you're feeling anxious by this slew of generational shifts, sit down with your beverage of choice and be honest with yourself about what you can do.

WARNING

We fear making you feel fear, but we also want to be 100 percent honest with you. If you haven't started grooming future leaders, you're behind. In the not-so-distant future, you may be in a company of Millennials who are unsuited (pun intended) and potentially unwilling to make that leap into the world of management. Picture the cowardly lion as a leader — all the potential to be great and powerful but ill-equipped to comfortably take the reins. The picture isn't perfect, but you can still make kings of the forest. We've listed four areas to focus on. Don't feel the pressure to do everything at once, but perhaps a combination will suit you.

Training

Though Millennials may carry the stereotype of being "know-it-alls," we're here to tell you that Millennials are arguably the most eager to learn new skills. From project management to emotional intelligence to phone etiquette, they want to be better and are (mostly) aware of their shortcomings. Of the statements that follow, how many are true for your company? How many are false? If you can't logically excuse the false answers, maybe it's time to refocus.

>> **T/F:** We offer internal training opportunities for both technical and soft skills.

>> **T/F:** The internal trainings are well-received and helpful.

>> **T/F:** When we can, we value the chance to invite outside experts to provide trainings.

>> **T/F:** When we can, we provide opportunities for young, high-potential employees (among others) to attend conferences.

Coaching

As we cover extensively in Chapter 7, Millennials are highly receptive to mentors and look to their higher-ups as great coaches and sources of wisdom. These one-on-one relationships aren't just about making Millennials better at their current jobs, but are also about inspiring them to see themselves as leaders. Now is the time for your best plays, Coach, so take the true or false (T/F) quiz. You may not be able to answer true to every one, but if there are more Fs than Ts, you will probably want to take a closer look at your mentoring approach:

>> **T/F:** My organization has a mentorship program.

>> **T/F:** Our mentorship program works well, whether it's formal or informal.

>> **T/F:** I always lead by example.

>> **T/F:** I turn every shortcoming/challenge/collision into a coaching moment.

Diversity and inclusion

To Millennials and all younger generations in the workforce, diversity and inclusion are critical. If you neglect any lens of diversity, you're going to feel the soft breeze of young'uns leaving your organization. They're looking to thrive in organizations that represent a diverse world — for example, if a woman doesn't see an equal representation of female leaders, she'll doubt whether her future is with that company and look elsewhere. The same could be argued for other lenses of diversity. Take our advice: Don't tiptoe around this. Be sure to include every lens. Take the T/F quiz, and as a reminder, if you can't logically excuse the false answers, it may be time to rethink your inclusion initiatives.

>> **T/F:** My organization has a diversity and inclusion department/team/initiative.

>> **T/F:** Our leadership represents the diversity that Millennials expect to see in organizations.

>> **T/F:** We are transparent about all lenses of diversity and build a safe space for everyone.

>> **T/F:** We embrace diversity as a celebration of differences.

WARNING

If you are someone who views humans as humans and believes that focusing on diversity drives people father apart rather than closer together, we can understand your perspective but can't ascribe to it. Too much research has proven that method a less-than-productive lens through which to view diversity and inclusion. Instead, embrace the differences.

Marketing

As you implement leadership development programs or initiatives, don't be bashful. Feel free to push out your chest and boast. Millennials want to know that leaders are taking an active interest in developing their skills and will undoubtedly do their research. Consider how you can use your efforts as a promotional tool and incentive for the next generation of hires. If you are ready to be bold and not bashful, make sure you get the word out by:

» Collaborating with your PR contact to spread the message of how great you are. After all, there's no such thing as bad press (especially in this scenario).

» Applying for "Best Place to Work" awards. There are many varieties, and you'll never win if you don't apply!

» Encouraging the use of social media at work. Millennials will be your own free spokespeople if they are allowed to post about how awesome their company is at leadership development.

YOU DOWN WITH LDPS? YEAH, YOU KNOW ME

Some organizations, like Unilever, GE, and McKinsey & Company, have done a fantastic job of creating formal programs to develop the next generation of leaders. These leadership development programs (LDPs) are often designed with the Millennial generation in mind and are no easy program to get through — often including milestone presentations, capstone projects, or consistently proving results have been met. They seek to train the most critical skills for future leaders. Sometimes, people don't make it through the leadership program, and that's okay! If you don't have a formal initiative, you can still take from their methods and create your own informal program by following these steps:

1. **Design the program.** Who is leading it? Is all leadership on board? How long will it last? What resources are needed? What training will participants receive? Who will those participants' mentors be? What is the final step of the program?

2. **Get the word out.** Market internally, and perhaps externally, about the program to get the right people interested. At the very least, it will get you some great PR.

3. **Recruit the crew.** Whether the potential leaders are nominated by peers or apply directly to the program, aim to attract a superior bunch of high potentials to then launch the program.

Predicting future leadership challenges

As you build your training programs, consider the areas where your Millennials may struggle in their future leadership roles. One simple way to do this for any person of any generation is to list that person's traits and values and then translate them into how they could manifest in a leader. As a start, we've listed the most common Millennial traits and values in Figure 15-1. Take five minutes (or ten if you're a deep thinker) to fill out the right column of this exercise. Knowing these traits and resulting leadership behaviors, what challenges do you see arising? How can you proactively help them with those potential challenges? How then can you ensure that they'll lead to their best potential?

Coaching the collaborative leader

It may not be all that surprising that a generation that excels at collaboration may want to apply that collaborative spirit to its management style. As any leader knows, it can get lonely up there on that mountaintop; big decisions, budgeting, and delegating often occur solo. Millennial leaders may struggle with the fact that the buck stops with them. Extra coaching on solo decision-making may prove fruitful to prevent a work environment that resembles universal democracy and paints independent workers as isolated lone rangers.

	Traits/Values	As a leader, they will …	What you can do … *(Fill in the blanks)*
Traits	Collaborative	Be democratic in decision-making.	
	Tech savvy	Organize and lead via technological platforms.	
	Socially accepting	Strongly value diversity and inclusion.	
	Disruptive	Seek and reward constant change.	
Values	Customization	Be eager to individualize their approach.	
	Authenticity	Have a tendency to be too informal.	
	Speed	Prefer to work and lead fast, for better or worse.	
	Flexibility	Be motivated to give flexibility, but may find that it's harder to manage than previously thought.	

FIGURE 15-1: Preparing to build Millennial leaders.

BridgeWorks. Minneapolis, MN. (October, 2016)

Forgetting formality

There's something to be said for formality in dress. The old adage "dress for the job you want, not the job you have" reflects the idea that if people see you dressed in a formal, powerful way, they will assume that you are a powerful and influential person. Consider football players' black paint on their cheeks. This doesn't just keep the sun's glare out of their eyes — it's a universal intimidation factor. If Millennial leaders are showing up at the workplace wearing their casual tees with slogans like, "But first, coffee," are they going to be able to inspire respect and buy-in with other generations? Millennial leaders will need to learn the balance required to build credibility with older generations without losing relatability with younger generations.

Feedback junkies

Millennials aren't immune to generational naiveté. If they haven't had a crash course in the generations, they may fall into that well-intentioned trap of giving feedback the way they wish they'd received it. It's one thing to have a manager who doesn't give you enough feedback (for example, Xers managing Millennials), but when your manager is flooding you with unsolicited and unwanted feedback or requesting multiple check-ins, it's going to feel like someone is continually poking your arm to get attention (or micromanaging). Millennials need to understand how to cater their feedback to specific generations and how to occasionally live at that 40,000-foot level rather than zooming right in.

ABW: Always be working

Millennials have taken the freedom technology offers and run with it, but there are signs that they may be over-integrating work and life. Because they're always carrying their phones with them, they never have an excuse for a delayed response. All of a sudden, everything is urgent. Did they send you an email at 7 p.m. last night? You didn't read it? For shame! Millennial leaders may struggle with turning off, and it will be important that they don't hold their employees to the same unrealistic expectations.

The Millennial martyr

Just like every generation has its favorite zombie movies, every generation has its share of zombie employees, in other words, the overworked, the exhausted, and those dangerously close to burnout. For Boomers, it was those who put in 80 hours a week. For Gen Xers, it was the workers with such an efficient work style that they hardly stopped to eat their lunch, let alone take a deep breath. Millennials have their own manifestation of the overworked. It's those who don't turn off email notifications *ever* (seeing work email pings at 3 a.m. in the morning) and those who act like not taking vacations is a badge of honor. This style of overwork is bad when it's an employee, but absolutely detrimental when it's the leader.

> "Having [the] freedom and flexibility to have a life when life comes up . . . I value that. [It's] great to feel enabled to do that, whereas at my last job [there was] a stigma against not working." —*Clayton H., Millennial*

Bringing Out the Best Millennial Leadership Skills

With a fresh new wave of leadership comes a brand new set of leadership skills. Millennials, like any generation, have many natural talents, some innate and some as a result of the conditions they grew up in. Unsurprisingly, they'll be bringing their generational traits with them as captains of leadership. To get a grasp on where to focus your efforts as you groom the next batch of leaders, it's helpful to understand the areas where they'll knock it out of the park, where they'll do just okay, and where they may fall short without your training and assistance.

While it's natural to manage how you want to be managed, don't try to make Millennials into mini versions of yourself. You'll end up frustrated and potentially damage relationships if you try to force a square peg into a round hole. Instead, think of how you can focus on making the most of their unique talents, and grant them generational self-awareness so they can adjust appropriately in the areas where they may be lacking (especially when they manage other generations).

Where they will shine

How do you bring out the best qualities of potential Millennial leaders? It's up to you to find the best ways to highlight the following shining stars:

>> **Collaborating:** They'll excel at building consensus across the team.

>> **Coaching:** More than being "bosses," Millennials will embrace a compassionate leadership style that is carrot (not stick) centric.

>> **Innovation/disruption:** They will inspire their direct reports to think in new, unexpected ways and to take the road less travelled.

>> **Accessibility:** The work-life integration that Millennials so love will make them extremely accessible leaders both from a time perspective (always on) and from a communication perspective (no need for formality).

>> **Customization:** They understand the value of customization and will strive to cater their approach to each employee.

>> **Open-mindedness:** They'll naturally create an inclusive environment because diversity in opinion will be just as important as diversity in employees.

"[Millennials have] seen a lot of change in the world and, as a result, we're going to hopefully be pretty adaptable in our leadership positions. We also might be a little more open to change." —*Alexa S., Millennial*

>> **Employee-first mentality:** Millennials value people above profit, and the welfare of their reports will be a high priority.

>> **Holistic approach:** They'll focus on promoting employee well-being — physical, mental, and emotional health — because they know how it can impact the bottom line. Yes, that means treadmill desks near windows and meditation/yoga rooms at work.

>> **Team building:** Millennials value a strong team (#workfamily) and will make great efforts to promote the ties that bind across their reports.

Which generation will Millennials shine at managing? It shouldn't come as a shock that Millennials will probably shine brightest when managing their own generation. There are many easy points of connection from a cultural standpoint, and they will share many of the same traits and values when it comes to the workplace and perceptions of work. Collaboration and feedback styles will be similar, and ideas around formality will likely align.

There is, however, a slight possibility that Millennials will get a taste of their own medicine. Managing one of their own could send them into a whirlwind of confusion. Thoughts of "Wow, this is harder than I thought" may cross their minds as they have to manage the stereotypes that are so often spread (and sometimes true!) about their own generation.

Where they could coast

Millennials, like other generations, will earn a solid B-average in some areas of leadership. As *their* leader, find the right times to coach as necessary. Remember to focus more energy on the shining moments than the ones that will require too much energy to buff out.

>> **Informality:** A relaxed attitude with both dress and communication can make it a challenge for Millennials to earn respect from other generations.

>> **Technology:** While their technology savvy will generally be a big asset, other times it can demotivate those who find the reliance on it crippling, distracting, or alienating.

>> **#workfamily:** Having close, open, authentic relationships with direct reports may lead to some display of favoritism or the inability to give critical feedback when needed.

>> **Communication:** They love texts, IMs, and emails, but with some generations they'll need to learn the importance of upping the face-to-face game.

>> **Burnout management:** Millennial managers will do their best to prevent burnout but may do a bad job of leading by example (for example, by not taking their vacation time or sending emails at all hours of the night).

>> **Rewards:** Influenced by their own generational lens, Millennials may initially struggle with giving rewards that appeal to each generation (rather than the ones they wish they'd received).

Which generation will Millennials be okay at managing? There are undoubtedly points of connection between Millennials and Boomers. Natural relationships will blossom because of the familiar generational dynamic, whether it's aunt-niece, father-daughter, and so on. Additionally, both generations share an optimistic spirit and lean toward positivity. The areas that may give Boomers pause could be Millennials' lack of formality in dress, communication, and general workplace etiquette, as well as eschewing, for the most part, a competitive work style.

Where they might struggle

While we don't advise focusing on Millennial weaknesses, we can't turn a blind eye to the reality that Millennials won't excel in all areas of leadership. We know, shocker! To ensure that you bring out the best, don't focus on the struggles but carry an awareness of what they may be so you can appropriately redirect.

>> **Struggle to work independently:** Collaborative work may be the Millennial go-to, but it could morph into a serious demotivation factor for some generations, primarily the hands-off Gen Xers.

>> **Oversaturated feedback:** The constant flow of feedback and check-ins that Millennials value may feel, to some, like micromanaging.

>> **Democracy overload:** Not all decisions can be made with group-think, and sometimes Millennials will need to just buckle down and make a decision without group consensus, uncomfortable as they may feel.

>> **Earning respect:** Older generations may feel some resentment toward a younger person managing them and will need Millennial managers to prove why they're qualified for their position.

> "The biggest [struggle] would be [that] now you're in a place of power and you have to create boundaries with people who were once your friends. How do you get them to respect you?" —*Lauren W., Millennial*

>> **Expecting immediacy:** Because Millennials are always on, they're going to expect speedy responses to communication, even if it's sent at 11 p.m.

>> **Discipline:** Millennials lead with a friendly, good-cop approach, and it's going to be extra hard for them to flip a switch and become the bad cop.

Which generation will Millennials struggle managing? Millennials will likely struggle the most when managing both Gen Xers and Gen Edgers. Xers raised their Gen Edge offspring to embody an independent spirit and to go for the win (not just the participation award). Millennials may have some hurdles to overcome when it comes to connecting with a generation much more practical, pragmatic, and direct than their own.

Preparing Millennials to Manage Up

Imagine that you are a 55-year-old employee named Michael. You have been working at your organization for 25 years. You are loyal, ambitious, and content with your career. You've got a few plaques for achieving great things and proudly wear a company T-shirt when you go out. In the past year, you've learned that you're getting a new manager, Ryan, who has been alive as long as you've been working.

For some reason(s), this situation is unsettling for Michael, but perhaps equally daunting for Ryan. Preparing Millennial leaders like Ryan for this quite common scenario will be key as you groom the next generation of leadership. Teaching Millennials to understand what it's like for veteran employees like Michael to work for a "youngster" will be critical.

Preparing to deal with potential negativity

Michael is not alone, as more and more Boomers and Gen Xers are being managed by blossoming Millennial leaders. If only it were an easy task! Leadership and management are not easy, especially in a "managing up" scenario. As you prime Millennials to reverse the traditional flow of management, check yourself.

Getting past the "haze the freshmen" mentality

Whenever a new group enters the pack, everyone's hackles seem to rise. It's the discomfort of the new, the unfamiliar, and the unknown. Unfortunately, this often leads to feelings of resentment. Grumblings of "I had to work tooth and nail to get to where I am," become rumblings of "I didn't have anyone to help me get where I am, *you* figure it out." If, as a manager yourself, this is your initial reaction to the idea of Millennial managers, there's no need to feel bad about it. This trial-by-fire or sink-or-swim mentality goes centuries back, and it's a way of having newbies prove that they deserve to be among the esteemed rank. If this is you,

>> **Ask yourself: Who does this help?** If you have wisdom and experience that can help streamline management, why would you hold back? To prove a point? No one benefits from this.

>> **Simmer in the feeling privately for a few minutes.** Then, compose yourself and lead the new bunch of managers. Don't be reticent about teaching them the wisdom you've acquired.

>> **Get ready to be a proud papa/mama/leader bear.** You'll find that one of the highest achievements you can accomplish as a leader is to be the one responsible for the next group of amazing leaders.

Dealing with the "upstart syndrome"

Beware of the "upstart syndrome." When a younger employee is managing an older direct report, there's always a risk of inspiring the upstart syndrome: *What's this kid doing managing me? How is she more qualified than I am? Why should I listen to her? She's going to have to prove herself.* Not everyone will feel this way, but for the ones who do, Millennials will be starting the managerial relationship at a serious disadvantage. So, do them a favor:

>> **Prepare Millennial managers.** You can provide the honest insight and tools for tackling this potential challenge and overcoming it.

>> **Emphasize the importance of humility.** The biggest favor Millennials can do for themselves is to develop a keen sense of self-awareness so that they exude humility in everything they do and say. They may feel pressured to come in as *"the boss,"* but this will only disengage everyone around them. Coach them on how to invite input and ask for guidance without appearing unqualified.

REMEMBER

The best gift that you can give potential and current Millennial leaders is generational training and know-how. By nature of reading this book, you've obviously made generational awareness a priority, so we applaud you and welcome you to the not-so-secret club of generational junkies. Impart this wisdom to Millennials so they can learn how to best work with Boomers and Gen Xers.

Millennials managing Boomers

It's time for a mind meld. As best you can, don your gen lens to get inside the mind of another generation. In Figure 15-2, you see a feedback form written for a Millennial manager from a Baby Boomer direct report. It's annual review time, and the Boomer is being as honest but polite as she can. If you want to challenge yourself, spot the generational collisions as you read.

Here's what you should take away from Figure 15-2:

Reasons Millennials will earn an A+ at managing Boomers:

>> Giving Boomers the positive and optimistic outlook they thrive on

>> Keeping Boomers involved and up-to-date on technology

Reasons Millennials will be on the struggle bus managing Boomers:

>> Overcoming the "you could be my kid" prejudice/uneasiness

>> Being overbearing about what technology Boomers should be using and how often

>> Approaching relationships too informally

Manager Feedback Form: *Please give feedback about your manager.*
Reviewer: Baby Boomer employee Bridget
Manager: Millennial manager Lyra

Communication is clear.

Lyra's communication is always forthcoming. She's not shy about complimenting me on a job well done or suggesting a resource or tool if my performance might be improved by it. I do think that she might favor technology tools (instant messaging and emails) a bit more than I would like. She's great about face time in big group meetings, but I'd appreciate a bit more one-on-one in-person communication.

My manager fosters a supportive team environment and handles conflict effectively.

Absolutely. Regarding a supportive team environment, this might be one of her greatest strengths as a manager. I feel very connected to the other members of our team, and there is something both inspirational and aspirational about the way she's led us through this year. I haven't, however, seen her handle conflict very much. From what I can tell, she'll seek out her own manager to help her address it. As long as it's getting taken care of, that's fine with me.

Feedback, good and bad, is timely and fair.

I struggle here because Lyra is not shy about giving feedback frequently and in the moment, if not VERY shortly thereafter. So, as far as the timely piece goes, yes. Honestly, too much yes at times, because I need a moment to breathe before hearing feedback. Sometimes she's so informal that I'm unsure of where I stand. I suppose I'm not used to having such a "friendly" boss. I appreciate the informality at times, but it can be hard to understand where to draw that line of manager versus friendly co-worker. It's different than my previous, more "dictatorial" leaders. When my previous manager told me to do something, there was no second guessing what she meant or what she wanted. Now, though, I do sometimes wonder.

I feel respected and that my hard work is appreciated.

When a Millennial first started managing me, it was a bit of a hard pill to swallow. I've been working in this industry for over 30 years, and to be told I was going to be managed by someone half my age ... well, needless to say, I felt the sting. We've definitely had our challenges along the way, but I appreciate the stream of positive feedback that comes my way (sometimes a tad more than I would like; see above).

Additional Comments:

Not to stereotype, but Lyra is such a tech addict. One part of me loves it, because I feel like we're staying on the cutting edge with the latest and greatest tools. The other part of me feels like I can hardly keep up with the constant switching and upgrading. Not that I'm bad at new tech stuff, I actually think I'm pretty good. But I'd appreciate more check-ins. Also, I like to learn new things beyond technology. I'd love to find more opportunities for learning in the next year.

FIGURE 15-2:
Baby Boomer employee to Millennial manager review.

BridgeWorks. Minneapolis, MN. (October, 2016)

Millennials managing Xers

While many people assume that the Boomer versus Millennial relationship is most challenging, in reality the struggles are more real between Gen Xers and Millennials, especially when it comes to management. Check out Figure 15-3 for a common tale.

Manager Feedback: Please give feedback about your manager.
Reviewer: Gen X employee Scott
Manager: Millennial manager Camila

Communication is clear.

Communication is clear enough. I find sometimes there's over-communicating happening, or it's done inefficiently. Still don't get the pinging me on IM thing instead of just getting up and asking me in person. Also, I think direction can be even clearer at times — articulating expectations is completely fine. Camila doesn't have to worry that I'll get defensive or sensitive.

My manager fosters a supportive team environment, and handles conflict effectively.

The team environment is there, but I think it's a bit overboard sometimes. Collaborating is fine, and I understand the need for a brainstorm every now and then, but I do my best work when I'm by myself. Would appreciate fewer ideation sessions and team outings and more time to do independent work. Also, I've found that she wants to run any and all new ideas by the rest of the team. It truthfully takes the wind out of my sails — seems like she has no confidence in my ability to get the job done. This is my biggest frustration with her. As far as conflict handling goes? There's something to be said for calling a spade a spade. I wish there was less beating around the bush and more nipping issues in the bud. Just say what you mean.

Feedback, good and bad, is timely and fair.

I find Camila to be a perfectly competent manager, but sometimes she really makes me feel like I'm being micromanaged. I understand the importance of feedback, but there are times when the dust can settle. Right after a presentation gone a bit wrong, she's stopped me in the hall to give me feedback. On any given project, she checks in with me at least a handful of times before the week is over, and I honestly don't think I need it. This could be just a preference thing, and I don't mean to sound mean, but there are too many exclamation points in emails with "harsh feedback." Tell me what I did wrong, and I'll avoid it next time. This whole compliment sandwich thing just slows me down.

I feel respected and that my hard work is appreciated.

For the most part, yes. I do feel that I'm a valuable member of the team, and Camila goes out of her way to compliment good performance. She also gives me the work-life balance I need, and I greatly appreciate how flexible she is.

Additional Comments:

I wish some attention was paid to the limits of technology. We've incorporated so many new systems/programs/apps in the last year that it's hard to keep up. I love new tech just as much as the next person, but do we even know it's going to work? There seems to be no testing outside of using us as guinea pigs. Not only is it hard to keep up, but it feels like I've just wasted my time when some of these things fail. I wish there was more of a vetting process before we adopt these things.

BridgeWorks. Minneapolis, MN. (October, 2016)

FIGURE 15-3:
Gen X employee to Millennial manager review.

Here's what to take away from Figure 15-3:

Reasons Millennials will earn an A+ at managing Xers:

>> Being transparent about company decisions and direction

>> Continually streamlining workflow, making things more efficient

>> Fostering a flexible work environment for everyone

Reasons Millennials will be on the struggle bus managing Xers:

>> Wanting to adopt too much technology without vetting its usefulness first

>> Collaborating by default and planning work events/outings without regarding Xers' fiercely guarded personal time

>> Finding the right balance of checking in to make the Millennial manager feel good, but also keeping the Gen Xer engaged and not feeling micromanaged

Getting Millennials Ready to Manage Across and Down

It seems obvious that Millennials who are tasked with the challenge of managing up, sometimes to employees twice their age, will have some challenges to work through. A savvy leader knows that these leadership issues aren't going to disappear just because a Millennial leader is managing down or across, but will instead manifest as slightly different, and sometimes unexpected, challenges.

Millennials managing Millennials

Here are some words Millennials may use to describe their managing style, especially when it comes to others of their same generation: bestie, biffles, coach, and so on. How does that play out when they're managing others within the same generation? Many older Millennials may learn the tough lesson that managing the younger version of themselves is complicated; there's a reason that the media is obsessed with talking about Millennials. Figure 15-4 gives some insight into what the dynamic may look like.

Manager Feedback: *Please give feedback about your manager.*
Reviewer: Millennial employee Rachael
Manager: Millennial manager Ahmed

Communication is clear.

Yes, communication is super clear! I love that he's one of the few managers who doesn't mind if I text him. He seems to always be available to answer any question I have whenever I have it, even if it's 8 p.m. in the evening. I really appreciate that no matter the time or the place, I can pretty much count on him to get back to me in a timely fashion. There are times that I feel like I don't get enough structured direction in how to do something — just be clear with what you want and I'll do it.

My manager fosters a supportive team environment and handles conflict effectively.

We all spend so much time at work, and it's always seemed silly to me that we don't connect with each other on a deeper level than just professional colleagues. Ahmed is amazing at building a team environment to the point that I can confidently say I've made some amazing friends. My teammates are more than just people I work with. I respect and love seeing them every day! I credit my manager for building a safe and fun environment where we can all collaborate, share our ideas (no matter how dumb they might seem), and work together toward an end goal that benefits us all. It's one of my favorite things about working here. Admittedly, conflict, when it has happened, has felt awkward. It seems like we're both trying to feel each other out when sometimes things just need to be said.

Feedback, good and bad, is timely and fair.

Like I said above, Ahmed seems to always be on. He is so quick at delivering feedback, whether it's words of encouragement or how I could improve next time around. It's so much easier to respond to feedback when it's almost in-the-moment as opposed to getting it six months or a year later (when I might not even remember what it was I did or didn't do!). I also appreciate that he's not über formal in his approach. I feel like I'm having a conversation with a coach rather than a talking to by a superior. I admire his positive approach and that even when the feedback is constructive, he gives me tangible ideas for how I can improve my performance.

I feel respected and that my hard work is appreciated.

Without a doubt. I'd say that the biggest way Ahmed shows me this is by having candid conversations about my future in this company. He sees potential in me and has invested a lot of time in developing skills that I know will be invaluable to me if I become a leader or manager in my own right sometime (hopefully soon!). I will say that I thought I'd get just a little more flexibility. I feel like it's a waiting game to be able to work from home, and I wish I could have done that in my first few months. I get why not, but it's just a comment.

Additional Comments:

I'm not sure if this is the right place to mention this, but I guess the one area of improvement might be … well, it's complicated. Ahmed and I have such a great working relationship. He's super authentic and chill, but I sometimes forget that he's my manager. Those few times he does put his foot down on some decision or needs to discipline someone, it feels jarring in a way. I'm not sure I want anything changed necessarily, it's just an interesting observation. But overall, Ahmed's management style is refreshing and fun, and I am glad to be a part of his team!

BridgeWorks. Minneapolis, MN. (October, 2016)

FIGURE 15-4:
Millennial
employee to
Millennial
manager review.

Here's what you should take away from Figure 15-4:

Reasons Millennials will earn an A+ at managing Millennials:

>> Growing an authentic, #workfamily relationship built around a shared understanding and shared history

>> Easy, streamlined communication

>> Embracing change

Reasons Millennials might be on the struggle bus while managing Millennials:

>> Falling into the "cool boss" syndrome, to the point that they hesitate to pull out the "stern boss" card

>> Over-authenticity leading to outward favoritism to those they connect with best

>> Learning how to manage the areas that so many others have struggled with, for example, allowing flexible work arrangements when they're not that easy to dish out

WARNING

Keep an eye out for the "I'm Not a Millennial" Millennial manager. These managers shrug off the "Millennial" designation because they've seen all the negativity that surrounds that title, want nothing to do with it, and will actively try to disassociate from the term. They may overcompensate by trying to squash Millennial-like tendencies and activities in others, and they may end up doing more harm than good.

Millennials managing Gen Edgers

Amid all this attention on Millennials, another generation has arisen, and it may turn out to be the thorn in Millennials' sides. We say this kindly, but if history proves anything, it's that the successor has the most conflict with the predecessor. Figure 15-5 offers some proof of what that may look like.

Manager Feedback: Please give feedback about your manager.
Reviewer: Gen Edge employee Huan
Manager: Millennial manager Eric

Communication is clear.

Yes! But also no. Communication on the smaller, tactical assignments is clear, but when it comes to more complicated projects, I don't feel like I get all the information I need. I think Eric is trying to let me have some freedom in deciding my approach, but I mostly just find it confusing. Some more clear directions and guidelines would actually give me more freedom, because once the framework is established, that's when the creativity can come in. Honestly, blue sky feels uncomfortable to me … I'm new here, and I want to make sure I'm not screwing anything up. A framework feels more safe.

Fosters a supportive team environment and handles conflict effectively.

Eric makes the team environment a priority, and I like that! In general, it's more team-oriented than I thought it'd be, especially based on how my parents described work. I enjoy the feeling of working with a group of supportive people, but I think we can sometimes forget that however much we like each other, we're all working on our individual careers. Sometimes, I wish there was a bit more individual working time and a bit more competition. I think that there are times that I might be able to do my best work if I did it by myself. This may sound boastful, but I want the chance to show off my skills!

Feedback, good and bad, is timely and fair.

There's a lot of feedback coming my way, and I appreciate it in one sense — I can adjust the way I'm approaching a task in almost real time — but it's also a bit distracting. Eric wants to help coach me through some of the feedback he gives me, instead of just giving me a tool or an online resource that I can look through and digest at my own speed.

I feel respected and that my hard work is appreciated.

There's a ton of verbal appreciation, and Eric gives a lot of little mini bonuses like gift cards to coffee shops or planning a team lunch out to a nice restaurant. These are fun, and I hope this isn't reading as unappreciative, but I'd rather just get money or a bump in my pay. I do like the rewards, and it's not that I want them to all go away. I just feel like salary bumps or monetary bonuses are building up toward something, rather than the experiential stuff or the coffee I'll just drink away, which seems good in the moment, but … I dunno, I guess I feel like it doesn't do much for my future? Or another option I'd love would be donating to charity or volunteering because we can all do so much to make the world a better place.

FIGURE 15-5:
Gen Edge
employee to
Millennial
manager review.

Additional Comments:

My career and the skills I develop here are really important to me. I like the added perks we get, but I'd like Eric to give me the option to participate (or not) in some of our group activities. I just feel my time might be better spent picking up a new skill than going on a team excursion.

BridgeWorks. Minneapolis, MN. (October, 2016)

Here's what you should take away from Figure 15-5:

Reasons Millennials will earn an A+ at managing Gen Edgers:

>> Embracing front-line technology and finding ways to incorporate the new tools to improve workflow

>> Understanding the importance and need for switch-tasking; just because they're on Facebook or Snapchat doesn't mean they're not working

Reasons Millennials might be on the struggle bus while managing Gen Edgers:

>> Appealing to the more practical rather than idealist nature of the Gen Edge mentality in the workplace

>> Focusing too much on interpersonal activities and team trainings rather than allowing space for self-directed research and individual learning

>> Restricting the set hours and balance they're seeking by filling work time with fun team activities instead of working time

>> Failing to provide the right amount of structure

Chapter **16**

Preparing for the Next Generation in the Workplace: Gen Edge

Time and tide wait for no woman. Yet again, another generation is blossoming from their teens years into a unique flock of young professionals, and everyone is wondering: Who are these newbies, and what changes will they bring to the workplace? Managers are wondering: How will this generation be different from Millennials, and how will I need to flex my management style? How will I train Millennials to lead this generation? Researchers have been forecasting who this group will be for a long time, and their place in the generational line is intriguing. They're succeeding the most researched — and perhaps most contentious — generation to date, but there is little to suggest that Generation Edgers are the new Millennials. This generation has been formed by events like the Great Recession, cyber-attackers, and terrorism at home and abroad. They've also been influenced by the election of the first African-American President, great strides made in the LGBTQA community, and ever-increasing access to information and opportunity via technology since their elementary education.

We'll be the first to admit that we can't currently know everything about Generation Edge. In fact, people haven't even completely landed on the name of this generation (more on this later). They are still in the midst of their formative years and, as such, are still being impacted by the events and conditions surrounding them. Like wet cement, the impressions have not quite dried, so we can't say definitively one way or another who they will be. What we can do is present some educated predictions based on what we've seen so far.

We know that you are still puzzling over how to manage Millennials, so why should you add an entire other generation to the mix? Well, for starters, the best managers are ahead of the curve. Consider that Generation Edgers are currently entering the workforce as both interns and full-time employees. Furthermore, the Millennials you manage will likely work alongside or manage Generation Edge, so you'll ultimately shoulder the responsibility of managing their generational clash points. If you haven't started peeking at information on the group after Millennials, it's a perfect time to start.

In this chapter, we first clarify the reasoning behind the term "Gen Edge." Then we examine other influential factors like population size and life stage. We take some time to break down the events and conditions that have shaped this generation's personality, traits, and values — all with the goal of helping you adapt your leadership and management style. Finally, we give you insight into potential clash points that may arise with this generation.

WARNING

As we uncover more about Generation Edge in this chapter, an important message to heed is that this isn't "out with the old, in with the new." While it may be tempting to throw the Millennial cohort aside in favor of these newcomers — whether from headline-fatigue or eagerness to discover something fresh — remember this information is best consumed in relationship to the past (or present, wherever you put Millennials on the generational time spectrum or depending on what stage you are in your Millennial education), as no generation lives in a vacuum.

Warning: This Generation Is Still in the Works

While there's a solid understanding of who each generation is in today's work environment, that insight didn't form overnight. As mentioned in Chapter 2, generational theory is based on brain development: What happens during your formative years shapes who you are. Gen Edgers are still in those formative years, so we can't claim that we know exactly who this generation is. It's like when you meet a new friend and have hung out a handful of times: You have a pretty good idea of who the person is, you definitely like him and want to keep hanging out, but you have yet to map out all his nuances and quirks. We're still getting to know Gen Edge and are getting closer to BFF status, but we're not sure what their favorite ice cream is yet. We promise that the friendship will be further evolved by the third edition of this book.

Why tell you these things? To put it frankly, we've been wrong before, and it sure isn't fun to come back with our tail between our legs. For example: There was a time when it was believed that the events of 9/11 would be the most impactful event for the Millennial generation. While it arguably remains one of the memories they can recollect most clearly, their generational traits and values were more strongly impacted by the introduction of social media and technological innovations. With Gen Edge, we're not ready to write an entire textbook with definitive conclusions, but we can give you valuable insight into trends we've seen thus far.

Sizing up Gen Edge

They're another large generation, right? Not really . . . we estimate. By our calculations, Generation Edge will fall somewhere closer to Generation Xers' size in the United States. We hesitate to state their actual population size because we aren't certain what the cutoff date will be for this generation. The pivotal events and conditions that bookend the generational birth years will ultimately determine the birth years, and since we can't predict the future, we are unsure of what all of those driving pivotal moments will be. For the sake of giving you some clarity, and maybe a little sanity, we are capping Generation Edge at 2010. It's logical to assume that their generational birth range will fall between 14 to 20 years like generations past, and as technology is so rapidly advancing, it's arguable that their segment will fall into a smaller birth-year range.

As we cover in Chapter 1, the population sizes for generations at their peak are:

>> Traditionalists – 75 million

>> Baby Boomers – 80 million

>> Generation Xers – 60 million

>> Millennials – 82 million

Drumroll, please, for the population size of Generation Edge . . . 61 million, based on CDC births per year 1996–2010. However, there is one consideration that isn't taken into account in this measurement — immigration. On that note, we could estimate that their population may peak around 68 million, based on past impacts of immigration patterns.

Considering their smaller population size, they may feel like a slightly smaller force than when Millennials started working. But don't discount the amount of preparation you'll need. They are entering the workforce at a time when Boomers are leaving in droves, so recruiting and retaining top Generation Edge talent is critical.

Playing the name game

The generational "sorting hat" has yet to decide what the generation after Millennials will be called. There are plenty of research houses, demographers, journalists, politicians, and yes, generational junkies like us that come up with these names, but no one has quite settled on a winner yet. There are a smattering of attempts, some good, some bad, and some . . . interesting:

>> The Homeland Generation

>> iGen

>> Gen Z

>> The Rainbow Generation

>> Plurals

>> Centennials

>> Founders

>> The Matrix Generation

>> The Offend Generation

By nature of this chapter's title, you've probably already guessed that our favorite designation (first released by The Sound Research) is Generation Edge. Why? There are a few reasons that we think it stands out from the bunch:

>> **They're on a demographic edge.** Edgers are the last generation with a Caucasian majority in the United States, so they're on a precipice (or "edge," if you will) of an ethnic shift.

>> **They have an edge.** They've grown up in a transparent world that begs the philosophical question: When do we reach the point of *too* much? Every economic dip, political scandal, international trauma, refugee crisis, protest, and shooting has been visible from a young age, in the palm of their hands, in real time. As a result of this exposure, they've developed thick skin and are proving to be a highly resilient generation.

>> **Other monikers don't capture this generation's edginess.** Not in a critical way — okay, maybe in a critical way — the other monikers don't capture the substance of this generation. They aren't super powerful or meaningful to the generation itself. "Generation Z" flirts with laziness; it simply follows the alphabet (Gen X, Gen Y, Gen Z) and doesn't carry meaning like "Gen X" did. iGen stereotypes them as a group solely defined by technology, and the Homeland Generation seems to be inspired by a show starring Claire Danes. Gen Edge hints at their generational personality while still being unique, a bit enigmatic, and cool. (As generational researchers, we could use a little coolness.)

Other generations have an edge, of course. They've had to react to what they grew up with and find a way to rebound in the face of change and adversity. Gen Edgers, however, have had to develop theirs from a very, very young age and that edge is only getting more defined over time.

When will we get concrete answers? Not to sound like a parent on a road trip, but we'll get there when we get there! Media publications are usually the ones that end up deciding. Through what will become increasingly frequent coverage as the Gen Edgers start to enter the workplace, there will be a name that sticks.

Decoding What Gen Edge Events and Conditions Will Mean for Managers

The world that Generation Edge grew up in has given them a unique generational personality. For the sake of understanding each event or condition, consider that if Generation Edgers are born from 1996–2010, the pivotal moments and trends that shape them in their formative years roughly cover 2009–2028, give or take. If you want a few "Whoa, they're young/I'm old/time flies" factoids to throw around with fellow members of your generation, here they are:

>> The iPhone was released when the oldest Gen Edger turned 10.

>> For many young Edgers, Barack Obama is the first president they can remember; they have no memory of anyone other than an African American in the White House.

>> High-school freshmen in the year of this book's publication (2017) were not yet born on Sept. 11, 2001 and will learn about it as a moment in history, not something they themselves experienced.

>> Edgers will not understand the outrage that accompanied Pluto's demotion from planet status. Heartbreaking, really.

Many of the events Gen Edgers have witnessed have been, needless to say, rather turbulent. Homeland violence, the Great Recession, social-justice movements, and repeated news coverage of international terror have rocked Gen Edgers' lives since before they could turn on the TV, computer, or smartphone. But paired with that turbulence is an era of change for the better, rapid technological innovation, and a continued battle against injustice.

The unforeseeable future is scary — especially for leadership. But one of the best ways that you can prepare for what comes next is to find out about what we know and understand what is yet to be determined. The following table is a good place to start. You can joke about "kids these days," but those kids determine trends that older generations embrace and emulate. Just as Millennials rocked the workplace, Gen Edgers are going to challenge the way that everyone works, and we suggest that you start the preparations: revisit your communication standards and expectations; rethink the task-list you have to give new, young hires (they get bored easily); and don't dismiss Millennials as has-beens when all attention goes to a new generation. Understanding their events and conditions is a way to make informed predictions about what that future might look like. Emphasis on the "might."

What We Do Know	What We Don't Know
They are different from Millennials.	Every detail about how their events and conditions shape them today
They are less collaborative, more inclusive, and more structured than Millennials.	Every way they'll clash with other generations
Technology has significantly shaped their life and communication styles.	Whether their technological expertise will promote or hinder future business
They're going to bring change into the workplace.	Whether they'll cause a ripple or a tsunami when they enter the workforce

The event that gave them an edge

REMEMBER

There have been watershed moments that shaped every generation — Boomers can recall exactly where they were when JFK was shot, when Neil Armstrong landed on the moon, and the first time they, perhaps embarrassingly, tried a move from *Soul Train*. Gen Xers recall the Challenger explosion, their anticipation while watching the O. J. Simpson trial, and when President Reagan exclaimed, "Mr. Gorbachev, tear down this wall!" Gen Edgers are a bit different: Due in large part to technology broadening the definitions of time and space, they are more shaped by a series of collective events, while generations in the past were more defined by singular moments. Also, even more importantly, they are still in their formative years. While we have a very good idea that certain events will have a significant impact on them — the Pulse nightclub shooting, the Brexit, and the election of Donald Trump — enough time hasn't passed to know how it influences them as a whole.

The Great Recession

When the Great Recession hit, Gen Edgers were waiting for the bell to ring in fourth period. Millennials learned to reach for the stars, that nothing was impossible; Gen Edgers learned that you couldn't trust the promises of anyone, let alone monstrous institutions. They likely saw their parents or their neighbors lose their home, lose their job, or at the very least, tighten the purse strings. Edgers saw their Millennial siblings move back home, entering adulthood with a heavy heart and deep pockets of debt.

What this means

As a leader, understand that Gen Edgers are going to be practical about their careers and their finances in a way that Millennials weren't at the same age. Their mission is stability, and their tactic is to save instead of spend, so prepare to have honest conversations about retirement accounts, pay increases, and negotiating in a competitive talent market.

What could happen

Time will tell whether this comes true, but studies, including our own, have shown that Gen Edgers plan to stay with organizations for a longer period of time, in contradiction to the stereotype of job-hopping Millennials.

The conditions that sharpened their edge

Many conditions contribute to what makes Gen Edgers who they are and who they will become. From technology to politics to homeland violence to who their parents are, Gen Edgers draw from a diverse pool of influences.

Tic, tac, tech

There are too many technological advances to boil down to just one that impacted Edgers, so we've chosen six instead. (Call us overachievers.)

>> **YouTube:** While Millennials first used the site to watch the evolution of dance, Gen Edgers use it to learn, share their views, and spread others'. YouTube has

become a sort of informal education: With tutorials on almost any subject, learning is at their discretion, at their pace, and on their time. Get ready for a generation seeking on-demand trainings and tutorials.

» **WiFi:** Access to Internet sans the beloved (or begrudged) dial-up modem means this group expects unprecedented speed and unlimited access to information and networks of people. They can filter and process content faster than generations past, and multitasking is second nature. Much like headphones at work for Millennials brought out the lazy and entitled stereotypes, Gen Edge will look distracted when they most definitely are not.

» **On-demand media:** This generation knows how to have themselves a good binge-watch. They'll bring their bingeing behaviors to work — in a good way — by diving into tasks, accomplishing them, and then moving to the next project quickly.

» **Social media:** This medium reinvents itself so regularly that we can't assume Edgers' loyalty to one platform over another. An entire book could be written about how they use social media platforms, so we'll save our breath. Of course there are negatives to social media use: cyberbullying, self-shaming, unhealthy social comparison. But on a positive note, Gen Edgers have used the platform for social awareness and as a free lesson in self-branding. They'll have a carefully crafted image before they enter the workforce — whether it's for employers' eyes or not.

» **Virtual "face-rooms":** The likes of Skype and FaceTime give this generation the gift of communicating digitally — in person. While they may appear distracted by devices or unlike the persona crafted online, they've learned how to master a communication style that the other generations haven't.

» **Minecraft:** This game has changed the name of the video-game game. It demands creativity from a generation that is stereotyped as having none. It also gives insight into how this generation can thrive: within a defined world of structure and logic but given rules when creating. Strategy optional.

Tech gadgets are a metaphoric third arm for Edgers. They're going to seek a work environment with top technological devices, if not the opportunity to use resources to make them better (think apps, project management tools, and so on). They will binge on work and then go home to binge on life and are experts at filtering through information while switching tasks. Their social media use and presence may lessen but won't cease, so don't expect it to.

CYBERBULLYING

Bullying is certainly not a new phenomenon; in fact, it's something that transcends every generation. For Gen Edge, however, social media has built formidable walls preventing escape from every kind of attack, and perhaps even worse, adults have a harder time intervening because they aren't privy to what's happening. Young girls are slandered for their looks, their clothes, their bodies, and their appeal. Preteens get threats because of their gender identity or sexuality. We are not parenting experts or child psychologists, so we can't dissect or diagnose, but awareness and empathy are the first big steps in doing something. While other generations could escape the bully, grow up, and distance themselves from their pasts, Generation Edgers carry more of the bullying baggage with them, mostly in the form of being keenly self-aware. Always being on the hunt to create an ideal picture for the masses has made this generation one who, at work, will want to vet ideas before speaking them off the cuff. They may hesitate to ask questions in a meeting just in case it isn't the best question to ask. As a leader, you'll need to give them the time and resources they require to feel comfortable bringing their ideas forward.

THE CODING BOOM

Silicon Valley has long been a breeding ground for technological advancement and genius. In return, young people are encouraged to go to coding camp and start paying for their education at 13, so that at 19, someone will be paying them (and paying well). It's a great way to give them a head start in the working world. However, even though the United States has become more and more famous for its technological stamina, they are not topping the world in STEM (science, technology, engineering, and math) education. According to the world economic forum, the United States hovers around the 51st spot in the world for quality of math and science education. There's a contradiction at play: Gen Edgers are encouraged to master coding because it will be essential to lucrative futures; however, the STEM education that supports it is suffering. If you are in the STEM field, work in an organization that has STEM jobs, or value the education itself, ask yourself:

- Are there good STEM programs in this organization?

- How am I helping with these programs? *OR* What more can I do to make them happen?

- Are minorities represented in that field at my company?

- Are there good mentors in place?

If you answered yes to these questions, give yourself a high-five and make sure that you are as involved as you can and want to be. If you answered no, see yourself as a catalyst for STEM change. The more that managers contribute to Generation Edge in STEM now, the higher the amount of quality candidates who will fill and stay in organizations.

Political milestones

Wow, has this generation been privy to political changes! While generations past worked decades to see the fruits of their labor, Edgers have already seen a lot of the fruit. Regardless of political opinion, you can't disregard the monumental advances:

>> **The first African-American President was elected.** President Barack Obama was in office when the oldest of Generation Edgers were preteens. While they may not have been tuned into the election itself, the only President during their formative years until 2017 was an African-American man.

>> **Gay marriage was legalized.** It was a long and difficult fight for gay rights activists for almost half a century. Gen Edgers saw it legalized in secondary school.

>> **Marijuana became legal in some states.** Greenery is legal in more American areas than ever before, which could make Generation Edge another generation to shorten the list of taboo topics.

>> **A new brand of #Activism emerges.** Battles are still being fought for the rights of several groups to raise awareness of others and to create effective societal change where it matters. Gen Edgers are shifting the political conversation by becoming their own brand of activist — rather than clicking "like" on Facebook, they're using social platforms like Twitter and hashtags like #BlackLivesMatter to unite people in a movement for systemic change. Gender-equality activists are proclaiming their conviction with #feminist or #banbossy. To them, the way to start a movement is to market your beliefs to your online network, build a conversation, and act. For the most part, the Millennial "slacktivist" trend is disintegrating as more and more Gen Edgers take a digital and physical stand.

>> **Seeing a rise in citizen journalism.** Generation Edge knows the value of their peers' thoughts and puts trust in them above others. They won't trust big corporations, politicians, or even media outlets because of the potential puppetry behind them. Live streaming and first-hand commentary are ways they are trying to expose truths and injustices — and many news and media outlets are relying on these sources to inform their stories.

As a result of these political changes, quite simply, Gen Edgers expect acceptance, period. When it comes to social issues, they want to work for leaders who aren't shy about taking a stand on topics they care about — or taking a stand, period.

Homeland violence becomes the norm

Generation Edge has grown up during an era when acts of violence and terror are the norm. For generations prior, violence existed in isolated incidences, but the high frequency of occurrences now has made violence a condition for Gen Edge. The Sandy Hook shooting, the Boston Marathon bombing, the Orlando night club massacre, the Charleston Church shooting, not to mention countless instances of police brutality against men and women of color . . . this list could fill this entire page. Research has shown that Gen Edgers have higher rates of anxiety and stress. While there are many factors that contribute to these rates, the foundation of truth is that Edgers are coping with what they're seeing in their own way. For some, this means adopting a #YOLO (You Only Live Once) mentality. For others, it means continuing to fight for change or simply creating balance and stability in their lives that can't be found elsewhere.

Prepare for what you do as a company when tragic events occur at home or abroad: What do you say? What do you expect people to do to carry on? Do you create safe spaces for discourse?

Gen X parents

If Boomers were helicopter parents, Gen Xers are jetfighter parents. They don't need to hover over every element of their kids' lives, believing more in the power of independent work and the need to fail from time to time. But when it counts, Gen Xers will forcefully fly in to solve their kids' problems for them — whether it's defending their kid's choice to quit the basketball team or challenging a report-card grade.

Gen Edgers know the truth game maybe a little bit too well because of their honest parents. So, they've learned to be honest with themselves about what's possible and what's not, what's affordable and what's not, and what's a hobby and what's a skill that can become a career.

REMEMBER

Gen Xers grew up with complete independence — this group had a lot of unsupervised time because their parents weren't consistently present. It makes them who they are today but, at the same time, they are reacting to how their parents parented by parenting differently. They sought to be around and give structure to help their kids compete in a tough education and job market. As a result, Gen Edgers seek structure to their days, weeks, and time. Heavily scheduled lives create a normalcy that they will seek at work, so prepare for time-specific expectations and needs.

Adapting Your Management Style to Accommodate Gen Edge Traits

Look into the crystal ball of generations, and you'll see a young demographic with countless valuable traits. While you struggle to count them all, we've narrowed them down to four that we deem most conceivable of impacting the work environment. (See Table 16-1.)

It's interesting to note that Gen Edgers are absorbing some of their Xer parents' traits: They're practical, straightforward, and competitive. You won't find any participation trophies with this generation — it's winner take all, or work harder next time.

TIP

It's easy to stereotype and find the negatives of this generation, even though they're still growing up and forming a generational identity. Please stop yourself when any of the following thoughts cross your mind:

» "They have no attention span."

» "They aren't creative."

» "They are losing the art of the written and spoken word."

» "They can't look someone in the eye."

» "They never put in extra effort."

Pause, put on your GenLens Ray Bans, and see the world through their eyes. Stereotyping is counterproductive.

TABLE 16-1   ## Gen Edge Traits

Traits	What That Means	How to Adopt Your Style
Resilient	They'll bounce back from workplace challenges. They'll absorb critical feedback and move on. They may be resilient in front of you but show a vulnerable side in safe spaces.	Avoid the compliment sandwich during feedback and tell it like it is without dipping into ridicule. While they are resilient, they also seek safe spaces and settings that are transparent about trigger warnings — think about how you'll approach this before you start recruiting them en masse.

Traits	What That Means	How to Adopt Your Style
Learn via imagery	They use images to communicate (think: Snapchat, Instagram, emojis).	Design trainings rooted in visuals, not just text.
	They're extremely comfortable with FaceTime and may find ways to use it at work.	Communicate in sound bites and image cues.
		Don't underestimate the power of the emoji, meme, or GIF.
Pragmatic	Their decisions will be logical and not necessarily out of the box.	Get ready to talk a five- to ten-year path at your company during interviews.
	They appreciate systems and order.	Clearly articulate what it takes to climb, lead, and advance in your organization.
	They're aware of their competition at all times and work as needed to reach their desired level of success.	Acknowledge that articulating the structure equates to communicating transparently.
	They're aware of the importance of paycheck before other workplace luxuries.	
Self-reliant and resourceful	They have a DIY mindset that they'll apply to their work.	They'll work quickly and then be done. If you need more, be very, very clear about it.
	They may ask you fewer questions than you're comfortable with (especially those of you who are Millennials).	If you want them to ask questions, tell them that early on.
	They're essentially "digitarians" and will rely on consumption of information to thrive.	Provide intrapreneurial opportunities so they can use their DIY mentality at work (instead of seeking another company to use it).
	They'll be confident in their ability to filter through content and will work mostly independently as a result.	

Getting in Their Heads and Hearts: Gen Edge Values

Generational values play a large role in getting the most out of your employees, but it's never an easy nut to crack. Where do the motivations and impetus for change lie for Gen Edgers? See Table 16-2.

TABLE 16-2   **Gen Edge Values**

Values	What That Means	How to Adopt Your Style
Compartmentalizing	They prefer to work in environments that foster efficiency and independence. They'll be eager to have flexibility and a schedule in which they can come and go precisely when they requested.	Stay on topic as much as possible to keep their focus. While they may seem to be distracted by functioning across multiple screens, it's their way of getting things done most efficiently in the time given. One task = boredom. Set expectations for schedules and when they can be adjusted.
Stability	An element of their work happiness will derive from elements of predictability. They'll prioritize financial security and stability.	Strategize how to strike a fine balance between managing boundaries without micromanaging duties. Motivate them via conversations of security.
Personalization	They don't want to be seen as one of the masses. They seek to have a unique career path compared to their peers.	Individualize your management approach by allowing them to shape it themselves. You'll be there for guidance and structure along the way. Allow them to "design their own" career.
Inclusion	Diversity in all forms is expected in the workplace. They'll be sensitive to any word or action that appears exclusionary.	Be open to an overhaul of your diversity initiatives. Avoid any attempt to dilute diversity by saying everyone is the same; in other words, "be color-conscious" will resonate more than "don't be colorblind."
Making a difference	Like all younger generations before them, they want to make a difference in their work. They lead with their hearts and their heads — it's likely a tough balance in their own minds, and they will seek jobs that cater to both.	As a leader and as an organization, it's best to stand for something — most Gen Edgers are looking for companies that share their political, personal, and professional views. Political and social movements are in the forefront of their minds. Give them the opportunity to stand up for change.

Getting a Jump on Creating a Workplace that Works for Gen Edge

There is no reason whatsoever to change everything about your office environment for Gen Edge. Trust us; that's a bad idea. If you are the kind of person who likes to get an "A" for effort (or prefers to stay ahead of the curve) follow this guide to creating a Gen-Edge-friendly workplace.

>> **Up your tech game.** When was the last time you changed your technology? Do you budget the right amount each year? If not, begin the strategy session now, because even though people *can* work on six-year-old computers, that doesn't mean that they should (or feel motivated by doing so). Some Gen Edgers will likely find a lack of "techxpertise" frustrating. In school, Gen Edge lives in the cloud — papers, tests, and assignments are all turned in virtually. Do you have a good, protected, cloud-based file system?

>> **Review your time-off policy.** If you thought Millennials were the epitome of flexibility, think again. Gen Edgers will demand flexibility without knowing that they're doing it. They grew up with Gen X parents who fought hard for work-life balance and are thus familiar with cut and dried personal versus professional time. To them, it may seem silly that they'll have *to ask* to arrive at 8:00 and leave at 4:00; they should be able to request it and live that way because it's what works best for them.

>> **Take a look at your demographics.** As mentioned previously, diversity is essential. Pay attention to your diversity and inclusion initiatives — they're incredibly important and can make or break a talented Gen Edger choosing to work for you or, more importantly, choosing to stay.

>> **Prepare to talk the total package — with an emphasis on money.** Offering fast career progression will get Gen Edgers only so far — they're going to want fast career progression, a job that uses their talents, meaningful work, a fast-paced environment, innovative opportunities, and good pay. While Millennials view money as secondary to many of the aforementioned options, Gen Edgers believe — and are still in their youth, mind you — that to get everything they want from work and life, they'll need a steady paycheck first. Millennials prefer fun rewards like company-sponsored happy hours and color runs, but Gen Edgers are likely to seek bonuses and more responsibility, with just a dash o' fun.

>> **Begin to brainstorm how you will give direction with metrics and imagery.** "If you can't measure it, it's not true" is a common phrase for the left-brained, and, in some capacity, Gen Edgers have altered that into "If you can't research it, it's not true." In this sense, research doesn't mean pulling up the latest data from Pew Research Center; it means venturing to search engines and finding all the data they need to make a decision. Remember when you wanted to learn how to tie a tie and had to ask your dad? Remember when, to choose a class, you simply picked it without knowing who was teaching or how students felt about it? Google and YouTube have been the go-to how-to guides since Gen Edgers' preteen years and have been solid visual educators. How are you preparing for that resourcefulness and structure? There are no limits to the information they can attain, and limited access in a work environment will likely cause some frustration. Think of how you will give information, context to decision-making, and visual tools for

learning. For example: Give them an article to read with links to related articles and infographics for cross-comparison.

>> **Sing to yourself: "Let's get literal, literal."** If you instruct Gen Edgers with few confines and "the sky is the limit" verbiage, they may feel paralyzed. Make plain your intent and your direction. Leave nothing to question — except questions themselves.

>> **Familiarize yourself in the ways Gen Edge differs from Millennials.** Check out the following table.

	Millennials	Gen Edgers
Collaboration	Love it	Like it (especially when digital), but need independent time too
Making a difference	Critical	Important
Charming office perks: outings, happy hours, fro-yo trips, and so on	Love 'em, most of the time	They're fine, but not at the sacrifice of personal time
Career progression	Needs to be fast and furious	Slightly more patient if allowed to have side-projects
Management style	Democratic and warm	Confident and directed

Predicting the Future: Potential Gen Edge Clash Points

While Gen Edgers will get on swimmingly with members of each generation, we have a suspicion steeped in truth that Millennials and Gen Edgers may have some of the strongest clashes. Just like generations past, we hypothesize that the preceding generation will struggle most to build an agreeable relationship with the succeeding generation. That being said, Millennials won't be alone.

The clash — Millennials versus Gen Edge

Gen Edgers may fail to ask enough questions of the Millennial generation who champions collaboration and checking in.

Edward, the Millennial manager: Hi Elinor. I was wondering how you're doing on the project I gave you?

Elinor, the Gen Edger: Oh, I'm doing well, should be giving it to you by the end of the day.

Edward: So soon? Wow . . .

Elinor: Yeah! And then I'll be ready for another project.

Edward: (thinking) But I think you may be way off on this one because you haven't spoken to me about it once . . .

Reading between the lines: Gen Edgers are confident in their ability to stay on task and finish projects in due course. Unlike their predecessors, they don't incessantly ask questions because they're either using the inter-webs as their resource or calling upon their peers to ask questions. While this independence is praiseworthy, concerns may arise when the new kids on the block appear to put (too much) confidence in their own product. The generation who values the question mark above most else will wonder: "Do they really think they've figured everything out on their own? Don't get me wrong, I love a good Google search. But they'll learn more by collaborating with me and others in the workplace along the way."

The clash — Gen X versus Gen Edge

Gen Xers may feel that Gen Edgers' reliance on tech is too extreme, and having a face-to-face conversation seems not only difficult, but straight-up awkward.

Jordan, Gen X Manager: Hey, I got your pings this morning about a new communication system . . . I honestly didn't read through all of them. What's that about?

Nick, Gen Edger: I was just thinking that there are easier ways to communicate, and this new system came out that could help with project management. There was a lot of cross-conversation between platforms.

Jordan: Okay, how does everyone feel about it?

Nick: I mean, everyone I've spoken to thinks it's a good idea. I think we should do it. It'll make everything so much easier.

Jordan: Riiiight. (thinking) You mean every other person like you? I fear another system that's going to deter you from building in-person relationships.

Reading between the lines: Jordan is an Xer who's perfectly capable with tech changes and has been patient with Millennials' eagerness to change everything. Her Gen Edge employees are pushing even more boundaries, however, often without asking forgiveness. She needs to reset expectations of what's okay to change and what's not. In the process, she can give them lessons where they may need them most, in building personal, face-to-face relationships.

The clash — Baby Boomers versus Gen Edge

The Baby Boomer's take on Gen Edge looks something like this: "They appear so distracted by everything, all the time — can they focus on anything?!

Gale, Boomer manager: Kat, can you please take off your headphones for a second?

Kat, Gen Edger: (presses pause on her iPhone) Yeah, what's up?

Gale: I wanted to touch base about this morning's meeting.

Kat: (grabbing computer, iPad, and iPhone) Cool. Can we talk about it in the conference room?

Gale: Sure. (thinking, *why do you need* three *devices for our talk?* They walk to the room.)

Kat: So, yesterday.

Gale: First bit of feedback — when you have more devices than just your computer in the meeting, I doubt that you're following all the important information being discussed.

Kat: (loud internal or external sigh) I'm not checking Instagram or anything . . .

Gale: Well, it's hard to know and also difficult for the more senior partners to know that you're not, because they feel like you can't look them in the eye.

Reading between the lines: Kat can easily function across screens but hasn't mastered the ability to do so in a nondisruptive fashion. Gale knows that Kat is intelligent but questions her emotional intelligence. What happens if Kat goes out in the field and works with clients? Will she know how to build a relationship? Just like Millennials caused a ruckus with their devices, Gen Edgers are going to exacerbate it but in the process add a whole new level of communication skills.

Chapter **17**

Forecasting the Great Unknown

We regularly encounter leaders and managers asking us to look into our generational crystal ball and make predictions about the future. They have an insatiable curiosity about what happens next, what the future of the workplace looks like, and who the generation *after* Millennials — and then *after* Gen Edgers — will be. It's not surprising. These people are the forward thinkers. They're doing their best to anticipate trends and stay ahead of the game. They want to preemptively prepare as much as possible for whatever's on the horizon so that when those cultural workplace shifts take place, they'll be ready to face them head-on.

This topic begs the question: Can one use generational knowledge to examine past cycles and predict what may happen in the future? As you can imagine, the answer is all kinds of complicated. In our humble experience, to some extent, yes, but with a giant grain of salt. Maybe more an iceberg of salt. We are not fortunetellers, or time-travelers, or even futurists. The future promises exponential change — revolution in some cases and evolution in others. It's unpredictable and uncharted territory, and exploring that world of the great unknown is scary. What we can safely offer you, though, are some educated guesses about what the future *might* hold — informed, of course, by generational theory.

In this chapter, we uncover information about how generational cycles and parenting trends can be used to forecast upcoming trends. We then explore how some of the most anticipated variables of change — technology, the economy, and what's "on fleek" (we use this term knowing very well that it will be out of favor by the time this book is published) influence what's coming next. Finally — for our skeptical Xer readers, don't worry — we're as transparent as cellophane and delineate the things we simply can't know. Our insights are focused on a future timeline extending to about 2040 (in other words, 15 to 20 years or so out from the writing of this book). We're not daft enough to think we can shed light on where we'll be in 100 years. Though wouldn't that be something?

Using History to Predict the Future

They (whoever "they" are) say that history repeats itself. It's true that when you look closely at generational dynamics over the years, some cyclical patterns start to emerge. Certain behaviors, traits, and attitudes appear and reappear on the generational timeline. We've seen how the past informs the present, and following that logic we should be able to use the present to make cautious predictions about the future. In the following pages we tap into generational history as well as present circumstances to predict what could be.

Yes, the generations are cyclical

If you've had any exposure to the generations topic, you may have found yourself pondering this thought: "Isn't this generations thing just cyclical?" The basic punchline is yes, generations are cyclical because humans do behave and act in patterns. Thousands of pages of information are devoted to addressing that specific topic in depth. Neil Strauss and William Howe are arguably the grandfathers of modern generational theory and have penned transformative works that include *Generations, The Fourth Turning,* and *Millennials Rising.* The theories they present are incredibly complex, and boiling them down into a small, digestible nugget of information is almost impossible. We do our best to present the need-to-know pieces that illustrate the cyclical nature of the generations.

Generations occur in a pattern of four (see Figure 17-1). The idea here is that generations are, to some degree, products of the society and the conditions they're born into. As the tides shift from a societal high to a period of awakening, unraveling, crisis, and then back to a high, different generational identities emerge as a reaction to what they experienced at the time:

1. Idealist generation (Baby Boomers)

Born in a time when crime was rare and spirits were high, people of this generation live up to their name, bringing an optimistic and idealistic energy that focuses on improving the world and effecting positive social change.

2. Reactive generation (Gen Xers)

The conditions for this generation were marked by a self-focused society and an uptick in crime. Because of previously low crime, they weren't necessarily protected by parents, whose focus was elsewhere. As a reaction to these new conditions, they developed practical survival skills, often showing up as skeptical and independent.

3. Civic generation (Millennials)

Here, the societal unraveling is in full swing, and the members of this generation focus on how they can fix a seemingly broken society. They put their energy toward rebuilding and improving, leading with optimism and teamwork before self-tendencies.

4. Adaptive generation (Traditionalists/Gen Edgers)

Because members of this generation enter at a time of high crisis, they are overprotected (to the point of smothering) by concerned parents. They tend to grow into highly pragmatic, risk-averse, and rule-following adults.

FIGURE 17-1: The cyclical nature of generations.

Traditionalists/Gen Edge
Grow up in a crisis period
Not individualistic, proceed with caution, institutions are strong.

Millennials
Grow up in an unraveling period
Institutions get rebuilt, authority gets reestablished, and have a can-do optimism.

Baby Boomers
Grow up in a high period
Fight against institutions for societal change, seek autonomy and authentic self-expression.

Gen Xers
Grow up in an awakening period
Institutions are distrusted, authority is weak, and individualism is high.

Strauss, W., & Howe, N. (1997). The fourth turning: What the cycles of history tell us about America's next rendezvous with destiny. New York: Broadway Books.

Using parenting trends to predict

Each generation of parents wants to give their kids what they didn't have. Parents also do their best to try and make the world a better place for children to grow up in. In trying to meet those goals, parents can sometimes go against the way they were raised. The result is generations of parents passing along traits that manifest in different ways in their children, as shown in Table 17-1.

TABLE 17-1 Parenting Styles and the Values They Instill Across Generations

	Traditionalists	Baby Boomers	Gen Xers	Millennials
Parenting style — how they treat their children	Children are better seen, not heard	Self-esteem movement	Honesty is the best policy	You will be the change I couldn't be
Parenting style — how they protect their children	Bike-riding instructor	Helicopter	Jet fighter	Lawnmower
Children's values	(Baby Boomers + Gen Xers): "My skinned knees never hurt anyone." "I speak when spoken to." "Making mistakes is a part of life."	(Millennials): "My opinion matters." "I appreciate the safety net." "My parents are my cheerleaders."	(Gen Edgers): "My parents are my reality check." "I have skills that will be applicable to whatever job I'll have someday." "My parents are my friends."	(Baby Alphas*): TBD, but something akin to "I am safe."

Generation Alpha is a very early name for the generation after Gen Edge.

Making sense of Millennial parenting and its implications for the workforce

Why are we putting the microscope on Millennial parents? Not to get too cheesy, but they're raising the future. Though it's taken many Millennials a good long time to enter the parenthood life stage, many of them are finally there and in the midst of raising the next wave of talent that will hit the workforce in twenty or so years. Just as the way Gen Xers raise their Gen Edge kids has direct implications on next-generation talent (see Chapter 16 for more on that), we can examine Millennial parenting trends to try and predict characteristics of the generation after Gen Edgers.

Here are some predictions about Millennials' children:

>> **Their children are being raised under a microscope.** Millennials' children learned to identify their parents' faces at the same time they learned about a smartphone's face — to them, technology has always been a part of their lives, and they know to turn on a smile at the sight of a phone. As they get older, there may be uproars from a generation of angsty preteens who shudder at the number of pictures and stories that exist on the Internet.

>> **Parenting in the social world is riddled with comparisons.** Do a Google search of "#PinterestFail" and you'll find a series of images where things just didn't go as planned. Millennial moms and dads face the pressure of being the best parents who give their kids the all-organic diet, multivitamins sourced from the most-trusted sources, and gender-neutral clothing made of hemp. This need to be perfect parents may create a world of comparison in the classroom, in turn creating a generation of highly competitive individuals.

>> **Millennials are becoming parents later in life.** If age equals wisdom, then the children of older Millennial parents are children of people who have more life skills that they can pass on to their kids than the average parent. Part of being experienced parents translates to doing all that is possible to make the world a safer place for their kids . . . Millennials are the lawnmowers — they clear every potential obstacle in their kids' lives.

Keeping Watch on Technology, Economy, and Trends

As you explore the world of the future unknown, certain factors will remain unpredictable but entertaining to think about. Back in the day (choose your time period), technology was rapidly changing, the economy was at a high or a low, and some cutting-edge trends emerged; vague statements these may be, but the way society finishes the story behind these statements defines a generation. Though the variables of technology, the economy, and public opinion are unpredictable, you can use their non-patterns to write a future tale.

Technology

Each generation has seen great technological change — Baby Boomers saw the first printers, fax machines, and computers. Generation Xers saw the first personal computers, email systems, and mobile communication devices. Millennials have grown up on an upgrade cycle of Apple products and anxiously await the next tech and social innovation. Though *The Jetsons* painted a futuristic society far removed from our current times, it was set in 2062, and that date is growing ever closer (it's less than 50 years away from the date of publication of this book . . . yup). While you may not be driving flying cars or enjoying the clean house kept by your robot Rosie, some technological changes are going to warp the future and influence generations at work.

The future of driving

Young people have a declining interest in cars and driving with each churning of generations. While Baby Boomers worked tooth and nail to afford their first ride, Millennials and Generation Edge find cars an annoying necessity and, at times, a nuisance. Look no further than teens in your neighborhood to see kids who rely on parents and sharing car services like Uber to get from place to place. Though less of the youth demographic finds interest in driving cars, more envision a great world with self-driving cars. We're going this way fast, and society is (for the most part) ready.

Potential workplace implications include the following:

>> **More flexibility for working parents:** They won't be restricted by having to drop off or pick up their children at school or extracurricular events.

>> **Shifting working hours:** Employees can start working as soon as they step into the car (effectively shortening the workday as their work time can include their ride time).

The future of wearable technology

Recently we've seen a huge movement toward wearable technology. The wearable tech market has introduced smartwatches, glasses, activity bracelets and rings, earpieces, and even belts aimed at either keeping you in-the-know and constantly informed or tracking some data about your life — or a combination of the two.

Potential workplace implications include:

>> Incredibly efficient access to information at work.

>> Priming people to be constantly on the alert to any workplace notification and/or request. "Always on" will transform from a figurative statement to a literal one as well.

>> A higher emphasis placed on constant data tracking, since people will be used to track data on a day-to-day, constant-feedback basis.

The future of the workplace

In general, technological changes will continue to affect where and when you get work done. They will also affect what jobs are created and what jobs are left vacant. The impacts of a tech-increased work world are extensive and include the following potential workplace implications:

>> New jobs will be created for every new technological change; there is no limit.

>> You can work anywhere, at any time.

>> There will always be more innovative ways to get work done.

>> There will be an even wider array of potential workplace distractions.

TECHNOLOGY HINDERING CREATIVITY AND THE ABILITY TO WONDER

Many adults who grew up with seven channels on television or parents who wouldn't let them back in the house until dark, fear that the imagination required to stay entertained in generations past is being replaced by technology. With technology, argue some, there is no opportunity to wonder what could be, because instead of letting your imagination run free you can just look for the answers to everything online. While this fear isn't entirely unfounded, we encourage you to view wonder and imagination with a different lens. It takes creativity to pick up a device and choose how you research any given topic. It takes wonder to imagine a safer world free of injustice, and Gen Edgers fight for that all the time. The way that they wonder and the way that they imagine relies on structure. That's a good thing! Appreciate that skill to imagine within a linear world and let them wonder to *their* hearts' content. Don't forget that just because it's different than the way you were creative, that doesn't mean it's not creativity. Not to mention, members of Generation Edge have already accomplished feats like the following:

- At age 15, Jaylen Bledsoe turned his IT company into a $3.5 million global company.

- At age 7, Zora Ball created a mobile video game.

- At age 18, Denzel Thompson co-founded a nonprofit in Philadelphia whose mission is to revitalize urban areas and create sustainable gardens that grow healthy foods.

- At age 15, Jack Andraka invented a pancreatic cancer detector.

- At age 17, Malala Yousafzai became the youngest Nobel Prize Laureate.

Economy

From experience, we know that the economy is fickle and will have its highs as well as its lows. We do not claim to be economists, so we aren't going to theorize when the next dip will come, but we do know that where generations fall on the economic parabola shapes how they work.

>> **In high times:** Generations whose formative years occur during a booming economy are generally optimistic. Take older Millennials as an example — though many of them graduated into a recession, for the most part, they grew up in an economically high time when conversations about money were uncommon.

>> **In low times:** When a generation comes of age during a low economic time, their view on the future is more bleak, they are more pragmatic in their life choices, and they tend to save instead of spend. Take Generation Edge as an example — when they entered middle school, they learned the important lesson of saving when people around them suffered the impact from the recession and are now a generation of savers.

Overall, as the economy ebbs and flows, take heed of how that impacts the amount of work your employees do. Between 1973 and 2013, wages increased only 9 percent while productivity increased a steep 74 percent. Now take into consideration younger workers, working from wherever they want and whenever they need to in the next 5 to 15 years . . . chances are they'll be putting in a lot of hours and getting by with even fewer wage increases.

Trends

The element of "cool" is ever fleeting, but one thing remains steadfast: Youth have a powerful voice in determining the current trends. With each generation comes a new set of slang, ideologies, or even complaints about the older generation. Trends may seem unimportant, as many of them are connected to pop culture, but they tell us more about the people you work with than you might think at surface level.

TIP

If you want to be on-trend, do the easy thing and just ask a young person. Develop a solid mentor relationship and ask the right questions. Most importantly, when you get those answers, don't sit with your feet in cement, unwilling to change! Do your best to absorb the trend, consider how it works for you, and move on. To give you an idea of just how fleeting trends are, take a look at the shifts over time shown in Table 17-2.

TABLE 17-2   **Trends Across Generations**

Trend	Traditionalists	Boomers	Gen Xers	Millennials	Gen Edgers
Slang	Hip, no sweat, cruisin' for a bruisin'	Groovy, outta sight, far out	Fly, fresh, total Barnie, what's your damage?	Talk to the hand!, Whatever!, As if!, tight	On fleek, #ratchet, lit, turnt, yaaaas
Fashion	Hoop skirts, three-piece suits, greasers	Polyester suits, go-go boots, bellbottoms	Shoulder pads, big hair, neon clothing, members-only jackets	Hip-huggers, scrunchies and butterfly clips, Zubaz, trucker hats	Leggings, athleisure wear, skinny jeans
Music	The Rat Pack, big band	Rock 'n' roll, bubblegum pop, The Beatles, glam rock	Grunge, hip-hop, alternative rock	Teen pop — boy bands/girl groups, punk rock, R&B	Mashups, auto-tune, acoustic
Music shows	Radio shows	*American Bandstand*	MTV	MTV, BET, CMT, VH1	YouTube, Vimeo
Tattoos and piercings	Tattoos are for the Navy	Hippie earrings, hippie tattoos	One ear piercing for men, multiple piercings for the ladies	All the tattoos as a form of self-individualization	TBD

What We Know We Don't Know

All in all, as humans, we know very little. Reasonable logic will have you understand that in comparison to all the things that one could possibly know, you know only a tiny sliver. See Figure 17-2.

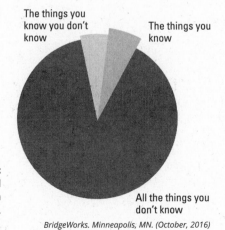

FIGURE 17-2: The sum of all human knowledge.

The things you know you don't know

The things you know

All the things you don't know

BridgeWorks. Minneapolis, MN. (October, 2016)

Here's the truth: We know a lot about generations and can guarantee that our trends forecasted throughout this book are indicative of the Millennial generation. What we don't know is how the future will unfold, how new presidents will shape the future, and how new devices will change the way we work. The best we can do is rest on the foundation of what we already know and what others project could be. It's up to you to decide what you want to do with it.

5

The Part of Tens

Get insight into the top ten things that motivate Millennials other than money.

Discover ten underutilized Millennial strengths that can be an asset to your organization.

Understand where ten Millennial stereotypes come from and why they are false.

Find out ten ways to become the #BestBossEver in the eyes of a Millennial.

» Discovering unexpected win-wins

» Knowing where to draw the line while granting Millennials freedom

Chapter **18**

Ten Things that Motivate Millennials Other than Money

With a group as complex as Millennials, it can be easy to believe there is a holy grail that will unlock them. As generational researchers, we're happy to tell you that there *is*, and by picking up this book you've found it. Did we just equate this book to the holy grail? Yes, yes we did. But the "secret" to deciphering Millennials isn't a secret at all. It simply takes an understanding of who Millennials are, where they come from, and what motivates them to get the most from them in the workplace. And it may not come as a surprise that what motivates them isn't what motivated generations past. Salaries are great, because, as it turns out, adulthood is 50 percent paying bills. But cold hard cash won't ensure Millennials are working to their full potential or challenged and happy enough to stay at your organization.

This chapter explores nonmonetary methods to light the passion flame in your Millennials. We uncover how to incentivize them while also setting boundaries that work for you as a manager. Lastly, we show how, oftentimes, these rewards are win–wins that benefit you and your Millennial so you can get the most bang for your (non)–buck.

Providing Exposure to Other People in the Organization

When it comes to being networked, Millennials have never known any other way. They grew up with the ability to email their high-school principal and tweet at the POTUS (President of the United States). Millennials are keenly aware that it's not what you know but *who* you know. Giving them exposure to people across the organization is a great motivation method: It shows them that the company is invested in their growth (without adding a budget line).

One way you can help Millennials build their networks is by developing a mentorship program, but it doesn't have to be that official either. As a manager, you likely have connections both internally and externally and are primed to make connections. Introduce the Millennial you manage to a supervisor in another department. Try setting up lunches between the Millennial and people who can expand their skill set. New perspectives will help Millennials connect the dots and feel that they're more than a cog in the corporate wheel.

TIP

Don't feel pressured to get the CEO to agree to lunch with your employees. Millennials will appreciate just about any kind of exposure. That could be someone in a cross-functional role, a completely different department in a different office, or maybe even someone who works on the factory floor. In the end, all of these outlooks will help Millennials see the bigger picture.

Giving a Good Old-Fashioned Thank-You

Feel free to categorize this one in the "duh" category. But believe it or not, we find that a heartfelt acknowledgment is one of the most overlooked (and cost-free) motivational strategies. All too often, managers wait for a performance review or year-end celebration to thank people for their hard work, successful projects, and day-to-day dedication to their work. While these celebrations are nice, sometimes a thank-you when it's least expected can make an employee feel more valued than a plaque at the annual award ceremony. And, they *do* say that gratitude is one of the keys to happiness, so you'll probably feel darn good yourself if you up your thank-you game.

TIP

When you do say thank you, remember to attach it to something meaningful. Nothing is worse than a slew of empty thank-yous. Choose exactly what you're going to thank a Millennial for before diving into the thank-you deep end.

REMEMBER

You may be thinking, "I never got a thank-you for simply doing my job." With that in mind, would you have liked that? Why should that stop you from complimenting someone else? Recognition for a job well done will show your people that you see their hard work through thick and thin, and that their contributions are exactly that: contributions to the company's overall goals, not just tasks to be completed.

REMEMBER

This tip is clearly effective well beyond the Millennial generation. Saying thank-you is a universal and cross-generational way to bring out the best in people.

Tossing Out Tailored Treats

Millennials grew up in the age of customization. They don't agree with the concept of one-size-fits-all. Managers who take the time to listen and get to know their employees can use what they learn to better reward Millennials. Sure, it may not be totally cost-free, but personalizing rewards can show big results and help you save even bigger bucks in the end.

Does your employee have a favorite local coffee shop? Does she have a taste for sour candy? Rather than giving something from the company catalog, get creative. You may only have ten dollars to spend, but giving a ten-dollar Target gift card (that'll probably be used to buy groceries and toilet paper anyway) won't go as far as a ten-dollar mug featuring an employee's favorite *Harry Potter* quote.

REMEMBER

As with many of these tips, if you're worried that personalization means you need to dig into your employees' personal lives, fear not. Don't cross your own personal/professional boundaries to find the perfect incentive for your Millennial. Often enough, ideas can come out of small talk and simply working side by side every day.

Having Fun with Co-Workers (Yes, That Means with You Too)

Many working adults spend most of their waking hours at work, and they often see co-workers more than their own friends and family. Millennials take this fact and, rather than get upset about it, get excited about it. Having fun and spending quality time with co-workers is hugely motivating for Millennials. It plays a big part in their preference for work/life integration over work/life balance, but it plays an even larger role in how Millennials view work. No one wants to spend 40 hours a week in an environment that implies people aren't the greatest asset.

It's easy as a manager to see Millennials as a bunch of kids just goofing off. After all, you're the one held responsible for what goes on and what gets done. While there need to be limits as to how much is too much, realize that enjoying your co-workers is more than just fun and games. People who actually like working with their colleagues are more likely to push through projects even when they're tough. And just because you are the "boss" doesn't mean you can't join in on the fun too. Not only does it show your Millennial employees your more authentic side and drive results, you may have fun in the process too.

REMEMBER

How much "fun" you have is up to you. Every manager has a different rule of thumb when it comes to how much he is willing to let his hair down in front of his employees. Be honest with yourself and your employees — it all goes back to being authentic. If you're forcing fun or putting on appearances, Millennials will see right through it. If you don't want to be Facebook friends with the new hire, don't. If you only want to show up to happy hour for 20 minutes and scoot, feel free.

Showing a Path to Promotion

A common Millennial plight is their slowly advancing career. To them, they aren't getting promoted as quickly as they would like, and therefore their future career is suffering. You, their manager, can feel frustrated because even if you want to, you may not have the power or authority to promote employees whenever they see fit. There are budgets and calendars and HR departments that often make it very difficult for managers to hand out promotions. So what is a manager to do?

Even if you can't promote your Millennials right now, show them the path. Demystify what it will take to go from "here" to "there." Your confidence in their abilities and the fact that you do see them as leaders is a reward in and of itself.

TIP

Shorten your time horizon. If you start speaking in terms of ten-year plans, Millennials' eyes will glaze over. Most of them are thinking more short term — this is a generation who has seen so much change in their lifetime that they have a hard time grasping the concept of a decade-long plan. Talk in terms of weeks and months, maybe a year or two tops.

WARNING

Don't get mad. This piece of advice sounds more appropriate for teen drama, but it applies here. Too many managers let their anger interfere with the ultimate goal of keeping Millennials engaged. Ask yourself whether you're having any of these thoughts:

>> Why is it *my* job to show them the path forward?

>> Why am I investing all this energy if they only intend to stay for three years max?

>> If they are really hungry for it, they will figure out their own path to promotion.

>> Can't you just focus on the job you have right now and not worry about the next best thing?

If you find yourself having these thoughts, you may be letting your emotion get in the way. As Queen Elsa says, *let it go*, and just remember that Millennials are eager for more ways to make a positive impact on the company, not just ladder-climbing for the sake of it. If you become defensive, your Millennials may feel frozen in their careers and pursue leadership positions elsewhere.

Giving More Responsibility

As we said previously, managers don't always have the ability to promote their employees. However, giving Millennials added responsibility can be an unexpected way to motivate them that not only costs zero dollars, but helps push a project, initiative, or even the entire company forward.

Many Millennials come to the workplace with a decent amount of leadership experience. Whether that comes from volunteering with a nonprofit, serving on the board of a fraternity or sorority, or being the captain of a sports team, this generation may be green in the workforce, but they aren't strangers to being held accountable. Hiring a high-performing college student for an entry-level position simply because she's new and has to "pay her dues" can be demotivating at best and demoralizing at worst.

Managers may assume that no employee in his right mind would want to do more work for the same pay, but that's not what we find with Millennials. Put them in charge of a committee; involve them in a new task force or project; or even involve them in things not directly related to their job, like leading your community-involvement efforts. For Millennials, more responsibility means more engagement.

And if all that weren't convincing enough, putting them in charge of a finite task or short-term effort gives you a chance to see what they are made of. Before you officially promote them or give them more difficult clients and so on, use these added responsibilities as both a training course for them and a testing ground for you.

WARNING

Avoid giving Millennials busywork or tasks you simply don't want, repackaged as "leadership" or "opportunity." There is a line between responsibility that motivates and responsibility that disengages, and if a Millennial catches the scent of time-wasting tasks, he'll jump ship.

Utilizing Half-Day Fridays or Part-Time Tuesdays

Workin' 9 to 5 may have been the way for generations past, but the world, as they say, spins madly on. For many positions, people can work from anywhere and at any time, and often do. While all the generations have made it a habit to bring work home with them, Millennials have always pushed managers to answer the question: "If you expect me to be flexible and do work after hours, can you be flexible with me *during* work hours?"

From wanting to do yoga over the lunch hour to leaving early to take advantage of the beautiful weather, Millennials have gotten a bad reputation for asking for too much. But like it or not, it is incredibly important. In fact, in our recent national survey, leading-edge Millennials cited this kind of flexibility as their number-one motivation.

Caveat: You may be thinking, "But I work in [retail, healthcare, manufacturing, and so forth]. There is no way we can offer that kind of flexibility." Our response: You're right! There are absolutely some industries that this piece of advice does not apply to. If that is you, move on and focus on the other nine items on this list.

WARNING

Avoid the "but I didn't get that" trap. Just because you entered the workplace without these kinds of options doesn't mean Millennials are crazy for wanting them. If you find yourself starting your sentences with words like, "In my day," you're probably getting in your own way. Like we said, the world spins on! You have to accept the changing times without bitterness.

Allocating Time for Passion Projects

A newer practice that some Fortune 500s are utilizing is the *passion project.* Employees are given a certain percentage of their time to work on whatever they want. It can be work related (and much appreciated, if so), but it can be personal in nature as well — as long as it's developmental and fulfills an itch they don't have enough time to scratch. Some of the most innovative ideas can be traced back to giving employees total freedom to explore.

While this idea resonates with all the generations, Millennials are uniquely attracted to it because of the world in which they grew up. This is the group that saw Uber and Lyft overturn the cab industry, Netflix overturn cable TV, and even Twitter and Facebook overturn traditional communication. Disruption and innovation is in their nature, which can work in your favor. When you set them on passion projects, Millennials get a chance to feed their innovative spirit and you get some fresh ideas. You're also showing them that you are investing in them as people, not just moneymakers.

Dressing Down the Dress Code

Dress code: The phrase itself raises hairs on the back of Millennials' necks. It implies rules and formality. This generation grew up with idols who wore tees, hoodies, and shower shoes to work everyday. (You can guess who we're referencing.) And with the mantra of "results, not hours" in their minds, Millennials are questioning why it matters if they're wearing a sweatshirt if the work gets done, and gets done well.

As much as you can, give Millennials the ability to "dress for their day." Whether that's athleisure or a suit, this type of freedom motivates them and also serves their desire for authenticity. ("My T-shirt designed by a local artist tells you much more about me than a suit and tie.") More important than the attire itself is your confidence that they'll know what's appropriate for their schedule.

REMEMBER

Like so many of these motivations, set boundaries. Tell Millennials exactly how informally they can present themselves. Some would wear pajamas and a Snuggie to work if they could. Others only want to be seen in a suit. Just be honest with them about what's expected and what could potentially change in the future, even if you don't have direct control over the dress code.

Offering Up Team Wins

Throughout this book, we exhaust the synonym of Millennials and collaboration. In school, Millennials worked on group homework projects before running off to basketball practice, and then they'd go home to log onto chat rooms with friends. They have a unique affection for the group, and those teaming skills come in not only before and during a project, but also after all is said and done. When it comes to celebrations, Millennials want group-oriented wins. Maybe the entire team gets a nice dinner out when a project is completed, or everyone gets a bonus if a sales goal is hit. Some things must be solo sports, like raises, but the things that can be rewarded collectively will give tribal Millennials pride in their team and company.

WARNING

Make sure team wins don't turn into a competition. Avoid pitting one team against another.

Chapter **19**

Ten Millennial Strengths to Capitalize On

Where there is light, there is also dark. Okay, that's a bit melodramatic, but as is the case with almost all strengths, many are often double-edged swords. In the case of managing Millennials, you may sometimes feel that what makes Millennials an asset to your organization is exactly what bothers you most about them. Tech-innate can quickly become tech-obsessed. Team-focused can devolve into dependent and needy. Eager to help can be misinterpreted as entitled. Managers who can resist turning these positives into negatives will be able to truly capitalize on the natural strengths that Millennials bring to the office.

Though hardly exhaustive, the following are ten Millennial strengths that, when honed and harnessed, can have real bottom-line benefits. Drum-roll, please . . .

REMEMBER

Just because we have labeled the following qualities as Millennial strengths does not in any way imply that they are weaknesses of the other generations. If you find yourself saying, "Millennials aren't the *only* generation who are innovative around here," or "I was the exact same way when I was that age!" we hear you, and we agree. Think of these as Millennials' hidden strengths that more companies should be encouraging rather than neglecting.

Taking Advantage of Tech-Innate

When we say to non-Millennials that Millennials are tech-innate, we usually get one of two responses: "Duh, everyone knows that!" or, "Just because I'm not a Millennial doesn't mean I'm tech inept!" Let's take these reactions one at a time.

The "Duh" Response

Yes, most people recognize that Millennials are a tech-savvy group. However, many people don't understand exactly how to capitalize on that strength because they're too convinced that Millennials' savvy is an obsession. It's true that this cohort may turn to tech far more than generations past, but remember, Millennials grew up alongside the burgeoning tech industry and therefore find ways to include its advancements in much of their daily life. While dependence on technology can definitely have its drawbacks, it is hard to deny that it allows everyone to work more efficiently, more creatively, and more globally.

At the same time, the transition to new technologies or systems can be rocky for everyone involved. Here's where Millennials are key: They're early adopters of new technologies, they learn systems quickly, and they're willing to help those who struggle to embrace technological change. Viewing and utilizing them for how they can help will not only benefit your entire employee pool; your Millennial will feel like a valuable member of the team.

TIP

Many progressive organizations have found an exceptional way to take advantage of not only Millennials' strengths, but every generation's: reverse mentorship. Pairing young employees with more experienced ones creates a two-way street of learning and knowledge transfer. In this scenario, you, the manager extraordinaire, would mentor based on your experience and knowledge. In return, a Millennial could teach you the ins-and-outs of the newest CRM system, a recent intra-office messaging system, or even Snapchat. At all times, leading with the question "What might this Millennial teach me?" can boost not only your knowledge, but also your Millennial's engagement level.

The "But I'm Tech-Savvy Too!" Response

Of course you are! If you have had any level of success in the workplace in the last two decades, you've had to become comfortable with certain technologies, or at least the changing nature of them. But the difference is that while other generations have been merging onto the information superhighway, Millennials were born in the fast lane. They have never known a world without the tech upgrade cycle. Of course, this can have its own disadvantages like impatience and a need for constant change, but having a generation of people who use technology as "their first language" can be a huge plus. They may think of using technology in a way you've never considered, they may be more aware of trends and cutting-edge innovations, and they may be more in tune with social-media platforms and networking systems. Leading with a defensive edge by bolstering how tech-savvy you are too will not bring out the best of this Millennial strength. Know what you don't know, and allow Millennials to fill in the gaps.

Tuning in to Team-Focused

Millennials grew up in the era of the group project/discussion/sport/club. In school, it was a rare occasion to have an assignment that didn't require collaboration. Many Millennials sat through middle-school lessons on team building and conflict resolution. (If they were especially responsible, they were nominated by their teacher to be a mediator for their peers.) This emphasis on teamwork-makes-the-dream-work is quite different from generations before, who lived by the motto, "If you want something done right, do it yourself." Traditionalists and Boomers grew up in more rigid, structured environments, where Mom and Dad had the final word, and command-and-control was the way of the world. Millennials, on the other hand, grew up in families with a much more democratic approach.

Millennials, in turn, entered the workplace uniquely suited to be excellent team players and team-before-self leaders. They are good at encouraging all voices and opinions, and often find unique ways to build consensus among their peers. As their manager, strategize the best place for them on your team; for example, they'll likely excel on teams that have historically struggled. Even if they don't have the most knowledge about the project, they can act as a catalyst to get the team-mojo flowing.

As Millennials continue to take on more leadership roles, don't expect this team mentality to change or evaporate. They are much more likely to be democratic leaders and less likely to choose favorites among team members. The key will be to coach Millennials on how to make decisions, especially if those opinions are unpopular.

Motivating by Meaning

Raised by optimistic yet overworked Boomers, Millennials were often coached with the idea of, "If you are going to work as hard as I have, be sure you do something that's meaningful to you." The mantra stuck; Millennials aren't solely interested in the numbers and the bottom line. They care about the bigger picture.

Don't get us wrong, Millennials still care about the paycheck. This is not an excuse to pay them in Pogs and Beanie Babies, though that would probably make a great Throwback Thursday photo. This is an opportunity for you to celebrate how meaningful a Millennial's work is in the company. When they know that their work has a direct, positive impact on the community and the world around them, it feeds a deep motivation of theirs, whether they know it or not. This can have several natural benefits to employers:

>> **It can save you money.** When you have a generation who can see the intrinsic value in doing work that has meaning, there are ways to give promotions or "raises" that aren't measured in dollar bills. And, as a manager, it gives you something to talk about other than money — an uncomfortable subject in any situation, especially if it's out of your jurisdiction. Giving them a seat on a charity committee or asking them to look for community outreach opportunities are ways to keep them motivated while "promoting" them. Two birds, one stone.

WARNING

Millennials will know if you're placating them. While Millennials' desire to do meaningful work can save you money, don't cut corners when you owe them more. They'll know when you're attempting to do that. View this more as a bonus than a mindset to have when motivating them.

>> **It can be utilized as an efficient training opportunity.** As the generation after Millennials continues to march into the workplace, they will undoubtedly need some workplace training and support. Enter Millennials, stage right. Millennials will find meaning grooming the next generation of talent and advising based on mistakes they wish they hadn't made.

>> **It can be the match that starts a motivation fire.** One of the most positive consequences of motivating Millennials by meaning is that it catches on. Thanks to their collaborative and tribal nature, once you've ignited the flame within one Millennial and made them feel motivated in their work, they are likely to pass the torch to their fellow Millennials. Like a wildfire, a group of passionate Millennials can spread their message quickly and possibly reignite other generations who are feeling burned out. (No forests or property were damaged in the making of this metaphor.)

TIP

Tap into your Millennials when running community involvement endeavors. Whether it's organizing a team to build a house with Habitat for Humanity or taking a leadership role within your United Way campaign, Millennials will want to be involved. It will not only energize them, but it may also breathe new life into initiatives that could be getting stale.

Embracing Diversity

By the numbers, the United States is growing more and more diverse every year. However, all too often we hear organizations describe their leadership as "male, pale, and stale." This will not go over well with Millennials who not only respect diversity, but expect it. As your pipeline of talent continues to become more diverse, you'll need more diverse leaders to attract them. How can Millennials help you achieve this?

Millennials have greatly broadened the definition of diversity. To them, diversity includes race, age, gender, sexual orientation, even diversity of thought. Millennials are often passionate about starting employee resource groups in the workplace and getting involved in initiatives that ensure an inclusive work environment. Use this passion to move your organization forward and appeal to top talent both in the Millennial generation and the following generation.

Of course, there are times when appealing to a pool of talent with diverse thoughts can slow things down (as much as we hate to admit it). It's just *easier* to get things done when everyone already agrees. However, easy doesn't equate to good, and no one believes that more than Millennials. Growing up, they were constantly told to voice their opinions and value everyone's point-of-view because you never know what innovation and disruption can come from the smallest voice. Let your Millennials be the Robin Hood of opinions.

Urging an Eagerness to Help

Millennials grew up in a time when a "well-rounded" resume was what got you into college, which would in turn get you your dream job. If you were an athlete, stretching your skills by joining the debate team doubled your appeal on paper. If you were an athlete, *and* in debate, *and* on the honor roll, *and* volunteered in your spare time . . . well, you could basically walk into class at any college you applied to. Needless to say, the worst thing you could do for a successful future was go home when school ended at 3:00. In the workplace, this means that Millennials are usually more than willing to learn about other positions and take on tasks that may not fit their job description, but less than willing to lead with a "that's not *my* job" mentality.

If you put out a call for volunteers to attend a meeting or help on a new initiative and/or committee, it is likely that a Millennial will raise his hand to get involved. It's possible that this "eager beaver" mentality can be chalked up to being young, green, and not yet jaded by the realities of the workplace. Or it could seem that he is taking on too many extra things when he should just be doing his job. On the farthest end of the stereotype spectrum, you may even consider this Millennial an entitled goody two-shoes. But it's a grave mistake to let that enthusiasm go unnoticed — tap into this pocket of energy within your walls.

REMEMBER

One thing that can make managers nervous is that, often, enthusiastic Millennials are willing to learn but lack relevant experience, and the young people making decisions could in fact be in over their heads and acting on adrenaline alone. Good news! Great Millennials find little shame in admitting what they don't know, and know when to call in the experts.

Capturing Innovation

Breaking news: Millennials grew up with rapid technology advancements. You've only heard that 100 or so times by now. Don't let this "Captain Obvious" news cloud your view of the important reality that Millennials saw innovation play out in two notable ways: industry disruption and the upgrade cycle.

>> **Industry disruption:** While each generation has seen its share of major innovation, the technology that Millennials grew up with has disrupted industries that had been stagnant for decades. Whether it was something huge like the advent of the smartphone, or something more simple like Uber, Millennials witnessed that no matter the history of the product or institution, nothing is here to stay the same. (Note that the inventors/disruptors themselves are not Millennials; the invention/innovation was created during Millennials' formative years, often by Gen Xers.)

Playing spectator to these advances, Millennials learned that one great idea can lead to an entirely new way of doing things. At work, it's historically been easy to fall in line and do things the way they've always been done. Cue a cacophony of "If it ain't broke, don't fix it." While this motto sometimes holds true, organizations that thrive are malleable and flow alongside change. Allowing Millennials to imagine the possibilities could take your organization to a new level.

>> **Upgrade cycle:** To use an age-old and very weird expression, sometimes it's not necessary to throw out the baby with the bathwater — improvement can be more than enough innovation. By the time Millennials got their first computer, they were already primed for Version 2.0, then 3.0, and then Version 10.1.4. They have learned to expect constant development and will expect the same at the office. While some may say, "This is how we do things," Millennials are more likely to respond to that with, "This is cool. Now how do we make it better?" Managers who choose to embrace this mentality rather than fight it may be surprised at how their organization will change for the better.

Staying Networked

Imagine if every person you'd ever met since middle school was in your Rolodex. Imagine that you'd never lost touch with any of your summer camp buddies or your fellow cross-country skiers. And you also didn't lose touch with any random person you met at your semester at sea. Well, if you're a Millennial, you don't have to imagine what this would be like because it's reality. Growing up with social media, Millennials have amassed huge networks of contacts, starting at incredibly young ages. The contact list they've been building since age 11 is one that even the most experienced executives could have only dreamed of decades ago.

And not only do Millennials have the ability to contact any of these people, most aren't afraid of actually doing so. While it may seem more awkward for other generations to reach out to someone they haven't seen since high school, Millennials don't see it that way. They've kept their contacts in their peripheral vision and usually have no qualms with tapping into their networks for anything from a new idea to looking for their company's next hire. Unknowingly, Millennials could be your most valuable, and least expensive, recruiting tool.

WARNING

As willing as Millennials are to use their social networks for professional use, make sure you, as their manager, give them clear guidelines about when it is and isn't appropriate to use social media at work. Are they crowd-sourcing for ideas around a highly confidential project? Are they posting pictures of proprietary systems or equipment? While these scenarios may seem laughable or obvious, we've seen them happen. Make sure Millennials know what is and isn't acceptable. One more thing — don't forget to articulate your personal expectations as their manager.

Recognizing a Fear of Failure

Okay, we admit that this one may fall under weaknesses rather than strengths, but stick with us for a minute. Millennials do not like to fail. Or maybe more accurately, they aren't good at failing. It's easy to make fun of the seventh-place ribbons and participation trophies that lined their childhood bookshelves, but remember that Millennials never asked for those trophies or ribbons. In the office, managers are often baffled when Millennials are deeply upset — or sometimes shed a tear — when others point out their shortcomings. Sure, it's critical for Millennials to have thick skin at work, and many who don't have the thick skin right away build it in short amounts of time.

If you want to capitalize on this strength that doesn't seem like a strength, rethink it: Perceive this fear of failure as a willingness to do whatever they can to do something the right way. This is a generation of people who *hate* to fail. They aren't used to doing it, and they don't want to start now. It can be their growing edge and a give them a strong sense of competition to achieve a level of greatness that only you can see.

TIP

To get the most out of Millennials that you manage, show them a clear path to success. Don't make them guess. You can even go so far as to start your feedback by saying something like, "I know how much you want to succeed here and how much you don't want to let anyone down. If you are serious about that, here's what needs to get done." This kind of messaging primes Millennials to push any sensitivity aside, listen to you, and work hard to improve.

Showing Informality at Work

This one can take managers aback. We have heard from leaders who can't believe what Millennials will say or do: They show up on their first day with facial piercings or brightly dyed hair, they admit to being a bit hungover on a Monday morning, or they even call their boss "dude." Millennials have definitely pushed the envelope when it comes to informality in the workplace, but they're doing so for a good reason. Anything less would be inauthentic and fake.

So, why is informality a good thing? First, as their manager you don't have to do a lot of guesswork to know where they're at. Many are keen on checking in to tell you how they're doing. Conversely, when you are managing older generations who prefer a more formal environment, it's possible you won't know their true feelings until you are blindsided by a scathing review or a letter of resignation. This is less likely to happen with Millennials.

WARNING

Millennials know their generation's reputation of being a more sensitive generation. Do your best to avoid stereotyping the Millennials you manage as all the same, and get to know their level of informality on an individual basis.

Secondly, it can save you time by relieving you from overthinking how you communicate with them. Millennials are more than fine with drive-by feedback or one-line emails that ignore basic grammar rules. You may need to coach your Millennials on when and where this is acceptable, but let's face it: Not every email needs to be written in corporate jargon complete with sign off and signature. Instead this is your opportunity to show your own personality and humor, and connect with your Millennials. Ultimately an informal managerial approach can save time and also create more authentic relationships in the workplace.

Being Ready for Fun

Millennials aren't afraid to let their hair down at work. People have told us stories of Traditionalist bosses saying, "casual day is Sunday" because, for them, suits and ties were required and — perish the thought — jeans were strictly out of the question. Traditionalists and Boomers grew up in a world with much firmer lines between work and home. For Millennials? Home is work and work is home. Their thought process: "If I'm going to spend 40+ hours a week at the office, I better enjoy my time and my co-workers." This is not a generation willing to wait until 5 p.m. on Friday to let loose — and that goes beyond wearing jeans or yoga pants to work on a Tuesday.

Millennials have been known to fawn over things like foosball tables and Xboxes in the office. While these kinds of requests can send some managers reeling, ask yourself, "Who is this helping, and is anyone really being hurt?" It goes without saying that if this push for fun gets in the way of productivity (or employees are getting physically injured), you'll need to step in. But many offices have found that infusing fun into work has benefitted not just the youngest generation, but every generation.

If you aren't ready to install a basketball court in the lunchroom or a treehouse in the atrium, fear not. You won't be turning off Millennials. But do look for ways you can embrace fun in a way that works for your culture.

TIP

You may be thinking, "Great. Now on top of doing my regular job and managing these Millennials, I also have to figure out a way to bring fun into the workplace too. What am I, a camp counselor?" No, you're not, and we certainly don't expect you to be the DoGT (Director of Good Times). Luckily, you don't have to come up with a darn thing — let the Millennials do it! Give them parameters and a budget, and you may find yourself having more fun than anyone.

Chapter **20**

Ten Millennial Stereotypes that Are Misinterpreted

When looking at different areas of diversity and inclusion, you will be hard-pressed to find a topic as full of stereotypes and misconceptions as generational diversity. You'd be surprised at just how many labels people are willing to slap on Millennials (or any generation) — not even behind their backs, but right to their faces. In a world that is becoming increasingly politically correct, sometimes honesty is refreshing, and the ability to openly discuss how other generations view one another is what makes this topic so powerful. But who wants to be defined by stereotypes? No one, surely, but especially not Millennials, who have been pigeonholed from the moment they started entering the workplace.

It's not that all of the stereotypes we cover here are completely false. Most stereotypes start with at least some kernel of truth, whether or not you choose to agree with it. In this chapter, we explore stereotypes that have stuck with Millennials, how they are often grossly misinterpreted, and how you can confront them in a positive and impactful way.

Hating Face-to-Face Communication

The assumption that Millennials don't like face-to-face communication is understandable. Walk into any coffee shop, bar, or office and you will be greeted with downturned heads, faces lit by screens, and silence, with the occasional laugh-out-loud — even if he or she is sitting at a table alone. To make matters worse, Millennials are the first generation to use instant-messaging tools to "talk" to their co-workers rather than stand up, walk 15 feet to their manager's office, and speak words.

While Millennials do spend many hours communicating via screens and feel quite comfortable doing so, it does not mean that they hate face-to-face interactions. Millennials are the generation that are often begging for mentorship opportunities and love to interact, network, and socialize with others; heck, many would sell their smartphones for a chance to get an audience with the company's executives. (Okay, maybe not sell their phone, but perhaps give it up for a few hours.)

TIP

While Millennials do not *hate* face-to-face communication, they may struggle with it and need your help. This may be especially true for younger Millennials. They're used to sending texts and instant messages because it's their default mode of communication. Even phone calls, with the slightest suggestion of a human at the other end, can make Millennials nervous. Rather than stereotype and scold them, coach them! It may seem remedial, but ask them if they'd like to listen in on your conference calls or audit your meetings. And even simpler than that: Model the behavior you'd like to see. If you'd rather a Millennial walk to your desk versus instant-message you, set the precedent by doing the same. And if all else fails, just straight up tell them what you expect or prefer. Millennials are a lot of things, but "mind reader" isn't one of them.

REMEMBER

The oldest Millennials are in their mid-30s and have a pretty good grasp of face-to-face communication. Many of them are now facing the challenge of managing a generation who can successfully function across five screens at work and have never lived a formative year without Wi-Fi. These Millennials may need your guidance to help them train in a skill that was once taught to them in a different way.

Having the Attention Span of a Goldfish

We've all walked by that Millennial in the office who has 17 browser tabs open, a Twitter feed scrolling, a phone buzzing, and headphones in. Managers may think, "Either you've made your coffee with Red Bull and can conquer all these tasks at once, or you're disorganized, undisciplined, and unfocused." Welcome to frustration station.

It's true. Millennials probably aren't going to work on a single task for eight hours, but don't mistake multitasking or switch-tasking as an inability to focus. Unlike previous generations, Millennials grew up in a fast-paced world fueled by the infinite and ever-changing Internet. Their attention is constantly being drawn to the latest, greatest, and craziest. Novels turned into articles, which turned into lists, which turned into 140-character tweets. Rather than getting upset, ask yourself two questions: Why does this have to be a bad thing? And, how can I use this to my advantage?

Of course, there are some jobs where multitasking isn't a good thing. We'd venture a guess that no one would want his surgeon reading a book or checking her email with a patient on the operating table. That example may be a no-brainer, but in jobs where it makes sense, managers who worry more about results and less about process will find that the ability to switch focus rapidly and efficiently isn't a bad thing at all — it's a skill.

Operating with No Work Ethic

A hiring manager at a financial advising firm once told us that if a Millennial candidate asks in an initial interview whether 8 to 5 is the hard and fast schedule, she immediately disregards them as a viable candidate. They're added to the pile of *those* Millennials who'll never succeed in the workplace: the lazy, entitled, no-work-ethic types. While we understood where she was coming from (kind of), we also ventured to guess that she hadn't reached the simple truth that hard work looks very different these days. People work from their phones and tablets at all hours, and they can get just as much done at a coffee shop as they can at their desk. The once-clear understanding of working versus not working is more fluid now than ever before.

At this point, you may be internally screaming, *"Just tell me: Do Millennials have work ethic or not?"* First, calm down. Second, yes, yes they do. It just looks *different*. Keep in mind the following points before giving any Millennials the pink slip:

>> **Focus on results:** We're starting to sound like a broken record here, but it bears repeating. Ask yourself what you'd rather have: a Millennial who's at the office when you arrive, stays late most nights, and appears to be working very hard but doesn't achieve the results you desire, *or* a Millennial who is in and out of the office, leaves for yoga at lunch, and takes care of some personal to-dos during business hours but always knocks it out of the park? Personally, we'd choose the latter every time.

>> **Assume the best:** All too often, we hear from managers who believe that if their employees are working from home, they are secretly watching *The*

Bachelor and eating bonbons. Or if they see a colleague perusing a social-media site during the workday, they believe that he clearly cares more about their social lives than work. In our experience, these people are the exception to the rule. Withholding these kinds of freedoms from everyone to protect against the very few will hold you back as an effective manager. If you find yourself questioning an employee's work ethic, reread the preceding bullet and refocus on results.

Plot twist: Gen Xers are actually looking to telecommute more than Millennials, yet Millennials are the ones who get the bad rap. If you're an Xer who would love to work from home but would hate it if people called you a slacker, assume Millennials are in the same boat as you.

Wanting to Have Fun All Day

Most people can remember complaining to a parent or grandparent about work and being met with a response like, "Well, there is a reason it's called the *work-*place and not the *fun* place!" [Insert eye roll here.] The fact is that Millennials (and hopefully all generations) believe that work and fun do not have to be mutually exclusive. No, Millennials do not think every working moment will be spent playing video games and drinking beer. (Nor would they feel too successful if that were the case.) But they do expect a little something every now and again.

So what gets misinterpreted here? It's easy to assume that the more time you spend having fun, the less time you spend actually working. While there is a time to buckle down and get the job done, studies have shown that having fun at work not only builds stronger ties with co-workers; it can also improve the bottom line. A few stats for your enjoyment:

>> In a 2013 survey of more than 40,000 employees at 30 companies around the world, TINYpulse, a survey and research company, found that the number-one reason people liked their jobs was because they enjoyed the people that they worked with.

>> At Google, employee satisfaction rose 37 percent as a result of initiatives dedicated to employee satisfaction — suggesting that financial incentives aren't enough to make for highly productive employees.

>> A study by economists at the University of Warwick found that happiness at work led to a 12 percent spike in productivity, while unhappy workers proved 10 percent less productive.

>> According to LinkedIn, 57 percent of Millennials say that work friendships make them more productive.

Refusing to Do Work that Is "Beneath Them"

Much like Gen Xers have never been able to rid themselves of that pesky "slacker" label, Millennials have been granted an "entitled" designation that they would do anything to jettison. Where does it come from? In many cases, it can be boiled down to Millennials asking one question that can seriously irk managers: *"Why?"*

For generations past, if a manager asked an underling to do a task, no matter how big or small, it was expected that the employee would hop to it, no questions asked. Millennials, as is probably clear, don't typically do the same as generations past. So, while they may push back and ask why a lot, it doesn't mean they are unwilling to help, believe they are too "qualified" for the task, or just copping an attitude. They're simply curious about your reasoning and how their actions will benefit you, the team, and the organization.

TIP

If you ask a Millennial to do something he may consider below his pay grade, take time to explain why you are doing so. It may be a great growth opportunity, an integral project to the company, or sometimes, it may just be something that needs to get done and no one else has the time to do it. All of those reasons are totally valid. But instead of barking orders, explain the reasons behind the task. In response, you will see a generation that is not only willing to help but eager to do so.

Being Young and Inexperienced

Many managers have to pick their jaws up off the floor when their new employee tells them they were born in the 80s or even, yes, the 90s. We've heard managers say things like: "It's just so easy to dismiss them as a bunch of kids playing 'office.'" This is hardly a new phenomenon: Everyone likes to poke fun at the newbie, and everyone got their share of teasing when they started working. However, there are a couple reasons to shift the hazing-the-newbie mindset:

>> **They aren't "kids" anymore.** Sure, younger Millennials are still in their early and mid-20s, but leading-edge Millennials are in their mid-30s. In just a few short years, they'll be celebrating their 40th birthdays. Many Millennials already have kids of their own. Yet somehow, since the term "Millennial" entered the daily vernacular of popular media, it's been used to reference *all* young people. That simply isn't accurate. As a reminder, Millennials were born between 1980 and 1995, and in many cases already, they aren't the youngest generation at the office.

>> **They have no real-world experience.** Millennials may have been less likely to work the cash register or flip burgers as youths, but if you ask any Millennial about her unpaid summer internships, you're bound to get a long list of previous employers. What's more, they're coming to the workplace with a different type of experience: life experience. No, we don't mean paying a mortgage or navigating the ins and outs of typical adulting. Millennials are more likely to have taken advanced-placement courses, travelled abroad, built a Habitat for Humanity home, or served in some sort of leadership capacity in their community. While some managers would prefer X amount of years in X industry or organization, try to figure out how you can capitalize on the experience Millennials *do* have.

Fearing Going Solo

Millennials are an inherently collaborative generation, so this stereotype is a trickier one to break down. But there is a huge difference in the subtleties between "haven't had to," "don't like to," or "don't see the value" in doing things solo. We take these one at a time:

>> **Haven't had to:** As we mention many times, Millennials are a collaborative bunch. They grew up truly believing that two heads are better than one and that there is no "I" in "team". They played team sports, completed group projects, and were often raised in homes where democracy ruled. It's important to realize that, as their manager, when you ask them to do something solo and you're met with hesitation, they aren't balking at your request; they just haven't done it that often. It doesn't mean they can't, but it may mean they need some extra coaching before they're comfortable riding solo. (If they are using "I can't" as an excuse, you should dig deeper, because that's a red flag.)

>> **Don't like to:** Millennials generally prefer working in teams for all the reasons mentioned earlier. This generation helped bring about the era of open floor plans and group ideation sessions. There will be times when Millennials need to get work done independently — a fact they can and do understand. But if working in teams is what they prefer and there's no good reason not to, why stop them? Just be sure they know they're there to work, not socialize.

>> **Don't see the value:** As a whole, Millennials believe that collaboration fosters better results. They crowdsource their friends, brainstorm with colleagues, and use the almighty Google in the hopes of building consensus, comparing progress, and delivering a stronger result. Two heads are better than one, but 20 heads are better than two.

Keep in mind that working alone can be a bit of a life stage/age thing. In the grand scheme of things, younger Millennials are still relatively new to the workforce. To them, it's comforting to have a team to back you up when you're green. On the flipside, if you work with a lot of Early Millennials, they'll likely profess their love of working alone and meetings-free. As a manager, gauge appropriately.

What's more, working independently versus collaboratively can come down to personal preference. Just use your generational lens sensibly, and you'll be fine.

Thinking They're All the Same

For a group as collaborative and socially-linked as Millennials, you'd think they'd all be quite similar. While they do share some overarching traits, one of the most offensive things you can say to a Millennial is, "You're all the same." You'll promptly be met with a searing glare and a clenched-teeth response of, "I really don't think all Millennials are the same." This is one of the biggest hazards of the generations topic: the risk of putting every member of a generation into a box without leaving room for differences among them.

Cards on the table: Pigeonholing is the last thing we intend to do, and we hope that none of our readers assume all Millennials — or members of any generation — are carbon copies of one another. Unfortunately for those who don't study the generations in depth, it can simply be easier to understand any group of people through a collective lens. But beyond all the factors that unite Millennials as a generation are the many distinctions that make each Millennial unique. Some are parents. Some want to stay with their company for 25 years. Some have older siblings who influenced them growing up, and therefore identify more with Xers than Millennials. The list goes on.

The key is to use your generational lens as a guide, not a finite list or definition encompassing an entire group of people. Remain curious and attentive, and remember to ask plenty of questions.

Note: For more information on the nuances between different types of Millennials, refer to Part III in this book.

Having No Ambition

This one is confusing. In one corner you have people who love to accuse Millennials of not being ambitious. In the other you have managers who are constantly complaining that Millennials are trying to race to the top of the ladder in three years.

So which is the truth? The answer is both.

Sure, sometimes Millennials are looking for the reward for just doing their regular duties. As their manager, seek clarity via transparency. Show them the direct steps it takes to get where they want to be. If they balk at the road ahead, you've found a tool for weeding out those who probably aren't the best fit for your workplace.

The other piece to keep in mind is that what ambition looked like for you and your generation may look vastly different to a Millennial. In some industries, the only ambition recognized is the one-track kind: one career, one job, and one goal, which is probably either CEO or retirement. For Millennials, it's not that straight-forward. A Millennial's goal may be landing her dream job, making more money, making an impact, having flexibility, taking a mid-career break to travel, or even just experiencing different workplaces and fields. These goals may not be attainable at one position, let alone three or four. Before you judge how ambitious your Millennial is, be sure you aren't using only your own personal definition of the word.

Relying on Mom and Dad for Everything

When Xers were entering the workplace, they would have rather lost a limb than move back in with their parents. Extreme, yes, but it definitely shows the extent of Xers' independence. Millennials have clearly chosen a different path. This generation is notoriously close with Mom and Dad. They were raised in the self-esteem movement and often name their parents as their greatest heroes and influences. Many Millennials are still on their parents' phone and insurance plans.

And it doesn't stop there — parents are following their Millennial kids into the workplace as well (sometimes literally on Take Your Parent to Work Day). We've heard stories of parents coordinating their kid's interviews, wanting to attend their review sessions, and calling their managers to hear how their kid is faring at work.

All this is to say that you aren't imagining things. Parents are showing up in the workplace in new, surprising, and, at times, frustrating ways. So what can you do?

>> **Draw the line.** If Millennials involve their parents at work in a way you aren't comfortable with, tell them. Explain why you aren't comfortable with it and that you expect it to stop. Don't assume Millennials know your policies here (it's not like there's a precedent), and definitely don't assume that because you didn't need to be told that they don't either. Also, don't assume that Millennials know. Sometimes Mom and Dad step in unannounced and without permission.

>> **Realize that there is a difference between relying on Mom and Dad and tapping into them.** Millennials don't see their parents as crutches but coaches. They're looking for guidance and comfort, not handouts and favors. Is that really so different than seeing a career coach or speaking with a friend? Parents of Millennials are likely to give sound advice coming from decades of experience, work and otherwise. As a manager, see parents as allies, not enemies, and it's possible Momma Terri's famous banana bread might make it into the corporate kitchen.

WARNING

While Millennials are close with their parents, many of them have cut the cord. Just like the stereotype prior, don't assume that all Millennials are the same.

Chapter **21**

Ten Tips on How to Become the #BestBossEver

Think about your favorite boss you've ever had. Have him/her in your mind? Good. Now, think about how great you would feel if your employees thought of you when people asked *them* who *their* favorite boss was. Even when leaders pretend not to care, most would be honored to be called the best boss ever. Figuring out the best path to popularity with this next generation can be rough, but it's definitely not unattainable. Whether you push your people to reach their full potential or tap into the personal connection, you can find a way to earn the title of "Best Boss." It won't be easy, but once you do, prepare to see your team flourish.

This chapter lists ten things you can do to go from being a great boss to being the #BestBossEver.

Asking Them Questions — All the Time

Many experienced leaders grew up during a time when the parenting mantra was, "Children should be seen and not heard." When they entered the workforce, they were expected to listen, learn, and put their heads down to get the job done.

REMEMBER

Millennials grew up under vastly different circumstances than Boomers and Gen Xers because adults in their lives wanted, perhaps even expected, to see and hear them. These adults — parents, teachers, coaches, counselors — constantly asked questions and were genuinely interested in the answers. Whether they asked about what piece of technology the family should invest in or if they felt safe during the aftermath of 9/11, adults raised Millennials in an environment that encouraged the sharing of opinions and feelings about every matter, no matter how mundane or extreme.

As a manager and leader, one of the most powerful tools you have in your tool belt is the question mark. Ask them about their weekend. Ask them about the project they are working on. If you are feeling particularly brave, ask them for input on a project *you* are working on. You don't necessarily have to heed their advice, but the simple ask will score major points with this generation of natural consultants.

Learning to Like Them, Genuinely

Making office small talk is easy; you've probably been doing it for years. When you ask your co-workers about their kids or compliment them on last week's presentation, you probably don't even realize how effortlessly you can make them feel appreciated and heard (regardless of whether you *really* care to hear the whole story). This skill, for decades, has been a necessary one in the work world, dominated by written and unwritten rules. Pause and think: How do these conversations change when you genuinely like the person you're speaking to? Seasoned workers are pretty good at playing the game, positive or negative, because it was necessary to get ahead, but that also means that people are equally good at spotting when you're playing the game. And if a Millennial spots it, he'll be rubbed the wrong way. This is the generation that values authenticity in a boss above anything else.

TIP

The key is to actually learn to like and care about each of the people you manage. Sure, you may not like everything about a given person, but find things you do like and focus on those. Humans are good at trying to show they care for one another, but sometimes they put minimal effort into it. Just know that when you're only putting in 10 percent, it's pretty easy to identify. Make the effort to take your next generation employees out to coffee, get to know who they are outside of work, and experience the gift of building a strong working relationship with them.

REMEMBER

This is the generation that grew up watching Barney, whose theme song started with "I love you, you love me . . ." and ended with the question, "Won't you say you love me too?" Don't leave them hanging; give them some love (or at least a like).

Individualizing Your Approach with Each Millennial

Some managers tend to take a "same equals fair" approach with their management style, which can backfire with Millennials who have been raised in a world that celebrated the individual. No one wants to feel like they're getting the short end of the stick, but everyone's opinion of what the stick looks like is different, and Millennials expect an advanced level of personalization.

Customizing your approach is critical with a generation that has been able to personalize everything from their song playlist to their sneaker color for as long as they can remember. If they see you using a one-size-fits-all managing model, you risk them checking out, or worse: leaving. They don't want to be grouped with every other Millennial, especially not as the Millennial that the media consistently describes.

Consider all the ways that you can change your ways, within reason. There is no reason to do guesswork here — you aren't psychic. If you aren't sure of the best way to customize your approach for a certain employee, just ask:

>> How do you best receive feedback?

>> What would be the most impactful way I can help you through this project?

>> What time of day do you feel like you do your best work?

>> Do you work better in a team or alone?

>> What can I do to make your work life better?

>> What is your ideal reward?

Giving Them an "A" for Effort (Even if the Results Are More Like a B+)

Rewarding effort is definitely one of those things that both gives Millennials a bad rap and also gets under their managers' skin. Yes, Millennials are the generation that got trophies for seventh place and a participation award for every activity they showed up for. It's not that Millennials don't understand the need to drive real results and win, or try for that matter. Of course they do. It's just that they *also* believe that there is inherent value in the results *and* the effort they put in.

TIP

You don't need to completely abandon your instincts. At the end of the day, it's about results. But look for opportunities where you can meet Millennials somewhere in the middle. Recognize their effort. Point out specific times they exceeded expectations and met challenges head-on. Then talk to them about the results. If they didn't achieve them, let them know. When you show them that you aren't blind to their efforts but also believe in constructively criticizing the areas that could be better, they'll feel motivated instead of inert.

The good news? This trend is fleeting with the next generation. Gen Edgers are showing up to work with a much more competitive spirit and truly believe that a participation award is *not* a real award.

Challenging Them to Do More

Think about the best teacher or professor you've ever had. Chances are, you aren't picturing the teacher who gave out the "easy A" and rewarded anyone in class who had a pulse. This teacher probably challenged you to stretch yourself beyond what you initially thought was possible, and though you may have been irritated at the time, you later thought it a valuable growing experience. Many managers and leaders think they're helping their Millennial employees by trying to make their lives easy. Any time a really challenging situation presents itself, too many leaders say, "Let me take that off your plate" instead of empowering Millennials with the responsibility.

Millennials were raised in a time when they were pushed to pack their schedules with strenuous advanced-placement courses and time-consuming extracurriculars. They'll rise to the challenge when dared to do more and will not only show you what they can really do, but that they can also be trusted with increasingly difficult tasks.

Sharing Yourself with Them (Yes, This Means Beyond Your Work-Self)

If you want to get the best out of your Millennial employees, you need to take time to get to know "the real them." However, in turn, *you* also have to be willing to share "the real you" with them. This can make some leaders very uncomfortable: accepting a social media friend or follow request, sharing details about their family, or sitting down for an unexpected tell-all lunch about their past, present, and future. We understand how unnatural this can feel. To manage these situations, take a two-step approach:

1. **Understand that your employees aren't inquiring about your personal life to be nosy.**

   It's not as if Millennials want you to solemnly swear that you're up to no good. With the advent of social media, Millennials have been exposed to the personal sides of everyone from their pastors to the President. And those people aren't just posting this week's sermon or their next political agenda — they're uploading pictures of their dogs and heartwarming stories from their past. It's no surprise that Millennials show up to work wanting a glimpse into what makes you, you. Find a way to share your authentic self without compromising your own values.

2. **Figure out boundaries that you are comfortable with.**

   You don't have to broadcast an exposé on your personal life at the office. If you don't want to talk about politics or religion but you're comfortable sharing your passion for the outdoors or discussing the latest documentary, great! Take some time to discover what you're willing to share and then step aboard the sharing train.

Giving Some Good Ol' Tough Love

Despite their efforts, Millennials have earned a reputation of being a little soft. As much as they may try to deny it, it's true that this generation is quite different from the Traditionalists, Baby Boomers, and Gen Xers who grew up in a more authoritarian, top-down, command-and-control world. This next generation of employees grew up in a flattened, democratic world, so they're more likely to view you as a counselor than a general.

That said, there's a time and place for tough love. If you want to get the most out of your Millennials, you will need to dole out some kudos paired with tough news.

This might come in the form of direct and honest feedback from a Gen Xer. Or, you could give them an assignment you know they will struggle with. While it may be painful to deliver the feedback at the time, and a box of tissues may be needed, the rewards will be great for both you and your Millennial.

REMEMBER

When it's time to deliver tough news, it will be most effective if you explain to your employees *why* something is so critical for them to understand or do. Giving them context will help Millennials see why they need to listen, and they won't disregard it as you overreacting.

Making Sure You Don't Let Them Down

No boss begins a work relationship thinking, "I can't wait to mess this up!" Most manager-employee relationships start out great: Employees bring their A-game and managers are engaged and supportive. The issue comes into play when, despite a strong start, managers let their employees down over time. Just because the newness has worn off, don't forget that Millennials still need your support from time to time.

TIP

Do your best not to blow off those weekly check-in meetings you were so religious about keeping at the start. Continue to seek manager training or find a mentor who can provide ongoing guidance. If you want to be especially diligent, set a reminder in your calendar every month that says something like, "Don't let them down," just to give yourself a moment to reflect.

You're bound to let your people down a time (or two) — it's only natural. Instead of ignoring this when it happens and living in a nice bubble of denial, recognize it. Talk to your employees. Tell them you realize that you missed the mark on this one and how you plan to do better next time. Not only will this help you earn the trust of your people, but it will also give them an opportunity to see you as a human who taps into the authenticity that Millennials crave.

Setting Clear, Structured Expectations

A very fine line exists between micromanaging and setting clear expectations. It's arguably one of the toughest distinctions that you will face, and it's a dance you'll be perfecting as long as you choose to lead.

REMEMBER

Don't forget that for the Millennial generation, the last thing they want is to feel that they're on a deserted island without the necessary tools. While fiercely independent Gen Xers may love the freedom to tackle a project by themselves, Millennials want clear guidelines to follow. Before setting them on a project, ask yourself:

>> How much do you expect them to work by themselves versus with you?

>> What are the check-in points?

>> How are you structuring those check-ins, if at all?

>> When is the deadline? How are you tracking it?

>> In what format do you expect them to deliver the final project? How are you going to give them that direction without micromanaging the situation?

For most projects, you will have some very clear expectations (deadlines, deliverable structure, and so on) and some flexible expectations (PowerPoint or Keynote for the presentation, agenda for check-ins, and so forth). Be sure to point out both sets of expectations and what items fall into which category. Explain why some things are nonnegotiable, but also highlight where you are giving them freedom.

Inviting Their Input

If you are a leader or manager, giving feedback to your employees on how they perform is part of the job description. However, asking your employees for *their* feedback on how *you* are doing is less normal. Some managers welcome and thrive on this two-way conversation. Others may find it to be the hardest pill to swallow on this list of ten objectives.

For those of you who find it difficult, you're not alone. It is easy to fear not only what they may say, but also how their input will affect your leadership. Can you trust their advice? Will they be too hard on you? Do they lack the emotional intelligence to see the situation for what it really is? If you fall into the camp of the latter, don't worry:

>> **Millennials don't view your soliciting input as a weakness.** If anything, it will only boost their confidence in you. Keep in mind, this generation has been reviewing everything from books to hotels to restaurants for as long as they can remember. If a website doesn't allow them to share feedback, they are very likely not to trust it. The same can be said about their manager. Soliciting feedback builds trust.

>> **They will freely give constructive feedback, but not without accolades.**
Millennials grew up during the self-esteem movement, so they know how to dish out the good feelings. So while many managers may walk away from these conversations with areas to consider changing, just as many leave the conversation surprised and much more confident in the job they're doing.

Before they know it, they'll find out that they've earned the title of #BestBossEver.

Index

About the Authors

Hannah Ubl, an information junkie to her core, quickly rose in the company to her current role as Research Director. She leads BridgeWorks' national research efforts, most recently overseeing the latest endeavor comparing Early Millennials, Recessionist Millennials, and Generation Edge. Whether running focus groups, diving into data analysis, interviewing a C-Suite executive, or speaking one-on-one with every generation, her research has unearthed valuable tips, actionable solutions, and key marketing strategies for generationally diverse workplaces and clients. Hannah especially thrives when connecting quantitative and qualitative data to a message for the masses, overseeing the keynote speaking side of the business, and giving generational insight to numerous publications. She has been fortunate to work with scores of companies such as Adidas Group, Deloitte, L'Oreal, and Lockheed Martin. Hannah graduated with honors from Boston University and launched her career in marketing and human resources for the non-profit and healthcare sectors. She has worked at BridgeWorks since 2012. In her spare time, she can be found reading in her favorite haunt, promoting the arts in her community, or persuading her friends to join her at the adult night at the Science Museum.

Lisa Walden is the Communications Director at BridgeWorks. She is a seasoned generational expert who co-leads the conception of hard-hitting, forward-thinking, and incisive management and marketing insights. A sought-after expert who has been featured in publications nationwide, Lisa has lent her expertise to many of BridgeWorks' largest initiatives. She's led her team in developing a generational portal for a prominent national financial advising firm, helped a master-planned community design a Millennial-friendly neighborhood, and worked closely with organizations to develop impactful recruiting and retention strategies. Prior to joining the company, Lisa worked in human resources and has first-hand experience managing the influx of Millennials into the workforce and the challenges such drastic demographic changes present. Lisa is a voracious reader who consumes everything from generational research to classic literature to graphic novels. She has a bachelor's degree in comparative religion from Boston University.

Debra Arbit is CEO, integrator, and motivator at BridgeWorks. What started as an internship blossomed into Debra playing a key role as a contributor and generational voice for BridgeWorks' second book, *The M-Factor*, which outlines the essentials needed to understand Millennials and their mark on the workplace. Her business acumen and natural leadership prompted the co-founders to offer Debra both the role of CEO and the chance to become majority partner in 2009. Now, as the sole owner of BridgeWorks, Debra dedicates her time to the growth of the company and its clients. She continues to help organizations narrow generational divides, and her favorite clients are the ones with the most complex issues to solve. Debra has a passion for all things generations, but one topic close to her heart is how parenting styles have shaped Boomers, Xers, Millennials, and Gen Edgers. Debra came to BridgeWorks after a successful career in promotion marketing at General Mills. She has an MBA from the University of Minnesota and is a sought-after commentator in the media on generational issues. Debra currently lives in Minnetonka with her husband, her three children, and her ridiculously fluffy dog Daisy.

Dedication

This book goes out to all the generations: The Traditionalists who put their own needs aside and got the job done. The Baby Boomers who never took no for an answer. The Generation Xers who taught us the unending value of asking tough questions. The Millennials who brought a renewed sense of hope and optimism. And to all future generations for whom we are working tirelessly to build a better world.

Authors' Acknowledgments

This book would not have been written without the intelligent and dedicated team at BridgeWorks. We extend gratitude to Kel for his ever-entertaining dad jokes, Skylar for his leadership support, Timm (Nicole) and Mara for their keen eye on content and above-average interviewing skills, Austyn for her precision, and Phil and Scott for their drive and champion spirit. To our interviewees, thank you for sharing your valuable time and unique generational perspective.

Furthermore, we couldn't have asked for a more seamless, encouraging, and motivating partnership with our acquisitions editor Tracy at Wiley Publishing, and editors Linda, Christy, and Erin. Thank you for the back-and-forth and education on how Millennial-minded some of our phrases and writings could be.

Hannah: If you'd have asked me ten years ago if I'd be writing a book before turning 30, *and* be writing it with the assistance of an incredible team, I'd have laughed at the preposterous notion. Needless to say, I have a multitude of strong women and men in my life to thank.

First and foremost, I have to fully embody my Millennial-ness and thank my family . . . starting with my parents. Thank you, Ma and Pops, for supporting every path I've tried and modeling how rich life can be when you do what you love and share that with the world. Thanks to my late grandfather who taught me how to revel in intellectual pursuits and never underestimate the power of wit. To my grandmother, thank you for passing on your progressive, competitive, and ambitious spirit. You are my idol. Thanks to my brother Ben for being my greatest champion and strongest force in closing my confidence gap. You have been, and always will be, my rock. Thank you, Kellen and your orange cat, for always providing calm in a writing storm.

Second, thank you to the support that I've been fortunate to have, from speech coaches in my past to professional mentors in my present. And to those who made me doubt my skills, talent, and abilities, thank you for giving me a reason to keep persisting.

Third, thank you to the providers of sustenance: Urban Bean for the caffeine fixes, New Bohemia for the hoppy elixirs, and Volstead's Emporium for the celebratory cheers.

Finally, thank you to my co-workers, co-authors, and friends. Debra, thank you for hiring me, leading me, and always believing that I can do more. Lisa, we met and bonded in college over the love of a book. Now, we've written a book together. And to my fellow GenJunkies of BridgeWorks, I am humbled to work alongside a group of such intelligent, creative, and thoroughly singular people, whom without your support and help, this labor of GenLove would not have been written.

Lisa: I'm not a dummy — there's a mammoth list of people I've been grateful for during this journey. For brevity's sake, I've narrowed it down to three major buckets of thanks:

#1 The powerhouse team of generational experts: This project would have been nigh impossible without the unflagging support of the entire BridgeWorks team. From contributing their brilliant brains to help refine our content, to deftly discovering omitted Oxford commas during edits, to bearing with us on those dark and dreaded days of writing blocks, you were with us from beginning to end. Thank you, thank you, thank you, my dear #workfamily.

#2 The local haunts: Urban Bean and New Bohemia were second (and third) homes to me while this project was in the works. I consumed more iced lattes and cheese curds than is advisable, but the supportive smiling staff at both locales served as the delightful backdrop for this incredible experience. And sometimes you need to write where everybody knows your name.

#3 The family: To my brother Andrew, who plays devil's advocate for all my theories, thank you for challenging me to think critically and formulate logically sound arguments. To my sister Karen, who has faithfully read my writing since before her age hit double digits, thank you for being my first and most ardent fan. And lastly, in proper Millennial fashion, I must thank my parents. You cracked open the world for me before I could stand on two feet. Whether it was inspiring my love of books or taking me on adventures around the world, you both, in your own ways, taught me the inestimable importance of exploration, curiosity, and creativity. Los amo con todo mi corazon. Thank you for your enduring love and support. I carry them with me always.

Debra: The older I get, the more I realize how true clichés really are. The fact is, it honestly does take a village. Especially when you are attempting to own a business, raise three kids, and not lose your sanity in the process. To my parents (by birth and through marriage) who make everything possible. From the big stuff like believing in this whole crazy dream to the really big stuff like taking kids to ballet and swimming, none of this could happen without you. To Alex who believes in me the most when I believe in myself the least. You are my everything. And finally, to my kiddos. Margot, Ben, and Levi . . . you are my reason. Thank you for greeting me every night with sticky fingers and silly outfits and for reminding me that BridgeWorks is just my day job.

Publisher's Acknowledgments

Acquisitions Editor: Tracy Boggier
Project Manager: Linda Brandon
Development Editor: Linda Brandon
Copy Editor: Christine Pingleton
Technical Editor: Erin Patton

Production Editor: Antony Sami
Cover Photos: © Dave and Les Jacobs/Kolostock/ Getty Images

Apple & Mac

iPad For Dummies,
6th Edition
978-1-118-72306-7

iPhone For Dummies,
7th Edition
978-1-118-69083-3

Macs All-in-One
For Dummies, 4th Edition
978-1-118-82210-4

OS X Mavericks
For Dummies
978-1-118-69188-5

Blogging & Social Media

Facebook For Dummies,
5th Edition
978-1-118-63312-0

Social Media Engagement
For Dummies
978-1-118-53019-1

WordPress For Dummies,
6th Edition
978-1-118-79161-5

Business

Stock Investing
For Dummies, 4th Edition
978-1-118-37678-2

Investing For Dummies,
6th Edition
978-0-470-90545-6

Personal Finance
For Dummies, 7th Edition
978-1-118-11785-9

QuickBooks 2014
For Dummies
978-1-118-72005-9

Small Business Marketing
Kit For Dummies,
3rd Edition
978-1-118-31183-7

Careers

Job Interviews
For Dummies, 4th Edition
978-1-118-11290-8

Job Searching with Social
Media For Dummies,
2nd Edition
978-1-118-67856-5

Personal Branding
For Dummies
978-1-118-11792-7

Resumes For Dummies,
6th Edition
978-0-470-87361-8

Starting an Etsy Business
For Dummies, 2nd Edition
978-1-118-59024-9

Diet & Nutrition

Belly Fat Diet For Dummies
978-1-118-34585-6

Mediterranean Diet
For Dummies
978-1-118-71525-3

Nutrition For Dummies,
5th Edition
978-0-470-93231-5

Digital Photography

Digital SLR Photography
All-in-One For Dummies,
2nd Edition
978-1-118-59082-9

Digital SLR Video &
Filmmaking For Dummies
978-1-118-36598-4

Photoshop Elements 12
For Dummies
978-1-118-72714-0

Gardening

Herb Gardening
For Dummies, 2nd Edition
978-0-470-61778-6

Gardening with Free-Range
Chickens For Dummies
978-1-118-54754-0

Health

Boosting Your Immunity
For Dummies
978-1-118-40200-9

Diabetes For Dummies,
4th Edition
978-1-118-29447-5

Living Paleo For Dummies
978-1-118-29405-5

Big Data

Big Data For Dummies
978-1-118-50422-2

Data Visualization
For Dummies
978-1-118-50289-1

Hadoop For Dummies
978-1-118-60755-8

Language &
Foreign Language

500 Spanish Verbs
For Dummies
978-1-118-02382-2

English Grammar
For Dummies, 2nd Edition
978-0-470-54664-2

French All-in-One
For Dummies
978-1-118-22815-9

German Essentials
For Dummies
978-1-118-18422-6

Italian For Dummies,
2nd Edition
978-1-118-00465-4

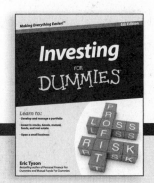

Math & Science

Algebra I For Dummies,
2nd Edition
978-0-470-55964-2

Anatomy and Physiology
For Dummies, 2nd Edition
978-0-470-92326-9

Astronomy For Dummies,
3rd Edition
978-1-118-37697-3

Biology For Dummies,
2nd Edition
978-0-470-59875-7

Chemistry For Dummies,
2nd Edition
978-1-118-00730-3

1001 Algebra II Practice
Problems For Dummies
978-1-118-44662-1

Microsoft Office

Excel 2013 For Dummies
978-1-118-51012-4

Office 2013 All-in-One
For Dummies
978-1-118-51636-2

PowerPoint 2013
For Dummies
978-1-118-50253-2

Word 2013 For Dummies
978-1-118-49123-2

Music

Blues Harmonica
For Dummies
978-1-118-25269-7

Guitar For Dummies,
3rd Edition
978-1-118-11554-1

iPod & iTunes
For Dummies, 10th Edition
978-1-118-50864-0

Programming

Beginning Programming
with C For Dummies
978-1-118-73763-7

Excel VBA Programming
For Dummies, 3rd Edition
978-1-118-49037-2

Java For Dummies,
6th Edition
978-1-118-40780-6

Religion & Inspiration

The Bible For Dummies
978-0-7645-5296-0

Buddhism For Dummies,
2nd Edition
978-1-118-02379-2

Catholicism For Dummies,
2nd Edition
978-1-118-07778-8

Self-Help & Relationships

Beating Sugar Addiction
For Dummies
978-1-118-54645-1

Meditation For Dummies,
3rd Edition
978-1-118-29144-3

Seniors

Laptops For Seniors
For Dummies, 3rd Edition
978-1-118-71105-7

Computers For Seniors
For Dummies, 3rd Edition
978-1-118-11553-4

iPad For Seniors
For Dummies, 6th Edition
978-1-118-72826-0

Social Security
For Dummies
978-1-118-20573-0

Smartphones & Tablets

Android Phones
For Dummies, 2nd Edition
978-1-118-72030-1

Nexus Tablets
For Dummies
978-1-118-77243-0

Samsung Galaxy S 4
For Dummies
978-1-118-64222-1

Samsung Galaxy Tabs
For Dummies
978-1-118-77294-2

Test Prep

ACT For Dummies,
5th Edition
978-1-118-01259-8

ASVAB For Dummies,
3rd Edition
978-0-470-63760-9

GRE For Dummies,
7th Edition
978-0-470-88921-3

Officer Candidate Tests
For Dummies
978-0-470-59876-4

Physician's Assistant Exam
For Dummies
978-1-118-11556-5

Series 7 Exam For Dummies
978-0-470-09932-2

Windows 8

Windows 8.1 All-in-One
For Dummies
978-1-118-82087-2

Windows 8.1 For Dummies
978-1-118-82121-3

Windows 8.1 For Dummies,
Book + DVD Bundle
978-1-118-82107-7

Available in print and e-book formats.

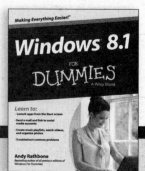

Available wherever books are sold. **For more information or to order direct visit www.dummies.com**

Take Dummies with you everywhere you go!

Whether you are excited about e-books, want more from the web, must have your mobile apps, or are swept up in social media, Dummies makes everything easier.

For Dummies is the global leader in the reference category and one of the most trusted and highly regarded brands in the world. No longer just focused on books, customers now have access to the For Dummies content they need in the format they want. Let us help you develop a solution that will fit your brand and help you connect with your customers.

Advertising & Sponsorships

Connect with an engaged audience on a powerful multimedia site, and position your message alongside expert how-to content.

Targeted ads • Video • Email marketing • Microsites • Sweepstakes sponsorship

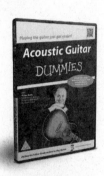

Custom Publishing

Reach a global audience in any language by creating a solution that will differentiate you from competitors, amplify your message, and encourage customers to make a buying decision.

Apps • Books • eBooks • Video • Audio • Webinars

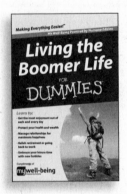

Brand Licensing & Content

Leverage the strength of the world's most popular reference brand to reach new audiences and channels of distribution.

For more information, visit www.Dummies.com/biz